Travels in Paradox

Travels in Paradox

Remapping Tourism

Edited by Claudio Minca and Tim Oakes

ROWMAN & LITTLEFIELD PUBLISHERS, INC.
Lanham • Boulder • New York • Toronto • Oxford

ROWMAN & LITTLEFIELD PUBLISHERS, INC.

Published in the United States of America
by Rowman & Littlefield Publishers, Inc.
A wholly owned subsidary of The Rowman & Littlefield Publishing Group, Inc.
4501 Forbes Boulevard, Suite 200, Lanham, Maryland 20706
www.rowmanlittlefield.com

PO Box 317, Oxford, OX2 9RU, UK

British Library Cataloguing in Publication Information Available

Library of Congress Cataloging-in-Publication Data

Travels in paradox : remapping tourism / edited by Claudio Minca and Tim Oakes.
   p. cm.
 Includes bibliographical references and index.
 ISBN-13: 978-0-7425-2875-8 (cloth : alk. paper)
 ISBN-10: 0-7425-2875-8 (cloth : alk. paper)
 ISBN-13: 978-0-7425-2876-5 (pbk. : alk. paper)
 ISBN-10: 0-7425-2876-6 (pbk. : alk. paper)
 1. Tourism. 2. Tourism—Social aspects. 3. Culture and tourism. I. Minca, Claudio.
II. Oakes, Tim.
G155.A1T684 2006
338.4'791—dc22

             2005035010

Printed in the United States of America

♾™ The paper used in this publication meets the minimum requirements of American
National Standard for Information Sciences—Permanence of Paper for Printed Library
Materials, ANSI/NISO Z39.48-1992.

Contents

Preface: Places and Performances

John Urry

The modern subject is a "connoisseur" of places. The language of landscapes (and of townscapes) is a language of mobility, based on judgments of abstract characteristics. Mobility is necessary to develop the capacity to be reflexive about places. And talk about the respective characteristics of place expresses the life-world of mobile groups, of academics, tourists, young travelers, environmentalists, the early retired, students, business people, and so on. Almost all places across the world are "toured" or may be "toured," and the pleasures of place derive from the connoisseurship of difference. This involves the emotion of movement, bodies, images, and information, moving over, under, and across the globe and reflexively monitoring places through their abstract characteristics, such as having good views, being a fun place to party, having a good heritage, being strong on "culture," having outstanding events, being good to do business in, and so on.

Such mobilities do not reduce the significance and experience of place, but they change them; places are intermittently toured, performed, and experienced. This book is about the changing place of places within the contemporary world. Places are not authentic entities with clear boundaries just waiting to be visited. Places are intertwined with people through various systems that generate and reproduce performances in and of that place (and by comparison with other places). These systems comprise networks of hosts, guests, buildings, objects and machines that contingently realize particular performances of specific places.

What I have termed elsewhere the "new mobility paradigm" tries through detailed social and geographical analyses to reveal this "contingent mobility." These analyses have been inflected by the cultural and spatial turns in the social sciences, and by recent analyses of the body, performance, and objects.

This new mobility position sees places as material, embodied, contingent, networked, and performed.

Moreover, in such performances there is no simple and unmediated relationship of subject and object, presence and absence. There is a hauntingness of place, through voices, memories, gestures, and narratives that can inhabit a place for locals and for visitors, although this distinction too becomes increasingly difficult to sustain (as this book shows). These ghostly presences of place are in between subject and object, presence and absence. This "atmosphere" of place is irreducible either to physical or material infrastructures or to discourses of representation.

This present book is part of a growing move within tourism studies to interrogate more closely the place of *place* in relationship to mobilities. Related works to *Travels in Paradox* include Coleman and Crang's *Tourism: Between Place and Performance;* Bærenholdt, Haldrup, Larsen, and Urry's *Performing Tourist Places;* and Sheller and Urry's *Tourism/Mobilities: Places to Play, Places in Play.*[1] In *Performing Tourist Places* analysis of the role of place in relationship to mobilities is organized through the metaphor of the "sandcastle" that I now briefly develop here.

Sandcastles are tangible yet fragile constructions. They only come about through drawing together certain objects, mobilities, and proximities. Their building involves children and parents working together, placing sand, buckets of water, and objects for decoration and stability within a network. The resulting collective performance is a castle of sand towering over the beach and drawing together memory flows, objects, and matter.

This "place" of the sandcastle contingently stems from various intersecting mobilities. There are imaginative mobilities in which people may dream of sun-drenched summer beaches, the globally universal place to play in the contemporary world. There are corporeal mobilities, such as the journey to a holiday region, a day trip, and the dense choreography of a family moving around and building the sandcastle. Then there are such mobile objects as fish, stones, and mussels at the shore or on the beach that may have traveled thousands of miles, waiting for their starring role. The tools for building, such as buckets and spades, are brought in the family car (maybe from abroad) but will have been manufactured and transported from a low-wage country. Performing the sandcastle necessitates the road network, widespread access to private cars, holiday housing, camp sites, beach hotels, restaurant / bar districts, marketing, Internet, advertisements, public holiday acts, planning legislation, road maps, guidebooks, ideologies of domesticity, the nuclear family, and so on.

These elements stabilize and regulate the sedimented practices that result in the humble and transient sandcastle on the beach. This transformation of the beach into a performed space is unthinkable without multiple networks that contingently necessitate certain proximities. The sandcastle is a social project involving face-to-face, body-to-body proximity among the family who both construct it *and* act as impressed audience. For a couple of hours the castle in the sand forms center stage for the performance of play and the applause of admiring spectators. The sandcastle, the sea, and the sun are central to staging a carefree, "timeless," not to be forgotten, experience of place.

These elements provide the backcloth for moments of pleasure to be remembered and recorded, before the tide of history washes the castle away. Through the sandcastle, the space and materiality of the beach is domesticated, occupied, inhabited, embodied. The sandcastle transforms the endless mass of white, golden, fine-grained or gravelled sand into a habitat; a kingdom imbued with dreams, hopes, and pride. Nature is reconstructed as the social space of an embodied family performance. But of course the sea rises and slowly the fortifications erode and the family leaves. Waves remove all trace of the day's performance. All is washed away and the castle remains only in the memory of the family and in its photographs.

This metaphor of the sandcastle captures aspects of tourist places examined in the chapters below. A particular physical environment does not itself produce a tourist place. A pile of appropriately textured sand is nothing until there is embodied activity, sociality especially around family life, memory especially as recorded photographically, and image of places. Indeed places only emerge as "tourist places" when they are appropriated, used, and made part of the memories, narratives, and images of people engaged in embodied social practices. Such places are inscribed in circles of anticipation, performance, and remembrance. Places entail multiple mobilities that are very limited *and* very wide ranging.

A sandcastle is not fixed and given but is fluid and changing. Tunnels and towers may collapse as the sun shines, the fortifications may get undermined. The work of erosion and sedimentation may slowly alter the sandcastle or there may be sudden ruptures as the walls collapse. Erosion and sedimentation are also found in tourist places that, like sandcastles, can turn out to be transient castles in the sand.

Thus analogously places are economically, politically, and culturally produced through multiple networked mobilities of capital, persons, objects, signs, and information. And it is out of these complex movements that certain places to play are contingently assembled. So places are not fixed or given or simply bounded. It is more profitable to see them as "in play," in relationship to multiple mobilities and varied performances stretching in, through, over, and under any apparently distinct locality.

So, like sandcastles, places are dynamic—"places of movement." They are like ships, moving around and not necessarily staying in one location. They travel, slow or fast, greater or shorter distances, within networks of human and nonhuman agents. Places are about the placing of peoples, materials, images, and the systems of difference they perform. But at the same time as places are dynamic, they are also about proximities, about the bodily co-presence of people in that place at that time, doing activities together, such as building a sandcastle *and* family life. There are intermittent moments of physical proximity between people that are desirable or even socially obligatory (the not-to-be-missed family holiday).

Also hugely important in mobility practices is "imaginative travel" to place. We "travel" forward in time to places only known through visual images, experiencing in one's imagination in advance what we imagine the atmosphere of place to be. And we travel backward in time to places that possess haunting memories. Wordsworth (1888) referred to the latter as "spots of time" (line 208), very short memories of a place that can "retain a renovating virtue" (lines 209–10). In the context of daffodils observed along Lake Ullswater he described how haunting memories can unexpectedly occur; they "flash upon that inward eye" even though we may be unaware that we are haunted by such vivid "spots of time." The apparently absent can dramatically and unpredictably make itself become particularly vivid.

The chapters in this book thus show how tourist activities are part of the places that get visited. The places depend upon what is routinely practiced within them. They depend upon performances by "hosts" but especially by "guests." Moreover, many such performances involve intermittent mobilities "within" the destination place itself; travel is not just a question of traveling in order to get *to* that destination. And the "place" itself is not so much fixed but is itself implicated within complex networks by which hosts, guests, buildings, objects, and machines are contingently brought together so as to enable contingently certain tourist performances in certain places at certain times.

The studies reported here thus de-center tourist studies away from "tourists" but not from their patterned performances, and onto the networks that contingently enable various places. Places are thus (re)produced through systems of tourist performances, made possible and contingently stabilized through networked relationships with other organizations, buildings, objects, and machines. Such performances can be more or less organized or formal. Each involves complex practices, a contingent and complex network operating through multiple times and spaces.

This then is the way forward for other tourism research, to leave behind the tourist as such and to focus rather upon the contingent networked performances and production of places that are to be toured and get remade as they are so toured. Places at home and away are all components of the modern world being toured and subject to the abstract characteristics of connoisseurship. Places are destined to be toured as modern subjects "on the move." Places are in the thick of such "touring."

NOTE

1. This preface and especially the metaphor of the sandcastle have been influenced by the various collaborators and contributors to *Tourism/Mobilities: Places to Play, Places in Play,* and especially *Performing Tourist Places.*

Introduction: Traveling Paradoxes

Claudio Minca and Tim Oakes

This is a book about the paradox of travel. It is a topic that perhaps conjures images of the ambivalent outsider, the wanderer who is at home everywhere and nowhere. But we wanted to work against simply laying down another take on the well-rehearsed theme of modern mobility and its associated restless anxieties. We began instead with the idea that any study of travel must also raise questions about the meaning of home, about belonging, about how places get made and remade. Travel, we thought, occurs in places, places that are homes to others. And travelers have homes that they have left for some reason but to which they will most likely return. While we like to think of travel as an escape from place, we have come to believe that such an escape is at best a comforting myth and at worst an ideology of control. Raising these questions about travel led us to consider the placed nature of identity and subjectivity in the highly mobile cultures of modernity. While we considered the experience of travel as part of the broader problem of "being modern," we mainly wanted to think about travel as part of place instead of thinking about travel as something that only happens between places. Travel, we believe, is part of place-based experience, and in this sense entails negotiations of meaning, identity, and otherness in specific places. Travel is about experiencing and making sense of place, of many places (rather than the rejection of place). We wanted to think about "being modern" as a particular kind of experience in place, one in which place-making is fundamentally infused with travel and all the baggage that gets shipped along the way—difference, strangeness, alienation, nostalgia, homesickness, inspiration, fear, frustration, hopes, and expectations fulfilled and dashed.

So that we might get a better *feel* for these ideas before sitting down to write about them, we took a trip to Venice. It was a very short trip for Claudio, who at the time was living very near and working within the city, and a much longer one for Tim, who lives in Colorado. How appropriate, we thought, to start writing this introduction in one of the world's most traveled-to places, a place so clearly "infused with travel." We found, however, that walking around Venice with, as Claudio called it, the "ghost of reflexivity" following us at every turn made us realize anew the impossibility of thinking about travel without thinking about home. It is not just that travelers must pursue their craft always in the home of someone else, but also that one's own sense of home is so often informed by travel. And this is the *problem of modernity* that we're after: being at home, being in place, these become a kind of traveling consciousness, a reflexive act informed by travel. The paradoxes of travel are also the paradoxes of place, of home. That much was abundantly clear to us after a day in Venice.

Our dual narratives of that day—first Tim's account, and then Claudio's—are offered here as a way of introducing the themes of the book. The narratives are followed by what some readers will recognize as a more "proper" introduction, picking up the threads and tying them to the broader fields of scholarship on travel, tourism, and modernity.

FISHING IN AN AQUARIUM

A Trip to Venice with Claudio

The afternoon of my arrival, Claudio and Luiza take me to Trieste, where Claudio grew up—the place he still considers home. I think visiting Trieste creates an opportunity for Claudio to perform his Italianness. "This is what Italians do," he says a number of times, with that nod of his head, a slight gesture of the hand. In Trieste, we do what Triestini do on a hot Sunday, swimming in the Adriatic, strolling around the pier as the sun dips into the bay and sets the city square aglow with twilight. Claudio points out the architecture of the city: this one fascist, this one "liberty," this one deco. The historical layers in the landscape are astonishing—amid the dominant nineteenth-century neoclassical architecture, interspersed with an occasional fascist building, hides a Roman theater, while above the town towers a fifteenth-century castle. Claudio and Luiza comment on how the city's public spaces are genuinely democratic, claimed and used by the people who live there. They are spaces that invite people to come out in the evenings, to enjoy the bay and the sunset, to drink and talk in historic outdoor cafes ("this one's leftist, this one used to be the place for Italian nationalists at the beginning of the twentieth century") and in the vast town square—spaces, in other words, not privatized, not seducing one's consumption. Our walk through the city streets delivers us to a neighborhood pizzeria. "This is what Triestini do," says Claudio. "They eat pizza on Sunday night after a day on the beach." We sit down and order beer. "Beer is for pizza," he continues. "Beer is the only thing we'll drink with pizza, never wine." The pizza is delicious, and we finish the evening with a late night gelato and a sleepy drive back to the house in San Dona' di Piave.

It occurs to me that Claudio may have wanted me to experience Trieste as a kind of prelude to Venice. Trieste doesn't really *look* Italian, at least not in any touristy way. It looks more like Prague or St. Petersburg, which is perhaps why very few tourists go there. And maybe it's also why some public spaces appear so democratic and uncommodified. Trieste has a kind of *realness* and a normalcy about it; Claudio presents it to me as a place where you can go and simply see everyday life. People occupy the city space just doing what they do, and they are, for the most part, residents. There are others too—Slovenians, Croatians, Serbians, Albanians, Senegalese—shopping, looking for work, smuggling goods, selling trinkets, or just hanging out on the street. But it is as if the normalcy of Trieste has been offered as a contrast to the abnormality of Venice. And here things get confusing for me. After visiting Trieste, Venice—which *looks* so "Italian"—strikes me as very *unreal*, not really an Italian city at all. Venice, in fact, looks *too* Italian; it looks like a theme park. And so, here's the irony and the paradox. Venice *is* a real city; residents still live there (although only about 65,000 of them are still hanging on); there are two universities, with students and faculty, markets selling fruit, vegetables, and fish, and plenty of "everyday life," just as in Trieste.

It is perhaps the oddity of Venice, more than the normalcy of Trieste, which encourages Claudio to perform his Italianness. In the morning of our visit, we ride his Vespa to the train station in San Dona' di Piave. Breakfast is an espresso or cappuccino—standing—at the station, with a croissant. "This is what Italians do," he says. "Have our morning coffee standing up, in a hurry, on the way to work." Claudio has finished his cappuccino before I can barely get my first sip in. The train arrives on time, from Budapest, and whisks us away to the city in the lagoon. Claudio's first task is to generate the right first impression of the city. To that end, we take the ferry along the Grand Canal to Piazza San Marco. Here the paradox of Venice reveals itself most clearly to me. The Piazza is full of people, thousands and thousands of people, *and they're all tourists*. It gives me that feeling—Claudio says it's common for visitors—that the whole city had been built for tourists, and tourists are the only people inhabiting the space of the city. And the tourists get to do their touristy things freely and with abandon, just as in a theme park. Everywhere they turn is another beautiful facade, another charming scene, another stunning vista; all seemingly created just for the camera. There is no unevenness about the Venice landscape. It is *all* beautiful, *everywhere.* Claudio calls it a fantastic laboratory. Being a tourism scholar in Venice is like fishing in an aquarium, he says.

And yet, this is also Claudio's city. It's where he has lived (for four years, until getting fed up and moving to San Dona' di Piave) and where he has worked. And so he is the destabilizing element to my visit; Venice is not just a theme park, much as the tourism industry might like it to be. It is a place where people live and work. Claudio doesn't try to show me the *real* Venice because, of course, the real Venice is everywhere. It's not that the real Venice is a fake, a theme park, but rather that there is a *tension* between the theme park and the everyday, the habitus of "what Italians do." And Claudio embodies this tension; he performs it when I arrive to visit his city for a day.

We walk the usual tourist circuit and then visit his department, where he gives a radio interview about the war in Iraq. The interview intrudes on my day in the theme park in a most welcome way, reminding me that yes, people do live and work in Venice. We have a quick lunch — sitting down this time — before walking around some more. Claudio tries to show me some kinds of "backstage" spaces in Venice (the fish market, the shipyard where gondolas are built, alleys where tourists are seldom seen, where laundry hangs and where facades need rebuilding). But it's an ambivalent effort, because we both know that the backstage idea is a false construction. These spaces are no more or less "real" than the junk market at Rialto Bridge, the occasional pigeon here is no more "real" than the thousands flocking to San Marco as if they're paid to be there (although in some senses they are paid, since tourists regularly purchase the seeds to feed them there).

In Venice with Tim

Tim is coming to Italy: what should I do with him? He is an academic, he works on tourism and we are collaborating on a book on modern paradoxes. I think (with some concern) about having to re-interpret "my" places for an "outsider," because it obviously involves both my judgment on the visitor's background and what I want to show of Italy, Trieste, Venice, and myself in all those spaces. And in this case, it is as though a ghost is traveling with us: the ghost of self-reflexivity, the syndrome of the post-structuralist tourism scholar.

After some hesitation about what would be the right start, we decide to have lunch at the Venice airport: not a very Italian/Venetian beginning. Or maybe it is. But we are hungry and Tim is not naïve, "like we think most tourists are."

Now, the very problem is how to represent myself to a post-structuralist scholar who has never been to Italy before, on what is supposedly "my turf."

What did he have in mind? And how important should this be for my choices about what to do in Venice? How were our shared taken-for-granted understandings of tourism and traveling influencing my feelings? How would he perceive my planned path through Venice and its surrounding region? Should I think of him as an American first, or as a fellow scholar? How could I translate my experience of meeting Tim in Italy and showing him around into a language that would not be banal? How could I translate into English my own rather strange and ambiguous Italian-ness? How would I see myself in Italy—and in this somewhat uncomfortable role? Would I be able to be "spontaneous"?

Luiza, my partner (and also a geographer), suggested that Tim should see Trieste, my hometown, "because it is beautiful and different." I was not completely convinced about this choice, but I accepted and we drove away. One thing was sure: Trieste was a city where Tim (and we along with him) could have a completely different experience compared to the quaintness of Venice. In our paradoxical anxiety of being different from the tourists, it turned out to be a good choice (certainly very few foreigners would start their first Italian experience in a place like Trieste, not quite enough "Italian" for a landscape seeker).

But despite the fact that I was born and had spent most of my life there, I do not live in Trieste anymore. Only recently have I begun to enjoy it with a strange and somewhat disturbing aesthetic detachment: I like it because I know it very well, but I would not be happy—or able—to live there fulltime anymore. I allow myself to have an almost paternalistic vision of the city's problems and the very particular ideas of the Triestini. What I once perceived as unbearable constraints, I now find reassuring: signs of continuity with the past. Exploring this context with a sophisticated mind like Tim's is proving an interesting enterprise. Throughout, I try to keep a very low profile: showing both the spectacular side of the city, but also some less attractive corners in order to do *what many Triestini usually do* (it would be interesting to question why these hints of reality became so subconsciously important during that experience). Despite my attempt to avoid traditional tourist routes—which are very few, anyway—we end up walking through the historical center and up to the hill where the cathedral and the castle stand. Beforehand, we stop in Miramare, where the city's student population hangs out on hot days, sunbathing and swimming. The "beach" is actually not a beach, but a long stretch of waterfront sidewalk along the main road into the city where people walk, jog, and sunbathe in the summer. For some reason, I find it particularly important to stress to Tim the democratic nature of this space, of this piece of "sidewalk-riviera," implicitly comparing it to the rampant privatization of the American city. A pinch of European pride lies beneath my explanation of the workings of this space, and perhaps this is why I had chosen it as an overture to the city. I do not realize how much I actually stress the *normalcy* of Trieste—only Tim's comments make me think about this—and all my efforts to offer him a concentrated set of fragments of "real life" ("this is what the Triestini do," which I apparently repeat quite a few times throughout the evening).

Venice, after a Vespa ride and a fast "standing" breakfast at the train station bar, is literally *waiting for us*. I realize that we are getting ready for the shock of Venice—Venice is always a shock—because we joked about the "perfect Italian experience" that Tim is being treated to in such a short visit. We both know that there are prejudices and expectations that we cannot escape. We are also both concerned about avoiding the tourist language. But, at the same time, the two of us are clearly not in the same position: in the process of essentializing the Italian experience produced by the tourist literature and the tourist economy, I am thrust into the rather uncomfortable position of being—by definition—part (an object?) of that experience; I am a representative, after all, of *Italianness in place*, since I am Italian.

So Venice is between us even before arrival, and I prepare myself to get into the right mood to experience my reading of Venice, the quintessential tourist city, aware that, after all the articles and books that we have both written on tourism, modernity, and subject formation, it would not have been easy to find the "right" way to be there *together*. A partial and somehow dangerous way out is offered by my work commitments that day and by the fact that we have to spend some time talking about the book—a great opportunity to go back to "real" things.

I decide to play with the ways the tourists experience Venice and to approach the city from the water. The water bus stop is packed with tourists. It is unseasonably warm and I am immediately tempted to show Tim the difficulties that tourism creates for many residents: our "tour," in fact, takes place on a regular public bus/boat, and despite the different fares paid by residents and tourists for the service, all of Venice's transport system is essentially kidnapped by the tourist army of image seekers. This, of course, is not a new issue in tourist literature, but now I am wearing (as I had been wearing during the four years that I lived in Venice) a double mask: that of a tourist scholar as well as that of a resident, that is, member of an (often idealized) "local community" that some scholars have been so concerned about protecting and preserving, but also the same "local" that, here in Venice, tourists are eager to frame in their pictures, and to approach in order to get some hints of real Italian-Venetian life. After strolling through the predictable landscapes of Piazza San Marco and the Rialto Bridge, I was tempted to take Tim to the backstage—but in Venice, as we all know, the backstage is simply another "special effect."

The only thing left for me to do is to try to ironically depict the Venetian tourist experience and to distance us from it—a very modern attitude, I admit. At the same time, we are both aware of the fact that the "Venice performance" is an amazing and unique spectacle—and that there is no way of escaping from it.

Some interesting questions come up during our final break at an outdoor café ("where my colleagues usually go," I announce in order paradoxically to reassure Tim about the fact that we managed "to step off the scene," maybe, for a few minutes or so). The questions are: how had the tourist scholar and the former inhabitant of Venice interacted in shaping my performance that day with Tim? Who was I that day in Venice? Why was I so concerned about showing what "typical" Italians do? Why was I so preoccupied about distinguishing tourist behavior from what "real" Italians do? Why did Venice provoke—as it has always done—such disturbing and intriguing feelings for a semi-resident like myself? Could I have refrained myself from falling into the traps of my modern language and its paradoxes, especially when performing my subjectivity on my own turf? What really happened that day between Tim and myself? Why did we feel the need to write about this— actually realizing that we couldn't start our book without narrating such a schizophrenic experience? What could we learn from this experience in order to better understand subject formation and modern tourism in place? What did the relationship between us and the tourists in Venice consist of? Why did I feel the need to compromise my self-reflexivity as a scholar with a set of very modern assertions about what Italians do and what tourists do, just to spatially mark this distance?

It is perhaps understandable, then, that I feel more comfortable when we leave Venice and return to San Dona', feeling literally overwhelmed by the unavoidable weight of the countertourist experience of the tourist city par excellence, and by the difficulties in positioning ourselves that this experience created. We end up eating dinner in a restaurant out in the country where, after a great meal, I apparently stress to Tim (again . . .) how un-gentrified that space was (and how different from Italian restaurants abroad) and, of course, how we are doing again something that . . . "Italians usually do."

PLACES TRAVELED-TO

The visit is always easier for the traveler. Claudio's account of our day in Venice narrates the ambivalence of those who must make homes out of places traveled-to. In the case of Venice, of course, ambivalence may be too soft a word. For many locals, the disaster of tourism in Venice generates powerful feelings about which there is little ambivalence. But it remains true that travel turns locals into ambivalent and self-conscious place makers. In her account of "*heimat* tourism," later in this volume, Soile Veijola captures a similar ambivalence with a set of questions:

> How do you know and experience a place you knew as a child; and how does that place know you? At which point do strangers turn into friends, tourists into neighbors, locals into visitors, and places into tourist destinations? Can *Heimat* be revisited? How is ontological security, guaranteed by being at home and having a home, produced and managed in the modern world? How does one trust a place?

Tim did not really *trust* Venice, but that is perhaps to be expected. Most tourists don't trust the places they visit—at least not on their first date. That Claudio could trust neither Venice nor himself *in Venice* is both more troubling and more revealing of the paradox of travel. Travel, it seems, turns locals into self-appointed packagers of place. But in packaging place for travelers, locals tend to acquire a kind of schizophrenic subjectivity, scrutinizing themselves and their own homes from an outsider's perspective. Locals often turn themselves into ambivalent objects, and it is precisely this schizophrenia that strikes us as peculiarly modern and paradoxical. When Veijola takes a friend to her native place she finds that "all I could do was gesture at the visible, picturesque landscape, like a tourist guide—lost for words, information and concepts." Turning her place into a viewable object for others renders it impossible to experience as home. She becomes an inside outsider and an outside insider, a paradox. In the Venice narratives, this paradox reveals itself on at least two levels.

One is on the level of place-making. A dualism creeps into Tim's account of the difference between Trieste and Venice, in which the traveler measures places with the yardstick of authenticity. For the modern traveler, places can be real or fake, or they can be real and "hyperreal," that is, so "fake" that they seem real (Eco 1986). In either case, travelers find themselves wondering what places visited are "really" like. What must it be like to live there, to be at home there? This is because the traveler—almost instinctively—does not at first *trust* the places s/he visits, and so assumes that there is a hidden realness somewhere just out of view. This is because, just as we all define ourselves according to a world of others, the traveler applies a binary of *real* and *unreal* to evaluate the world she travels through. At the same time, places traveled-to get remade with a self-consciousness about this lack of trust. This results in places that are increasingly packaged versions of themselves, "hyperreal" places. And so, "reality" is put on show for the traveler, to gain her trust, to *convince* her that this place is indeed authentic. But its authenticity must be marked as such (Culler 1981). Yet while places may be consciously marked and packaged with a particular kind of authenticity—that is, an authenticity explicitly sought by the visitor—they continue to be remade through the daily practices of the subjects living within them. Such places thus experience a schizophrenic dualism of paradoxical modernity. People both living in and visiting such places must negotiate this paradox in one way or another. Indeed, it is the very quality of place that the paradoxes of modernity make manifest and palpable (Oakes 1997). And while a phenomenology of place would argue that such is the quality of *any* place (Casey 1997, 240–41), we find that places receiving a greater share of travelers reveal this quality all the more clearly.

A similar level of schizophrenia is revealed by the Venice narratives in terms of subject-formation. Travel is often thought to induce what Victor Turner has called a "performative reflexivity" for both locals and travelers alike. Turner defined this reflexivity as a condition in which sociocultural groups or particularly perceptive representatives of such groups "turn, bend or reflect back upon themselves, upon their relations, actions, symbols, meanings, codes, statuses, social structures, ethical and legal rules, and other sociocultural components which make up their public selves" (Turner 1986, 24). Such reflection is especially inspired at moments of intersubjective encounter between travelers and locals, when both find themselves to be the objects of the other's contemplation and gaze (Urry 2002b, 156). Through such encounters both locals and travelers consciously experience subjectivity and objectivity simultaneously, an experience that often produces Turner's "performative reflexivity," as locals become self-conscious place-packagers and guides, while visitors assume the role of consumers.

Invoking performance theory at this point risks a detour into a complex and diverse body of work, but more needs to be said about how performativity speaks to the question of paradox and travel. As Schein (1999, 369–73) indicates in her brief review of the field, performance theory has genealogies in philosophy and linguistics, performance and theater studies, and sociology and linguistic anthropology. In cultural studies, though, it has been the work of Judith Butler that has perhaps most inspired a sustained questioning of the often taken-for-granted categories of social being. Butler (1990; 1993) develops the idea of gender as a kind of reification of social norms about difference, a consequence of repeated performative enactments of male and female conventions in a given society. As Schein (1999, 369) summarizes it, "The significance of this argument lies in the notion that there is no essence, origin, or reality prior to or outside the enactment of a multiplicity of performances. It is the recurring regularity in performances that makes certain social norms acquire their authority, their aura of inevitability." Extending from this, one could further argue that recurring enactments might transform, in addition to gender categories, other binaries from arbitrary distinctions into seemingly essential conditions. This would include subject and object, mind and body, self and other, among many others that Western epistemology relies upon to order the world and make it knowable.

As Edensor (2001) has pointed out, there is nothing necessarily *reflexive* about such re-enactments. Indeed it is precisely the unreflective and habitual nature of repeated performances that assures the "realness" of the resulting binaries. Thus, Edensor argues that tourism is a kind of unreflexive performance and that it is a *lack* of reflection that preserves the tourist's sense of relaxation and "getting away from it all." Yet precisely because it is an *enactment* of arbitrary categories (tourist-subject and exotic-object, be it a native person, an unusual landscape, or an exotic cultural event), performativity preserves the possibility that reflexivity *might* disrupt our taken-for-granted view of the world. Performativity both encrusts hegemonic social conventions *and* creates opportunities for the disruption of those conventions. What we notice about travel is that it often creates exactly those kinds of opportunities for reflexive disruption even while it provides the option of unreflexive bliss on the beach (or in the shopping street, festival marketplace, heritage center, or wherever else tourists would go to "get away") (see also Franklin and Crang 2001, 18). Jacobs observes this disruption, for instance, in her account (this volume) of European women tourists in the Sinai who "take on the supposedly masculine subjectivity of travel" by, paradoxically, turning local men into hypermasculine objects. Similarly, Veijola's movement between "masculine countryside and feminine city" disrupts more conventional notions of "masculine mobility and travel as opposed to a feminine notion of dwelling and belonging."

And indeed, the savvy of the tourism industry has even tried to turn this possibility of disruption into a commodity. Citing Featherstone (1991, 78–82), Edensor (2001, 78–79) argues that,

> Tourism as performance can both renew existing conventions and provide opportunities to challenge them. Yet many stages devised by the industry are typically designed to promise a carnivalesque experience but are usually "sites of ordered disorder" which encourage a "controlled de-control of the emotions."

This echoes Wang's (this volume) analysis of tourist itineraries as the commodity form of tourist experience, in which the itinerary promises the freedom of escape but instead acts—as with all forms of consumption—more as a constraint on freedom. Wang is right in arguing that this marks the paradox of consumption itself. The above is also true for places like Las Vegas, as shown by Raento and Flusty (this volume), where the commodification of placeness and of the tourist experience of place is taken to an extreme (see also Minca 2004). While commodified subversions of social convention may ultimately be merely another kind of conformity, commodification is nevertheless incomplete because, in tourism at least, it is places that must be commodified and places always will resist and disrupt the social closure necessary for absolute control. It is the placed aspect of travel, not its commodification, that provides for those moments of reflexivity that prove disruptive to our taken-for-granted ideas of subject-object distinctions. Thus, in Flusty's (this volume) analysis of Zapatista muñeca dolls, their value as commodities is continually disrupted according to the places—and thus the social contexts—which they travel through upon being dislodged from their production origins in Chiapas. As commodities themselves travel, their capacities of order and standardization are compromised.

Similarly, travel in places introduces new contexts that can threaten the unreflexive calm waters provided for by the industry (Urry 2002b, 152). "An unreflexive disposition characterizes much tourism and where this is not the case, where reflexive improvisation and a critical disposition are mobilized, the resultant ambiguity can threaten the sense of well-being that is one of the main aims of tourism—to relax and let go" (Edensor 2001, 62). While we may think of tourism as a performative enactment of the subject-object binary, that performativity means that such a binary is always vulnerable to disruptive reflection. In his analysis of ethnic village tourists in China, Oakes (this volume) thus argues that intersubjective tourism encounters reveal authenticity to be a void, momentarily exposing the real/fake binary as the arbitrary construction that it is. It is the embodied and paradoxical nature of places traveled-in and traveled-to that makes this possible. As suggested by Crang and Coleman (2002, 1), as well as emphasized by Crang in this volume, places should be viewed less as fixed and stable entities than as "fluid and created through performance." Thus, while the performativity of tourist "places" seeks to make them unreflexive stages where subject-object binaries are maintained and where particular experiences are regularized and commodified, that performativity always renders this process of order and control incomplete and vulnerable to disruption, as Minca (this volume) also highlights in his discussion of the (re)construction of the Jamaa El Fna square in Marrakech as an idealized space for ordered consumption.

In commodifying places as stages for "ordered disorder," tourism capitalizes on the traveler's need both to cognitively map or "freeze" the world (making it comprehensible through knowledge, order, and abstraction) while also "re-opening" the world (to reproduce the adventure, difference, exoticism, and risk that also lie at the heart of modern sensibilities), thereby creating new frontiers worthy of exploration. The tourist is always looking for an impossible balance between the need of finding and establishing order in the world—that means mapping tourist spaces, landscapes, and cultures—and the desire (possibility) of transgressing that same order, of going beyond and behind the map. She is caught between an unavoidable propensity toward putting places and people in their "proper" order and a fatal attraction toward disorder, between rationality and desire, between an essentialized sense of place and a progressive sense of place (Massey 1993). The commerce of tourism promises an impossible combination of attractions that can only be sustained through performative re-enactments: an *objectification* of the world as a knowable space and a subjective *experience* of the world as a place of difference.

In seeking to commodify this paradox, tourism requires a place in which to ground and display its patterns and codes, and to provide the stage for the tourist experience. It is interesting to note that it is only through the existence of specific *places* that the tourist discourse can be developed and can become believable as well as desirable. This, of course, makes the paradox all the more palpable, since *tourism requires places to express the traveler's apparent desire for displacement.*

In addition to the mobilization and commodification of places, tourism also repackages two characters, or "model subjects," that embody the contradiction between objectification and subjective experience: the explorer and the anthropological field researcher. Both figures are incarnates of the modern Man whose positionality and use of power (through the gaze and the map) are well known and analyzed (e.g. Mitchell 1988; Pratt 1992; Farinelli 1992; Minca 2001). Additionally, both Crick (1995) and Bruner (1995) have specifically addressed the disquieting yet striking similarities between anthropologists and tourists, suggesting that all scholars engaged in "field work" must consider seriously the implications of their own reproduction of binary categories of Western epistemology (Bourdieu 1990). Tourism, we believe, clarifies such issues quite effectively. Like Simmel's stranger (1971), both the classical anthropologist and the explorer justify their existence through the assertion of a defined set of contradictions: being *outside* and *part of* the observed object at the same time; believing in the existence of the real thing "out there" and relying merely on representation of the same thing at the same time; defining order through the description of others' disorder; a confidence in the binaries of subject and object, the map and the territories, the representation and the thing represented; the belief in the text as a means of narrating the world but also the ever-present readiness to "jump into" the real/world to experience it—and disrupt that order.

Tourism replicates on a mass scale the paths and the behaviors of these two modern heroes, making their paradoxes even more explicit and defining (in an aware or unaware fashion) their desires. The success of the tourist experience is often measured according to these two referents. In particular, cultural and ethnic tourism reveal very clearly where the deep contradiction lies. It is enough to notice the way everyday life is converted into an object of observation, or how through heritage preservation we map, freeze, and frame the past, while simultaneously desiring a "living history" that provides a spectacular background for the present. The modern tourist lives these tensions between freezing and preserving something "alive" in her/his attitude toward history, as well as social and cultural difference. The management of tourist places is obviously highly influenced by such contradictions since the never-tamed tension that derives from it is the real fuel of the tourist market. It is this tension that allows the sale of comfort and safety, exploration and excitement in the same "package"; that allows some "rough" travel guides to introduce millions of readers to the very same "off the beaten track" itineraries; that allows the alternative traveler to believe in the possibility of meeting and knowing the "locals," to believe in an unspoiled "out there" to be found, to believe that there is a way to escape the ordered landscapes of the tourist traps.

What we're suggesting is that travel-tourism derives its power by providing a stage upon which to act out the binaries by which we make sense of and order the world. Yet by definition the provisioning of such a stage must acknowledge the "constructedness" of such binaries. This is why travel-tourism makes such binaries vulnerable even while propping them up. That travel-tourism must occur in places is why this is so. For while places are objectified as destinations and scenes by travelers and commodified as tourist attractions, they remain at the same time inherently deconstructive of these processes. To return to the idea of "performative reflexivity" in tourism, we can perhaps characterize such reflexivity as not one that cognitively puts everything in order but rather does precisely the opposite. By producing the "special effect of order," what is actually enacted is a process of *social ordering* (see Hetherington 1997), where the subjects involved are not properly "put in place," as many postcolonial critics have argued, but rather are endlessly "replaced" through a subtle strategy of ordering.

The placed quality of travel and tourism—a quality that we are suggesting as a space of disrupted categories and universalisms rendered arbitrary and absurd—induces an embodied reflexivity that defies our more standard notions of cognitive reflection. It is closer to what Lash (1999)—referring to the "self-reflexive conscience" of modernity—has termed "aesthetic reflexivity." But we prefer the term *paradox* to describe it, because it resists epistemological closure. And it is for this reason that Crang (this volume) calls for a "thinking through the ontology of tourist places rather than the epistemology of their representations." This recasts the problem as an epistemological paradox, rather than a problem of not knowing the "truth" about a place. "In other words," Crang (this volume) continues, "we shall see the paradox of experiencing a place is that it depends on other absent places."

In the Venice narratives, Claudio's performance of "Italianness" marks the habitual way that travel induces us to perform the subject-object binary, as well as revealing the arbitrariness of such constructions when subjected to the reflection that travel (in places) *also* inspires. That Claudio resorts to performing Italianness perhaps indicates how such performances are the only option when we are confronted with the task of packaging a place for an outsider's consumption. Performance, then, is a way of putting order in an otherwise disordered and unruly world. The narratives from Venice reveal a deeper desire to put order to the world, by both visitor and local alike, as a way out of our epistemological paradox.

Travel, we suggest, emerges from an impulse to order the world; it can be conceived as a kind of escape from the disorder that confronts us in place. To take to the road, to disavow, if only temporarily, one's home place for the open space of mobility, is to pay homage to our need for order. And the space of movement, of travel, seems to offer a refuge of sorts. The apparently empty space of travel offers "a special form of comfort, a reassuring presence" (Casey 1997, 338). Travel seems to bring us closer to the abstract qualities of space as opposed to the lived messiness of place, to the universal categories that space allows for.

Thus, through travel we set the world right. We find the real lives, peoples, and places that we've expected to be there, and reify those abstract representations of the world we've expected to find.

All of this is, perhaps, counterintuitive. Doesn't it seem more the case that we travel to introduce a bit of disorder to our regulated and routinized daily lives? Doesn't travel refresh and revive us because our narrow views of the world become disrupted as we expand our horizons? Such views, we feel, constitute more an *ideology of travel* than actual traveling practice. As many observers have noted, tourism is a highly regulated and routinized activity that seeks to transform places into standardized and interchangeable attractions (Urry 1995; Hughes 1998, 20–21). Indeed, tourism has been referred to as "a vast system of social control" (Dann 2003, 468). Yet it also seems to succeed to the extent that consumers feel that they are *not* being controlled and that places are *not* turned into commodities. Travel must therefore maintain an ideal of freedom (and its many variants of risk, danger, transgression, disorder, adventure, exploration, discovery) while provisioning the consumer with the necessary amenities to make him or her comfortable. This becomes quite disturbingly evident in the practices and the fetishism of "war tourism," as shown by Adams in this volume. In that case, the tourists' feeling of being in touch with the real "event," of being able to confirm and go beyond the mediatized experience of death and destruction is accompanied by the implicit need to be able to come back home safely and to relocate/re-signify that experience in their own sociocultural context. It becomes just another way of negotiating (the traveler) identity and subjectivity through the experience of the paradox of/in place. Thus, it seems unavoidable to regard tourism, as Edensor (this volume) does, as an inherently ambivalent activity, reflecting both a desire to escape and an enjoyment of the pleasures of conformity.

This ambivalence begins to acknowledge that travel is on the one hand very much about ordering the world and making sense of it in epistemological terms, while on the other hand a rather unsuccessful project in these terms. If travel were to occur in some sort of vacuum of space, never touching down, we might actually be able to speak of the universal abstractions to which the escape from place aspires. But instead travel never really escapes places. Despite our desire for order, and despite relying on an industry that seeks to provide for this desire, travel nevertheless results in a paradoxical experience of *ordered disorder.*

The more we seek to order the world through which we travel, the more it confronts us with disorder. The result is an endless process of *ordering*; a process that is the product of this very tension—and of the real, ontological impossibility of ever reaching the desired order (Hetherington 1997). Subject formation, in the tourist experience, is based on a set of spatial special effects that impose their paradoxes *in place* by eternally *deferring the order* toward which the subject is drawn to find her/his place in the world. The modern transcendent knowing subject, by displaying categories of order, actually performs ordering strategies: not freezing each subject in its proper place, but endlessly producing the conditions for that subject's emplacement in the world. The modern tourist thus constantly re-writes the world, while, paradoxically, trying to freeze it within a static image able to reflect his/her own Self.

TRAVELING PLACES

"Travel" has held a prominent place in cultural studies scholarship for some time now, and this has in some ways come at the expense of a better understanding of place. But this is not necessarily always the case, nor do we seek to construct a dichotomy between traveling theory and place theory. Instead, we hope to bring these bodies of work together in fruitful ways. If the study of tourism is to contribute to traveling theory's ongoing "revitalization" of the concept of culture, as called for by Sørensen (2003, 864, cited in Crang this volume), we believe that place must be a fundamental part of such a contribution. Early work on traveling theory and traveling cultures sought to correct what was regarded as a privileging of dwelling over mobility in the human sciences (Clifford 1992; Pratt 1992; Wolff 1993; Robertson et al. 1994; Kaplan 1996). This diverse body of work has emphasized that the erosion of boundaries as stabilized territories are replaced with hybrid and fluid borderlands where identities are forged through diaspora and mobility across space, rather than within a bounded place. While this work has directed our attention to the importance of mobility and porousness in conceiving the conditions of subject and identity formation, there is the danger of constructing a "straw-man" of place as a foil to make this point. Traveling theory rests upon an assumption of place as bounded and closed. Put in these terms, the spaces of travel take on a liberating quality—precisely the same quality, in fact, that attracts tourists to temporarily leave home and head down the road and jet through the skies.

But a large body of work on place has long dispelled the notion of place as necessarily bounded and enclosed (Pred 1986; Agnew and Duncan 1989; Entrikin 1991; Massey 1993; Casey 1993; Oakes 1997; Dirlik 1999; Gieryn 2000; Escobar 2001). All of this work tends to argue that place is a fundamental quality of human spatial experience and that, as such, it derives as much from conditions of mobility and linkage across space as it does from any *absence* of these things. This is why Crang (this volume) argues that any critique of tourism must take into account the open and unstable quality of places since "virtually every culture is constructed as much, if not more, by links and attachments with people in other places as it is by internal homogeneity." Only when we fail to see place as a basic part of our *experience* of the world, and instead regard it as simply a sectioned and closed-off portion of space (that is, simply a smaller or derivative version of space), do we make the mistake of viewing it as parochial, isolated, or otherwise antithetical to globalization and all the mobility with which much of the world lives today (see Herzfeld 1991; Agnew 1993; Massey and Jess 1995; Feld and Basso 1996; Gupta and Ferguson 1997).

Again, rather than set up a confrontational dichotomy here between theories of travel and theories of place, we instead seek to reconfigure traveling theory to consider how we are always traveling in place. Rather than ask what travel tells us about postmodern identity and subjectivity, we ask what the experience of travel teaches us about place. This can be put in yet another way: what does placed experience teach us about travel? Place is a fundamental concept to start with because we hold that place is something in which the abstract dualisms and categorizations of modernity are rendered arbitrary and absurd in the face of complex local knowledge, bodily experience, and the disordered order of everyday life. This quality of place is noted both by phenomenologists like Casey (1997) and materialists like Massey (1992), who has argued that "home places" are not the ordered secure worlds many (men) take them to be but are rather fraught with the ambiguities, tensions, and contradictions of modernity. In place, we are both subject and object. It is the seductive escape from place promised by travel that leads us to perform, to repeatedly reenact, a (subject-object, mind-body) binary that helps us make sense of the world in more generalized and abstract terms.

Travel is thought to be placeless, and as such has long been seen as evoking a distinctly modern subjectivity of freedom coupled with detachment and alienation. For Bauman (1991), the modern subject was an ambivalent stranger, an exile, pilgrim, someone out of place yet longing for a place, obsessed with anguish and fear yet seeking a sense of control and a unifying gaze upon the world. Simmel's (1971, 145) mobile stranger, for example, was an exiled foreigner who was free from the obligations and repetitions of everyday (placed) life. Such freedom from routine and obligation was refreshing to the senses and mirrored the bracing freedom of modernity itself (see also Touraine 1995, 202). The stranger was thus an *objective* person, ideally positioned in a space "out there," capable of abstract clarity where "placed" people were not. The stranger "examines conditions with less prejudice; he [sic] assesses them against standards that are more general and more objective" (Simmel 1971, 146). But the stranger also embodied a paradoxical synthesis "composed of remoteness and nearness, indifference and involvement" (Simmel 1971, 145). Travel allowed for an outside position that was the source of some comfort and control even while it conjured its own kind of existential anguish. The displacement of travel, exile, and exploration engendered a paradoxical and schizophrenic *experience of detachment* that was at once liberating, terrifying, and commanding of power (see also Pratt 1992).

This schizophrenic quality emerges from the process of subject formation whereby subjectivity is conceived as an articulation of self to others (Foucault 1978/1990; Butler 1997). This articulation marks the schizophrenic practice by which the subject always "objectivates" itself. Berger and Pullberg (1965, 199–200) thus argued that it is a necessary human condition to know the self by establishing a subject-object binary. We all "objectivate" our world, they claim. Objectivation is a process "whereby human subjectivity embodies itself in products that are available to oneself and one's fellow men [sic] as elements of a common world." Objectification is, therefore, "the moment in the process of objectivation in which man [sic] established distance from his producing and its product, such that he can take cognizance of it and make it an object of his consciousness." Humans are thus continuously "making their world" as they act to modify the given, structuring it into a meaningful totality (a process that is never complete). The object-world, in other words, must be made and remade over and over again. "The world remains real, in the sense of subjective plausibility and consistency, only as it is confirmed and re-confirmed" (Berger and Pullberg 1965, 201). As with the performativity of tourism discussed above, this continual reenactment of the world both makes it "real" and creates opportunities for our taken-for-granted views of ourselves and our world to be disrupted.

Such disruption might occur, for instance, when the distance of objectification is closed by an "other" asserting its presence in unexpected or even unwelcome ways. It is in these contexts that *representations* of the world achieve their power, for they promise a reenactment of the world without the threatening possibility of that reenactment being disrupted by the "other" world itself. This is why, as Timothy Mitchell (1988) has observed, Europeans of the nineteenth century were inclined to see their world of empire as an "exhibit" of something, rather than as the thing itself. This was, for example, illustrated in the "great exhibitions" of this period, which offered elaborate displays that sought to replicate as faithfully as possible the far-flung places of empire. According to Mitchell (1988, 12), the *world itself* was for nineteenth-century European metropolitans a kind of exhibition, objectified and displayed before them to gaze upon:

> Outside the world exhibition . . . one encountered not the real world but only further models and representations of the real. Beyond the exhibition and the department store . . . the theatre and the zoo, the countryside encountered typically in the form of a model farm exhibiting new machinery and cultivation methods, the very streets of the modern city with their deliberate facades, even the Alps once the funicular was built . . . [e]verything seemed to be set up before one as if it were a model or the picture of something.

This speaks to the possibility that the great exhibitions drew upon a deeper need for a particular kind of *representation* that faithfully met certain expectations necessary to European subject-formation (as pointed out by Minca in this volume).

What this leads to, then, is the idea that while we may travel in order to transgress, if only for a day, the boundaries and routines that order our lives, we find that travel becomes more of a routinized homage to shoring up those boundaries; it merely reifies boundaries by reinforcing a subject-object binary. Indeed, such a reinforcing is extremely empowering in many ways. The search for order—for example, through the framing of a perfect tourist landscape or place—does not accomplish what it is there to do but, rather, produces a process of social ordering, changing the spatial rules of the place and its very geographies.

We perform this binary repeatedly through the practice of travel, and thus make it real. MacCannell (1976, 13) saw this when he argued that "sightseeing is a kind of collective striving for a transcendence of the modern totality, a way of attempting to overcome the discontinuity of modernity, of incorporating its fragments into unified experience." That this sense of power comes more from visual aspects of travel than other senses is captured by Urry when he states that "focusing on the gaze brings out how within tourism the organizing sense within the typical tourist experience is visual. And this mirrors the general privileging of the eye within the long history of Western societies. Sight is viewed as the noblest sense, the most discriminating and reliable of the sensuous mediators between humans and their physical environment" (2002b, 146). Similarly, Tuan (1974) points out that the world perceived visually is more abstract and thus more amenable to order, objectification, and control (see also Berger 1972; Jay 1992). This issue is picked up by Edensor (this volume) who argues that,

> visual techniques are widespread within both tourist production (in brochures, holiday programs, guided tours, and guidebooks) and in tourist practice (through photography, video recording, and journal keeping). Such techniques tend to banish the ambiguity of the world, bringing "otherness" into representation in contradistinction to the unpredictable, indescribable effects of the sonic, the tactile, and the aromatic, which are far more difficult to visualize and textualize.

What is crucial to understand, then, is that such power and order are not so much illusory as incomplete and always vulnerable to disruption by other senses that are inherent in placed experience. This is because, despite the assumption or even hope that we might escape place to become "strangers" and thus achieve an ordered and empowered sense of the world, *place travels along with us*—it is never left behind. While we are trying to build our cognitive mapping of modernity and to achieve some sort of order within which we can place ourselves as relatively stable, immanent, subjects in place, we actually travel; and places and their representations travel as well, accompanied by the theories that attempt to make sense of them. By traveling, we challenge that same order, for the purpose of our travels is both the definition *and* the transgression of that mapping, of its reassuring stability and the fascination with what is not only behind, but also beyond the map.

What is important about place is the idea that it cannot be subsumed by the universal categories conjured to explain away chaos and paradox. We pick up and travel—we forsake place—in order to order disorder. But at every step of the way, because we always travel through places to other places, we re-encounter disorder.

Place is deconstructive of the binaries through which we seek to order the world because it is simultaneously subjective and objective. According to Casey (1996, 36), these binaries include:

> pairs of terms that have enjoyed hegemonic power in Western epistemology and metaphysics. I am thinking of such dichotomies as subject and object, self and other, formal and substantive, mind and body, inner and outer, perception and imagination (or memory), and nature and culture themselves. It is always from a particular place that a person, considered as a knowing "subject," seizes upon a world of things presumed to be "objects." The reduction of persons to subjects — and, still more extremely, to minds — and of things to objects could not occur anywhere other than place. Yet to be fully in a place is to know — to *know* by direct acquaintance as well as by cultural habitus — that such a double reduction delivers only the shadowy simulacrum of the experiences we have in that place.

Place, in this sense, is the holder of paradox, the unifier of things held separate by abstract modern epistemology. But it takes movement, indeed travel, for us to really experience them as such. Movement of the body, for Merleau-Ponty (1962), is what constitutes place itself, and movement brings with it encounter with "the realist ontology of the larger place-world" of others. Places are at once the sedimented layers of historical experience, cultural habit, and personal and collective memory *and* continually remade by "lived bodily movement." For Casey it is precisely this combination of the objective realism of history and habit, and one's embodied subjectivity, that allows place to contain and hold paradox, rather than explain it away.

> The world of places is densely sedimented in its familiarity and historicity and its very materiality while, at the same time, it is animated and reanimated by the presence of the lived body in its midst. In the end, *both* factors — one realist in significance, the other idealist or transcendental — are required for a full determination of what it means to be bodily in a place. If the body/place nexus allows us to conjoin realism with transcendentalism — itself a deeply paradoxical combination — it also permits us to see that the bond between body and place is further paradoxical in being at once subjective and objective and, more especially, private and public. (Casey 1997, 241)

To the extent that these paradoxical aspects of place are the product of a combination of movement through space and experience through time, the condition of travel only heightens, and indeed makes more accessible, these paradoxes. Travel intensifies those moments in which we are at once shoring up the binaries of subjectivity and epistemology, making the world abstract and knowable, and creating opportunities for the disruption of these binaries and abstractions. Traveling in places, we seek out an object of difference to reconfirm our sense of order, while at the same time opening ourselves to the possibility that others will not always re-enact their expected roles, and that our order will be transgressed and deferred.

CODA

In Venice, we experienced *in place* the resilience of modern epistemologies that force us to travel, seeking an order that will never be. Traveling is not a choice, then, but a way of coping with the anxieties of the modern condition. By traveling to Venice and *in* Venice we did not escape; rather, we embodied the paradox, we found ourselves translated into mobile subjects faced with endless paradoxes every time we "touched down"; every time, by being in place, we were bound by its tentacles.

At the same time, the metaphysics of representation in which we were ensnared relied on the putative existence of some order in Venice, somewhere "out there," waiting to be discovered and reached. For this reason our traveling had to go on, with its endless enactment of performances and the related production of paradoxes.

There is no such place as a "tourist Venice," just as there is little sense in addressing the possibility of reaching a "non-tourist" Venice. Venice, after all, is nothing but a place where all the anxieties and difficulties of "living *with* and *within* the paradox" come to shore quite blatantly; it is just another modern place, where the recurrent regularity of tourist performances makes "things tourist" real (and often unpleasant); where we cannot help but fight the traps and cages of binary thinking. Venice is where we realized that while we were searching for a sophisticated and alternative order, that order could never be, but was always in the making.

Following our troubling experience of Venice, this book is just another modern journey—books, indeed, travel—a journey through the paradoxes of traveling, an exploration of how such paradoxes are enacted by tourists' performances in place and how they travel and are reproduced within a specific set of epistemological fields, mobilizing the hearts and minds (and bodies) of hundreds of millions every year in the search for a liberating order, an order that is promised but, always, endlessly deferred.

1

Sensing Tourist Spaces

Tim Edensor

INTRODUCTION

> The ability to replicate cultural identity is a material practice embedded in the reciprocities, aesthetics and sensory strata of material objects.
>
> —Seremetakis (1994b, 3)

This chapter explores the kinds of sensory experiences that are fostered by contemporary tourism. While the tourist gaze has been subject to much analysis, the senses of smell, tactility, hearing, and other senses have been less considered. I propose to link tourists' sensory encounters with different forms of tourist space and place, and discuss how they emerge out of the contradictory modern desires for order and its transcendence.

Certain recent accounts have usefully attempted to put the body back into tourist theory (for instance, Veijola and Jokinen 1994). While these have been particularly useful in accounting for the embodied identities of different kinds of tourist, it is also pertinent to recall that "the human body is not principally a text; rather, it is consumed by a world filled with smells, textures, sights, sounds and tastes" (Stoller 1994, 119). Tourists are inevitably embodied, although never "merely pairs of eyes" (Saldanha 2002, 43). The tourist body, like all phenomenal bodies, is active and experiential, and develops practical dispositions toward circumstances through experience, including sensory experience. Embodied tourist performances, perceptions, and experiences emerge from active subjects practically oriented toward durable shared skills and meanings. Yet this should not be conceived as purely subjective, for ways of sensing are partly produced out of "a shared world of intermundane space which crosses over and intertwines with that of similarly embodied human beings" (Williams and Bendelow 1998, 53) through intercorporeal relations. Through the expansion of mobilities, we might expect that sensory experience expands in and through multiple, complex, and uneven global flows, including tourist flows.

Crucially, embodied praxes may be subject to reflexive assessment but are often habitual in familiar spatial and social circumstances where they are informed by sensory information—via regular tactilities, smells, sounds, tastes, and textures. However, they may be confounded where social and sensory familiarities are absent. In such circumstances, sensual experience may overwhelm practical enactions.

In Western processes of modernity, there are powerful tendencies to organize bodies and spaces according to particular imperatives, producing distinct forms of ordered and commercial space as well as regulated bodies. Experiential modes of operating within disciplined spaces can reproduce both regulated bodies and space, and disciplined space likewise conditions bodily praxes. However, these spatializing processes are complemented by the radical destabilization of the familiar engendered by modernity's dynamism, so that both understandings of space/place and habitual corporeal sensation are apt to be threatened. Moreover, the production of experiential order may lead to the variable search for transcendence of a mundane state of being in the world, a quest for sensory "otherness" outside an apparent matrix of spatial predictability.

In contemporary Western modernity, rational and commercial forces are currently preeminent in the tourist industry, although in tourism—as elsewhere—alternative forms of modern desire find outlets in other places and spaces. This distinctly modern paradox of simultaneously producing order and disorder, of confining desire but producing desirable spaces and occasions, saturates tourism. However, modernity is often inaccurately characterized as solely the dissemination of Western processes of development that universalizes globality. It is far better to conceive of overlapping multiple modernities constituted by disjunctive global flows that are mediated by particular cultural and historical contexts that impact upon public cultures, social imaginaries, bureaucratic designs, technologies, industries, and spatialization (Appadurai 1996). Accordingly, the global distribution of order varies greatly with consequences for the production of distinct spatial qualities and sensory experiences.

In what follows, I discuss the sensual experience of spaces within a framework that distinguishes between different modern tourist contexts. First, I question the theoretical preoccupation with the ways in which tourists experience other spaces and cultures through their eyes by foregrounding other, nonvisual sensual experiences. Next, I explore how the habits and conventions of tourism produce tourist "taskscapes" in which specific forms of touristic habitus are mobilized but are also constrained and enabled in their experience and actions by the spatial and material affordances of these distinct spaces. I then go on to discuss the contrasting sensualities between "enclavic" and "heterogeneous" tourist spaces before concluding.

SENSING TOURISM

It is not my intention to criticize studies of vision and tourism but to suggest that the assertion that the visual is central to tourism is an exaggeration that downplays other touristic ways of apprehending the world. While John Urry has recognized that tourist experience is constituted by far more than the gaze, he still insists that "the organising sense within the typical tourist experience is visual" (2002b, 146). The notion that there is a "typical" tourist experience is somewhat arguable, for while modes of sightseeing are important to tourism, they are far from central to all touristic practices. Indeed, the emergence of sightseeing out of romantic, modern techniques to improve and enlighten the self (Adler 1989) has always been accompanied by numerous other sensory experiences, and with the proliferation of tourist activities and venues this is expanding. Urry has broadened his initial typology of the tourist gaze (1992), a move which chimes with my own attempt to identify different gazing practices at the Taj Mahal, where, for instance, many Muslim visitors adopt a reverential gaze at variance to normative Western ways of seeing (Edensor 1998). This proliferation of gazing practices should be similarly accompanied by an acknowledgment of multiple sensory practices and experiences.

Arguments that the visual is central to tourism may also veer toward those rather dystopian, Baudrillardian versions of the postmodern condition, which assert that the proliferation of empty, free-floating signs overwhelms attempts to perceive and understand the world. For instance, recently Garlick found it necessary to ask why people still travel to see and photograph otherness in an age when images of otherness proliferate (2002, 303)—a suggestion that otherness is only manifest in sign form and apprehended only through the gaze. Undoubtedly the nexus between mediatized imagery and tourism is highly pertinent in an increasingly spectacular culture, but we should be wary of producing over-general theories about such image-culture and hence, about its impact upon tourism. This tendency is perhaps understandable if we acknowledge that the visual is a more identifiable element of the tourist experience whereas the nonvisual senses are somewhat ineffable. For instance, smells "yield experiences which are inherently discontinuous, fragmentary and episodic." In contradistinction to visuality, "(I)ntensity, complexity and affect replace considerations of perspective, scale or distance." Moreover, "environmental and immersive," smells are "inhaled and thus become intimately bound with the body; they permeate the atmosphere and are thus inescapable" (Drobnick 2002, 33). More obviously, with regard to tourism, odor is a key marker of cultural differences based upon dietary, natural, climatic, sanitary, and industrial contrasts.

It is difficult to avoid the suspicion that most writers have generalized about tourism by accounting for the touristic dispositions and experiences of a small group of middle-class, Western tourists in particular kinds of tourist space and have neglected, for instance, working-class seaside holidays and carnivalesque adventures, as well as numerous non-Western tourist practices. In addition, the focus on purposive gazing has often conjured up an instrumental, disembodied tourist so that undertaking tourist pursuits in a state of relaxed distraction—where tourists "switch off," for instance—has been underplayed. Accordingly, as Constance Claessen contends, "(W)e not only think *about* our senses, we think *through* them" (1993, 9, her italics). In what follows, I argue that many tourist endeavors are mundane and informed by an unreflexive sensual awareness, and hence not particularly dissimilar to everyday habits and routines.

Claessen (1993) insists that rather than trading in generalities, it is better to refer to the distinct ways in which the senses are culturally shaped, that we perceive according to norms that prescribe what is sensually desirable and acceptable, and what must be kept at bay, and thus accord value to particular sensual experiences. For instance, smell can justify "not only essentialist views of inferior or superior places, but also desirable and undesirable people" (Drobnick 2002, 37). The senses are thus "cumulative and accomplished, rather than given" (Stewart 1999, 18) and do not provide an unmediated access to the world as purely "natural" tools. Moreover, the senses are "shaped and modified by experience and the body bears a somatic memory of its encounters with what is outside it" (Stewart 1999, 19), so that sensing is always in process. General sensory paradigms are therefore wholly inadequate to understand particular ways of apprehending the world, which depend upon culturally located modes of sensory experience and conceptualization. For ways of conceptualizing senses are imbued with cultural values, hence the prioritization given to sight in Western modernity: "sensory values not only frame a culture's experience, they express its ideals, its hopes and its fears" (Claessen 1993, 136), its social relations, its cultural practices, and its forms of practical living. Thus Western modernity has valorized the use of scopic approaches to understanding and classifying the world and consolidated the power of the visual by adopting authoritative techniques of representation that have become common-sense epistemological tools (Jay 1992). Such visual techniques are widespread within both tourist production (in brochures, holiday programs, guided tours, and guidebooks) and in tourist practice (through photography, video recording, and journal keeping). Such techniques tend to banish the ambiguity of the world, bringing "otherness" into representation in contradistinction to the unpredictable, indescribable effects of the sonic, the tactile, and the aromatic, which are far more difficult to visualize and textualize. However, despite the persistence of these dominant conventions about the meanings of sensual experience, in increasingly complex societies, contesting values may proliferate.

While the visual is the pre-eminent sense engaged in cultural and heritage tourism much of the time, a quick appraisal of other forms of tourism indicates that it is certainly not always the dominant sense. This is most obvious when we consider the mantra of beach tourism, "sun, sea, sand, and sex," a phrase which immediately conjures up a series of nonvisual sensualities. The sensation of heat beating down on the relaxed, unclothed body is primarily haptic. The view is often occluded by sunshades while the gaze does not generally strain to witness the marvellous; indeed, the eyes are often closed while sunbathing. The tourist's body becomes more actively engaged as it enters the sea, leaping over waves, swimming and floating. It is sensitive to temperature and the eddies and currents of the water, and is careful not to taste the brine. The particular textures of sand are all sensations with which the regular beach-goer is well acquainted: the pleasures of its graininess, the way it slips through the fingers, irritation when it gets stuck in the body's cracks. What is more, the scent of sun tan lotion and the smell of the sea, the "ozone" that is consciously breathed in, provide a powerful sense of place that is not necessarily connected to geographical familiarity.

Other forms of tourist experience equally center upon nonvisual sensation. The adrenaline-charged activities of adventure tourists as they hurtle into a bungee jump, cascade along a river with a raft, or abseil rapidly down a cliff (Cloke and Perkins 1998) produce a whirl of intermingled sensualities fueled by rapid and uneven movement, in which the weight, strength, and elasticity of the body becomes foregrounded. The same could be said for the sensations engendered by ever-more elaborate "white-knuckle" attractions of log flumes and roller coasters, which likewise scramble the senses through the foregrounding of rapid movement. The experience of a pop festival can be considered as absorption in a somatic response to auditory stimulation, and provides a haptic stimulus in the crush of the crowd. Walking holidays render the body receptive to different senses over time. The walker may commence with a bouncy step and a keen eye, but after several hours, the ache of the limbs may override the stimulus of the visual (Edensor 2000). And Saldanha (2002) shows how Goan beach raves are a complex amalgam of music, smells of sweat, kerosene, and cannabis, the sight of the moon and coconut trees, the tactilities of moving bodies, sand, and humidity, which combine—together with the varied effects of sensory-enhancing drugs—to produce a subjective, intensely kinaesthetic experience. A similar sensory immersion might be attributed to the rave tourism of resorts such as Ibiza and Ayia Napa if we take notice of Reynolds's account of a contemporary dance scene: "the listener is hurled into a vortex of heightened sensation, abstract emotions and artificial energies. . . . Rave provokes the question: is it possible to base a culture around sensations rather than truth" (1998, xix). The expansion of the global tourist flows through the proliferation of the kinds of tourist pursuit, and destination multiplies these diverse sensualities.

In order to rethink the sensual experiences embodied in tourism, I draw on a range of tourist spaces to explore how they may be conducive to particular sensual experiences, to examine the possible intersections between particular touristic dispositions and forms of tourist space. Before this, I need to discuss tourist taskscapes, the affordances of tourist space, and modes of tourist performance and the ways in which they paradoxically produce a serialized sense of place in the realms of the unfamiliar but also provoke a desire for sensual experiences that transcend normative apprehensions of place.

Tourist Taskscapes

Tourism is usually considered to occur during extraordinary periods of time and is marked against the habitual routinized world of work and home. However, this dichotomy has become much more tenuous as commercial strategies have increased opportunities for pleasure. Notions that the body becomes dulled in its daily grind, that it becomes desensitized though the imposition of routine and can be re-awakened on holiday are unrealistic because of the proliferating opportunities for pleasurable everyday leisure, but also through the instantiation of highly predictable tourist routines, habits, and dispositions. Thus many tourist ventures resemble both the mundane rituals of domestic life and the responsibilities and planning required in workday employment. With this in mind, I want to put forward the idea that the increasing range of tourist spaces can be described as "taskscapes," simultaneously exploring how the instantiation of routines shapes sensual experience through everyday interaction with familiar space.

Ingold and Kurttila (2000) describe "taskscapes" as everyday spaces that are fostered by the ways in which habits and habitation recreate local and domestic space and render it comfortable and homely. Strikingly, despite the geographical focus of space as text, as representation, or as power-laden, the most common spatial experience is that sensed through everyday life, where familiar space forms an unquestioned backdrop to daily tasks, pleasures, and routine movement. This is the taskscape, the terrain on which quotidian maneuvers and modes of dwelling are unreflexively carried out, a habitat organized to enable continuity and stability, and recreated by regular existential practices. As I argue, although taskscapes have been conceived as local and everyday, they can also be likened to the many tourist spaces to which we become accustomed. Enmeshed in our tourist routines, we possess a practical, unreflexive knowledge of such spaces; what to do there, where to go, how to look, and what to look at.

One way of conceptualizing place is that it "exists through the realisable projects and availabilities, patterns of use and users, all of which are practically negotiated daily." This "unnoticed framework of practices and concerns is something in which we dwell" as "habituated body subjects" (Ingold and Kurttila 2000, 90–91). Thus there exist spatial constraints and opportunities which inhere in the qualities of places, and these mesh with the bodily dispositions emerging out of the routine practices of its inhabitants that become embedded over time. In this regard, it is clear that space is not only understood and experienced cognitively. Rather it is approached with what Crouch (1999) calls "lay geographical knowledge," a participatory disposition in which the influences of representations and semiotics are melded with sensual, unreflexive, practical knowledge.

As Casey (2001) outlines, place is apprehended by means of habitus, through habitation and via incorporation into the body. While this underplays the importance of understanding place through the representation of place and space—highly pertinent to tourist spaces—it foregrounds the customary, embodied modes through which people dwell within and move through places, refuting overinstrumental portrayals of subjects in space. The "taskscape" foregrounds unreflexive modes of dwelling, of "being-in-the-world," of mundanely organizing and sensing the environment of familiar space. The operation of the senses is thus central to understanding the interplay between people and space. For example, Ingold and Kurttila (2000) explore the ways in which the Sami people of northern Finland "understand" the weather they confront. Unlike the more abstract, quantifiable, scientific modernist approach of climatologists who *record climate*, the Sami *experience weather*. As a sensuous form of knowing, weather is part of the everyday experience of work and play and is part of a practical knowing of familiar space, a flexible skill which adapts, for instance, to such new forms of transport as the snowmobile and motorbikes, which require different forms of knowing weather, of *feeling* forms of snow and maneuvering vehicles appropriately. The apprehension of weather is typified by a multisensory awareness that facilitates spatial orientation and coordinates activity, an immersed, space-making practice that embeds identity. Here, then, is a situated, sensuous engagement with the environment, one that continuously emerges out of an unfixed and improvisatory disposition, which nevertheless is influenced by conventions and traditional practice. Thus such sensual, knowledgeable practices make space, are part of the ways in which people inhabit place and come to belong in it.

Sensual and practical engagement with familiar space also requires that the *materialities* of such spaces should not be neglected. All too often in geographical accounts of place and space, and in accounts of human experience and practice, materiality is ignored, implying that subjective understandings emerge out of broader discursive and representational epistemologies. Seemingly there is no sense that embodied subjects physically *interact* with space and objects, gaining sensory experiences that shape an apprehension as to their feel and meaning. It is therefore essential to reinstate the *affordances* of place and space, those qualities which are spatial potentialities, constraining and enabling a range of actions. Here, space is conceived as "a concrete and sensuous concatenation of material forces" (Wylie 2002, 251) that possesses an agency to impact upon the sensibilities of those who dwell and move within. The surfaces, textures, temperatures, atmospheres, smells, sounds, contours, gradients, and pathways of places encourage humans—given the limitations and advantages of their normative physical abilities—to follow particular courses of action, producing an everyday practical orientation dependent upon a multisensory apprehension of place and space.

Accordingly, "the sensory is not only encapsulated within the body as an internal capacity or power but is also dispersed out there on the surface of things as the latter's autonomous characteristics, which can then invade the body as perceptual experience" (Seremetakis 1994b, 6). While such processes of spatial interaction are never merely "natural," since all human action and apprehension is enmeshed within learned cultural, practical techniques and conventions, particular physical phenomena impact upon people and influence their spatial practices, their sensory perception and sensual evaluations. Affordances thus inform a practical engagement that becomes part of "second nature" where people are familiar with space. And as we see below, the dissolution of sensual familiarity may render visitors unable to develop any practical sense of what to do, how to move, and how otherwise to behave, but conversely, may provide a stimulating experience in its distinction from the familiar.

The practical knowledge informed by the sensory apprehension of place instantiates particular norms of performance that make up the taskscape. I have written elsewhere that performance be conceived as unreflexive and habitual as well as conscious and instrumental (Edensor 2001, 2002). This notion can be furthered by conceptualizing tourist spaces as stages upon which particular enactions take place and which are maintained—stage-managed—according to particular imperatives. Besides the conventions that guidebooks and tourist workers uphold, and fellow tourists reproduce, performance also emerges out of the communication between senses, spaces, and things, and is thus "embedded in, and inherited from, an autonomous network of object relations and prior sensory exchanges" (Seremetakis 1994b, 7). Thus, "the sensory landscape and its meaning-endowed objects bear within them emotional and historical sedimentation that can provoke and ignite gestures, discourses and acts" (Seremetakis 1994b, 7). Spatial sensual experience is thus always contextual, being constituted out of a practical engagement with familiar kinds of space, action which becomes habitual and unreflexive, and is thus part of the place-making process that both domestic and tourist routines perpetrate.

Tourist spaces are realms in which particular kinds of tasks are accomplished and reproduced, constituting the *work* of tourism. These performative habits—dispositions which, for instance, promote the desire to visit particular sites, to learn something about the culture visited, to develop the self, to pamper the body, to restore health and relax—involve a series of techniques that help to achieve these aims. Modes of walking, listening, gleaning information, relaxing, and socializing reveal persistent and regular forms of bodily hexis and embodied praxes. Much tourism is carried out in a langorous state of distraction, but more purposive actions to reach desired states of being are facilitated by the familiar amenities and an infrastructure comprising tour operators; health, sports, and beauty facilities; shops; banks; and information spaces that infest many tourist spaces. Many such spaces are devised to accord with familiar and comfortable sensual experiences, and therefore possess serial affordances. And these stages are organized to accommodate and perpetuate performative conventions, which are also consistently reproduced by the enactions of tourists who have ingested notions of how and where to perform in these settings. As an immersed practice, the accumulation of repetitive events becomes sedimented in the body to condense an unreflexive sense of being in place. Individually, a sense of place is consolidated through the instantiation of routine, and collectively, as these individual paths and routines coincide. Thus the meaning of place becomes sedimented in time not only through external constraints imposed upon tourists but also through the consistent enaction of performative norms—modes of strolling around, comportment, and so on. These conventions are helped by the familiar affordances of place that condition sensualities sedimented in the body. To summarize, becoming a tourist is about accommodating oneself to the affordances that are dwelt within and passed through, and out of these adaptations sensuous apprehensions and practical epistemologies emerge. Modes of apprehension evolve that tie people to an extended sense of place. Thus place is reproduced by the enaction of habitual performances and touristic forms of habitus find their expression in particular spaces.

As I have said, the phenomenological experience of the world is always mediated by the cultural context in which it occurs, for understandings of the senses are loaded with cultural values, despite the elusiveness of certain sensual experiences. A further problem lies with the tendencies of phenomenologists to portray bodies themselves as undifferentiated in their interaction with space rather than freighted with dispositions and modes of perception shaped by class, gender, ethnicity, age, and a huge range of other contextualizing factors (see Hooper 2001). Such variations generate an understanding of place as multiple and unenclosed, potentially thwarting the attempts of tourist managers to produce "coherent" and bounded places. Nevertheless, the production of a tourist habitus through the reproduction of conventional touristic performances and the materialities and affordances of distinctly produced space "brings together the placiality of its setting and the temporality of its ongoing re-enactment" (Casey 2001, 686). International tourism thus produces ways of dwelling within widely distributed taskscapes.

Yet this modern extension of mobilities and generic space does not necessarily diminish the salience of the local, which may become more central as resistance to the homogenizing tendencies of global capitalism proceeds—and in tourism this might be understood as re-emphasizing the specifically local. But more generally, a sense of place is increasingly mobile, so that we are able to serially belong to a diversity of interconnected and unconnected locales, each with its own set of attachments, whether familial, political, social, functional, or sensual. This spatial expansion may lead to a thinning out of place, but it extends a sense of place across space. Part of this spatial familiarity can be found in proliferating globalized spaces in which we find ways to "orient ourselves and feel at home" (Casey 2001, 685). The global "disarray of place" is complemented by the postmodern "scattered self," which possesses a habitus attuned to such placial thinness (Casey 2001, 684). However, the sense of place here might prove unsatisfactory because of its predictable and habitual character, and those other elements of place longed for—the complex and dense socialities, the unassimilable otherness of unfamiliar places, the multiple connections and external intrusions from outside, and, not least, their peculiar, surprising sensual qualities—might be sought. First, however, I focus on the sense of place engendered in more predictable tourist spaces.

The Sensualities of Tourist Enclaves

One way of utilizing the notion of the taskscape with regard to tourism is by looking at the serial, homogeneous spaces that proliferate globally wherever large-scale tourist industry develops, and the kinds of practice, disposition, and experience they foster. The home-from-home characteristics of many tourist destinations are highly familiar. The international standard resorts and hotels, the beach, the air-conditioned bus tour are all sensually apprehended and practically engaged with on the basis of prior knowledge and sensation. Here, networks of familiarity are not effects of local knowledge but extend through a kind of parochial cosmopolitanism.

Craik points out that trends toward the production of large-scale, customized, themed tourist developments, referred to as "built environments," "spectacles," "property markets," and "festival markets," "entail a convergence or blurring between tourist and everyday leisure activities" (Craik 1997, 125). Thus the distinction between peoples' local leisure and shopping spaces and those they inhabit as tourists may be more contextual than material, for the affordances encountered at this panoply of designed realms may produce familiar sensual experiences. Accordingly, much of the sensualities of tourism and tourist space are learned and expected. As Urry remarks, tourist performances "fold notions of movement, nature, taste and desire into, and through, the body" (2002b, 152). The technologies characteristically provided by the tourist industry (modes of coach travel, guide services, tours) and the techniques learned by tourists (how to comport oneself, what to move toward, what to photograph) mesh with each other at intensively managed tourist sites to constitute powerful ways of organizing sensual experience.

In tourist enclaves, often impugned as aspects of the environmental bubble, harsh sensations are kept at bay and moderated soundscapes, tactilities, smells, and scenes are maintained. The increasingly themed spaces of leisure and shopping (Gottdiener 1997) produce visual codes or spectacular landscapes in which gazing is enjoined. The centrality of the visual inheres in the interior design, the uncluttered spaces, the carefully placed local paintings, textiles, and sculptures, and also in the technologies utilized in such enclaves, such as the tour bus, the exhibition, and the spectacular show (Urry 2000, 95). As Rojek maintains, the design of purified tourist spaces is devised to shut out "extraneous, chaotic elements" and reduce "visual and functional forms to a few key images" (1995, 62). By framing views, sights, photograph points, and cultures, the visual design of highly commodified and regulated tourist spaces direct the tourist gaze. Rather redolent of the museum or the parlor (see Seremetakis 1994c), this homely décor represses the kinaesthetic qualities of seeing, desensualizing vision by removing the tactile, auditory, and aromatic qualities from artifacts. In heritage sites and theme parks, on guided tours and bus journeys, the tourist gaze is directed toward particular selective items and features by means of commentary, information boards and markers, signposts, and signs that recommend photographs be taken. Other sensate experiences are rarely remarked upon so that the visual predominates and tourists are able to "take possession of objects and environments, often at a distance" (Urry 2002b, 147).

In keeping with the olfactory regulation—and the commodification of scent—that persists in most Western urban environments, tourist enclaves tend to monitor smell so that local incense may waft through hotel lobbies and scented blooms thrive in the gardens, but the everyday smells of sewage, food, and industry are minimized. This helps to produce the "blandscapes" described by Drobnick, namely those "aseptic places, created by the modernist drive towards deodorization, that are so empty that they lead to an alienating sense of placelessness" (2002, 34). A disdain for strong smells pervades highly regulated tourist spaces, for they continue to signify poverty, disease, decadence, and decay, the antitheses of high modernity (see Bauman 1994, 24), and hence, must be confined to particular areas, well away from suburbanites, shopping centers, and tourists. Subverting the regulation of and behavior central to such spaces, strong smells transgress "social conventions in regard to enjoyment, discipline, functionalism, corporeal deportment" (Drobnick 2002, 35). Similarly, sound is carefully controlled. Little is permitted to disrupt the calm, toned-down atmosphere that has become synonymous with relaxation, and soundscapes made up of the tinkle of fountains and piped music drift through restaurants and hotels. Often, this soundscape is composed of pale versions of local music or familiar western tunes in muzak form. Hotel shows of "local" culture also tend to feature skilled musicians able to play westernized versions of music and dance, as well as "global" standards. Here, like the few selective local artifacts on display, the sensual experience of otherness is gestured toward but tamed by its emplacement within a carefully controlled environment and its contextualization within an "international" ambience.

Tactility is also organized so that smooth surfaces prevail on walls and floors, clutter and dirt are eradicated, and evident routes are maintained. The seamlessness of linear movement and the even surfaces of polished floors and paving underfoot mean that the body remains undisturbed in its progress and is able to perform unhindered movement toward destinations. Linen sheets, cushioned furniture, and air-conditioning enclose tourists so that familiar standards of comfort ensure that bodies relax in habituated fashion, and hands and skin sense little that is jarring. Similarly, guided tours proceed at an even pace along distinct, regulated pathways.

Admittedly, then, in these regulated spaces, the visual is the predominant sense by design and touristic accommodation to space. Direction, stage management, and choreography maintain a sense of how space should be used (Edensor 2001), and repetitive, performative conventions about comportment, movement, and the volume of conversation are largely sustained.

These archetypal, modern spaces have emerged out of several interrelated processes. First of all, the designs and schemes of modernist planners to rationalize the landscape are embodied in the structure and organization of much tourist space. For instance, Ritzer and Liska (1997) demonstrate how Weberian rationalization is extended to produce spatial predictability through "McDisneyization," a term which connotes the "efficiency" and "calculability" of the Disney theme parks as exemplary rationalized tourist spaces. The Disney techniques for control and entertainment have been adopted in the production of numerous other leisure environments, which seem to typify what Lash (1999) calls the "machinic episteme," the belief that an all-encompassing design can order meaning through the logical placing of people and things within a gridlike system. The rational production of such landscapes is described by Berman as emerging out of a dialectical process whereby "one mode of modernism both energises and exhausts itself trying to annihilate another" (1982, 165). This "other" modernism is discussed below.

Such spaces—which may again be conceptualized as stages according to a consideration of tourism as performance—are venues for particular kinds of enaction. Rational(ized) space is supposedly conducive to the formation of "good habits," akin to the bourgeois, Victorian forms of "rational recreation" devised to inculcate improving norms of conduct and personal development in such purpose-built sites as parks, libraries, and promenades, developed to accommodate these rational activities. The inculcation of "good" tourist habits has been further consolidated by the commercial imperatives of calculability that supposedly ensure success with the consequent diminution of spontaneity and intensity of experience. The rationalization of the body through state education and health regimes has long permeated leisure, a sphere in which "the modernisation of the body and the senses can be described as a process containing experience, discovery, as well as instruction" (Frykman 1994, 65). And beyond this, contemporary reflexive projects of self-fashioning are mediated by scientific knowledge concerning appropriate nutrition and exercise, and the ingestion of information to foster a disposition that seeks out these spaces of "improvement." For instance, in certain forms of rural recreation, the body is instructed to become aware of certain stimuli and objects of interest. Through valorizing certain forms of sensual experience, such instructive regimes aim to create a reflexive body which "became the training ground for the double process of educating the senses and making good use of them" (Frykman 1994, 67).

Accordingly, both planners and advocates of "productive" forms of leisure envisaged an ordering of space and, subsequently, a clarifying of sensory experience. In regulated space, the senses perceive and enjoy the precision of the environment. For instance, Le Corbusier, doyen of the international style, conceived leisure as a necessary and healthy social pursuit that could be enabled by the development of appropriate spaces devised to maximize rational leisure experience in an orderly fashion. The provision of plentiful supplies of light, clean air, and space would, it was believed, encourage the rational development of healthy persons whose eyes, noses, and ears would be uncluttered by sensory rubbish. Clear, linear sight lines would allow purposive progress and an undistracted mind. These modes have percolated into popular social conventions and cultural tastes associated with notions about what is "civilized" and reflexive self-development, so that the acquisition of sensory capabilities—taking the seaside air, cultivating a nose for perfume, developing a finely tuned ear for music and a taste for good food—extends into tourist modes of acquiring distinction. These conventions about what and how to sense the world are upheld through the bureaucratic monitoring of noise and smell and through the instantiation of touristic norms.

There are indicative trends that within these touristic spatial complexes processes of tourist management are evolving that allow a greater range of customized experience, within the security of packaged provision. For instance, Torres (2002) shows how the massive complex of enclavic tourist resorts in Cancun, Mexico, is offering an increasingly varied range of activities and excursions further afield, so that tourists are able to tailor their vacations within more flexible limits.

Despite these tendencies, the pre-eminent drive is toward the production of spatial order, regulation, classification, and rationalization in accordance with the bureaucratic and commercial imperatives of the tourist industry. As such, this spatialization echoes the wider production of functional differentiation and single-purpose spaces, the division of space into a gridlike structure in which specialized spaces for play, work, and reproduction are assigned. This has culminated in "a spatially and socially segmented world—people here, traffic there; work here, homes there; rich here; poor there" (Berman 1982, 168).

The Sensualities of Heterogenous Tourist Spaces

Although the ordered, packaged, enclavic tourist experience may resonate with modern imperatives to plan and manage space, there are modes of tourism which are drawn closer to the flux and contingency of modernity, to spaces in which unpredictable happenings, incongruous juxtapositions, diverse social and cultural activities, and a low level of surveillance promote a rich and varied sensory experience. Such spaces are often sought precisely because they confound familiar forms of comfort and mundane sensual experience, and perhaps because tourists might bypass the rather rigid regimes of representation through which sensual experience is conditioned and reclaimed.

Rojek (1995; also see Wang 1996) contends that in contemporary forms of leisure contradictory tendencies of modernity are evident. "Apollonian" impulses tend toward the "timid freedoms of respectable leisure" (1995, 80), where the "capacity for arousal and pleasure associated with the passions is denied because the passions themselves are reined in by the requirements of respectable society" (1995, 82). On the other hand, "Dionysian" urges seek out the antithesis of this ordered pleasure, revelling in the carnival and the unbounded, in excess and obscenity, in the sensual delights that flow through flux and the mixing of people, activities, and desires. Similarly, in contradistinction to classifying and regulatory tendencies, Lash refers to the "aesthetic reflexivity" of modernity, a sensibility that accepts indeterminacy. While sensations pertain to reality, they can only indicate potential meaning and are therefore "not graspable by concepts, but only via feeling, only via the imagination" (1999, 200). Emerging from the romantic imagination and fueled by the dynamism of modernity, this sensibility wallows in the contingent and the indecipherable in search of sensation.

This countertendency within modernity is captured by Berman's enthusiastic embrace of its inherent dynamism and continual change, which turns all that is solid into air. The emphasis here is on romantically conceiving of, and imaginatively engaging with, the constant flux of modernity and the stimulation it brings. Here is a "maelstrom of perpetual disintegration and renewal, of struggle and contradiction, of ambiguity and anguish" (Berman 1982, 15). This is what Lash calls "the anti-foundational undecidability of reflexive modernity" in which the fluid modern self is able to avoid fixity, moving from place to place (1999, 7). This constant disruption inevitably brings with it a continual reordering of the sensory constituents and the affordances of place, and opportunities for being stimulated by diverse and multiple sensations.

Although a dominant rationalizing modernity continues to consign the carnivalesque to specific times and marginal spaces (Shields 1991), there remains a lingering fascination with the possibilities available at such weakly regulated occasions and spaces (see Stallybrass and White 1986). The infusion of both the everyday and the supposedly "extraordinary" holiday with routine instantiates a habitual concern with epistemological and sensory security but simultaneously there is a desire for its transcendence, a shaking up of the experiential order that can be partly satisfied by the sensual experience of street markets, popular music festivals, large carnivals, and raves. Rather than comparable to medieval carnival, such spaces have been described by Featherstone (1991) as places wherein a "controlled decontrol of the emotions" can take place, are "liminoid," only pertaining to liminality. A sensual frisson may be experienced rather than an enveloping of the senses and emotions. For *signs* and *spectacles* of the carnivalesque are apt to be commodified by the tourist industry, reinstating the ordered primacy of visual representation. Nevertheless, certain occasions, such as the Notting Hill Carnival which draws huge crowds, mix people, roadside food stalls, sound systems, and spectacles to produce a rich sensory experience markedly different from that sensed in everyday urban settings. On the other hand, in other contexts, practices at variance to preferred norms of touristic conduct can be subjugated. For instance, at Stonehenge there is the normative visual consumption of the site, subject to challenge by the more sensual pursuits of music-making, dancing, and other invented rituals practiced by New Age travelers, which have been harshly prohibited, a policy which has delimited the auditory, tactile, and aromatic possibilities of experience at the site. Cohen and Taylor (1992) have suggested that people continuously attempt to escape the tedious "paramount reality" of the overregulated life world in leisure practices ranging from sex to sport, from DIY ("Do-It-Yourself") to drug use. While this perhaps portrays a somewhat dystopian view of the everyday, it usefully identifies the tensions between the contradictory modern desire for order and desire for transcendence that the tourist industry capitalizes upon in devising its various products.

In general, such leisure and tourist opportunities are spatially and temporally restricted in most Western contexts, although such marginal spaces as industrial ruins (Edensor 2005) can provide the mystery, incomprehensibility of function, and sensual onslaught, which I go on to describe, that confound the regulated sensual experiences discussed above. However, tourist spaces outside the west can appear wildly sensual and disordered to Western tourists. I am referring here to the bazaars, backpacker "honeypots," villages, fetes, and urban life which are regulated according to different principles, not lacking regulation but subject to contingent, local, and informal administration rather than state and bureaucratic control. Accordingly, these different modes of spatial organization produce a more variegated space in which the mixing of social activities—for instance, of tourist practices and facilities with other local business, domestic, educational, leisure, and bureaucratic activities— create a series of affordances that constitute a rich sensory space. Typically, a perceived sensory onslaught envelopes the Western tourist, not only because unfamiliar smells, sounds, tactilities, and sights arouse an awareness of sensual difference, but because their diversity and intensity contrast with the pale impressions gained in the highly regulated Western spaces of most tourist adventure. While such apprehensions may come as something of a shock to the normative apprehension of space, these spaces may be sought by desensitized bodies as a sensual restorative.

To give some idea of the bewildering but intoxicating effects of unfamiliar sensations, I will describe my first visit as a tourist to India many years ago, when after briefly dallying in Delhi, I spent a number of weeks in a small Gujerati village. The first striking thing for me was the baking heat, which ensured that my body remained fully clothed to avoid burning, and also disabled my movements since I could only move very slowly. Next were the sounds, which needed decoding for me: the sound of the temple bells, the numerous unfamiliar bird and animal noises, the harsh cries of traders and hawkers, the sulphurous noises emitted from several archaic motors, and in general, the human noise, the levels of conversation, the laughter, all slightly at variance to my habitual life world. Equally powerful were the smells: the scent of buffalo dung, the fruits produced by the village, the earthy aroma of rain on dust, the *bidis* and smell of kerosene. The textures were also drastically unfamiliar at first—of the furniture, the dusty ground, the air—so that a tactile apprehension of the village only became familiar after a few weeks. Finally, the sights of village life were equally startling: the colourful saris and other clothes, the huge bats that flew overhead, the lush greenery of the mango groves, the almost fluorescent yellow of the frogs in the village pond, and to my eyes, a host of obscure signs and activities. This overwhelming sensory defamiliarization was accompanied by the equally baffling social mores that confronted me. For instance, people I didn't know would walk through the house I was staying in, and the old woman next door would come inside uninvited and sleep on the bed.

In terms of a response to this sensory overload, there was little else I could do but give my body up to such sensual stimuli, and to accept the unknowability of cultural mores and activities. In fact, with the absence of any epistemological framework to comprehend difference, I was thrown back onto the senses, which overrode any meaning-making facility. In retrospect, it was this immersion in an unfamiliar sensual world that made this a memorable tourist experience for me. In actively seeking difference and "otherness," I was part of the modern tourist tendency to go beyond the packaged experience of enclavic tourism, which can only provide pale hints of sensual difference.

Certain modes of tourism are undertaken to engage in these different sensualities as well as to confound the habits and commonsense epistemologies of home, notably, certain kinds of independent travel and backpacking. To be sure, backpackers and other sensualists are driven by a desire for cultural capital and are apt to follow conventional practices replete with technologies and epistemologies through which experience is gained and interpreted (Desforges 1998; Edensor 1998; Munt 1994; Riley 1988). Backpackers usually follow highly prescribed routes, share "alternative" values, pursue particular practices, and altogether adopt regular dispositions toward other tourists, toward

self-development, and toward engagement with difference, and part of this involves valorizing a more "authentic" sensual experience of "otherness." Backpacking is, accordingly, part of the structuring of the tourist product in accordance with ideas about marketing order and (conditional) disorder. Yet
crucially, irrespective of the conventions of backpacking and the slogans of
tourist marketers, the spaces in which backpackers dwell and move—the sites
of cheap hotels, restaurants, and bars—possess different affordances from the
tourist enclaves referred to above. Elsewhere, I have described these environments as "heterogeneous tourist space" (Edensor 1998; 2001).

Certain kinds of tourist space outside the west contain tourist facilities as
well as workplaces, schools, meeting and eating places, extemporized leisure
sites, transport termini, bathing points, political headquarters, offices, administrative centers, places of worship, and temporary and permanent dwellings
that defy dichotomies of public and private, and work and leisure. Typically,
such spaces are characterized by mild regulation and a labyrinthine structure,
enabling the multidirectional flows of different bodies and vehicles and facilitating a wide range of movement. In contrast to a themed or manicured appearance, a bricolage of designs and signs mingle among carefully decorated
and unkempt facades. Additionally, distractions and diversions, and a shifting
series of juxtapositions, can provide surprising and unique scenes that interrupt the tourist gaze. In terms of bodily movement, unlike the linear progres-
sion experienced on guided tours, in heterogeneous tourist space it is difficult
to move in a straight line. Instead tourists must weave around obstacles and
be alert to other people, traffic, and animals. This jostling means that there is
continuous touching of others and weaving between and among bodies, and
the different textures brushed against and underfoot render the body aware of
diverse tactile sensations. For instance, in India, a differently modern spatial
order and experience might be symbolized by the *pheriwalas*, the mobile urban traders who set up stalls on pavements, or continually keep on the move
(Rajagopal 2001). In these habitats typified by "the unruly energy of the
bazaars, the assault of different sensations, varieties of costume and counte-
nance," shoppers must participate in a "typically fluid, dialogical encounter"
(2001, 99), also described by Buie (1996) as a "sensual dance." The
"smellscapes" in such spaces may be rich and varied, jumbling together pun-
gent aromas to produce intense "olfactory geographies," and likewise, the
combination of noises generated by numerous human activities, animals,
forms of transport, and performed and recorded music produces a changing
symphony of diverse pitches, volumes, and tones. Moreover, these aromas
and noises are part of constantly changing soundscapes and smellscapes, in
contrast to the regulated sensory and aromatic environments of enclavic
tourism. The body must continually confront a more variegated set of sensual

stimuli than prevails in enclavic tourist space. These diverse sensual stimuli produce *affect*. Distinct from an ordered and qualified emotion domesticated through its representation, affect is that intense and sensual experience of otherness that escapes signification. Here, in a Deleuzian sense, the body is a site of "surfaces, affects and desires that perceive and connect with other planes of existence, energies and affects" (Fullagar 2001, 74).

These more heterotopic spaces are far from pre-modern but testify to the unevenness of modernity and the distribution of different forms of spatial regulation. More akin to aspects of the early modern cities of Europe and the United States than the hyper-themed spaces of contemporary Western urbanity, the social and cultural mixing that occurs provokes responses that chime with accounts of the late nineteenth and early twentieth centuries.

The exemplary modern figure who best exemplifies a tourist disposition that seeks out sensual stimulation in the flux of the non-Western urban is the flaneur (see Smart 1994; Bauman 1994; but for an opposing view, see Morawski 1994, 184). Mobilizing distinct modes of strolling and looking, and developed ways of representing the city, using "a multifaceted method for apprehending and reading the complex and myriad signifiers in the labyrinth of modernity" (Frisby 1994, 93), the flaneur's approach is not merely concerned with detachedly acquiring impressions, but also in developing a "tactile ability." Roaming, discovering obscure experiences and residual processes, revealing "things hidden to those intent on purposive, linear goals" (Savage 1995, 207), the flaneur dwells among the multitude and wallows in the fleeting and contingent, in the flux of modernity. The figure of the flaneur undoubtedly has drawbacks in terms of the elitist and masculinist character attributed to him (see Wolff 1985; Wilson 1992) and has usually been presented as a rather detached figure. However, another reading can draw on a necessary sensual immersion—and not only the visual—which is part of the flaneur's existence within the crowd and is counterposed to the rational, scientific interpretation of social processes. For although the focus of many accounts of flanerie has been upon the visual clues and spectacles interpreted by the flaneur, the tactile, aromatic, taste-ful, and noisy experiences of wallowing amid the urban maelstrom of sensation have been downplayed (Frisby 1994).

Unlike Simmel (1995), who puts forward the urban dweller as mobilizing a defensive disposition to insulate himself against the sensual shocks of the modern city, the flaneur opens out to receive contingent sensual stimuli (Shields 1994) as part of the restless search within modernity to embrace the shock of the new. As the flaneur benefited from the possibilities for anonymous, aimless wandering in the new modern cities of the nineteenth century and thrived on the multiple characters, fleeting incidents, and continual flux, so does the tourist in the heterogeneous spaces of certain non-Western spaces. The onslaught of sensory information, rather than provoking neurasthenia or a blasé attitude to insulate the self from these shocks, provides a host of stimulating sensations and material for imaginative speculation. Definition and fixed meaning is not sought but delight is found in the contingent and the opening up of the body to sensation.

Debate persists about whether the flaneur is tethered to a specific time and place, namely, the early modern urbanity of nineteenth-century Paris as depicted by Baudelaire, or has mutated into several forms in a later modernity. Some contend that the flaneur disappeared as the arcades and less-ordered spaces of the early-modern city were extinguished in favor of highly rationalized, commodified spaces. Bauman aptly notes that "not all streets are, however, the proper grazing ground for the flaneur's imagination" (1994, 149). He maintains, however, that through the production of shopping malls, theme parks, and package holidays, flanerie has mutated into a ubiquitous contemporary habit, since designers have expropriated "the flaneur's own right and capacity to invent the rules of the game he would play and to supervise their execution" (Bauman 1994, 190). My own view is that this expropriation thwarts the individual agency to engage in adventurous wanderings that inculcate sensory and imaginative experience, and therefore cannot constitute flanerie. But rather than disappearing, flanerie has been globally redistributed and to be undertaken depends on specific spatial affordances. Like the early modern urban dweller's skill at performing "sudden, abrupt, jagged twists" (Berman 1982, 159) among the urban chaos, an embodied disposition oriented to this environment evolves which is attuned to sensual fluidity and mobility.

CONCLUSION

The mobilities of global tourism produce sensual experiences that are stretched out spatially rather than being confined to specific locales, for "we live out our bodily habitudes in relation to the changing spatiality of the scenes we successively encounter" (Casey 2001, 687). I have argued that this proliferation of spatial experiences does not necessarily engender confrontation with sensual difference and variety but may simply extend the familiar sensorium across space through the reproduction of serialized spaces and their affordances.

Tourist development is part of the complex redistribution of sensual experience across the social world as modern regulatory and rationalizing processes spread, as part of the globalization of Western capitalist, corporate, and bureaucratic imperatives. The Apollonian impulses within modernity are in the ascendant, and tourist space is increasingly subject to the bureaucratic, classificatory, rational imperatives that inhere in planning and commodifying culture. Yet this is a far from static picture. Novel sensual experiences previously confined to an elite band of travelers are being opened up through the evolution of niche-marketing and alternative forms of tourism. And even within highly regulated enclavic spaces there has been a move to diversify the Fordist management of tourism, to provide more niche marketing, as part of a strategy which is better conceived as neo-Fordism than post-Fordism (Torres 2002). In addition, the very processes by which a globalizing tourist industry produces sensual and spatial homogeneity are resisted: "The more places are levelled down, the *more*—not the less—may selves be led to seek out thick places in which their own personal enrichment can flourish" (Casey 2001, 685). Such is the paradox of tourist space, where homogeneous design and materiality not only render a sense of place comfortably predictable, partly through the comfortable sensual experiences engendered by these serialized affordances, but also provoke the sense that tourists are missing out on the dense social, cultural, and sensual experience of place they are also drawn toward.

Yet in any case, one of the spatial effects of modern planning is the illusion of permanence, for the underlying turbulence of continual economic and social change can destabilize the orderliness of the most carefully managed, exclusive spaces. This illusion of order needs to be continually recreated by workers and managers *and* tourists themselves. For attempts to regulate the conduct and the meaning of contemporary life are liable to be undone by the contradictions that inhere within it. For instance, conventional displays in shop windows and heritage attractions contain disparate elements that can strike peculiar relationships with a shift in the onlooker's perspective. Attempts to extinguish ambiguity are difficult to sustain for visual ordering; muzak and the feel of things can appear suddenly outmoded. The maintenance of order relies on keeping out of sight that which does not fit, or is abject, offensive, or disorderly, and this requires constant vigilance. Yet Massey's (1993) nonessentialist understanding of place, wherein places are fluidly constituted out of a dynamic multitude of connections with numerous other places, means that the people, objects, and energies that flow through and around places will inevitably intrude and interrupt upon touristic reverie.

Despite such regulatory procedures, then, the underlying chaos of modernity is apt to disrupt the best designs of bureaucrats and managers. Loud noises, powerful smells, rough contact, and jarring sights are apt to intrude on highly regulated space. For Richard Sennett (1994), the politics of disruption are an important counter to the individualism and pacified bodies that are eroding public space and modes of sociality. While I agree that the modern processes that instantiate spatial order are dominant, it is unlikely that such quiescent corporealities are all pervasive, for forms of resistance persist and alternative spaces are found in the interstices of the ordered. Moreover, the redistribution of sensualities has produced new experiences. For instance, car driving has enabled novel social, practical, and sensual experiences.

Academics and other tourists routinely disparage the attractions of regulated tourist enclaves in contradistinction to the experiences gained through apparently more adventurous pursuits. But it is important to acknowledge the pleasures of the familiar—a comfortable sense of place, a practical competence, and familiar sensations. Such experiences have been described as numbing, even erasing sensory capacities and social awareness, but I suggest that they are sought because they offer temporary escape from the everchanging nature of modern life. Similarly, the search for difference, continual change, and unpredictability also emerges out of a modern sensibility.

Infused with self-reflexivity, the modern self has been described as a project. The desire for self-development achieved through rational application persists, and there are a host of highly commodified and regulated places and times when improvement can be sought. Yet the self is also believed to develop through an encounter with difference, through an openness to unpredictable experiences in the modern ferment usually experienced outside familiar space, but liable to intrude upon it. Tourism, then, often consists of a movement between distinctive spaces and dispositions, namely between an embrace of familiar comforts and the sensualities of the unfamiliar, through a disposition that embraces both aesthetic and cognitive reflexivity. The interweaving of apparently paradoxical dispositions toward the sensual produces embodied subjects and fluid places that are distinctively modern.

For the sensory alterity sought and experienced by tourists, although often spurred on by nostalgic longings for that which modernity has obliterated, is as much a part of modernity as the desire for order. Uneven and disjunctive global flows produce spaces that defy hegemonic assumptions about the ubiquity of Western modernity and notions that sensual spaces and cultures belong to the past. Nevertheless, suffused with notions that "we" (the West) have fallen and can only seek recuperation in an "authentic" other, tourism encapsulates the "perspective and priorities of a culture that treats other cultures and epochs as insurance policies of its own vanished experience" (Seremetakis 1994d, 125). A rationalizing modernity has perpetrated the "disordering, institutional repression and perceptual discrediting" of sensual and material experience at a cost to the "narrative efficacy of material culture" and "the historical poetics of identity and memory" (Seremetakis 1994d, 136), thereby marginalizing and "discarding (the) sensory values, meaning and emotions attached to discredited materialities" (Seremetakis 1994d, 136). However, this commodification and regulation of the world can be broached by the multiple affordances that lurk, waiting to break out and bewilder and overwhelm the senses. And the possibilities offered through particular modes of tourism offer ethical opportunities for opening out to otherness and decentering the self through engaging with sensual alterity, through experiencing the affect engendered by the touch, smell, and sound of otherness. This contrasts with the experience gained through mobilizing a gaze that is directed toward a codified, commodified, and spectacular "otherness" that renders difference familiar. Here, the "desire to know that which is different to the western self is profoundly embodied, mediated by . . . senses that disturb and confound attempts to grasp at Hegelian notions of self-certainty" (Fullagar 2001, 72).

2

Circulation and Emplacement: The Hollowed-out Performance of Tourism

Mike Crang

Experience lives and proclaims itself as the exclusion of writing, that is to say of the invoking of an "exterior," "sensible," "spatial" signifier interrupting self-presence.

—Jacques Derrida

There is a story of tourism geography that begins with measuring flows of people as they go through points. In practice this means charting the movement of people as they pass through specific places—a story of "bums on seats," of number of overnight stays, durations of visits and distance traveled. This was then a geography of events—an event ontology of the measurable and visible. Emerging as a critique of this, so the story goes, is a geography of the construction of places through representations, a shaping of imagined landscapes. We should, however, quickly admit that this was not just a critique but also a reflexive recognition that the tourist industry was about precisely making and selling images. Perhaps the apotheosis of this is the "literary landscape" where, say, Britain is divided into Brontë country (west Yorkshire around Haworth), Austen Country (literary Hampshire as the local council has it), Lorna Doone Country (Exmoor), Hardy Country (Dorset) or more declassée Herriot Country (Yorkshire Dales around Thirsk), Heartbeat (North York Moors), or Catherine Cookson Country (South Tyneside), or to go further afield we might look at Anne of Green Gables (Prince Edward Island) or lately Captain Corelli's Island (the Ionian Island of Kefalonia). Even this quick selection starts to indicate ambiguities where, say, films or TV series overcode books, which, as we shall see, themselves may lean on other sources. This chapter asks a little more about the *instability of producing destinations*. First, it deconstructs tourism as a signifying system. That is, to see

47

tourism as precisely a form of geography—literally earth writing—or to put it another way, as inscribing meaning onto the earth. However, this vision of tourism inscribing meaning on the world, making the world as text, has limits. Both the semiological approach and the managerialist mapping of flows to destinations we might argue see tourism as being about structures and orders imposed upon the world. What both these approaches share is quite a strong sense that tourism makes places and those places are delimitable and definable—and that tourism occurs out there. They produce oddly fixed versions of the world for a mobile and fluid process. As Minca and Oakes note in the introduction to this volume, the tendency is to see places defined by immobility and travel as something that happens in a sort of nonplace between them. This chapter asks whether a refashioned sense of the eventfulness of tourism might enable us to tell stories that see places as more unstable, as themselves involving movement, and track circulation as a constitutive activity of representations. In other words, it is going to suggest that at issue are not just the representational strategies and structures that code places, but the ontological construction of places. That is, it is not about the image of places as beheld by tourists, but rather the processes and practices of signification—where tourism takes up discourses and representations and uses them in ordering places, making meanings, making distinctions, and thus making places through actions. It is not about what representations *show* so much as what they *do*. This picks up on accounts of the worldliness of texts and the textuality of world, but tries to find a way around some of the static or synchronic structures of textual models. It addresses the "bleed through" of "back here" to "over there" in overlaying and discordant geographies of social memory, personal memory, and social structure.

HOME AND AWAY: MAKING A DIFFERENCE

Many analyses of the bases of tourism have developed from a spatialized structural dichotomy of "over there" and "back here"—building from the banal yet important starting point that if destinations were no different than home people would not travel. This basic division has been reworked and connected with other binaries that have allegedly dominated modernity in a number of ways—for instance, self and other, secular and sacred, fallen modernity versus authentic experience, ordered and carnivalesque, quotidian and extraordinary. To take three well-known examples, Urry suggests the structure of the tourist gaze is one of directed attention focused upon the extraordinary away from the mundane, familiar, and everyday (Urry 2002b); alternately, MacCannell's thesis starts from a notion of modernity as alienating or incomplete experientially, whereas tourism is seen as promising the authentic (MacCannell 1976); while Shields focuses upon the ordered rational-ized dimension of the everyday home and the liminal and carnivalesque over-turning of that order in many destinations (Shields 1991). Clearly, then, one way of thinking through tourism is as the spatialization of these structural ten-sions in modernity. Or more accurately, as the spatial form of modernity that enables these tensions to operate. To tease out the implication of that latter sentence, then, in its strongest form, I am arguing that tourism is not only a product of the tensions of modernity, a symptom of deeper underlying struc-tures, but that it would be difficult to imagine a modernity without tourism, since tourism contributes precisely to a sense of modernity. Tourism is not merely emblematic, but an important vector in shaping late modernity. I en-deavor to show it does this by articulating many of the paradoxical senses of modern life—in this case how tourism works as an interplay of movement and fixity, absence and presence. That is, the tourist seeks to travel to be pres-ent at a place, but as we examine those places we find they are shot through by absences where distant others, removed in space and time, haunt the sites.

What we are seeing here is the etching of modern social practices onto the landscape through tourism. In a clichéd form it is as though the different ele-ments and trends with modernity were being regionalized—that is the spa-tialization of social meaning (Hughes 1998). To take a deliberately overstated position, the architectural collective MVRDV caricatures a borderless Europe as becoming one overlarge theme park for tourists encompassing not so much nations and peoples as a series of themed zones, with Norway turned from forest to supervillage; the Alps into a park with hotel cities; France trans-formed into a *Guide du Routard* landscape, in which the agricultural products became the instrument for "a gastronomically oriented zone penetrated by ho-tels and restaurants according to special nostalgic rules"; while Tuscany mu-tates into an "international villa park where Italians own less than 50% of the grounds" and "the farmer oriented landscape has become a villapark with gi-gantic private gardens maintained by the former farmers" (MVRDV 2000, 57). They go on to focus upon the Iberian coast and see it as a modern re-framing of traditional rites. "It is a space that has become the most effective substitute for the time of the breaking-up party, that countryside festival that industrialization eliminated from the calendar of Europeans," in effect a mod-ernized potlatch or center of Bacchanalian partying (MVRDV 2000, 107). It is this thematicization and scripting of places that has been characterized as marking a reflexive or postmodern sensibility.

> Suddenly it becomes possible that there are "others," that we ourselves are an
> "other" among others. All meaning and every goal have disappeared, it becomes
> possible to wander through civilizations as if through vestiges and ruins. The

whole of mankind becomes an imaginary museum. We can very easily imagine
a time close at hand when any fairly well to do person will be able to leave his
country indefinitely in order to taste his own national death in an interminable
aimless voyage. (Ricoeur 1965, cited in Neumann 1988, 19)

While clearly this is a one-sided picture, accepting too readily that the
tourist industry succeeds in "taming places" (Chang 2000a) and repressing
the polyvalence of these places to locals, different types of tourists and so on,
an issue to which I return later, this does flag up the important process of the
inscription of new meanings onto zones of the earth. This is a geography in a
literal sense, taking on Culler's dictum that tourists are indeed a great army
of unsung semioticians (Culler 1981). And the process of inscribing meaning
resonates with paradoxes of experiencing places, since the argument goes that

> The proliferation of markers frames something as a sight for tourists; the prolif-
> eration of reproductions is what makes something an original, the real thing: the
> original of which the souvenirs, postcards, statues, etc. are reproductions. The
> existence of reproductions is what makes something original, or authentic, and
> by surrounding ourselves with markers and reproductions we represent to our-
> selves . . . the possibility of authentic experiences in other times and other
> places. (Culler 1981, 132)

In other words it is the representations and discursive signifiers that not
only shape our understanding of the world, but actually stand to create our notions of authenticity. Although we may set out to see places for ourselves, all
our travels can take us to see are more signs of tourism, as the experience is
always mediated with markers of various kinds, from guidebooks to signposts
to other people, indicating what it is we are beholding (Morris 1988a, 10). One
example might be the *tau-tau* statuary at Tana Toraja in South Sulawesi, Indonesia, which have long been one of the key emblems of that local culture —
and as a result have been often stolen by visitors, to the extent that most are
now replacements. This is often a cause of disappointment to visitors, but visitors only notice because the guidebooks highlight it as a problem (McGregor
2000). So we can note the proactive shaping of attention through various discursive markers — from literal signs pointing out the historical significance of
buildings, through to guidebooks and marketing materials.

Perhaps an extreme example is that of the small town of Wall in South
Dakota "famed" for its drugstore. Eve Meltzer offers a detailed analysis of the
semiotic mobilization of place there. The store itself is located absolutely, by
a sign on it, at 43°, 59 minutes, and 63 seconds north, by 102°, 14 minutes,
and 55 seconds west. This small drugstore opened in 1931 and its only espe-
cial feature was the offer of iced water to serve a town of eight hundred resi-

dents. It was then a twenty-four by sixty foot structure. It is now a fifty-five thousand square foot emporium with chapel, art gallery, memorabilia store, and a vast array of kitsch artifacts for sale. The transformation was effected by its insistent location through signs of itself. By the 1950s there were some twenty-eight thousand signs to "Wall Drug"—and American servicemen and visitors planted them in Korea, Vietnam, Pakistan, Europe, and elsewhere. These are signs that over and again locate Wall drugstore, be that in a pulsing countdown along the highway ("Wall Drug only 200 miles," "Wall Drug only 100 miles," "Wall Drug next," "you are missing Wall Drug") or with the more ironic format of a direction arrow and a distance to the Wall drugstore (such as 10,728 miles in Pakistan). What is famous about the store is its celebrity—it is "a tautology of colossal proportions" (Meltzer 2002, 170). It is a place mobilized through transport—be that the real or discursive conventions of highway advertising, the billing of Wall as gateway to the Badlands, it is a place constantly inscribed yet also strangely dispersed since in the end it is rather less than the sum of its signs. As Meltzer argues, that final sign that we are missing Wall Drug is telling:

> it seems to offer itself to be taken at its very word. It directs us to look for the locus of that "missing." . . . Surprisingly the locus of that "missing" shows itself equally inside Wall Drug, once we have arrived. We are in other words, always missing Wall Drug and this, precisely, is the nature of the sight. This roadside sign alerts us that the quality of this place is most activated by the quantity of distantiated references to it. As such, I want to argue, Wall Drug has acquired its touristic value by dint of being absent. (Meltzer 2002, 162–63)

This begins to shift our attention, however, from the actual sights onto the discursive apparatus of tourism, away from the movements of people to the flows of images and words, from the phenomenon of the visit to what has often been treated as the epi-phenomenon of the ephemera of images, brochures, and so forth. Here work of late has flourished in providing critical examinations of how this might be seen as a coercive apparatus or "linguistic agents of touristic social control" (Dann 1999, 163). Several studies have highlighted how, through narrative voice, guides can occlude some images of places and reinforce others. Thus for instance, in discussing the Lonely Planet guide to India, Bhattacharyya notes how its authoritative style denies any contestability of its accounts of sites or events, while in its photographic depictions, it "is especially striking that the monuments of India's past are represented pictorially without human subjects, communicating a disjunction between the contemporary inhabitants of India and their historical past." This reinforces "the sense that 'the wonder that was India' is no longer connected to the lives of today's Indians" (Bhattacharyya 1997, 382). In so doing we might read it as shot through with the elegiac longing for premodern authenticity identified by MacCannell, or at least:

> This representation of India would appear to indicate considerable ambivalence toward modernity. To the extent that the traditional and the ethnic are perceived as attractive, India represents an escape from the modern. India in this context has a positive valence in relation to the contemporary industrial world. But to the extent that the country is portrayed as a *decayed* tradition and as a world of poverty and misery, India represents the dangers of the failure to become modernized. (Bhattacharyya 1997, 383)

The importance of these framings that draw upon long discourses of orientalism in the self-conceptualization of modernity is in shaping expectations and practices with a very selective choice of which elements of places are mentioned or depicted (Dann 1996; McGregor 2000). In one sense this is hardly surprising, as the art critic Lucy Lippard notes that having "plowed through piles of travel magazines with a kind of dead eye[, t]he manipulations and givens are so obvious they barely lend themselves to satire or analysis" (Lippard 1999, 52). However, it is not just guidebooks but also literary sources, films, and so forth that shape our spatial imaginations, so we should not underestimate "the power of secondary sources in general to forge expectations and bolster the urge to travel" (Pocock 1992, 243). And in several studies, "[i]nterviews with tourists suggest that pre-existing stereotypes are not dismantled by actual experiences, but instead serve as standards against which the visited culture is evaluated" (Andsager and Drzewiecka 2002, 403; see also Bruner 1991). To return to the Indonesian example mentioned before:

> The travelers' expectations had been so well shaped by their guidebooks that they were no longer surprised or astonished when they finally arrived at these "exotic" sites. Viewing the known, while an integral part of their trips, was not considered a fantastic part of their experiences because, in a sense, they have already done it. For one couple, pre-destination images made gazing upon the tautau a fulfilling experience, not because of the tau-tau themselves, but because they were at the very spot that had been made famous in their minds by countless previous exposures. (McGregor 2000, 40)

This is salutary and important work, but describing and unpacking the images (signifiers) is not the same as analyzing the practices of signification (Morris 1992, 264), even if the two are sometimes closely intertwined.

And I worry that this interpretative strategy has risks. Semiotic studies tend to work for an assumed reader working through the textual shaping of places or decoding the iconographic significance of images. In so doing they seem to position the analysts as "a 'cruising grammarian' reading similarity from place to place" (Morris 1988b, 95). There is indeed a sense in which this highlights that local difference may now be "a look, not a text" (1988b, 95) and a cruising glimpse, certainly not a contemplative gaze (Chaney 2002). And that tourism, as for Wall Drug or themed motels, becomes a scanning of the landscape where the difference of one place from another is indeed an optical illusion:

> The difference is mere variation apprehended in a high-speed empiricist *flash*. Indeed, the rapidity with which I "recognize" the difference is the sign of its pseudo-status. (Morris 1988a, 5)

However, by focusing on the epistemological paradoxes of representations produced by tourism, it leaves us stuck between a conceptual Scylla and Charybdis, where on one side is a constructionist renunciation of truth, that since everything is representation then anything goes, and, on the other, a position that sees these representations as somehow obscuring reality when what we need is either some form of vision that will lead us directly to truth, or an unmediated experience. This latter we might, after Morris, call the bad mirror (nasty tourist representation), good mirror (critical social theoretical representation) approach (Morris 1992). And of course this is the familiar argument between particular versions of a so-called postmodernism and a so-called modernism. The tensions of a fear of a "descent into discourse" and the realization of the discursive shaping of space is elegantly summed up by Taussig:

> But just as we might garner courage to reinvent a new world and live new fictions—what a sociology that would be!—so a devouring force comes at us from another direction, seducing us by playing on our yearning for a true real. Would that it would, would that it could, come clean this true real. I so badly want that wink of recognition, that complicity with the nature of nature. But the more I want it the more I realize it's not for me. Not for you either . . . which leaves us in this silly and often desperate place wanting the impossible so badly that while we believe it is our rightful destiny and so act as accomplices of the real, we also know in our heart of hearts that the way we picture the world and talk is bound to a dense set of representational gimmicks which, to coin a phrase, have but an arbitrary relation to a slippery referent easing its way out of graspable sight. (Taussig 1993, xvii)

Taussig highlights the seductive power of an urge to find "real" places and thus offer "real analyses" that get behind the images and representations of places. The examples in this section however, suggest that images do not just obscure a true place, but rather constitute the very sense of places themselves. We have then to look at the performativity of images and texts moving and making through processes of signification. This is subtly but importantly different from looking at images as depicting places with varying degrees of accuracy or truthfulness, because it shifts us to thinking through the ontology of tourist places rather than the epistemology of their representations. The ontological work done by various signs we shall see suggests places are made, and they are not bounded, fixed entities but are relationally linked to other places. In other words, we see that the paradox of experiencing a place is that it depends on other absent places.

WISH YOU WERE THERE: DISPLACING DESTINATIONS

This approach to the scripting and zonation of places, then, reveals the powerful role of discursive systems in carving out tourist places from the everyday world and etching new configurations of meaning into the landscape. However, the analysis of Wall should point out that not only are the effects on places profound, so too are the effects on our notion of place. Minca and Oakes, in this volume's introduction, suggest the importance of seeing a relational sense of place, of what we might see as a phenomenology of place, that sees its experience not in itself but only in tension with movement and absence from it. Thus "home" becomes invested with emotional charge through absence, while the distance of an outsider again transfigures places. And as Minca and Oakes demonstrate, these are not always unreflexive positions—where one becomes aware that they are being called upon to perform the role of the insider, for instance. One standard critical discourse is to opine that tourism obscures or, more strongly, erodes authentic places—making everything into a staged performance or an other-directed culture. One may want to argue about the desirability of specific changes, but crucially I want to suggest this critique misses the constitution of modern places. For a start it implies a privileging of "real" places as in some ways immobile places populated by "insiders" or locals. But there are surely many degrees of estrangement that we experience, and virtually every culture is constructed as much, if not more, by links and attachments with people in other places as it is by internal homogeneity. The implication of this view of authentic, immobile cultures tends to be that tourism is considered as "people traveling to places [conceived] as cultures mapped in space. . . . There is in this approach a presumption of not only a unity of place and culture, but also of the immobility of both in relation to a fixed cartographically coordinated space, with the tourist as one of those wandering figures whose travels, paradoxically, fix places and cultures in this ordered space" (Lury 1997, 75). What we have is an opposition of "authentic dwelling" as sedentary against a mobile tourist, in an unsurprising replay of a trope of lapsarian modernity (in the allegorical ideal typical figure of the Tourist) set against a premodern existential place.

This baggage of the valorized, sedentary sense of dwelling in place, then, positions tourism as producing a truant proximity that disrupts the wholeness of places by bringing in absent others and distant lands (Shields 1992). The presence of tourists inscribes absent locations into places. Tourist places are haunted by many others outside the locale, while, as we shall see, tourists seeking to experience sites, to be present in them, are haunted by other times and roles they play back home. This ephemeral presence seems so unstable that it gives rise to an almost desperate urge in many studies to pin down and fix both places and tourists. Although places are rendered unstable by the semiosis of tourism they are heavily reinscribed by the standard idiom of analysis. Studies have generally been restricted to a vision of tourism as a series of discrete, localized events, where destinations, seen as bounded localities, are subject to external forces producing impacts, where tourism is a series of discrete, enumerated occurrences of travel, arrival, activity, purchase, departure (Franklin and Crang 2001, 6). This leads to a binarized geography of local place versus global tourist industry, produced by the artificial closure of places and the expulsion of movement and connection to some space "in-between" places rather than inside them. This division is then all too often shackled to another series of binaries: authentic versus artificial, traditional versus modern, cultural versus economic; in which the destinations of tourism are depicted as suffering the impact of a vast and exterior industry. This "coercive conceptual schema" creates an "epistemological obstacle" by conceiving of the issue in terms of local bounded place, which is impacted upon by a delocalized, disembedded global industry that is rendered curiously placeless (Picard 1996, 104). This way of conceiving tourism is cycled back and forth between academia and policy analysis "not only in terms of the perception the local authorities have of tourism and its issues, but also and above all, in terms of the representation they come to form of their own society once it has become a tourist product for sale on the international market." This leaves us with a touching if naïve polarity of good tourism as "interested in the particularities of the place and able to fuse harmoniously with the host society" and projects all the problems onto bad tourism that is the converse (1996, 108). Now empirically there are many negative stories about tourist development and its interaction with aspects of local cultures and economies, but the study of "impacts" reinforces "the idea that cultural changes arising from tourism are produced by the intrusion of a superior sociocultural system in a supposedly weaker receiving milieu" (1996, 110). Picard's study of Bali for instance highlights a "touristic involution" whereby local arts and practices develop through tourism, becoming more "Balinized," more localized over time (1996, 21). This is not just a product of global commercialization but also a strategy that Picard suggests is promoted by local hegemonic Hindu actors to prevent the Islamization of the island. In other words, local Hindu leaders perceive external pressure of one kind, their location in a predominantly Islamic state with issues of migration and population movement threatening their supremacy, and respond by utilizing another "external force," that of tourism, which results in them accentuating the performance and practices of Balinese culture that mark them out as different from the rest of Indonesia. Thus we need:

> a more culturally complex rendering of tourism's "consumption" of places, one that sees not merely a globalizing force bearing down upon a once-isolated community, but also the dynamic ways local cultural meanings—which are themselves a product of a dialogue between local and extra-local cultural systems—wrap the tourism experience in an envelope of local meaning. (Oakes 1999, 124)

I have elsewhere suggested that instead "of seeing places as relatively fixed entities, to be juxtaposed in analytical terms with more dynamic flows of tourists, images and culture, we need to see them as fluid and created through performance" (Crang and Coleman 2002, 1). We might here first keep the semiotic focus upon the performativity of place and how it renders unstable notions of "being there." Tourism, if it does anything, trades upon precisely the notion of *presence*—it is the manufacturing of co-presence, taking people and putting them somewhere—to experience being there. My aim is to destabilize what that *there* entails. I want to show that when we say "wish you were here," the "production of hereness in the absence of actualities depends increasingly on virtualities," on elements beyond the physical destination, and that we travel to actual destinations to experience virtual places (Kirshenblatt-Gimblett 1998, 169–71).

One example might then be to unpack the creation of themed places in literary tourism, since we began with that as an exemplar of the process of scripting places in the carving up of the countryside into literary regions. Here we seem to see the tourist industry reprising the early geographical attempts to think through the relationship of fiction to landscape by seeking out and ticking off place references in the works in order to map writers and their writings onto regional territories (such as Thomas Hardy onto Wessex, see e.g., Darby 1948). The relations of fictive and real are complicated for writers such as Austen, though, since she rarely used direct references to existing places. So if we take Pemberley (*Pride and Prejudice*), it "is a fictitious literary landscape created in the same way that Gilpin said he composed his picturesque landscape; ideas are taken from the general face of the country not from any particular scene . . . the Pemberley chapters had almost certainly been written based on her concentrated reading of Gilpin" (Batey 1996, 76). Gilpin was writing a design manual for gardens collating numerous spatially disparate features into an ideal type. So Austen thus based a fictional place on a textual composite made by a writer who himself developed amalgams of key places. Austen also studied Repton's Red Books, as well as his actual work at Stoneleigh. It is not merely, then, that her landscapes are polysemic, in terms of our interpretations, but that they are polygenic, as they are themselves compound forms where text and landscape are not distinct categories. It also means that both textual and physical landscapes are now haunted by their counterparts, from film, novels, and design manuals. To this we can add that Austen's textual practice was about creating places as bounded, localized, and knowable entities—famously claiming that a village of three or four families was an ideal setting. This in turn meant her textual geography tends to repress external connections—most infamously Sir Thomas's Antiguan slave plantations that helped sustain the economy of her Mansfield Park. Her landscapes then are articulated through a constitutive outside, where they are made coherent by a textual closure that hides absent others.

If the places in her texts are rather unstable, as we move forward to current tourism geographies she seems to become pinned down, and places are anchored with suspicious firmness. The current mapping of Austen claims her for "literary Hampshire" although she set little significant action in the county where she dwelt for many years. In tourism related to her novels, we find not merely fictive landscapes founded upon theoretical landscapes but films and series that then seek approximations to those landscapes—looking for sites that offer both the right scene setting and resonances. Often the original site (if it is known) is not suitable for use in film versions of her novels, so a surrogate site is introduced. Of course this site has its own history that is thus drawn into the story. So, for instance, Pemberley is widely regarded as inspired by Chatsworth—although Cottesbrooke Hall and the grounds, but not the building (Ilham House), also have their supporters. However, its most recent film incarnation is as Lyme Park, but with Sudbury Hall being used for interiors. So we have a filmic compound, being layered over a literary composite. Putting Austen on the map then is not straightforward, but that does not stop a sizeable literary tourism industry offering tours through her landscape. Thus the National Trust "Pemberley Trail" at Lyme Park restages scenes of the film—making the location of Austen's fictional site more solid, and reading backward from film to text to society. I am not trying to depict some conspiratorial deception foisted onto unwitting tourists, many of whom are quite well aware of the role of sites in films and indeed of different sites in different screen versions, but to point to the creation of a stable visitable place where one can be in the presence of Austen's work. Perhaps a resonant example is in the marketing of "Proust's Normandy," where "Proust's identification with Illiers is important today not because it has made it possible to create a local shrine to the writer but because it encourages a convenient, idealized identification of reality with fiction, which always makes for easier reading" (Compagnon 1997, 226).

The way Austen is linked to places reminds me of Derrida's analysis of Joyce—where he speaks of traversing the haunted work of the text, where the authorizing signature is permanently displaced (Derrida 1991). Derrida suggests that disseminating the work, and reciting it, in the name of the original, inevitably buries and displaces that original. Indeed in *Ulysses* (1961, 731), James Joyce seems to offer a template for this overlaying of landscapes and sources. He sardonically notes that our concepts often "reflect that each one who enters imagines himself to be the first to enter whereas he is always the last term of a preceding series even if the first term of a succeeding one, each imagining himself to be first, last, only and alone, whereas he is neither first nor last nor only nor alone in a series originating in and repeated to infinity" (cited in Schleiffer 2000, 149). Joyce's textual practice of endless, unheralded citation seems to echo this touristic landscape of quotation (Roberts 1988, 545). In other words, places are precisely hollowed out, distantiated, and spread through other texts and sites. They are not self-present, independent entities. So in terms of destinations, "[t]he heart of this process does not lie in the satisfying object but in the needing subject" (Haug 1987, 122), where the figure for the consumer becomes Tantalus who reaches for satisfaction only to find empty space (Haug 1983, 35). We have only to think of the serial experience of tourism—moving from one site to the next—that is inscribed in the performance of an itinerary. What is suggested is less the plenitude and fulfillment of dreams come true than a continual quest driven by successive disappointments, or better, as Oscar Wilde said of cigarettes, experiences that are exquisite but leave one unfulfilled. It is to the subject's experience that I wish to now turn, to suggest that since the destination is not a simple place, then nor can we say tourism is located there.

LOCATING TOURISM

So far I have concentrated on suggesting that the destinations of tourism are "hollowed out" and not self-present. What I want to turn to now is the other side of this—the flows of tourists. I want to do this in two steps, first to link the tourist experience with the distantiated place, and second, to think about how, analytically, the events of tourism have been treated. To do this I want to start by thinking through what we might call the *re-mediation of tourism*. I choose this term to emphasize that we are not talking about some fall from grace—from unmediated contact into a distanced gaze, but rather about circuits of media laid on top of each other, tangled through each other, and functioning because of each other. In this sense, I want to see tourism as embedded in a media ecology of various elements and types of mediation. One starting point is, then, to think about the increasing overlap of the everyday and tourism. I do not mean here mediation as in a putative "virtual tourism" through Web browsing that clearly fails to deliver the experience of "real places," but firstly the way increasingly many of us perform tourist activities in our daily lives—thus, wandering in the city, or window shopping, or people watching, or watching the sunset are all activities that can overlap with tourist modes of apprehending the environment. And of course, the point that brochures so often skip across, and an omission with which analysts seem to collude, tourism is often full of the every day—from familiar belongings, to washing, to shopping, to dressing children, to inevitable family rows, to shared joys and intimacies (see Edensor in this volume). I shall return to this crosspollination of tourism and the mundane later, but here I want to stress not "Web-based" tourism, where so far the main effect on choice of destination seems to be comparative purchase technology, but instead point to the oft-noted similarity of screen visions and tourist gazes. Both tend to simplify and spectacularize, both set the observer as the diegetic center of knowledge and events, picking up the travel writer's imperative to survey and produce an encyclopedic knowledge. If we take something like IMAX technology here then we have the vaunted notion of presence with distant environments, especially films of the "natural world," through media, in cinemas that themselves become tourist attractions, with people traveling to one city to see films of a remote environment (Acland 1998). As noted at the start of this chapter we have brochure reading and other sources that shape tourist imaginaries about destinations. "Daydreaming of potential destinations precedes every act of voluntary traveling. The building blocks of these everyday dreams are large scale repertoires of images and narratives provided by what Appadurai has labeled mediascapes" (Alneng 2003, 465). These mediascapes are "representational realms" which the tourist normally encounters both before and after experiencing actual social destinations (Jansson 2002, 434). They intensify consumption, setting up a discourse where places fulfill, or disappoint, on the basis of prior mediatization. They form certainly a phantasmagoria but they do not "float free" or simply happen but instead "depend on the imagination as an elaborate social practice," meaning that with "tourism evaporating into overall society a clear cut opposition of mobility and immobility will not do; its point of departure lies elsewhere" (Alneng 2003, 464, 465).

Let us then think about the mediatization and its impact on experience. That media in general frame experience becomes clear when we hear how visitors whistle the theme tunes of spaghetti westerns when visiting ghost towns (DeLyser 1999). Or let us follow Alneng's example of Vietnam, which he argues to be radically overcoded by referents not to the American War, but to films of the American War, where "the Vietnam of backpackers is a war-movie with surplus physical appearance" even leading to "oneiric situations in which the physical landscape is not only interpreted in terms of cinematic events, but fiction is put into practice, in a sense experienced" (Alneng 2003, 471, 469). Alneng develops his argument by tracing the cross-referring networks of Alex Garland's novel *The Beach* (Garland 1996). At one level this is a story of backpackers, or long-term independent tourists seeking to find a perfect edenic beach, precisely the self-defeating quest for the unspoiled paradise that would be ruined the moment it became part of the tourist circuit—a beach found hidden in the forbidden exterior of the circuit in a national park. However, for the protagonist it is also a thinly veiled replay of the journey to the heart of darkness, a dissolution of the self, mediated not via Conrad's novel but Coppola's film *Apocalypse Now*. The anti-hero, Richard, is beset by drug-inspired hallucinations depicting the war in Vietnam, with the episodes themselves a reference to film versions of GI drug use, and is guided by a ghostly mentor who insistently poses the question "where are you?" The novel offers a textual replaying of contemporary Thailand through the lens of a filmic sensibility about the American-Vietnamese conflict. To this we might add the resculpting of a Thai National Park to create the perfect beach for the film version of the novel.

Now this self-referential circuit would be interesting but little more, were it not for the way it clearly chimes with popular currents, and thus my second concern with how the events of tourism are seen. Following this line of argument, books are not just texts but are actually transported and read. Books and not just meaning circulate. And what was the hottest book of 1997 on various Thai and Viet book markets in the quarters of cities where tourists clusters? It was *The Beach*. Alneng's reflections are in part due to being sold *The Beach* in a backpacker hotel in the Pham Ngu Lao area of Ho Chi Minh City (2003, 471). Or we find conversations between backpackers framed in terms of the novel where "experienced" backpackers distance themselves from newcomers by calling the latter "FNGs"—an abbreviation for "Fucking New Guys" used by U.S. soldiers in Vietnam and popularized by Garland's novel (Elsrud 2001, 610).

So the formal mediated environment can diffuse and frame experience in a variety of ways. This may be by differentiating ourselves from others—as in backpackers who deride the collective travel and organized packages of

Japanese tourists, about which they know little, but who form "imagined ghosts upon which to build difference narratives" (Elsrud 2001, 607) and thus define their own holiday in terms of adventure, solitariness as a particular form of freedom, and indeed a thrill of danger. Elsrud argues that the stories of hardship and danger, and the telling of these stories, are as important as actual events, so that "the journey becomes a spatial and temporal frame to be filled with identity narratives" (Elsrud 2001, 605). So in terms of events and locations a key place becomes not just destination but places *en route*—such as cheap hotels and districts where like-minded budget travelers congregate. Indeed, so much so that a character in *The Beach* quips, "You know, Richard, one of these days I'm going to find one of those Lonely Planet writers and I'm going to ask him, what's so fucking lonely about the Khao San Road?" (Garland 1996, 194). It is in locations like these that information and terms are swapped. Indeed we might look at these as key moments in a culture which travels and, unusually for the predilections of anthropology, is both spatially distantiated and not supported by a coherent enduring group (Hutnyk 1996; Murphy 2001; Sørensen 2003). The process of swapping stories, be that a competitive display of status, or the endless cycling of what Hutnyk calls Indo-babble, is a powerful force in shaping these tourists' practices.

More recently this has been compounded by the newfound ability to bring home along with them, and to maintain contact and collaborate with other travelers whose paths they crossed elsewhere. The factor that is enabling this is the humble roving e-mail account and the net café. Poste restante business has diminished enormously in some locations, along with all the attendant rituals of booking calls home. Instead there is a more continuous contact (Sørensen 2003, 859). Even the tourists most avowedly "away" are now in contact with home, those most adamantly "on the road" keep in touch with ships that formerly passed in the night. But if we turn to the mundane mass tourism we find the time and space of the vacation is distended. Recent figures suggest the text message is supplanting the postcard and that patterns of texting continue patterns of sociality from home onto holiday despite the much greater costs (Wainwright 2003). It is quickly evident that although tourism is often defined as synonymous with travel not only do we perform touristic activities at home but we also begin going on holiday while we are at home. Thus to take a cliché we begin our fortnight holiday not in August, but sometime in the depth of winter, as we surrender to the excitement and pleasures of brochures and holiday programs on TV, as we discuss options with friends and colleagues, and so on. It builds when we actually book, when we go shopping for appropriate clothing, or if we book into tanning parlors so we do not look like such newcomers on arrival. When we return then there is the cycling of memories and stories, the display of bodily capital—the tan—of cultural capital through souvenirs or so forth. "The full process of the anticipation of holidays, the act of travel, and the narration of holiday stories on return are all tied into an imagination and performance which enables tourists to think of themselves as particular sorts of person" (Desforges 2000, 930). So tourism is in part sustaining and being sustained by stories we tell that define ourselves, and these stories are sustained and worked through a range of objects. But these stories and objects spill out beyond containable episodes and boxes. Souvenirs are not just tokens of status, of "having been," but also mnemonic devices through whose materiality we reconnect with precisely those senses of presence that are discursively difficult to articulate.

> We do not need or desire souvenirs of events that are repeatable. Rather we need and desire souvenirs of events that are reportable, events whose materiality escaped us, events that exist thereby only through the invention of narrative. Through narrative the souvenir substitutes a context of perpetual consumption for its context of origin. . . . The souvenir speaks to a context of origin through a language of longing. (Stewart 1984, 135)

So far, then, in this section I have been trying to argue that touristic desires are rarely internalized wishes but rather parts of wider social imaginaries that are articulated through constellations of media and social practice. In other words that "over there" is powerfully framed "back here." Then I have tried to suggest that "tourism" cannot be located in a neat box as happening "over there," in that distant location during that discrete period. Rather our anticipation and memories spill out on either side. The issue this is beginning to raise here is how tourism diffuses into the rest of our lives. And here we have to note a couple of glaring lacunae in many studies—that is, other people and their things. So often we write of the prototypical tourist, who has desires and acts, who seems to exist only as the solitary figure or the collective plural of the mass. But not many people travel alone. So all our discussion of desires and satisfactions has to be mediated through tourists' shared and divisive aspirations, actual compromises, and negotiated actions. Moreover, all these things happen through the use of objects—from the obvious airplanes, to flip-flops, cameras, postcards, to souvenirs and sun hats. Very little critical theory has really engaged with the material cultures of tourism, and how they support and undercut notions of tourism destinations (for exceptions see Lury 1997 and Flusty this volume). We might then start to think of tourism as happening whereby a network of more or less spread out actors, in time and space, come together to form an event or "a hacceity, a mode of individuation not limited to a person or thing but consists of multiple relations between things and their capacities to affect and be affected" (Fullagar 2000, 64).

BRINGING IT ALL BACK HOME

My main aim here has been to try and dislocate tourism from a sense of being something that happens "over there" for a fixed period of time. I have tried to do this both by pointing to the instabilities of places constructed as destinations but also to the construction of tourist experience. Simply put, I tried to undercut the notions of self-present location and self-present visitor. The paradoxical nature of tourism is that it aims to produce an experience of "hereness," that is, a sense of being somewhere different and specific, but it does so through a number of constitutive absences. That is, it is the absences and gaps that make the sense of "hereness" possible. It is important that this lack of self-presence, this lack of closure, this openness is seen to apply to both places and tourists. I am wary that critical accounts of the semiological realization of tourist destinations can serve to affirm the dissolution or fictive quality of place while reinforcing a sense of centred human agency—as a resistant, practical bricoleur. I want most certainly to keep a sense of fictive places that are made through tourism and local and tourist practices. I do not want to slip toward a model whereby tourism forms some sort of distorting mirror or alienating representational layer covering real places. Instead I use "fictive" not in the sense of fiction, as opposed to reality, but in the sense of made and constructed. Far from being the static ground on which tourism happens, I am suggesting that places are themselves happenings. This ontological critique sees places as relationally constructed and thus linked and themselves distantiated. It is an ontological critique in the sense then of addressing what places are, how they happen, rather than how they are represented—although of course that too is affected. To do this I have tried to suggest how they are not simply created as individual places but always in relation to other places. While we might see this as a network of affiliations, or of debts and borrowings between places, the nature of travel as a sequence suggests instead a sense of places in a serried chain, perhaps less like Derrida's grammatology and more in the media ecology that, after Dienst, we might call "programmatology" (Dienst 1994). That is to emphasize not just a textual metaphor but one that incorporates a range of media. The sense then of places being encountered in a sequence and unfolding and being grasped through the affordances they offer to various travelers is important.

However, likewise I do not want to romanticize agency and presence for tourists. Perhaps Deleuze's use of Bergson goes too far in putting "phenomenology in reverse, spewing the inward out, forcing consciousness to become a wandering orphan among the things called images" (Dienst 1994, 148), but a certain reorienting of the subject in tourism seems important. Admittedly, focusing on people's agency serves as an important critique of the way tourists have been codified as objects of knowledge in tourist studies, pinned in ordered lattices through ever finer subdivisions and more elaborate typologies as though these might eventually form a classificatory grid in which tourism could be defined and regulated. While there is necessarily a role for thinking of typologies, the obsession with taxonomies and "craze for classification" seems often to produce lists that "represent a tradition of flatfooted sociology and psychology," which is driven by "an unhappy marriage between marketing research and positivist ambitions of scientific labelling" (Löfgren 1999, 267). Moreover, this seems the enlightenment encyclopedic model of visualized society writ over. It seems as though when confronted by the elusory and insubstantial subject of tourism the response is to try ever more desperately to fix it into analytical place.

The response to this classificatory mania, this objectification of the tourist, does not however have to be a celebration of autonomous agency, and instead I am suggesting desolidifying the object. The elusory sense of fleeting presence is what makes tourism a modern phenomena that speaks to and trains people in a "dwelling-in-travel" (Clifford 1989, 183). It functions as

a figure for different modes of dwelling and displacement, for trajectories and identities, for storytelling and theorizing in a postcolonial world of global contacts. Travel: a range of practices for situating the self in a space or spaces grown too large, a form both of exploration and discipline. (Clifford 1989, 177)

The implication of linking dwelling with mobility is not simply a change of classifications, nor even an epistemological challenge, but an ontological shift in characterizing social action. It is in this context, then, that work on tourism often seems to miss the potential of the phenomena it studies. As Sørensen notes:

In recent years Clifford and others have contributed to the revitalization of the concept of culture by insisting on a de-territorialization of its propensities, thereby allowing culture(s) to travel. Yet it is interesting to note that, despite the cognation between travel and tourism, the revitalization of the concept of culture has not been much inspired by insights from the tourism study. Allusions and anecdotal exposés apart, the revitalization has largely ignored this domain, and the theoretical and conceptual advances have not been challenged and tested by means of the tourism phenomenon. (Sørensen 2003, 864)

This chapter has been an attempt to suggest that we need to thoroughly *mobilize* both the tourist and the places in our analyses of tourism if we are to speak back to the issues raised for modern culture by social forms that are unbounded, temporally unstable, and yet immensely influential in shaping social imaginaries, about which the orchestration of life in places can revolve and upon which livelihoods depend.

3

Itineraries and the Tourist Experience

Ning Wang

INTRODUCTION

Tourism is a quest for experiences that are in contrast to, and sometimes an extension or intensification of, daily experience. In this sense, tourism is a pioneering example of the emerging "experience economy" (Pine and Gilmore 1999). The quality of experiences constitutes the key to the success of tourism development. However, despite the importance of the "tourist experience," this is still an ambiguous term. Although various constituents of the tourist experience, such as motivations (curiosity, novelty, change, authenticity, meaning, identity, self), satisfactions, feelings, and emotions, have been well researched in psychology, anthropology, sociology, and other disciplines, the literature on the tourist experience as a *gestalt* phenomenon has still been understudied. This is not to deny that there exists a small literature on the tourist experience per se (e.g., Ryan 1997). But many questions still remain unanswered. For example, how is the formulation of the tourist experience related to itineraries?

Itinerary is a frequently used term in the tourism industry, especially in tourist brochures, but it is rarely seen as an academic term. The reason for this situation could be simple. The itinerary is seen as too self-obvious, too simple, and too trivial to deserve serious academic treatment. At best, it is treated as a component of tourism linking to tour operation (see Poynter 1993, 136–54). Such a common-sense view of the itinerary should be challenged, however. Rather than being trivial, itineraries act as important media through which the tourism industry interacts with the tourist in the production and consumption of the tourist experience. Itineraries shape the formulation and organization of the tourist experience and become an arena in which the tourist experience is socially produced. As *temporal-spatial carriers* of tourist experience, itineraries are significant in the ways that tourism is consumed and in the ways that tourists' experiences are shaped.

Surely, the tourist experience cannot completely be equated with, or reduced to, itineraries, but it is equally true that the tourist experience is shaped by itineraries. There are at least two reasons that the itinerary deserves study in its own right. First, a number of paradoxes involved in tourism have their roots in itineraries. These paradoxes involve dualisms including authenticity and inauthenticity, autonomy and passivity, freedom and determinations, agency and structure. For example, while tourism is regarded as a quest for authenticity, what is experienced often ends up as "staged authenticity" of the front zone (MacCannell 1973), partly because of the temporary and transient nature of itineraries that constrain tourists from penetrating the back zone of toured reality. While tourism is hailed as freedom, it often ends up as the loss of freedom, partly because of the rigidity of itineraries. While tourism is thought to restore the autonomy and agency that have decreased in daily routines, it creates its own constraints over autonomy and agency because of the constraining, pre-determining, and disciplining nature of itineraries. As Minca and Oakes put it in this volume's introduction, tourism is a performance through which various binaries, such as subject and object, are constantly re-enacted. Relatedly, itineraries are performances in which the paradoxes of modernity are enacted and embodied. The itinerary is thus one of the best dimensions of tourism from which the paradoxes and ambivalence of modernity can be revealed.

Second, as spatial-temporal carriers of tourism commodities, itineraries constitute the media that bridge experiences and goods, services and products, hospitality and attractions, movement and rest, time and space, the quantitative side and the qualitative side of tourism, the ordinary supportive consumption and extraordinary peak consumption, tourist consumers and tourism suppliers. Thus, the itinerary is one of the best domains of tourism from which the mechanisms of social, economical, and cultural production of tourism can be better understood.

This chapter deals with the issue of how the production and consumption of itineraries bring about and reinforce a series of paradoxes in tourism, and how the formation of itineraries are related to wider social, economical, and cultural processes. Just as tourism reveals the ambivalence of modernity and globalization (MacCannell 1976; Wang 2000), the same is true of the itinerary. The itinerary provides an alternative perspective from which the paradoxes of tourism can, perhaps more clearly, be revealed.

The following pages consist of three parts. The first concentrates on the issue of how itineraries constitute the *commodity form* of the tourist experience and how the commoditization of itineraries leads to a number of paradoxes. The second examines how itineraries become a way of circulation of tourism products and the associated paradoxes. The third focuses on the role that itineraries play in shaping the consumption of tourism, and the consequential "consuming paradoxes" (Miles 1998, 5). Finally, in the conclusion, the paradoxes of tourism are discussed in relation to the rationalization of the tourist experience within the context of postmodernity.

ITINERARIES AS THE COMMODITY FORM OF TOURISM

In contemporary societies, the tourist experience is sold as a commodity (Watson and Kopachevsky 1994), which is a result of the commoditization of travel and associated pleasant experiences under the condition of modernity (Cohen 1972; MacCannell 1976; Graburn 1983, 27; Watson and Kopachevsky 1994; Rojek 1997, 58; Wang 2000, 188–99). However, what is the commodity *form* of tourism? This is still an unanswered question. For a commodity to come into being, it must have a form (Lee 1993). For example, for a commodity to become the object of desire, it must be designed in order to take a particular appearance of colors, shape, size, and so on (cf. Miles 1998, 36–51). This type of appearance can be called the *material form* of a commodity. However, in addition to the material form of commodities, there also arise *dematerialized forms* of commodities. In postindustrial economies, the commoditization of information and services leads to the *dematerialization* of commodity forms (Lee 1993, 135; Slater 1997, 194). The increasingly dominant part that the economy of services plays in postindustrial economies makes the nonmaterial form of commodities increasingly significant. As an integral element of the service industry, tourism also assumes a nonmaterial form, which is exemplified by itineraries.

The itinerary is a system of links between the temporal and spatial arrangements of tourist activities on the tourist journey. From the perspective of the tourism industry, an itinerary is a salable product that links, bridges, and puts together the various components that are necessary to the consumption of tourism. These components include accommodation, transportation, restaurants, attractions, entertainment, and tourist sites. Obviously, for tour operators and travel agencies, itineraries are the commodity form of mass tourism products. But they are the nonmaterial form, despite the fact that tourism contains such material elements as food, means of transport, and hotels. The itinerary is nonmaterial because it is "virtual" (somewhat similar to grammar, see Giddens 1979), existing in both tourists' and suppliers' imaginations; illustrated in tourist brochures, guidebooks, or TV programs; and only instantiated or materialized in the stage of consumption. Although itineraries are the non-material form, this does not mean that itineraries have nothing in common with the material form. The material commodity form consists of the arrangements of material elements. By contrast, the nonmaterial commodity form is constituted by the temporal and spatial arrangement of procedure, process, and activities. Thus, itineraries, as the nonmaterial commodity form of tourism, are temporal-spatial connections. They constitute the temporal-spatially organizing processes in which discrete tourist "raw materials" are integrated and sold as a packaged commodity. At the same time, they themselves become the boundaries organized and constrained by the larger economic, social, political, and cultural contexts.

Why does tourism take the commodity form of itineraries? The answer should be found from the process of the commoditization of travel experiences. First, the commoditization of travel experiences is confronted with the problem of *intangible* experiences. In order to turn intangible experiences into "tangible" products in managerial terms, a certain organizing form must be imposed upon the journey. Thus, itineraries are a way in which travel experiences are objectified, operationalized, and temporally and spatially "materialized." In a literal sense, we cannot sell experiences or pleasures per se, but we can sell the itineraries that are the "containers," carriers, or confines of experiences and pleasures. In short, itineraries are the "tangible" temporal-spatial carrier of intangible travel experiences, which can be produced, circulated (in the form of tourist brochures), and sold in the tourist market. Second, the essence of the commoditization of travel experiences is to make profit through creating an exchange value of tourism commodity. In so doing, travel experiences, as a qualitative subjective state, must be turned into precisely quantifiable and price-able products. Itineraries thus become the quantifiable, profitable, and saleable products of travel experiences.

Third, the commoditization of travel experiences reduces risk and uncertainty arising out of journeys. In order to transform the "raw materials" of risky and uncertain travel into tourism commodities, itineraries become a necessary form through which risks, chances, and uncertainties linking to journeys are eliminated or diminished (Meethan 2001, 75). For examples, flight seats, hotel rooms, and restaurant tables are secured; safety and hygiene are ensured; access to attractions is guaranteed with tickets booked in advance. With itineraries, the risk-related and uncertain journeys are turned into clearly arranged, certain, standardized, and predictable commodities of tourist experiences. Itineraries thus embody the rationalism in capitalist commoditization (Weber 1978), and hence act as a rational way in which the tourism industry controls and manages mobile experiences (Ritzer and Liska 1997). Itineraries are particularly attractive to *mass tourists* who want to create order out of chaos, risks, and uncertainties on their journeys to un-familiar environments, even though they might also want to defy that order at the same time.

Itineraries are thus an indispensable commodity form of modern tourism and act as an integral dimension of the commoditization of the tourist experience. However, while tourism is successfully commoditized with the help of itineraries, it also faces a paradox derived from itineraries. Part of the essence of the tourist experience is to get out of daily routines, order, schedules, and constraints. As mentioned above, in order to turn the tourist experience into a commodity, it is necessary to make tourism assume a commodity form, namely, itineraries. The latter, however, imposes an emergent routine, order, schedule, and constraint upon the tourist experience. Thus, tourism, the very act of escape from daily constraints, ends up as an alternative constraint.

In relation to the *elimination of chance, risk, and uncertainty* and the in-crease of security and certainty, tourism is wheeled to the position of dimin-ishing the real charms and appeals of travel, namely, a suitable extent of risk-taking, challenge, improvisation, independence, flexibility, freedom, creativity, and authenticity. Thus, while tourism is put on with the commodity form of itineraries, it paves a way to the demise of the authenticity of travel.

As a response to such a strong commoditization of tourism, an increasing number of tourists tend to abandon overscheduled and itinerized mass tourism and adopt more individualist, independent, and flexible forms of travel (cf. Cohen 1972). These individual tourists take responsibility for their own itineraries and leave enough room for adapting and changing primary schedules. The increasingly popular "backpacking" form of travel is such an example. This process can be called the *decommoditization* of itineraries. What Edensor (1998, 105–14) describes about tourist behaviors at the Taj is a typical example of differentiation of decommoditized itinerary from com-moditized itinerary. For package tourists, visits to the Taj are highly regu-lated, pre-determined, restrained, and disciplined in time and space. As a re-sult of commoditization of itineraries, package tourists are usually allowed to stay for a quite limited time and to walk around within a limited range when they visit the Taj. By contrast, backpackers have much wider room for im-provisation and for changing their itineraries as much as they wish. For ex-ample, they usually spend much more time and cover a wider spatial range at the Taj. Decommoditization of itineraries is thus a tourist action that seeks to transcend the rigidity, constraints, and disciplines of the itinerary of package tourism and that seeks more individual freedom, autonomy, and creativity.

However, after getting rid of the itineraries of package tourism, indepen-dent travelers find themselves involved in an alternative form of commoditi-zation. For example, independent travelers often have to buy guidebooks in order to plan an itinerary. Here, guidebooks, such as Lonely Planet and Rough Guides, are themselves a specific way of commoditization of itineraries, or more precisely, the commoditization of the *knowledge* of potential itineraries. In guidebooks, itineraries become the content, rather than the commodity form, of guidebooks. The consumption of this content accompanies independent travelers' journeys. The itineraries described in guidebooks are thus the *hidden* itineraries of the tourism system that shape and organize independent travelers' concrete itineraries.

These *hidden itineraries*, such as the network of schedules, traffic lines and prices, and booking systems of transportation and hospitality, constitute alternative constraints on travel. While the itineraries of package tours are the first level of touristic constraints, the itineraries of the tourism system as a whole are the second level of touristic constraints. Thus, while independent travelers can get rid of the first level of itineraries (overt itineraries) that are sold by travel agencies as packaged tours, they cannot get rid of the second level of itineraries (covert itineraries), itineraries that are hidden in the tourism system and are described by guidebooks and other travel materials.

ITINERARIES AS THE WAY OF CIRCULATION OF TOURISM PRODUCTS

Itineraries are not only scheduled journeys, but also mark a spatialization of those journeys. To put it another way, itineraries are about "what" will happen "when" and "where." While the issue of the scheduled journeys has been touched on above, we now turn to the issue of the spatialization of tourism, namely, the issue of "where" tourist activities will take place.

Itineraries are not only the commodity form of tourism, but also the form of access to tourist attractions. Itineraries are the way to circulate tourism products in tourist markets. In the market of goods, it is commodities that are circulated and delivered to consumers for consumption. In the market of temporal-spatial experiences of tourism, however, it is tourist consumers that are "circulated" and "delivered." They are taken to tourism products, products that are not deliverable in a literal sense. Thus, when tourists travel to destinations, destinations are in a sense "delivered" to tourists. Itineraries can thus be regarded as a way of the circulation of tourism products, despite the fact that itineraries are themselves an integral part of those products.

As a result, once tourist sites are visited by tourists, the "experiences" of these sites are in reality "delivered" and "circulated" to the tourist simultaneously. Therefore, the directions of tourist flows or itineraries are of significance to tourist destinations. Itineraries are thus not only the way in which people move, but also the way in which landscapes, cultures, and heritage are "circulated" (cf. Rojek and Urry 1997b, 10–11). The integration of places into the networks of tourist itineraries turns the places into "experiential commodities" circulated among tourists. Thus, it is no small wonder that tourist destinations compete for access to the network of tourists' itineraries. The simultaneity and synchronization of *circulation* and *consumption* of the tourism products makes the directions and coverage of tourists' itineraries vital to the success of tourism development.

Paradoxes may occur when tourist destinations vie for inclusion into the network of tourists' itineraries. In reality, to compete for this inclusion is to develop a favorable image that is in congruence with targeted potential tourists' tastes and demands. In this sense, to promote the circulation of a product of "tourist destination" is an issue of developing and establishing a desired image about the destination. In general, a favorable tourist image of a destination tends to allow tourists to include this destination into his or her itineraries, whereas a negative image, on the other hand, tends to deter potential tourists from visiting the destination. However, a favorable image of a destination may involve a paradox. For example, in sightseeing tourism, the inclusion of a destination into his or her itineraries this time simultaneously implies the exclusion of this place next time, for sightseers always want to seek variety and novelty (Cohen 1972). Therefore, while a favorable image increases a destination's attractiveness, it may at the same time pave a way to the demise of that attractiveness. That is why a destination has its own life cycle.

In postmodernity, with the help of mass media and the Internet, images increasingly become cultural fashions, whereas cultural fashions are always transient and temporary. Moreover, with the bombardment of images, images seem to become an autonomous world, a world that is "virtual reality." Thus, while image-making on the part of a destination is originally aimed at directing potential tourists' journeys and competing for the inclusion of the destination into their itineraries, it may often end up as distracting those tourists because they may get lost in the bombardment of tourist images. In this situation, word of mouth regains its significance in a world with too much information and too many images.

ITINERARIES AS MENUS FOR TOURISM CONSUMPTION

Tourism is essentially an activity of consumption (Urry 1995; Watson and Kopachevsky 1994; Baranowski and Furlough 2001a, 2001b; Meethan 2001; Wang 2002). What is consumed in tourism consists of two types of "materials." The first is the "material" serving of such daily consumption needs as eating, drinking, and sleeping. This does not mean that the material of this kind needs to be same with that of everyday life. Rather, a certain variety is necessary. Moreover, the consumption of this material takes place in a nondaily context, that is, the context of a journey, mobility, and an itinerary. New meanings of the consumption of the daily material can be derived from such a nondaily context. The second is the "material" of attractions at destinations and the journey itself. This type of material is beyond the reach of daily consumption. The consumption of the first type can be called "consumption *on* the journey," and the consumption of the second type can be called "consumption *of* the journey." The consumption *on* the journey is the primary tourism consumption, and the consumption *of* the journey is the secondary tourism consumption. The former is the extension of daily consumption to the journey; it is the base and support of the secondary consumption. By contrast, the latter is a transcendence of daily consumption; it is an extraordinary consumption. Both kinds of consumptions constitute *mobile* consumerism, or mass consumption *on the move*.

In both the primary and the secondary consumption, itineraries function as the temporal-spatial carriers of the two. In the primary tourism consumption, itineraries act as the nondaily *context* where daily functions of consumption are performed. In the secondary tourism consumption, itineraries become not only an *object* for consumption (journeys, services, and experiences), but also a *means* of "consumption *elsewhere*," consumption that takes place in other places and that transcends daily consumption. The secondary tourism consumption can thus be called "*peak consumption*" (Wang 2002).

The rise and the spread of mobile or touristic consumerism relates to the rise of tourist citizenship in contemporary societies. Tourist citizenship means a specific type of consumer citizenship, a democratized right to consume extraordinary experiences that transcend one's daily reach and that are accessible only through travel. In relation to this, itineraries act as the *carrier* of extraordinary experiences. However, problems arise with the question of "what is the extraordinary experience?" The extraordinary is always relative. What is extraordinary for children could not be so for adults. What is extraordinary for the first-time travelers could not be so for experienced travelers. For island residents, the sea is not the source of extraordinary experience. However, the sea is so for inhabitants from desert areas. Therefore, the extraordinary is relative to different potential tourists with different experiential backgrounds and characteristics. Relatedly, in tourism marketing, tourism is segmented into different typologies and packaged as various types of products in order to serve the varying needs of potential tourists with different tastes.

As a result, the functions of itineraries as illustrated in tourist brochures are similar to the functions of menus in restaurants. Just as menus help customers in selecting courses of foods that best fit their tastes and preferences, so itineraries presented in tourist brochures serve clients in choosing types of tourist experiences that best satisfy them. In short, itineraries function as menus for tourism consumption.

According to Levi-Strauss (1983), for foods to be edible, they must be cooked. In this sense, cooking is a cultural practice. The same is true of potential tourist resources. For these resources to be consume-able by potential tourist consumers, they must also be culturally "cooked." Itineraries are thus one of the cultural ways of "cooking" these resources. Just as menus represent certain cuisines by means of which foods are cooked, itineraries embody touristic "cuisines" by means of which potential tourist resources are "cooked" and "packaged." As itineraries are often displayed and illustrated in tourist brochures, it is more precise to regard itineraries *as presented in tourist brochures* that are the "menus" of tourist experiences.

Just like a certain type of cuisine produces some consistency in foods, itineraries also embody a certain theme or consistency in tourist experiences. A "touristic cuisine" that produces this consistency is "thematized." As a result of thematization, each itinerary is often centered around certain common themes, such as the itineraries of "Beautiful China," "Classic China," "China Adventure," and "the Silk Road." All these itineraries select some of the components from the "raw materials" of China and combine them as a thematic itinerary. Itineraries are thus the cultural combination of tourist experiences, in which the criteria for inclusion and exclusion of the components of tourist resources are culturally, as well as economically, determined. In short, it is culture that determines what type of packaged tourist experiences suit what kind of potential tourists. Via such criteria of selection, discrete tourist spots are integrated as a whole and objectified as an itinerary. Itineraries thus reflect people's views, evaluations, and imagery of the world. They are the categorization of peoples, cultures, places, and heritage in the world. In this sense, itineraries form *institutional circuits* in which contemporary people are "circulated" to examine and renegotiate the meanings of their relationships with the world.

Itineraries are not only culturally structured as thematic experiences, but also dramatized as progressive stories. Itineraries are *scripts* in which the tourist journeys—like courses for a meal—can be organized as the beginning, the middle, the climax, and the end. Accordingly, tourists are performers who make their own stories with the itinerary unfolding across time and space. Just as dramatization creates meaning, the intensified dramatization of human experiences in itineraries indeed helps foster and reproduce meanings in human life. Therefore, the consumption of itineraries is in reality a way of *consumption of meanings*, meanings that are created beyond the confines of daily life and that make human life more colorful and meaningful.

However, with the mass production and consumption of itineraries or tourism, there arises a paradox of objectification of meanings, a paradox inherent in what Simmel (1990) calls "the objectification of culture" in western modernity. Itineraries are the temporal-spatial carriers of tourist experiences and their associated meanings. Under the condition of the commoditization of tourism, itineraries are often supplied in massive, homogenized, and standardized ways. The new marketing strategy of the segmentation of tourism does not forsake these standardizations but merely divides them into several domains. As a result, the meanings related to itineraries are objectified, standardized, and thematized. In pre-modern ages, every single journey was linked to unique, subjective, and personal meanings. Under the condition of modernity, by contrast, such subjective and personal meanings of travel are increasingly diminished. Instead, tourism is packaged as various types of itineraries with thematic, categorized, homogenized, and objectified meanings. In tourism advertisements, there are a number of "musts." Once these "musts" are seen, this means "you have been there." If you go to Paris, you "must" find the scene of a romantic couple kissing each other. If you go to London, you "must" enjoy beers in a typical English pub. If you go to Beijing, you "must" see the torrent of bicycles on streets, Tiananmen Square, the Forbidden City, and the Great Wall at Badaling. All these "musts" signify the typical, objectified, standardized, and commonly acceptable meanings derived from the journeys to these places. Itineraries are thus organized in terms of socially, culturally, and objectively sanctioned and defined "worthiness" of visits. This site is included in our itineraries, just because everybody says it must be seen. That activity is also an item of our itinerary, just because everybody thinks such a kind of activity is a "must" in such a place. To miss such a "must" is not only a pity, but also a loss of value we pay for the journey. Thus, in a hidden way, itineraries lead to a cultural and social conformism to objectified and stereotyped meanings that are already circulated within society, mass media, and the tourism industry.

However, for individual tourists, the problem could be, "why 'must' we see this site or participate in that activity at such a place?" "Could we look at the place from our own perspectives and find something meaningful with our own eyes?" Yes, you could. However, even independent travelers are in pursuit of the experiences that are informed by guidebooks, brochures, maps, and holiday programs on TV that are seen at home. Thus, it becomes obvious that tourism is a kind of cultural practice in which each tourist participates to reproduce the code of meanings regarding the status quo, what is "sacred," and what is "heritage." The meanings derived from itineraries are thus unavoidably objectified and stereotyped. Accordingly, the consumption of these meanings serves to reproduce consumerist values of a society. Thus, tourists begin with a search for personal meanings but end up with the disappearance of *personal* meanings. Tourists want to keep a distance from reality but end up with a stronger conformity to the objectified semiotic order that a society needs.

Such a paradox is one of exemplifications of what Miles (1998, 5) calls the "consuming paradox." In this, the consumers' pursuit of freedom through economic means ends up maintaining "a dominant order that potentially constrains personal liberty" (Miles 1998, 32). He describes the consuming paradox as the idea that,

> on the one hand, consumerism appears to offer us individuals all sorts of opportunities and experiences, on the other hand, as consumers we appear to be directed down certain predetermined routes of consumption which ensure that consumerism is ultimately as constraining as it is enabling. (Miles 1998, 147)

Itineraries embody the same consuming paradox. As the form of circulation and consumption of tourism products, itineraries are the bearer of touristic consumerism. On the one hand, itineraries offer tourists "menus" for free choices and ease and order on the journey. On the other hand, itineraries direct tourists to the "predetermined routes of consumption" (Miles 1998, 147), which may trigger complaints about the very ease and order linking the itineraries because of their constraints on freedom and spontaneity. Itineraries initially offer tourists menus for free choice, but they finally deprive tourists of freedom of choice on the journey. Itineraries are thus constraining as well as enabling. While tourism becomes a reaction to the ambivalence of modernity (Wang 2000), it itself brings about its own ambivalence.

CONCLUSION

The quest for the tourist experience is essentially a reaction to the Logos-modernity which is about the realm of institutions characterized by reason and rationality (Wang 1996, 2000). However, in so doing, the tourist experience is itself rationally organized. The tourist experience appears to be an escape from the overwhelmingly rationalizing institutions, but finally ends up as the rationalization of that experience, with the tourism industry being its rational agent. Itineraries, then, become a way in which the tourist experience is rationally organized. In this sense, the paradoxes of tourism derived from itineraries represent the paradoxes of the Logos-modernity that is characterized by overarching rationalization in contemporary societies.

In effect, the rationalization of experiences often turns the tourist experience into its opposite, namely, the nonflexible and rigid schedules and itineraries that defy the very essence of the tourist experience. Tourism is thus rationally bounded, embodying as typical roles which are performed on itineraries. In this way, the antithesis between reason and feeling, rationality and romantic experiences, are joined to itineraries. And this joining of reason and experience becomes one of the sources of paradoxes and ambivalence of tourism.

For Tim Oakes (this volume), tourism, in the form of a quest for authenticity, can represent an attempt to negotiate the paradoxes of modernity. However, in seeking authenticity, tourists merely play a *role* of authenticity-seekers. In effect, the performance of the role of authenticity-seeking ends up as the disappearance of authenticity. That is why there is endless quest for authenticity and consequential endless frustration and disappointments, because, while tourism becomes a responsive action to the paradoxes and ambivalence of modernity, tourism itself absorbs the paradoxes and ambivalence of modernity in its course of rationalization of experience, as exhibited in the production and the consumption of tourist experiences via itineraries.

Even so, the tourist experience still becomes one of the most popular leisure, consuming, and cultural pursuits in postmodern societies, not for the reason that tourism is laden with paradoxes and ambivalence, but because there is no other way. Nobody can escape the hold of rationality and modernity, despite the fact that escape is initially a counteraction to that hold. Thus, while tourism begins with an attempt to escape from the control by Logos-modernity, it ends up as a return to that control. And this paradox becomes the very condition that tourism bears under postmodernity.

4

Heimat Tourism in the Countryside: Paradoxical Sojourns to Self and Place

Soile Veijola

INTRODUCTION

A few years ago, I showed my *Heimat* to my (then) boyfriend. We were sitting on a night train, just before Finland's midsummer festivities in June, traveling the long eleven-hour journey from Rovaniemi in Finland's Lapland, back to Helsinki. As we sat in the restaurant wagon, a sign flashed past us in the night, with the name of Ii on it. (I know, it is a very short name for a place.) Apart from the sign, the light sky, and the dark woods, there was nothing else to be seen. After a moment of hesitation, I gave up the idea of trying to explain to my companion everything worth seeing and experiencing that was hidden behind that sign. Thinking about it now, an account would have been useless. I should have pointed at myself and said: here is a part of Ii. Or I should have shown the darkness behind the sign: there is a part of me.

These "parts" are perhaps what much of contemporary cultural theory is trying to make sense of when conceptualizing modern subject and identity formation in relation to place and mobility (see, for example, Hall 1999; Oakes 1997; Urry 2002a). The obsession with the *authentic* we have witnessed in the heart of modern thought and sentiment for so long (cf. Mac-Cannell 1976/1989) is now being replaced by an equal quest for the *local*—as a basis for social life, identity, and belonging for both individuals and communities. But how are locality and belonging experienced, situated, and placed in a world of mobile societies, traveling cultures, and cosmopolitan individuals (Clifford 1997; Thompson and Tambyah 1999; Urry 2002a)?

In this chapter, I approach the broader question above, in inspired but light contact with certain threads of theorizing on place and belonging, focusing on a series of subjective experiences that have made me conscious of being *of* a place and, simultaneously, *cut off from* the same place. In these moments, I have felt like a tourist in my own homeland, a host and a guest at the same time. An analysis of personal experiences of moments like these, I find, may help in understanding the interplay between the local and the touristic in contemporary configurations of visiting, being in, and belonging in places. I shall do my best to accomplish the mission without falling into sentimental nostalgia for a unifying origin story that would try to "create order from the point of beginning" (Probyn 1996, 113). Nor do I wish to dwell on its opposite, a future with no strings attached to place, others, or self.

PLACES AND EXPERIENCES

Tim Dakes stresses that places are not mere physical spaces or objective locations on a map, nor are they to be confused with such territorial entities as regions, states, or communities. They are geographical expressions of interactions between historical processes, individual actions, and specific locations and sites. In this respect, they are sites of meaningful identity and action for individuals, derived from webs and connections across space and time (Oakes 1997, 510). These networks, however, have been transformed in the modernization process by global mobility and displacement.

Rearranged networks of time, place, and social life have resulted in detachment, disconnectedness, and lack of commitment (see, for example, Giddens 1990; Sennett 1999) which have, for their part, given impetus to a kind of *a new locality* which feeds, among other things, *nostalgia tourism* to former homelands. In Esa Sironen's (1993/1995, 221) view, this does not necessarily mean regression to the pre-modern. "It can equally well be understood as the genuine flip side of modernity, a way of working on alienation, and specifically, alienation from space and homeland. One searches for an identity at a close proximity. Dig there where you are standing, advises the new history writing."

One way to dig locally today, and to find one's position in the mobile society, is to investigate the discourse of homeland, *Heimat*. The term evokes a *memory of origin* while at the same time denying a possibility of return to it, since the past is already disintegrated and thereby forever lost (Morley and Robins 1993, 7, 10–11; Probyn 1996, 103, 111–16). For Edgar Reitz, who made the famous TV series *Heimat* shown in the Federal Republic of Germany (FRG) in 1984, *Heimat* is, as the place where one was born, "for every person the centre of the world" (cited in Morley and Robins 1993, 10). However, historically, the discourse of homeland is not an innocent one. The German word *Heimat* bears a connotation to a discourse that once was a synonym for race (blood) and territory (soil), with deadly consequences for those who did not "belong" (Kaes 1989; cited in Morley and Robinson 1993, 17). It may still be dangerous to ask to whom do the roots, heritage, and identity belong. A potential result is to close the borders to "outsiders," to exclude and annihilate exiles and refugees (Morley and Robinson 1993). Yet in this chapter *homeland* is used for reflexive rather than political purposes. It is a concept that interweaves time, place, identity, and history with the personal and the subjective, and, moreover, in the German language it does not emphasize the aspect of "land" in the concept.

Both feminist theorists (e.g., Haug 1983/1992; Braidotti 1994) and those in cultural studies inspired by the work of Michel Foucault (Hall 1999) have emphasized the fact that identities and subjectivities are not sealed and closed totalities, constructed by remembering or finding the time past as something whole and integrating (Hall 1999, 49). Rather than guaranteeing a coherent narrative of self as something simply found and reported as always the same, the retelling of this narrative in new situations results in something else: it displays the character of identities as names we have given ourselves when being positioned or positioning ourselves in certain ways in our narratives of the past (cf. Hall 1999, 224–27). Resistance and countermemory are embedded in the narratives in complex ways, disturbing the dominant and conventional ways of representing the self (cf. Foucault 1978/1990, 95–96; Braidotti 1994, 25). In other words, cultural identities and subjectivities are composed of silences, differences, discontinuities, breaks, and forgetting as well, not only of clearly articulated itineraries in time and place. Indeed, one could replace an idea of a stable state of identity with the notion of *belonging*—as "the desire for some sort of attachment, be it to other people, places, or modes of being . . . a process that is fuelled by yearning" to mark modern identity formation (Probyn 1996, 19).

Thus, *memorizing, remembering,* and *telling* a lost homeland are not exactly the same thing; nor does *experience* of having or having lost a homeland emerge in the narrative of self in a simple manner. According to Sironen (1993/1995, 203–4), experience includes a constant and complex emotional and intellectual arranging by means of which an individual recognizes in her mind the meaning of a thing or an event. Experience is "connected to the life history of the experiencing subject, the images and texts that have come across to each of us in the right moment and from the right angle" and have thereby been experienced (Sironen 1993/1995, 222). "'*Heimat,*' 'nature' would hardly exist in any other way than through the filter of one's own experience. Each has her/his own, but the very birth and structure are after all what is common to us all" (Sironen 1993/1995, 225).

What is also common to us all is that we remember those moments of *Heimat,* be they visual or mental images of a photo or a memory, that have a *punctum* in them: an arrow or a little hole or a scratch, a coincidence, which disturbs the *studium*—the historical or cultural evidence of the time. It is a punctum which pierces and bruises the subject through her or his armors of years, through all her experience of life (Barthes 1985, 32, 33). It is these kinds of moments with which I experiment in this chapter. I am not so much memorizing a life history for autobiographical or personal purposes but remembering a "place of origin" in order to understand the meaning of a sojourn to it and other places with a paradoxical identity of a local and a tourist.

For this purpose, the German language makes a useful distinction between *Gedächtnis* and *Erinnerung*. The former refers to *mémoire involontaire*, the involuntary memory that Marcel Proust was after in his famous volumes of books, *A la recherche du temps perdu*, whereas *Erinnerung, mémoire volontaire*, refers to conscious memorizing and active remembering. *Erinnerung*, memorizing, has been used as a research method, titled memory-work, *Erinnerungsarbeit*, by feminist scholars (Haug 1983/1992)—in a sense, against Proust. According to the method, one is a conscious seeker of the *in*significant which has not left a lasting memory, that is of the substance of which knowledge and experience are made. On this level, my underlying questions are as follows: How do you remember a place you have left behind and forgotten in order to become yourself? How does a place remember you?

But first: how do you describe your Heimat to a tourist?

TOURISTS AND LOCALS

If a tourist should come to Ii, a place located one hundred kilometers south of Torneå, the point where the Gulf of Bothnia separates Finland from Sweden, she might want to hear about the history of the place, how many people live there, what are the traditional means of livelihood and the most exotic corners and views to attend to, and what kinds of leisure activities are available in the region.

On a gray day in May 1999, I wanted to show the Gulf of Bothnia, "my sea," to a colleague in tourism studies from New Zealand. We had never met but had entertained a lively correspondence for a year. I asked an exboyfriend (they seem to pop up everywhere in this essay) who still spends his summers in the area to take us to the sea by boat. During the trip, I did not provide my guest with facts about the local fishing industry. I knew, of course, from a lifetime of experience, that people ate salmon, powan, and lamprey in Ii because generations of locals had always fished it and brought it home from the sea. When we pulled up onto the shore of a small island named Rontti, I proudly showed my guest the way to the little gray cottage that my grandfather and father had used as a base when setting or gathering the fishing nets. But we had to settle for taking turns peeking in through the window since I did not even know where the keys were kept! I knew this was an important junction in my family history as well as local history, but all I could do was gesture at the visible, picturesque landscape, like a tourist guide—lost for words, information, and concepts. Of course, the island had also been the site of many generations of midsummer night bonfires, including those of my young love with the boat driver. I could have described these events at length to my new friend, but not with the third party in question present, instead of safely locked up in the past.

The trip gave me another start on our way back. We were greeted by a fisherman inspecting his net. Our driver turned around and halted the boat for a chat. The man proved to be of my age, a familiar face. He had taken over his father's fishing business as a hobby. When he heard we had a New Zealander with us, he at once switched to fluent small talk in English, having visited the land himself. So much for local, unspoiled color, I thought. My ex was our guide to my family landscape; I was a guide to my new friend; and the first fisherman we had run into, still practicing the traditional local livelihood, had toured the homeland of our guest.

Was I being a host, or a guest, or a chance tour operator introducing people to one another in random places on earth? If I were a host, I knew the place by heart but not in a way that I could describe it to someone else. "This is what Finns do, are, and like" would have been too impervious a statement (cf. Minca and Oakes in Venice, this volume's introduction). If I was a local, I was a local *daughter:* a complete tourist in the male world of fishing and boating. I belonged to the gender that had been sentenced to the less heroic world of peeling potatoes for fish soup indoors, instead of combating the harsh elements and making a livelihood at sea. But since I was never really sentenced to the kitchen or other feminine spheres of the rural household either, but to the school bench instead, I lacked both the internal knowledge (know-how) and the external knowledge (information and facts) about life at sea—or the kitchen, for that matter. I was a complete stranger in my own homeland. I was a tourist, and I wished somebody would tell me what it was all about.

According to Michael Polanyi (1983), we always know more than we can tell or describe. He calls this aspect *tacit knowledge*, which for him is unformulated knowledge affecting people all the time, even though it cannot be expressed or articulated. Hannele Koivunen summarizes it as "all that genetic, bodily, intuitive, mythical, archetype and experiential knowledge that a person has which cannot be expressed in verbal concepts" (Koivunen 1997, 78–79). Local knowledge is tacit in various ways. It rarely needs be articulated or accounted for because everyone already knows what needs to be known. It is the arrival of the newcomer—the stranger, the tourist—that changes everything. This encounter is summarized by Yi-Fu Tuan as follows: "Only the visitor (and particularly the tourist) has a viewpoint; his perception is often a matter of using his eyes to compose pictures. The native, by contrast, has a complex attitude derived from his immersion in the totality of his environment." The visitor can state his viewpoint easily and confrontation with novelty also prompts him to express himself verbally, whereas the complex attitude of the native "can be expressed by him only with difficulty and indirectly through behaviour, local tradition, lore and myth" (Tuan 1974, 63).

Although Tuan's comparison captures my experience at sea in some respects, there is even more to it. The presence of a stranger also encourages a native of the area to explain and account for the stranger what is there to be seen, experienced, and sensed, and why. This telling may reveal the landscape to the one who already knows it in a different way because of the new social situation of looking at it and telling its stories. Thereby traditional, tacit, constitutive, and familiar knowledge may become visible and accountable, which makes formerly self-evident truths, practices, and values visible and, as such, contestable and changeable.

Local knowledge also contains knowledge of the matters a guest should *not* be told (where are the best woods or swamps for berry picking, for example). Unless, of course, one is very good friends with the stranger. But at which point do strangers turn into friends—and when does the need to articulate or to hide facts end? Or, to look at the issue from another angle, at which point do strangers become *tourists*—for whom the ready-made packages of information and stories are passed on without any necessary personal motivation to share a cultural experience with them; without a need to listen to the stranger's account in turn? At which point does the sign of my village of Ii start marking "the knowable (and 'do-able') point on a map" (Minca and Oakes, this volume) for both tourists and locals?

Or, turning the tables once more, when do the strangers become locals and get to claim access to places, views, and natural resources, even without military or violent interventions? As Orvar Löfgren (1999, 147) has stated, sometimes "it is hard to draw a sharp line between locals and summer guests. Who are the locals? The retired urban couple, the returned local boy, the commuting young family? It is a social landscape in which the classic categories of old and new, urban and rural, insiders and outsiders don't work."

But one could question the very distinction between locals and strangers as a feasible starting point. For Tuan (1974, 63), in a traditional and stable society strangers are few and relatively insignificant. Then again, and in contrast, Gilles Deleuze and Félix Guattari (1980, 535–36) claim that if it were not for the strangers, the locals would never become conscious of being locals and having their own language, as opposed to foreigners with foreign languages: "La langage est fait pour cela, pour la traduction, non pour la communication." Again, in Tuan's opinion, it is in the mobile society where "the fleeting impressions of people passing through cannot be neglected" (Tuan 1974, 63). Yet, it could be argued that when tourists come in uninterrupted flows, they become part of the scenery, not worthy of focused attention. Georg Simmel, for his part, has formulated the special relation between the stranger and the local as one with mutual confidence and openness unforeseen between those connected through established ties of kinship or locality (Simmel 1950; Jokinen and Veijola 1997, 29–30). In line with Tim Oakes (2005), the previous could be perceived as contributing to the process of place making through encounters in place rather than disengagement engendered by travel or mobility through space.

People passing through one's own scenery are evidently needed for a reflection of self and one's environment, just like seeing strange places oneself provides a new view on one's own ordinary life. Thereby, as demonstrated in the scene at sea, locals and tourists can engage in an exchange of their respective "lores and myths," since each may have occupied roles as both visitors and locals in turn. Lores and myths become a recognizable and interchangeable genre that travels and sheds light on both them and us (cf. Clifford 1997). A prerequisite to this is that both parties understand the difference between *Erlebnis*, "a moment of adventure and event," and *Erfahrung*, "familiarity with something, skillfulness and observation." The latter term emphasizes the aspect of "already known, already experienced," the past in the present; and the former the aspect of "never before," the future in the present. It is commonly believed that tourists go for *Erlebnis*, and locals start from *Erfahrung*. Yet, each encounter is an opening to new possibilities, rearrangements of fixed expectations.

So how do you *ask* a local how she knows a place and how the place knows her?

INVOLUNTARY MEMORIES

I am surrounded by thirty-four persons, most of whom I have not seen for over two decades. But between the years 1971 and 1975, I saw them in the same classroom every working day of the week. Now we are at our first class reunion, arranged in my hometown, the village of Ii. The year is 2000 and, fittingly, we are all forty years old.

Only a handful of us still lives in Ii; the rest of us are just visiting. The children of the locals race their skateboards at the very same curve of the road where I walked or rode my bike at their age but, still, the *place* is not the same. It is marked by a different historical constitution and by different meanings (Paasi 1991, in Riikonen 1997, 182) for their generation and mine. According to Heikki Riikonen (1997, 182), a *generation* is a "group of people connected by the experiences of certain stages of life that is social history." He calls these biographical communities, which corresponds to the definition by Benedict Anderson (1983/1991) of *imagined communities*, in which people do not need to know each other personally or ever even meet in order to have the experience of belonging to a community and the subsequent feeling of comradeship.

During our reunion in the local restaurant, the (then) only one in town, we evoke a reimagined concrete community, based on the shared history of the early '70s: of local figures, common habits, taste for music, styles of hair and clothing. Our generation witnessed the arrival of summer cottages, television, and nonmanual telephone centers in Finland. We grew into the culture of too tight, name brand jeans and disco fever, and the era of a couple of victories every now and then in international ice hockey. We call ourselves, ironically, "the children of the milk bay revolution," since we reached the age of adolescence in the early seventies, just in time to see milk bays, the unofficial platforms for cross-sex meetings, disappear from the roadsides. (Before them, the hay-houses had been the secret meeting points for couples courting.) At the reunion, we reminisce about one generational experience after another through the night and thereby strengthen our sense of belonging to one. Uncannily, we also realize the huge discord between our own images of ourselves and the others, and their images of ourselves and themselves at that time. It is as if we had known others better than ourselves.

But it was the following day that I first visited the past in a way that was more than a heartfelt inside joke. Our master of ceremonies had invited us all to his old family farm by a curvy gravel road. The six of us who reappeared decided to go swimming at some point. We, three women and three men, strolled through a sunny and, to use an accurate term, pastoral landscape to the seaside. The hay was piled in poles as it had been years before. My feet sank in the soft and muddy sand at the water's edge, and the water was just as warm as it had been in my childhood summers. And, when I stopped swimming and turned around to stand in the neck-deep water, I suddenly saw around me faces so unexpectedly *familiar* that I realized they must be the most familiar faces to me that I know or can imagine. (Of course one knows the features of one's family members by heart, but unless one loses them for twenty-five years and then meets them again, one rarely notices or reflects upon their familiarity.) Later it occurred to me that these classmates will probably also be *persons* to me in a way unlike anyone else.

This despite, or because of, the fact that they (we) had been hurt in our inmost hearts during those adolescent years by love, hate, or pure cruelty—pointedly as persons. I also realized that the sight of the circle of faces around me was the exact opposite of the urban excitement aroused and inspired by "the ocean of billowing heads" (for Edgar Allan Poe, in Benjamin 1974/1986, 16–17) to be found, and consumed to the point of nausea, in the anonymous, exotic cities of the world.

These persons are also the first *tribe* I ever belonged to, and in that respect, the first communion to which all subsequent ones are reverted to.

Still, it was not only the familiar faces that sent me back in time with a jolt. It was also the underwater domain: the familiar, salty substance and smell of the water, the sensations of swimming in something that combined sun and seaweed, lightness and darkness, memories of the past and the vivid moment of the now (see Edensor, this volume). The involuntary memory of the gestures of my body in the water. *Mémoire involontaire des membres*. (See Tuan 1974, 5–12; Macnaghten and Urry 2001; Jokinen and Veijola 2003.)

For Walter Benjamin, the involuntary memory, *Gedächtnis*, protects impressions by storing them, but "only that which has not been consciously and especially 'lived,' that which the subject has not encountered as an *Erlebnis*" (Benjamin 1974/1986, 19). Whereas *Erinnerung*, *mémoire volontaire*, conscious memorizing and active remembering, stores nothing of the time past; it aims at disintegrating the impressions by willpower or intelligence, which are, however, completely useless in conjuring up the past (Benjamin 1974/1986, 15, 18).

What if we had invited spouses to the reunion? We would have most likely not gone swimming. Too childish. Or even if we had, we would not have remembered and changed each other and ourselves at the same time. We would have met in time and place lost *as tourists*, with accompanying persons. "So this is where you all used to come swimming when you were kids?" "No. It wasn't as simple as that." "What was?" "Oh, just forget it."

PRIVACY AND NATURE

"Maan korvessa kulkevi lapsosen tie / hänt ihana enkeli kotihin vie. / Niin pitkä on matka, ei kotia näy / vaan ihana enkeli vieressä käy." The verse can be translated from Finnish into English as "In the wilderness of a land goes the way of a child / Guided home by an angel so fair / So long is the journey, with no sight of home / But the guardian angel is there."

This Finnish lullaby by Immi Hellén and P. J. Hannikainen, from the turn of the twentieth century, is often accompanied by a visual image of a guardian

Figure 4.1   The Guardian Angel

angel sheltering a sister and her little brother through the woods (see figure 4.1). Both the rhyme and the picture are familiar to all Finns. In the painting, one can depict the touch of a human hand and a social community: There is a footpath, a bridge, and peasant clothes on the children—all indicating a cottage or a village somewhere in the distance. The children, be they from the village or forsaken by passersby, have gotten lost somewhere between the wilderness and the city.

Going to the countryside in Finland means visiting the childhood of both the nation itself and a large majority of its citizens. It has enveloped, or at least bordered, the formation of both the subjective and collective Finnish identities of all generations, except perhaps the youngest ones. Finland was predominantly an agricultural country until the 1950s. In the 1990s, less than one-tenth of the population was working in farming and forestry since, by the mid-1970s, Finland had become an industrial and service economy—simultaneously. The Great Migration of the 1960s and 1970s, also known as the rapid modernization process, had emptied the villages and the back country, raised and filled the blocks in towns and, finally, turned the capital of the country, Helsinki, into a modern city.

Building a modern city and learning to live in it meant leaving the rural landscape behind, concretely and symbolically (cf. Tuan 1974). The future lay ahead, in the lights of an urban center. Today the countryside and its rural communities are, in a manner of speaking, both the past tense of the nation and a recreational present tense of domestic tourism. For Finns, the annual ritual of returning to their old family places in the pastoral countryside, seaside, or lakes for the summer (and again for Christmas) is an established social and societal pattern.

It is also what my sister and brother and I do with our own families. Each of us arrives from our own direction at our mother's house in Ii. The home is traditionally Finnish: red timber with white corners, built in the 1880s in the same yard as our grandparents' old house. Or else we drive ten kilometers further to the seaside and our summer cottage, a time-pocket that stores the long summer holidays of a teacher's family from the 1960s and 1970s. There is no electricity; none of the amusements that require engine power. A paraffin lamp is good enough for reading in the darkening nights of August; the nautical chart on the wall for ritual inspection on where we are. Fire is kept for cooking, making coffee, and burning all the waste wood that the sea, untiringly, donates to its coastal residents. An old adventure book by Zane Grey softened by two decades on the shelf punctures through the armor of the years. A sauna, swim, and subsequent long session of admiring the sunset from the balcony, accompanied by the unstoppable wind in the willow trees and birches, the divers and snipes in the sky, and the endless striking of the waves ashore, fills the evening. Fishing boats and sailing boats silhouette the horizon, and, on a clear night, we imagine we can see Sweden behind it.

In 1970, there were around 175,000 summer cottages scattered around the lakes and seashores of Finland. Now there are around 460,000 of them, with an increase of 20 percent in the last ten years (Skoglund and Hermiö 2002, 22). Interestingly, the new cottages are currently built by people in their middle ages, not by young families as was the case in the 1960s and 1970s (Skoglund and Hermiö 2002, 22).

This may indicate that a more collective form of holiday making is starting to tempt Finns, as family and kinship ties are increasingly replaced by bonding and public sociability between significant peers as leisure tribes (cf. Maffesoli 1988/1996; Jokinen and Veijola 2003, 271; for countertendencies see Jallinoja 2000). A nationwide breather "somewhere out of this networked world," to paraphrase Baudelaire, used to close up the whole country in July, to the dismay of international business associates, not to mention tourists looking for open dinner locales in the city. In the global economy this cannot be recommended. Successful or aspirant companies cannot afford losing their winning teams for weeks, and, generation by generation, even the need for such a break from the global connectivities may fade. *Unique places* in family history will be replaced by *generic spaces* of the present moment, shared by leisure tribes. Instead of visiting a certain place at a certain time of the year (going home for Christmas and Midsummer night), vacationers will migrate to social spaces (skiing resorts, spas, mountains to be climbed), which can be visited the year round. Winter holidays in the ski resorts of Lapland and summer holidays in the tent villages of rock festivals have, for their part, gradually paved the way for a new and active sociability and collectivity. Today, a sport, a hobby, or a profession unites people and makes them feel "at home" when they are on vacation and in everyday life. An illustration of the point came in the winter of 2002, when my Finnish mobile phone operator changed the brand name of its popular *home line* service into *tribe line*.

Another point of illustration could be the marginal but symbolically central social practice in the urbanization process of Finland in the sixties and seventies called the summer kitten. It was picked up from a farm in the neighborhood to link children, first-generation urbanites, back to the country life emotionally and conveniently during the summer holidays. But before returning to the city and the oncoming winter, the now outgrown young cat, "impossible to have in the city," was customarily dropped off out of the car on the way home. As the story line for the kids would go, it was released "back to nature." I guess the summer kitten experienced the centrifugal forces of modernity in full force: being thrown out to the wilderness of the winter on one's own, without knowing the way home.

WINTER IN THE CITY

"The path into town, and out of it, was nearby or had points of transition" (Bloch 1929/1991, 48). Identities have points of transition, too. My *Heimat* was not all about the countryside. Both imaginary and real visits to the city marked my childhood.

My mother was a city girl. She grew up in Kajaani, a city two hundred kilometers east of Ii. According to her testimony, she was the first girl in town to buy jeans, perm her hair, and tuck her loose shirttail under her waistband. So she would know about the charms of walking the streets and making impressions through appearances, borrowing identities from movie characters in the cinema and untamed characters in city novels for girls.

In her adult life, she saw to it that the family went shopping in Oulu, a city fifty kilometers south, or visited grandparents in Kajaani or Haparanda up north in Sweden on a regular basis. (There was also traveling abroad in the summer.) For us daughters, Kajaani meant the most rewarding city life experience, in the sense that there we could walk to the city on our own from our grandparents' house and take our time investigating the shops. In Oulu, by contrast, we were often locked up in the car (childproof locks on the back-seats) with the less invigorating presence of our father, to wait for our mother who would be buying the latest household accessories. Father had the power to control the transportation, as was common in the countryside; getting to places was a masculine routine and domain. (In the mid-seventies, my mother bought her own car and the "autocratic" paternal control of the family's mobility ended.) For my sister and me, visits to the city meant also being modernized by force. Our mother would drop us off at any barbershop that came our way, and our hair was always cut very short. In vain, I hoped one day to come out with longer hair, just like any normal girl!

In addition to the real visits to cities, there were the significant imaginary visits to the urban scene provided by the national newspaper, *Helsingin Sanomat,* which my parents read (for its supreme crossword, my mother later explained). The Swedish women's magazine *Femina*, to which she also subscribed, however, was the decisive thing; I devoured the best catwalk performances in the streets of Stockholm once a week.

No wonder then that for me the city meant *feminine space*: in the form of appearances, postures, clothes, style, and freedom. It meant a performative identity (Butler 1990) far from that of a rural one which was, in my childhood experience, based on place, tradition, and gender-based, task-bound roles and chores. The countryside was impregnated with what feminist scholars call the law of the father (see for example Irigaray 1977/1985). It was a masculine order of ownership, obligation, inheritance, and nonnegotiability of traditional identities based on such local parameters as family, gender, profession, and place. This order dictated suitable behavior for girls and boys as well as proper ways of making, maintaining, and using material objects—in a way that prevented any fusion of the two spheres of action and work between genders. Traditionally, women fed the families and kept the indoor spaces (including that of the livestock) clean and the home-fires on, while men tended to the fields and hunted in the woods and the sea. In the adult lives of my parents, as well as in their family friends', each with the same education and profession, women minded the household and men resisted the winds and storms of the outside world—after office hours, that is. From a child's perspective, women seemed to do all the bonding in the family's personal life while men expressed their thoughts by putting their newspaper down, getting up, and stepping out for a smoke (or even more violently, staying in to smoke).

Paraphrasing Marshall Berman's (1982) infamous book, in the countryside, all that was solid between the genders melted into soil. In sharp contrast, the city as a representation and experience promised freedom, autonomy, a less rigid gender order, and looser spaces and forms of interaction. So at eighteen, I left for the city and lived in a series of them.

Interestingly perhaps, my dilemma in combining the orders of masculine countryside and feminine city in my childhood and youth does not support the common notion of masculine mobility and travel as opposed to the feminine notion of dwelling and belonging (cf. Rojek and Urry 1997b; Jokinen and Veijola 1997; Thompson and Tambyah 1999). In Reitz's film *Heimat*, for instance, it was women who stayed (*die Dableiber*) in the village and men who left home and emigrated (*die Weggegangenen*) (in Morley and Robins 1993, 15). (For a richer picture of women in the city see for example Wilson 1991; Hochschild 2000.) In Finland, however, it was women who left the countryside in large numbers from the start. As a rule, the eldest son inherited the house and the farm, while the daughters were given a small sum of money and sent away, for marriage or an education or a job in the city. Accordingly, there were more men than women staying in the countryside, which led to a shortage of wives in the rural communities, still an issue periodically lamented in public. As for the men who left for the city, many got lost on the way, falling aside with a bottle and a handful of companions in misfortune.

I propose that women in Finland were more accustomed to losing their foothold. They could balance themselves better on the new surface of asphalt and office floors, giving up their dialects, traditional dress, and social manners in the urban melting pots more willingly than men did—adapting themselves to the constant change of modern life. After all, the soil of the countryside had never been really theirs to stand on.

There is another phenomenon that took place around the 1960s in Finland that leads me to a sociological, gender-sensitive interpretation of a generation experience. More than one of my same-age women friends was displaced from her home at a very early age, living with her grandmother for weeks, months, or even years. Could there be a more general pattern of gender relation and societal change behind these personal experiences, random as they may be? Namely, if young mothers in the 1960s needed or wanted to study or work after or between babies, but their husbands would not change their patterns of domestic responsibilities, the logical solution would have been to send their children to grandmother, in order for the mother to "emancipate herself." (Unless, of course, the family could afford a full-time maid in the house.) It may have felt sensible to send a girl away to the grandmother from the mother's side. And, usually, in the 1960s, grandmothers lived in the countryside.

Alas, when it was my turn to serve time away from home in the early 1960s as the price to be paid to women's liberation, I was sent to a city instead. I still remember the comforting sounds of the streams of cars driving past the house in the evening in Kajaani, their lights wiping the ceiling of the bedroom. For me the city became a place of both unbearable loss and its immediate, sensual consolation. (My grandmother was very affectionate and fed me well.) Whereas for many of my contemporaries, it may be the countryside that bears the mark of physical comfort in ontological insecurity: lacking the confidence in the continuity and reliability of a self-identity, the environment, persons, and things (see Giddens 1990, 92–100).

In other words, the women of my generation may have met the antagonism between the countryside and the city, home and displacement, at a very young age and with a price. We are the generation whose mothers modernized themselves before their husbands did. In this framework, modernity in Finland is a fundamentally feminine experience. We long for a language, a home, and a place that we could call our own. (All I have left of my local dialect are the vowels.) Perhaps it is for this reason that our generation of women travels in and out of both places and languages, looking for paradise lost.

Romance on the beach in the south. Why not? At least it is not wintertime and one is not alone. Crying in the aeroplane on return brings back heaps of involuntary memories.

MOBILITY AND BELONGING

How do you know and experience a place you knew as a child; and how does that place know you? At which point do strangers turn into friends, tourists into neighbors, locals into visitors, and places into tourist destinations? Can *Heimat* be revisited? How is ontological security, guaranteed by being at home and having a home, produced and managed in the modern world? How does one trust a place? How has the countryside configured in the identity-formation of my generation?

Where do I want to be buried?

There are those who trust that they have a home (ontological security), or they trust their home (belonging), or they trust other peoples' homes (their roles as guests and others' roles as hosts). Sociologist Taina Rajanti (1995) has read Finnish author Tove Jansson's novel *Magic Winter* [Trollvinter] (1957) against the process of becoming modern and learning to trust again. *Mumin*, a little troll who is the main protagonist, wakes up in the middle of winter, while his family and friends are fast asleep. He cannot get back to sleep and is faced with the challenge of experiencing winter for the first time, on his own. Winter in Rajanti's reading of the novel is the modern form of a social bond where the community lacks a base and consists of isolated individuals that are strangers to one another.[1] It is "separate from family, relatives, home, traditions and proper manners"; it is modernity. Mumin "longs for a member of his former world with whom he can communicate and by narrating, create and maintain the old communion," to encounter the winter by. But the only ones he meets are odd winter creatures saying things like "'We do not belong together but that does not prevent us from being friends'" or "'Everything is very insecure and precisely that makes me feel calm.'" The creatures of winter are not united by an immediately experienced communion; they are not there to be seen, heard, and understood immediately. Instead "alienation gives form to an individual's relation to others."

To his delight, Mumin finds his forefather living in the bathing cabin. This provides him with a frail connection to the world, something that exceeds mere coincidence, even though this connection is not as tight and warm as a family communion. It gives him a sense of history that is possible only after the concrete connection with his forefathers has been broken. But, as Rajanti phrases it, does belonging to a place equate to living amid old, forsaken, and useless things with one's ancestors?

Finally, in the middle of a snowstorm—a formless crowd and its billowing heads, the core of modernity—Mumin realizes that all he needs to do is fly along with the storm. The anonymity and infinity of modernity carries him forward, him and his relation to himself. After that, winter is something he has fought and conquered for himself; and not even spring releases him from the hostile world "as the experience of irreversible loneliness and separateness," since this very experience is now the basis of communion and constituent of an identity of someone belonging to a community. The challenge overcome becomes a grounding experience of one's "own" and of an "experience"— and that is universal. But this challenge being loneliness and isolation is something particular, something modern.

Jansson and Rajanti address the issue of our time on mobility and belonging. More and more people find it hard to construct one's home and homeland as an unambiguous and harmonious place and to have a relation to it. We may have more homes than one, and our sense of belonging may be dispersed from a place-based community to extensive and flexible networks of colleagues, friends, tribes, and places—different ones for summer and winter. Family members live on the opposite sides of the world (see Urry 2002a; 2004). It is a complicated issue even to own a place in the traditional meaning of the word since strangers and tourists have started to inhabit them as their *amenity landscapes* (Keskitalo et al. 2000; cf. Löfgren 1999). Relations between locals and visitors can no longer be categorized as either hospitality or hostility but are marked by ambiguity. Instead of buying or inheriting our homes or vacation spots, we—and our guests—rent them by the day or week, just like a deck chair in the sun: in a landscape of freedom, pleasure, and adventure without the burdens of ownership or stewardship. We encounter all these landscapes and places ready to wonder and to remember at the same time, paradoxically, being no longer free to commit ourselves to any of them.

> The winter does not wipe out family nor Mumin's sense of belonging. Families and kin do not disappear in modernity. Modernity does not mean a denial of emotions and the need to belong. Winter has changed Mumin himself so that the experience of loneliness and isolation does not separate him from the rest of the hostile world, but forms a bond between him and the outside world. Mumin now has "everything," also the irreversible experience of loneliness and isolation; which he memorizes with eyes closed, with the sun warming the stairs of the bathing cabin and the spring sea rolling against it. (Rajanti 1995, 154)

My efforts to situate my origins in the sunny countryside, a *locus amoenus*, a pastoral retreat (Andrews 1999, 53, 57), at the beginning of my journey, veiled my resistance to the rural order. This refusal underlies my desire to live in an open social space, rather than in the fixed geographical co-ordinates of a place. Without remembering the winter and the sense of nonbelonging, I could not reflect upon my entering the gender-specific and socially divided symbolic order of the time nor the ways in which I became a subject by contesting my relation to place, locality, and community as something given, constraining and unyielding. But in order to remember my homeland, I had to forget it for two decades and, upon return, accept that remembering the city and the winter, side by side with the summer and the countryside, brings along memories of pain and violence. All of this is unavoidably involved in questioning the law of the father, be that forced by a culture or a man of that culture.

EPILOGUE

As a child, one does not know one is a child.[2] That a place is just a place, one of many. That one is made of a place. Place for a child is home, and home is the place where a child lives.

Every summer my son, a city boy, visits the same landscape by the sea in the countryside that his grandfather used to cultivate and master when he was young. My son knows it differently. Together with the boy from the house nearby, they share their modern, placeless, young boys' culture of music and computer games. But, to end the day, they often engage in a drawn-out, scoreless game of badminton, shrieking and panting in the same summer night air which is embedded in the involuntary memory of my own childhood existence. Every time I step out into the yard in a summer evening, I automatically inhale, and remember. (Summer is not only about the sun; it is also about the odors and smells in the shadow, but this is something one learns only later in life.)

It would be useless to tell either my own or my father's stories about the place to my son. I have let him experience it. Now he is fifteen and can start forgetting.

I myself was finally taught what it was all about in the sea; I was treated with a readable narrative of my family history. In autumn 2001, with a group of tourism professionals, I visited a tourist destination in the Torneå area, in northwestern Finland, one hundred kilometers north of Ii. We were taken to an old school called Pekanpää, which had been turned into a museum storing the traditional way of life in the Torneå Valley, with the help of material culture and an animated drama of smugglers and customs officials trying to con each other, as well as performing their everyday chores in the farm house. A large room was covered with authentic household and fishing objects and tools. A few older men, probably locals, dressed in clothing my grandfather might have worn in the 1950s, explained to us how one fished in the old days or how one could tell a good knife from a bad one.

I suddenly realized that the knife that I had so many times seen my father use with skill, when making a fire or taking a splinter from a child's finger, was made there, in Pekanpää. I also realized that I was being shown and explained something neither my father or my grandfather bothered or were able to account or show to me in their lifetime. (I wonder if I would have paid attention had they tried to.) Equally, the demonstrations of making butter or yarn that the women presented reminded me vividly of my grandmother's smug smile when she postponed teaching me how to milk a cow until there were no cows left to milk on the farm. She knew better than I did that I was to learn and do something completely different in my life. I was never made to choose between the gender-specific chores on the farm; I was simply expelled from it, welcomed to visit in the paradoxical identity of a guest and a kin.

Incidentally, the experience of being expelled was repeated in Pekanpää. My efforts to talk back to the animators of my family history were not responded to. They did not step out of their roles nor welcome me to do the same. Evidently, for these hosts, the guests should come from outside the local culture, not inside. I was still an educated daughter: an outsider!

Heimat is not left behind in the past. For Ernst Bloch, it is "something that is familiar to us all from childhood but where no one yet has been" (Bloch 1959/1973, cited in Sironen 1993/1995, 222). We have not lost it for good, nor can we hold on to it as something that stays the same; it needs to be produced over and over again as something different. *Heimat* is an experience of knowing oneself, the moment of now, and the landscape (Sironen 1993/1995, 221, 222). Or, in the words of Niels Kayser Nielsen (1999, 288): "The feeling of home is based upon movements, experience and physical activities. It is therefore individual and diffuse, "unclean" and contingent, but therefore, also more durable than the firm nationalism with its demands for borders, system and order." The subject who is visiting her home and thus articulating herself for others, the place, and herself, is doing it by enacting an identity that is necessarily retrospective, as Rosi Braidotti has formulated; "representing it entails that we can draw accurate maps, indeed, but only of where we have already been and consequently no longer are" (Braidotti 1994, 35).

Some people raise their children into a place by not leaving it but staying. Others leave, or are forced to leave, and narrate their homeland and the family origin story to their descendants. Some stay, and their children leave—trying desperately to escape and forget. Others resort to tourist guides and information to learn about their past.

My son sees my homeland through my belated father's eyes and he sees the same landscape through my son's. That is as far as one can get from the tourist gaze. Or the conqueror's, for that matter. The connection, real and imaginary, is more than a coincidence even if it is a frail one.

My generation lived through the transition of the symbolic and concrete countryside in Finland as concrete, immediate, communities of classmates. This makes us "locals in our generation's experience" of a particular place and its formative role in our personal and collective identities. By having left those places and finding them and each other again in class reunions—from now on, as a peculiar and new form of *Heimat* tourism—we will continue changing the place, its meanings to us, and each other.

This we cannot invite strangers to share with us, but they can come along for a boat ride or a swim. The rest is new history.

NOTES

This essay has been drafted in three oral presentations. The first was given at "The European Summer School for Rural Sociology: Building Alternative Futures in the European Countryside," held from August 21–27, 2000, in Siuntio, Finland. The second was prepared for the Village Festival of Ii [Iin Kotiseutujuhlat] held in July 2001, and the last version was presented as a paper at the international Winter Academy of Amenity Landscapes Research Project in January 2003 in Rovaniemi. I am grateful for invaluable comments on the Winter Academy paper to John Bale, Lynda Johnston, Eeva Jokinen, Turo-Kimmo Lehtonen, Harri Veivo, Tim Oakes, and Claudio Minca. I also thank Terry Marsden for critical and supportive comments on the first and Otso Kautto on the latest draft, and Nenne Hallman for our conversation on a sunny day in July 2002 about homeland, the countryside, and grandmothers.

1. Quotes from Rajanti (1995) in this and the next two paragraphs are found on pp. 151–53.

2. "When the child a child was / it did not know it was a child. / To the child everything had a soul and all souls were one" (Peter Handke).

5

Three Trips to Italy:
Deconstructing the New Las Vegas

Pauliina Raento and Steven Flusty

I like Las Vegas. Admittedly, it is relentlessly vulgar, noisy, money-grubbing, deceitful and repetitive. Granted it screams bad taste from slot parlour to tower block, from gilded faucet to mirrored bedroom, inside and outside, day after night after day after night, glitz without end.

Despite all that, I like it. In fact I'll say it straight out: I LOVE LAS VEGAS. The point about it, which both its critics and its admirers overlook, is that it's wonderful and awful *simultaneously*. So one loves it and detests it at the same time. The fact that I keep going back, that I never miss the chance of making a detour from "real" life, is convincing evidence that I like it a lot more than I dislike it.

—Spanier (1992, 1, emphases in original)

These words by David Spanier, written a couple of years before our own first trips to Las Vegas, could be ours: we love and detest the famous city. Our first encounters with Las Vegas were a massive "jolt to the sensorium" (Zelinsky 2001, 6) that left us both exhausted and extremely curious. We were puzzled by how quickly the seemingly infinite variety of experiential options began to feel monotonous and how the constant overstimulation of our senses and our wallets made us want to get out. And it was this sudden transition, within a few days, that made us want to go back and to learn what was behind the tremendous impact this entertainment environment had on its visitor. We were equally fascinated by the contrast between Planet Fun; the surrounding city where people lived, worked, and lined up at the grocery store like in any other southwestern American city; and the barren desert around this particular urban island. Our mixed feelings about the city as an exciting night out and as a monument to hyperconsumption and environmental arrogance also seemed to reveal something about ourselves. This pointed to the significance of values, identity, and preferred lifestyles in the construction of a tourist's relationship with, and sense of, a place. To us, Las Vegas presented itself as an intriguing series of paradoxes we wanted to examine more closely. This romance eventually led to academic research and to repeated trips to Las Vegas.[1]

This article is an attempt to share some of our subsequent observations regarding the paradoxical character of Las Vegas, a destination that attracts 35 million visitors per year (in 2001; Visitor Statistics 2002). We offer one series of critical readings of its entertainment landscapes and spaces, deconstructing some of the most explicit messages of this environment. For this purpose, we made three trips to Italy in the Mojave Desert in the summer of 2001. In other words, we toured the three Italy-themed casino-resorts (Caesars Palace, the Bellagio, and The Venetian) on Las Vegas Boulevard, commonly known as the Strip. We approached these properties as "scripted spaces," or spaces designed as narratives (e.g., Klein 1997; Kranes 1999). Our purpose was to select representative segments of these spatial narratives to illustrate the idea and spirit of the so-called New Las Vegas. This is the Las Vegas of megare-

Figure 5.1   Longing for High Culture on the Strip (November 1995)

sorts that rides on an upscale, culturally sophisticated imagery (figure 5.1).[2] The Strip compresses world history and geography in one place for our convenient entertainment and for the entrepreneurs' profit, thus reflecting the dramatic and determined change of the city's entertainment landscape since the early 1990s. In this transformation, modernities both post- and otherwise fuse to realize elsewheres and elsewhens that cohabit in the same space and in the same time, overlapping in a paradoxical, indistinguishable manner. This points to "the changing nature of tourism" (Ritzer and Liska 1997, 96) and to the "paradox of consumption" (Miles 1998, 5), as discussed in Ning Wang's contribution to this volume.

Within our loosely set, empirically oriented agenda, we assigned a supportive but clearly secondary role to all those written sources, statistics, industry reports, interviews, and informal chats with fellow academics and industry experts we had gone through over the years of travel and research. For us, geography (our academic field) and traveling (our business and our pleasure) are "contact sports" that first and foremost require a visceral relationship with the surrounding world that is direct and personal, accommodates surprises, and welcomes critical questions that spring up from firsthand experiences. Our method can thus be characterized as "inspired voyeurism" (Zelinsky 2001, 8),

> fieldwork that is altogether informal, sometimes hovering on the margins of consciousness, a sensibility ecumenically attuned to all innovations in the sensed environment, to every manner of loss, gain, and the unexpected, dedicated to absorbing a dynamic world without a set agenda. (Zelinsky 2001, 7)

This type of approach is particularly suitable to a setting like Las Vegas (see Crawford 1992; Goss 1999). The approach has its foundation in the rich tradition of geographical fieldwork, especially in the intertextual interpretation of landscapes as constituents of ideological structures, hierarchies of power, and other social processes (e.g., Meinig 1979; Cosgrove and Daniels 1988; Duncan and Duncan 1988; DeLyser 1999). This kind of "reading" is grounded in the problematization of the myriad of meanings embedded in any landscape and in the ways of looking at (or otherwise sensing) it. The signs, the signifiers, and those signified form an unstable web where the relationships between the constituents and their contents are in a constant flux (Duncan and Duncan 1988, 188; Urry 1990, 1–2, 11). The New Las Vegas illustrates how (and why) spaces of recreation and consumption are designed consciously according to this principle in order to create entertaining, perhaps liberating, spaces for play—and for making profit. Most importantly, the New Las Vegas highlights "the more material aspects of tourism, without losing sight of the importance of signs" (Ritzer and Liska 1997, 104).

From this perspective, particularly useful in Las Vegas, is Wilbur Zelinsky's claim that people are capable of transforming themselves "anywhere and any-when mentally" instead of being "tied to the here and now" and that there is also a pronounced *craving* for "imagining and creating alternate existences" (Zelinsky 2001, 1, 7). The New Las Vegas serves the "post-tourist" (Feifer 1985) by underscoring this capacity and, especially, this craving. The themed megaresorts on the Strip are all about journey and transportation (see Goss 1999; Kranes 1999). These journeys can be made in both space and time: Ancient Rome is just across the street from medieval/Renaissance Venice. The opportunity is not only exciting but also convenient and safe, which is particularly appealing to the post-tourist who "finds it less and less necessary to leave home" (Ritzer and Liska 1997, 102). This is a powerful combination in a thrill-seeking postindustrial society increasingly concerned with physical safety, image, and lifestyle. Those who participate in this experience are active constituents of the fantastic story itself and main characters in the unfolding of the story, free to choose from a seemingly endless menu of options. "If what we do for entertainment tells us who we are" (Cooper 1995, 336), the New Las Vegas further confirms the significance of understanding our preferred experiential spaces in the context of contemporary consumer and travel cultures.

THE NEW LAS VEGAS AND ITS THREE VERSIONS OF ITALY

The business of today's Las Vegas is to create unique atmospheres and place-related fantasy entertainment that produce holistic recreation experiences for the city's customers. On the Strip, "[e]verything about casinos is designed to assist gamblers in slipping the perceptual boundaries of their worlds" (Campbell 1999, 289). The purpose of this "slipping" is to make money: to make the customers stay in for longer, spend more, and call again. The mechanisms of this persuasion range from architectonic details to physical comfort to an exciting stimulation of eyes, ears, mouths, and noses (see Friedman 2000). Following the finest tradition of contemporary consumer culture, the boundary between gambling, entertainment, and merchandising is notably blurred (Sorkin 1992; Christiansen and Brinkerhoff-Jacobs 1997; Bryman 1999; Wasko 2001). Behind the tourist's bliss is the industry's "efficient, calculable, predictable" and very carefully orchestrated approach, which relies heavily on "controlling non-human technologies" (Ritzer and Liska 1997, 97, see 99–100). The New Las Vegas thus illustrates the interoperation of modernist production principles with postmodern priorities and modes of experience.

The typical Las Vegas visitor still gambles, but there are plenty of other things to do as well. The customer can choose from a seemingly infinite list of entertainment options in settings that range from contemporary world cities to mythical places of the past. The Strip properties host casinos, thousands of hotel rooms, shopping malls, restaurants, live entertainment, thrill rides, luxury spas, and art collections. These casino-resorts fit both Jean Baudrillard's descriptions of a vast, self-sufficient "hyperspace" and Erving Goffman's concept of "total institution," where people "lead an enclosed, formally administered round of life" away from the rest of society (Goffman 1961, xiii, cited in Ritzer and Liska 1997, 106). Each property's entertainment narrative draws from fantastic geography and history, compressing the world's famous architectonic sights into one place for our travel convenience. And convenient it is, as this hyperreal journey in one Western city is void of many of the hassles related to traveling the world it seeks to represent (Eco 1986; Raento and Douglass 2001, 8).

The transformation of Las Vegas from a kitschy gambling town toward the world's entertainment capital and the "New Las Vegas" began in the late 1980s. The first landmark of the current era of megaresorts was the opening of the developer Steve Wynn's The Mirage casino-resort in 1989. This $620-million, 3,000-room property set the tone for the construction boom in the 1990s, responding to the increasing competition in the North American and global gaming tourism markets (see Raento 2003). The number of hotel rooms available in Las Vegas rose very rapidly as a result of this boom, from 77,000 in 1991 to almost 127,000 in 2001 (Visitor Statistics 2002). The revenue from casino gambling has kept rising as well, but it now accounts for less than one half of the total revenue. The annual visitor count climbed from 21 million in 1991 to 35 million in 2001 (Visitor Statistics 2002), and the length of an average stay has expanded from 3.9 to 4.6 days since the megaresort boom began (LVVPS 1991, 26; 2001, 45). An average Las Vegas tourist is a wealthy middle-class Westerner who now spends $548 on food, drink, shopping, and shows, which is a considerable increase from the $355 in 1991 (LVVPS 1991, 38, 40, 50; 2001, 60, 62). (S)he is certainly wealthier: the proportion of visitors whose household income is at least $80,000 rose from 11 percent in 1991 to 23 percent in 2001 (LVVPS 1991, 60; 2001, 88), highlighting the city's emphasis on the affluent middle-class market. One half of the visitors to Las Vegas come from the American West and especially Southern California (LVVPS 2001, 88).

Significant contributors to the appeal and revenue of the New Las Vegas are the three Italianate casino-resorts on the Strip: Caesars Palace, the Bellagio, and The Venetian.

Caesars Palace, opened in 1966, was the most expensive hotel-casino project of its time. As the first thoroughly themed property in Las Vegas, it was a significant predecessor of the current megaresorts, elaborating on the groundbreaking approach of Benjamin "Bugsy" Siegel's Flamingo resort (opened in 1946) (e.g., Moehring 1989; Smith 1991; Schwartz 2003). Most importantly, the Caesars developer Jay Sarno's new concept of entertainment matched the increasing significance of themed environments and leisure consumption in American society (Sorkin 1992; Gottdiener 1997). Since its opening, Caesars Palace has undergone several major "Additions to the Empire" and changes in ownership. Nevertheless, it has kept its position as one of the most popular casino-resorts on the Strip, being one of the few older resorts fully capable of adjusting to the change of scale and business outlook in the 1990s. In the summer of 2001, more parking space, new hotel rooms and restaurants, additional convention and retail space, and new "architectonic wonders" of Ancient Rome were being added, including the construction of the 4,148-seat Colosseum Showroom and Arena. The venue was finished during the first quarter of 2003 and was expected to host a major Celine Dion production under an exclusive contract for three years.

The other two Italian-themed properties on the Strip, the Bellagio (opened in 1998) and The Venetian (1999), are prime examples of the new generation of Las Vegas megaresorts that build on the idea first introduced in Caesars Palace. They are notably large, with over three thousand hotel rooms and tens of thousands of square feet of gambling space. Unlike contemporary Caesars Palace, however, they were built rapidly from scratch (figure 5.2), and the cost for each hovered around the $1.5-billion mark. Each is a product of one man's vision, that of Steve Wynn (Bellagio) and Sheldon Adelson (The Venetian). In both properties, the theme extends from the overall architecture to the smallest details in design, to the selection of the retail mix, to customer entertainment, and to souvenirs. Both properties are carefully targeted to a specific market niche. The Bellagio seeks to attract the wealthiest end of the tourist market with a special focus on foreign visitors, who account for roughly one-tenth of the Las Vegas annual visitor count (IGWB 1999, 6; LVVPS 2001, 88). This goal is reflected in the highlighted elegance of the design and the upscale, somewhat exclusive atmosphere and amenities of the property. The Venetian focuses on serving the middle-class professional—business travelers and conventioneers—which is again reflected in the available amenities: the property hosts half a million square feet of convention space and offers access to the adjacent convention center (Shemeligian 2000, 32). For some time now, conventioneers have been among the fastest-growing segments of Las Vegas tourism—in 2001, over four million convention travelers visited Las Vegas (Discover the Facts 2001).

Figure 5.2 The Venetian under Construction (December 1998)

The three Italys embody the long-lasting association with the ideals, excitement, "class," and "style" of ancient Greece and Rome in American national consciousness (Malamud 1998; 2001). This association is evident in architecture and toponyms across the country, witnessing the expansion of the "Jeffersonian Democratic" across the vast continent from the nation's initial hearth in the east (see Zelinsky 1967). That this fascination with Mediterranean classical exoticism has now become particularly prominent in America's Sin City points to the domestication of Las Vegas and the general acceptance of gambling by the American public (see Edwards 1992; cf. Parker 1999). The celebration of such themes as the indulgent excess and decadence of Imperial Rome is loyal to the history of Sin City, but at the same time it perfectly fits the ideals of modern consumer capitalism. Thus, the titillating lure of Las Vegas's bad reputation is still there, but in a tame and even predictable form that can be trusted in the same fashion as any other mass-produced commodity. Gambling (or *gaming*), the climax of capitalist logic, is now an acceptable middle-class pastime, sugared with a multitude of mainstream options that are produced by publicly traded, multinational corporations (Edwards 1992; Douglass and Raento 2004).

ALL ROADS LEAD TO ROME

A statue of Augustus, the first of the mighty Caesars of Imperial Rome, greets guests at the entranceway on Las Vegas Boulevard. He is a prominent sign, one that embodies the prime theme of this property, one of the largest in Las Vegas and "reminiscent of Caesar's world 2,000 years ago." We walk to the main entrance, where another, more conventional sign commemorates "the world's largest cantilevered structure of its kind, fabricated from 4,549 tons of concrete and steel." The dedication date on this sign is June 1980, in commemoration of the seventy-fifth anniversary of Las Vegas, a twentieth-century creation in the orbit of Southern California (Douglass and Raento 2004). Size does matter, we observe, and so do eternal beauty, youth, and the good life. The six statues at the main entrance conform to the image of Las Vegas as a constantly novel, carefree, and future-oriented place. Bacchus (god of wine and revelry) is accompanied by several goddesses of love, beauty, youth, and victory, and the nicely built David, whose "pose depicts the tense moment, of tightening muscles and rising excitement" (according to an explanation attached to a larger version of this statue inside the property). The door to the Empire has no locks, and no clocks are in sight: this is the tense moment of crossing a threshold between the linearity of the Strip's urban structure and a cyclical make-believe timeworld.

Following Jay Sarno's original vision, Italian marble is used for the property's oval motifs, fountains, and Romanesque statues (Moehring 1989, 116–18). The theming demonstrates a sophisticated attention to detail that contributes to the credibility of the fantastic narrative (Hausladen 2000, 1–31). The names of the property's segments, its architecture and decorative details, and its interior design all conform to the theme. Italianate music is played softly in the background, and staff dressed as Roman aristocrats and soldiers entertain the visitors in the casino (figure 5.3). The guest may stay at the *Centurion Tower*, see a show at the *Circus Maximus* ballroom, shop along the *Appian Way*, or insert a coin in *Nero's Nickels* or *Roman Rewards* in the casino's slot section (Raento and Douglass 2001, 15). The promise of "fine Italian cuisine" draws us toward the Forum Shops at Caesars, one of the most profitable malls in America since its opening in 1992 (see Malamud 1998).

We are determined to eat Italian to maximize the sense of *really* being in Italy. Besides, "eating out" has become a staple of the Las Vegas experience. The former "mecca for ALL YOU CAN EAT FOR $2.95 buffets" (Pileggi 1995, 340) now boasts highly rated, spendy restaurants and celebrity chefs. Signs that request "proper attire" and "reservations" suggest a new sense of exclusivity and class preference, helping to justify the price. The popularity of these restaurants is reflected in the increase of money spent on food and bev-

Figure 5.3   Roman Entertainment at Caesars Palace (August 2001)

erage by the Las Vegas tourist. In 2001, this amount was over $210 per person per an average trip, whereas five years earlier it had only passed the $110 mark (LVVPS 1996, 60–61; 2001, 59–60). It is somewhat unclear to us, however, whether the food budgets have gone up because of a general raise in price levels — there seems to be very little variation in the prices between selections in individual properties and between the properties. One can still find inexpensive options, but restaurant food it is for a pedestrian visitor to the Strip.

Several American-Italian options of "Finus Dinus" are available at the Forum Shops mall at Caesars. The differences within the selection seem superficial, so we choose a restaurant that gives us a good view of the legions of shoppers who crowd the mall. The menu points out that most of the items available have been *imported*. This intends to add rarity and quality to the produce, but, in our case, succeeds in pointing out that few things grow in the barren desert around Las Vegas. All roads that lead to this Rome come together on Interstate 15, usually overcrowded with huge trucks full of goodies to be consumed in the city. In Roman times, the main transportation arteries of the Empire were roads of extinction for several species. In this Rome, there is Chilean orange roughy on the menu — a replacement for the overfished Chilean sea bass, a potential counterpart of the Mesopotamian lion brought to extinction in the blood-sports of the Colosseum.

Las Vegas is fully dependent on the outside. The city and its entertainment business would not be without the consumers for whom they exist. This existence is critically dependent on the electricity that has dictated the development of the entire region, leading Las Vegas to seek outside energy sources by the 1950s (Brigham 2002, 104–6). The need for electricity in Las Vegas has been highlighted by the rapid growth of population, a scorching climate that requires air-conditioning, and the energy-hungry tourist industry. Since the 1990s, most of the electricity used in Las Vegas has been purchased on the open market, and the sources are located outside of Nevada—only hydropower is produced in the state (Brigham 2002, 108–9). Paradoxically, power generated in the surrounding Mojave Desert and the adjacent Hoover Dam flows out of Nevada, while the state's power company goes shopping on the free market or imports coal- or natural-gas-based energy from Utah, Arizona, and New Mexico (Brigham 2002, 111). In the flashing jungle of neon and electronic billboards, this energy-hungry, environmentally hazardous side of the narrative remains understated. The dangers generated by the tourism industry to the area's sensitive ecosystem are rendered invisible to the visitor who is willing to accept these dangers "as a modest cost to pay for the gains" regarding the leisure experience and its convenience (Ritzer and Liska 1997, 100).

A strong odor of chlorine creeps over our table from the adjacent Fountain of Gods, keeping us discussing the pleasantries we are used to and demand when traveling, and the costs of producing them (see Ritzer and Liska 1997, 99–101). The recycled, chemically sanitized water reminds us of Marc Reisner's (1986) influential book *Cadillac Desert*, an insightful discussion of the major political controversies related to the scarcity of water in the arid American Southwest. These environmental, economic, and energy-related controversies in the rapidly growing region and this particular desert city are hidden from the tourist's sight, behind the abundant and seemingly unproblematic usage of water on the Strip. It is used both inside the properties and in their outdoor landscaping to create a pleasant leisure environment and to enhance the sense of being someplace else.

This illusion of yet another infinite resource is based on the Colorado River, from which water is channeled to the urban areas via the Lake Mead reservoir at Hoover Dam (this source is supported by the remaining groundwater in the Las Vegas Valley). After complex negotiations in the 1980s and the 1990s, the city's future growth has been secured for the time being by the construction of a new pipeline from the Colorado River and new plans for sustainable water management (Christensen 2002). This process has solved some of the problems created by the rapid growth and the insufficiency of Nevada's allocation in the Colorado River Agreement, signed in the early 1920s, when only five thousand people lived in Las Vegas (Poyner 1998, 40). Beyond the Strip,

Figure 5.4   Golf in a Desert City (October 1999)

new problems are being created, as the city keeps growing: two-thirds of the water is consumed in the residential areas, and about two-thirds of that water is used to keep the lawns green (Martinez 1999, 142). Landing at McCarran Airport offers a glimpse of the lush green of golf courses, irrigated front lawns, and the abundance of swimming pools and artificial little lakes that stand out at a distance before the plane touches down (figure 5.4). The paradox between the "traditional temperate zone outlook" (Poyner 1998, 42) of Las Vegas developers and residents and the brown aridity of the Mojave is striking, but that, too, is edited out of sight—and out of mind—on the Strip.

The artificial sky above our restaurant is ready for a sunset at 8:45 P.M. Artificial skies are now a common feature in the Las Vegas entertainmentscape, as they are sophisticated tools for the manipulation of time and space. This sky controls perspective and perception by making the clouds appear as if they were moving when one walks underneath. The artifact "seems to suggest that the outside world has been obviated, transcended, or replaced" (Branch 1999, 287). For example: It never rains in this setting—unless an emergency activates the numerous sprinklers in the ceiling that conform to Nevada's strict fire safety laws. The sky is another element that promotes a powerful sense of a journey, perhaps even stimulating the passion for it. After the sunset above us, the night lasts for twenty minutes and is followed by a forty-minute day—and another sunset. This rhythm adds to the general sense of timelessness of the sealed space, supporting the engineering of a *new* sense of time. It is based on contrasts between past and present eras and between night and day within the interior microenvironment. But what looks like control of nature is control over "*human* nature" (Branch 1999, 291, emphasis in original). The designers of the New Las Vegas are masters of simulacra (see Baudrillard 1994), and we, too, become a voluntary part of this machinery by unwittingly serving as anonymous entertainers: dining in a simulated "street restaurant," we represent one detail in the restaurant's signage and the property's overall *streetmosphere*. Spending a full day on a meal makes us wonder whether we would age faster if we stayed in for longer.

LA DOLCE VITA

Next door, the Bellagio makes a reference to a similarly named small town on the shores of Lake Como in Italy. The property's promenade parallel to the Strip and the moving walkway to the entrance offer a view to the nine-acre lake in front of the property and the picturesque "Tuscan village" on its shores (figure 5.5). At the walkway's end, the Bellagio's wall paintings of bucolic

Figure 5.5   The Bellagio on Its Nine-acre Lake Como in December 1998. The Romanesque architecture of Caesars Palace is seen in the background.

landscapes suggest sophistication, unspoiled rustic and romantic peaceful-
ness. This is where the city returns to the countryside—where the elegant
aristocrats withdraw from the heat, dust, and noise of the city. What Caesars
Palace offers in fake Roman script is now elaborate longhand. An additional
association with prestige is evoked by the property's name itself, especially
by the classical implication and wholesomeness of the letters o and b (Room
1982, 15–16, 194–97; Raento and Douglass 2001, 14). Gold, black, and marble white change to warm, wholesome earth tones. This place shares few
things with the town it is named after. But that is irrelevant: what matters is
the *idea* of a small Italian countryside village in the American mind as the
aristocracy's bucolic space of leisure (Minca 2005; see Silverman 1986).

The carefully designed entity illustrates the scale-conscious, comprehen-
sive design logic of the new properties. The Bellagio is an example of the
dramatic redefinition of signage in casino design during the megaresort era.
The building itself is tailored to communicate to the observer what the property is about. In order to guarantee that people gaze in awe, "Fountains of
Bellagio," a hundred-million-dollar dancing fountain show with music and
lights, entertains the audience at intervals over the lake in front of the building. The spectacle is a typical "weenie"—a Disney term for a crowd magnet
that lures attention and draws customers in to the property (Wasko 2001).
Signs no longer focus on informing and identifying only, but form an integral part of the overall theme and the suggested entertainment experience. As
such, they are powerful "means of consumption" (Baudrillard 1988b, cited
in Ritzer and Liska 1997, 104–5; see Venturi et al. 1972). Signage makes a
difference and helps to differentiate one property from another: "The one
that catches your eye is the one you want to go to" (sign designer, cited in
Klepacki 1997, 50). It is also the (desired) image of oneself and one's identity as a traveling consumer that guides one's choice of a preferred space of
leisure and self-fulfillment.

The promise made outside must be kept indoors, and the tone set outside
must be supported and enhanced. The design's consistency inside the Bellagio gives rhythm to the vast property's spatial segments and their abundant offerings—signature restaurants, a luxury spa and pool, unique shopping
spaces, and an art collection that features original Picassos. There are four particularly significant spaces at the Bellagio in terms of the idea and spirit of the
New Las Vegas: the lobby, the garden, the shopping arcade, and the art gallery
(see the discussion about performance in the introduction of this book).

The Bellagio's lobby illustrates the emphasis on uniquely designed
nongaming spaces in the New Las Vegas. In the 1990s, the lobbies evolved
into important focal points that are meant to impress and satisfy the demands
of the upscale customer. The lobby "sets the tone of the resort and helps distinguish the property" (casino architect, cited in Parets 1998, 20), crystallizing

the idea and mechanisms of product-differentiation. Long gone are the times when arriving visitors had to haul their belongings through the congested casino. Now they use a separate entrance, which offers easy access to the gambling space but keeps its congestion and noise away. This separation marks a threshold, an axis, and a center, all important in constructing "a clear sense of arrival" and welcome (casino designer, cited in Parets 1998, 22; see Kranes 1995a, 94). Even the joining of carpet and stone on the floor repeats similar thresholds throughout the lobby. The lavishness of the lobby makes it an independent destination within the resort, and it is listed as an "attraction" on the property's Web page (www.bellagio.com). Above the gawking visitors, glass artist Dale Chihuly's two thousand colorful flowers (*Fiori di Como*) cover the ceiling and are both unique and uniquely appealing to the in-the-know upper-middle-class connoisseur of high folk art.

An extension of the lobby is a space titled "The Conservatory and Botanical Gardens," a seasonally changing collection of plant ornaments from the property's enormous nursery. The air is filled with a seductive scent, increasing the perceptual distance from the desert setting. A pacifying dimension of nature is brought inside to create an "interiorized, urban wilderness" (Branch 1999, 289). The visitors passively *contemplate* this lush scenery, thus following the refined traditions of the bourgeois landscape ideology in America (see, e.g., Nash 1983; Runte 1987; McClelland 1998) (figure 5.6). This wilderness, however, is rigorously controlled, from the degree of humidity to the design of the ornaments and the entire setting. This interiorized, intensely controlled nature is the ultimate refuge that provides "an attractive alternative to the chaotic and threatening world outside" (Branch 1999, 292)—or to the busy casino. It delivers a refinement of the sense of aesthetics, thus fulfilling the property's promise of elegance and upscale lifestyle. The imagineered harmony is shaken by a fellow visitor who, looking at one of the rich ornaments, whispers to his travel companion: "You don't think it's real, do you? It looks so fake."

The third landmark at the Bellagio is "Via Bellagio," the property's shopping and dining arcade that represents an entirely new genre of shopping space in Las Vegas. The selection of world-famous designer boutiques from Europe ranges from Prada of Milan to Hermès of Paris. The namescape is instantly recognizable, original, and carefully selected to enhance the credibility of the property's atmosphere. The signature restaurants and a "street café" conform to the "Mediterranean" touch; staff members are dressed in black and quietly nod to the customers as they pass by. The (h)earscape adds yet another layer to this imagined European elegance: classical music, some with Italian lyrics, plays quietly in the background. We detect a slight perfume in the air, which suggests that the designers did read their consumer inspiration

Figure 5.6   Christmas at the Bellagio (1998)

textbooks in the marketing class (see, e.g., Classen et al. 1994). Above the busy passageway, we are looking at a real sky, but seen through arches. The outcome is "a harmonious, elegant, and timeless atmosphere in which the hectic and congested sense of place" of the adjacent casino is miles away (Raento and Douglass 2001, 16–17). This is another space for contemplation, self-fulfillment, and confirmation of a (desired) lifestyle.

The fourth particularly illustrative space is the Bellagio's $300-million art collection in the "Gallery of Fine Art." For a fifteen-dollar entrance fee, the visitor can admire pastels and oil-paintings by such European masters as van Gogh, Renoir, Matisse, and Picasso, and in the fall of 2002, a visiting collection of Faberge's eggs. Again, the selection's name recognition is immediate. Like the other discussed spaces, the art gallery makes a strong statement of uniqueness, authenticity, aestheticism, and would-be elitism. It is a must-see destination for those who wish to belong to the high-art-admiring cultural literati but perhaps fear that not seeing the paintings would be *tacky*. The presence of the paintings contributes to the legitimization and celebration of the engineered opulence of the Bellagio, and the gallery is an icon of class identity and a monument to the power of money (Minca 2005).

Together, these four spaces highlight the Bellagio as a unique place for the performance of identity. The exact location of the Italian place in the property's name is irrelevant, but the image of a lifestyle associated with that place through popular culture makes the name significant (figure 5.7). This lifestyle is particularly attractive in the middle-class American touristic imagination that has recently demonstrated a general taste for things "aristocratic" (Malamud 1998, 23; see Silverman 1986). The property offers its visitors a feeling of "the chance to transcend economic constraints and social barriers" and to achieve a desired image of themselves, increasing the pleasure of spending (Malamud 1998, 14). This imagined lifestyle is constantly created and re-created by the people who wish to take this journey and who thus underscore their own identity as traveling consumers. In its overt emphases on "authenticity" and "uniqueness," the Bellagio of Las Vegas constitutes "a monument to gentrification" (Minca 2005, 107). This observation crystallizes the idea behind niche-marketing that reigns supreme in the New Las Vegas.

COMPARISONS AND CONTROL

In the popular imagination, Venice offers a kaleidoscope of images, from romantic gondolas to garish Murano glassware, from crumbling palaces on the Grand Canal to masked revelers at the Venetian Carnival. Summer presents the bustling splendour of Piazza San Marco while winter is swathed in mystery: the mist-laden, monochrome curtain of a city out of season. Then, the city conjures up the cultivated melancholy of Visconti's haunting *Death in Venice*, based on Thomas Mann's novel. (*Insight Compact Guides: Venice,* 1995, 5, emphasis in original)

We read this quote from a Venice guidebook while approaching one of the most impressive signages in the New Las Vegas—the architecture of The Venetian. The sensation of a journey is strongly evoked: the property is a compressed replica of the most famous sights of Venice, all described in our travel guide. Saint Mark's lion looks over the patio and the gondolas lulling in the shiny blue water in front of Doges' Palace. Archangel Gabriel stands atop the

Figure 5.7   The Outdoor Pool Area at the Bellagio. This is another significant space for the performance of identity at this casino resort; access to the area is limited to hotel guests, while others may contemplate the scenery from a sightseeing platform (December 1998).

Campanile Tower. The Rialto Bridge stretches over the driveway to Las Vegas Boulevard, right next to the Bridge of Sighs. It makes perfect sense that the theming in the New Las Vegas favors "cities"—nodes of diverse contacts and exchange, full of exciting opportunities for exploration, day and night. It also makes perfect sense that the most pedigreed cities of the Old World have been prominent themes in the upscaling of the Strip, allowing the celebration of stereotypes and place-specific romance cultivated in popular culture. The condensed containment of the urban wonders in one property and the lavish amenities also evoke a strong sense of self-sufficiency, in stark contrast to the dependency of Las Vegas on the outside. That The Venetian claims to be an "authentic re-creation" of the best in a particular city *demands* comparisons.

The gold and jewel tones inside the pleasantly air-conditioned property shine as brightly as the scorching desert sun outside. Everywhere, there is the promise and expectation of wealth. Beginning from the replica of the Ca' d'Oro, the number of references to gold is astonishing, bringing the New Las Vegas's "wealth and opulence syndrome to its full bloom" (Raento and Douglass 2001, 19). The "faithful masterpieces" of the works of such famed Venetian artists as Titian, Tintoretto, and Veronese in the ceiling above the entrance imply that this is a place where money falls from the heavens (figure 5.8). The polysemic character of "gold" makes references to it a valuable marketing device. The multiple connotations in the New Las Vegas suggest a golden opportunity and good luck, wealth and eternity, appreciated personal characteristics, and excitement and adventure in the entrepreneurial, risk-taking-oriented context of the American West (Raento and Douglass 2001, 23). Despite the new emphasis on entertainment and design, these places remain casinos after all (and, appropriately enough, the world's first casino was located in Venice).

The property's own travel guide booklets to the "Venetian Experience" evoke a confusion of time and place by introducing the visitor to the most "famous icons" in Venice, Italy, discussing Venice's history as though it were *here* and *now*. The *Resort Guide*

> has been prepared as a guide to the magnificent colonnades to the Doge's Palace, through the neighborhoods and palazzos of the Grand Canal Shoppes to St. Mark's Square. [We are invited to] experience the gondolas of the Adriatic Sea and the beauty of the masters of art displayed liberally for [our] pleasure.

We are told what to see and how to see it. From *The Venetian Experience* booklet, we learn about the Campanile Tower that it was

> [b]uilt as a guard tower in the 8th century and modified in the 12th, 14th and 16th centuries. Its base "Loggetta" was built by Sansorino in 1539. The classical sculptures celebrate the glory of the Republic. (Open gate fold to see location of these famous icons at THE VENETIAN.)

We also learn what to appreciate when shopping for the Venetian offerings at the property's "Grand Canal Shoppes," described to represent "the modern day trading tradition of Venice":

> In storefronts running the entire length of the *riva* and *merceria* district, visitors will encounter an unprecedented collection of shops and boutiques, many

Figure 5.8   Ceiling Art at The Venetian (October 2000)

premiering for the first time in the United States. Retailers offer spectacular presentations of the finest in goods and fashions and products of authentic Venetian retailers such as Il Prato (masks and costumes for over 150 years), and Ripa de Monti (Venetian art glass and Murano glass specialties). The vibrant sense of an open air experience culminates in a gondola ride to St. Mark's square, beneath a 70 foot ceiling filled with an early evening Venetian sky. The square offers a remarkable mix of shops, cafes, and live performances by masked and costumed Carnival revelers and famous characters of Venetian history.

The selected sights are made meaningful to the gawking visitor by stating their importance and "explaining" what they are about. The outside is again brought indoors, but the wind in the "open air experience" comes from air-conditioning. Similarly, boundaries between "high art" and popular culture, and leisure and learning, are blurred in a way that is typical of postindustrial, postmodern consumer culture (Urry 1990, 11; Selwyn 1996, 19–20). Historical factoids are conflated with entertaining fiction, and attention is drawn to details in tandem with the painstakingness of their recreation. The booklet offers a touch of *infotainment* and constructs an authenticity predicated upon visitors' very real perception that there is elsewhere an authentic Venice to serve as the property's referent, but any learning is optional and, in any case, superficial (Light 1995, 118).

The artifact selection in the boutiques of the shopping area conforms to the overall theme of the property by repeating the same stereotypes. The selection of unique items carved by "authentic Venetian retailers" with long traditions in mask and art glass making highlights the symbolic, identity-enhancing values vested in purchasing and owning such items. In this context, these artifacts are typical souvenirs, objects without much practical utility value but with strong symbolic content (Goss 1999). The decorative items and jewelry pieces at The Venetian crystallize the strong association between an individual artifact and the place they represent by bringing together Venice's romanticized reputation, landscape, and lifestyle (de Wit 1992; cf. Lury 1997). These items stand witness to how the upscaling of Las Vegas has transformed the idea of souvenir kitsch toward higher quality and higher prices, addressing the dreams, identities, and preferences of its wealthy visitors. "Kitsch" may no longer apply to these items in the word's most conventional sense, but it now points to a lifestyle where the act of, and the satisfaction produced by, purchasing matters more than the item that is purchased. *Where* it is purchased matters, too. On the wall or on a shelf at home the artifact thus becomes a status symbol, which communicates that its owner (or someone close to him or her) has traveled in exotic and romantic places. That the item is "hand-made" or "uniquely carved" adds to its individualistic value in the context of mass production and consumption (cf. Relph 1976). Unlike "classical souvenirs," few items at The Venetian have the name of the place written on them. The place-related message is nevertheless loud and clear, and perhaps the implicitness hides the fact of shopping in make-believe Italy. What matters is that the item *could* have been purchased in Italy, and it may have additional entertainment value because it *really* came from Nevada. Once more, the scale of Venice gets compressed, this time to the most intimate space of an individual souvenir shopper.

A leisurely stroll along the Grand Canal points out that the reproduced design is *better* than the original—in that *other* version of Venice the streets run only across the canal, because the canals are street alleys and thus essential parts of the infrastructure. In Las Vegas, the Canal is a linear centerpiece of the property, again highlighting the tactically rationalized concept of spatial design in the New Las Vegas (figure 5.9). The scale is intensely compressed: the world is brought to Las Vegas, and Venice is brought to Saint Mark's Square. Indeed, this Venice is suspiciously convenient. There are people dining inside the indoor version of the Bridge of Sighs. There are no pigeons, no unpleasant odors, no garbage in sight. But Venice, Italy, is neither so deodorized nor so free of pigeon droppings. Its narrow medieval alleys do not conform to the Americans with Disabilities Act, and they are packed with people from all walks of life—not only the clean-cut, consuming middle classes that we see around us in this casino resort. The reality of this Italy is considerably

Figure 5.9   A Gondola Ride beneath an Artificial Sky at The Venetian's Grand Canal (October 2000)

more adept at reconfiguring itself in accordance with what the customers prefer to exclude from their recreational spaces. The result is a safely exciting travel experience without the confusions and intimidations attendant upon the grand tour of Europe. In this Italy, passports are not required at the border, all customer clerks speak English and accept dollars, restrooms are clean, free of charge, and readily available, Italian food offers no Italian surprises, and any jet lag is purely optional. Perhaps there *is* "such place as a 'tourist Venice'" after all (Minca and Oakes, introduction).

"It's pretty European," comments a fellow visitor right at the moment when we have noticed a blond female gondolier who somehow seems to be *out of place*. Indeed, this *Pseurope* proves only as accurate as the stereotypes it is built upon and the messy realities it excludes, and the suspension of disbelief works as long as one wants to play along. The observation that many things about this place are "not quite right" is not necessarily disturbing, however — sometimes it is simply amusing. But either way, the divergences can be so extreme that they damage the required suspension of disbelief and bring to the fore subversive readings of the intended narrative. As we grow oddly irritable and are ready to leave, the singing gondoliers of the Gondolier Parade salute the crowd with a familiar song with a Las Vegas twist to it: *Arrivederci Roma* has become *Arrivederci Venezia*.

From the moving walkway inside the Rialto Bridge, the open space in front of the property looks like any busy regular street. Yet, very few people (if anybody) in this streetscape are locals carrying out their daily errands. Instead, the crowd consists of tourists whose demographic and socioeconomic profiles stay almost as consistent as they were indoors. A sign on the wall along Las Vegas Boulevard states that we are standing on private property: the casino corporation *owns* the sidewalk (figure 5.10). The camera surveillance that reaches every corner of the hotel-casino's interior extends its eye to the outside and is backed up by security guards. The division of ownership between the corporation and Clark County is marked on the ground discreetly by white strips of paint on the curb. For the mostly new-immigrant leafleteers who crowd the narrow street corner half a block down the Strip, fishing for customers for the city's "adult entertainment" services, the paint tells where the no-go zone begins and ends. For the casino corporation, it marks sovereign territory where people are judged according to their desirability and appearance as consumers. In this Italy, public space is an illusion (Flusty 1994; 2001; cf. Minca and Oakes, introduction).

Figure 5.10   A Sign Indicating That the Sidewalk Belongs to the Casino-resort (December 1999)

A PLACE OF PARADOX

Today's America likes to think of itself as the bastion of freedom, democracy, and egalitarianism. Yet America is fascinated by the "class" and "style" it situates in Italy's past and present, and it covets the corollary images of imperial grandeur and elegant, understated noblesse oblige. As America's self-proclaimed beacon of classy entertainment, the New Las Vegas advertises itself by promoting an image of egalitarian elegance, lavishness for all, and an almost aristocratic freedom of personal experience—"What You Want. When You Want." The new Italianate theming reinforces the implication of grand living and unrestricted privilege no longer confined to select elites. There is no apostrophe in *Caesars Palace*, suggesting that this is a place where everybody gets to be a Caesar (Raento and Douglass 2001, 15). But the democratic character of a palace is constrained by definition, and crowds do not necessarily qualify as markers of democracy (Klein 2002, 28–29). The egalitarian freedom of an individual tourist is an illusion in Las Vegas, as our three trips to Italy suggest. The modernist concept of straightforward, even brutal control has been hidden and made persuasively gentle in the New Las Vegas—a sense of freedom and excitement has been successfully married to the machinery of predictability, efficiency, and calculability (see Foucault 1979). This union serves us with both order and excitement. If done skillfully, we do not sense the control nor do we question it, but contribute to the profit of the property—and if doing that gets us what we came for, do we ever care to resist?

We are allowed some choice, however, as the properties in the New Las Vegas differ in their degree of interpretative determinism. The role and freedom given to the customers in writing their own entertainment micronarratives varies considerably in the three Italies. At Caesars Palace, the tone is "loonius toonius," honoring the good old Ratpack and offering positively redneckish, optional fun for the masses. Nevertheless, the property has remained popular among the wealthiest end of the tourist market, confirming that wealth does not require a rigorous focus on "class" or "style." Perhaps it is the property's simultaneous capability of self-parody and sophisticated segmenting that has guaranteed the success of its constant reinvention through decades.

The Bellagio, in turn, has managed to refine the New Las Vegas's romance with upscale recreation, art, and luxury to a rarified level. Its messages are multivocal, often understated, and allow a variety of equal readings. The utilization of this power of seduction makes the property very credible, confirming to the lifestyle-conscious customers that they are *right*. The Bellagio stands in stark contrast to The Venetian, the most thoroughly Disneyesque of the three Italys in Las Vegas. It is also the most exposed: by claiming to be a replica of one particular place, it excludes the possibility of self-criticism. Hence, it is a thoroughly imposed and tightly controlled narrative. By repeating known stereotypes put forward in travel books it becomes an openly predictable story that is good for a once-over but wears thin very soon, as there is little room for discovery. It is an example of kitsch as a way of being, where a considerable part of the society wants, and can afford, to consume mass-produced commodities as badges of distinction, and where the uncritical attitude of such consumption so renders it complicit in the production of "triviality, artificiality, and cuteness," "mediocrity, and 'phoniness'" (Relph 1976, 82). The uncritical suspension of disbelief is thus absolutely required at The Venetian, whereas it is not needed at the Bellagio and optional at Caesars Palace. The observation highlights the significance of niche marketing in the New Las Vegas and the emergence of new class differences in this "democratic" city. It also points further to the New Las Vegas's success in wrapping modernist profit making into a new, appealing package. As George Ritzer and Allan Liska (1997, 101) aptly put it, "the future of McDonaldization lies in being able to apply its principles to smaller and smaller market niches."

Indeed, the center of this particular experiential universe, the consuming traveler, has as many choices as (s)he can afford. For those with a generous credit line, the range of opportunities in the experiential realm is obviously broad. One dollar buys the Las Vegas customer one vote, but it is not good for much on the new Strip—we look at our souvenir statues of Caesar Augustus and David and think of them as evidence. The surrounding setting and the composition of the consuming crowd suggest that, in keeping with the broader sweep of American history, white property-owning males are perhaps more equal than others in the New Las Vegas. Similarly, the egalitarianism of such public spaces as piazzas and forums is overshadowed by the fact that in the New Las Vegas they are owned and operated by private corporations whose rule is sovereign and absolute in limiting access according to each individual's desirability as consumers.

Nor does the egalitarianism of the New Las Vegas include its most indispensable participants: the thousands of people who keep these three Italys (and the rest of the Strip) in operation are mostly invisible. The food gets transported into the kitchens and the beds get made, but this is carefully edited out of the visible narrative (Bryman 1999; Wasko 2001). The tourist exchanges occasional pleasantries with the locals in service positions, but most of the time these people are anonymous parts of the scene. Their residential city, life experiences, and personal narratives are rendered both invisible and irrelevant on the Strip's fantasy planet (see Littlejohn 1999; Rothman and Davis 2002). That city is also rather inaccessible to a pedestrian tourist with no prior knowledge of the neighborhoods or experience with the local public transportation system. Yet, these workers add a significant dimension to the casino-resorts' external dependency: the business relies on this largely unskilled, inexpensive pool of labor. A new segregation has emerged in this city that used to be one of the most segregated cities in America. Neighborhoods, schools, workplaces, and entertainment venues are now more mixed racially than they were just a few decades ago, but there is a widening gap between socioeconomic classes on the tourists' Strip and the rest of the city that supports it. Furthermore, there is a strong segregation of experience in each entertainment space: the perspectives of those who stroll leisurely along the Grand Canal in a postmodern bliss and those who keep the setting clean as the necessary nuts and bolts of the modernist grinder differ dramatically from one another.

Each of the three Italys, abetted by the disappearance of their human and mechanical infrastructures, thus come to serve as a monument to the entrepreneurial one-upmanship of both Las Vegas and the American West as a whole (Douglass and Raento 2004). This narrative of emperors (or caesars and doges) gone mad en masse is the penultimate expression of the capitalist ideals of individualism, opportunity, risk-taking, and acquisition. These new emperors, whether in the person of the tourist on the Strip or that of the high-profile megaresort developer, reiterate past industrial tycoons that maximized their earnings by feverishly investing their values, worldviews, and even their lifestyles in their products and in the mechanisms of their production.

Indeed, the mechanisms used in creating the seemingly unique, individualistic experiences of the Las Vegas visitor are essentially "modern," and even Fordist, in their industrial uniformity. The entertainment product is created through efficient linearity and punctuality, and the outcome is safe, clean, and convenient. Many of the underlying mechanisms are deeply rooted in the science of geography: in the manipulation of scale, time, space, and sense of place; in the manipulation of sense of distance and spatial perception, boundaries, freedom, and control. We could have journeyed to someplace else on the Strip and made similar observations, or we could have made most of our observations in any one of the three Italys. In the New Las Vegas, the standardization of differentiation makes it possible to be in more than one place at the same time, or in two times in one space.

Nevertheless, the product we have observed and experienced cannot be separated from its uniquely relentless postmodernity, one that assiduously devotes all the modern has to offer to the production of individual and place-specific images, identities, and lifestyles (Bryman 1999, 43–44). Each of the three trips to Italy thus ends in the heart of contemporary America, as the New Las Vegas appears as a place of paradox. The New Las Vegas is a place where the tourist can encounter excitement and strangeness in a setting that is utterly safe and even homely, a place where uniqueness entirely depends upon the most rigid standardization for its production and maintenance. It undergoes constant transformation, but it still stays the same. Economically and demographically, the city has grown like few other places have. The growth has created an urban structure that is both compartmentalized and highly linear, but its concepts of time and lifestyle are relentlessly cyclical. As a further irony, Las Vegas visitors necessarily participate in the production of this everyday reality through their purchase of a reality no less manufactured but infinitely more fantastical, one in which the problem of which historical epoch to sojourn in for the afternoon supercedes such mundanities as overstressed infrastructure and water scarcity.

Thus, Las Vegas may be egalitarian and even democratic in nature in the sense that it allows the freedom to choose one's experience, but, simultaneously, that experience is carefully constructed and takes place in a carefully manipulated and strictly controlled space. Much of the satisfaction the properties create is based on surprise, but it "is never random or chance; it's highly engineered, determined" (Kranes 1999, 301) and may soon wear thin because of its underlying predictability. Further, the credibility of the egalitarian illusion correlates with the thickness of one's wallet—every experience in the New Las Vegas comes with a price tag and the visitor is entitled to as wide a selection of experiences as (s)he can afford. So the mass product that is Las Vegas may offer the same for everyone, but each experience is different and conditioned by each individual's perceptions, desires, and credit line (Raento and Douglass 2001, 24–25). For those who experience the New Las Vegas, then, the key to affection or rejection can be found in the beholder's eye (Meinig 1979).

In many ways, Las Vegas continues to exhibit the spirit of postindustrial America well before any place else (Venturi et al. 1972; Findlay 1986, 1990; Gottdiener et al. 1999). Las Vegas is "an other-directed place" (Relph 1976, 93–95) and fully dependent on the outside, but, simultaneously, a powerful center of innovation, capital, and know-how. It sells postmodern frontier adventures where the values of individualism, hope of making it, eternal growth, and future-oriented movement are reproduced and consumed for the maintenance of identity. And as Las Vegas has become a global entertainment destination, this frontier has brought together (and has been peddled to) people from all over the world. But this frontier is suspiciously homogeneous— the adventurers' outlook, appearance, and taste suggest that the recently confirmed multivocality of the history of the American West is suddenly being rewritten backwards (Limerick 1987; White 1991). For us, the fundamental beauty of this beast is exactly this paradoxical quality that points to the shaky, often artificial separation between "modern" and "postmodern," the decline and fall that necessarily abides within every ascendant empire. David Spanier's words in the beginning of this chapter are still valid, but Las Vegas's schizophrenia has changed in tone and content since the beginning of the megaresort era to better meet the condition of its customers, whose hunger for the thorough ordering of experience impels a reciprocating and ravenous thirst for the spontaneous, the exotic, and the free-spirited.

We look at one of our acquisitions from this engagement with the New Las Vegas: a souvenir statue of Caesar Augustus, a notorious gambler (figure 5.11). We believe that the statue summarizes much of this new essence of Las Vegas, pointing to the city's exemplary tradition of inventing images, identities, and new needs (Douglass and Raento 2004). In real life, the famous emperor had bad teeth, jaundiced skin, a limp, and a filthy beard (Kivimäki and Tuomisto 2000, 30–31). He did have prominent ears, which add a boyish look to the image carved in—well, in this case—cold-cast resin. But this is perhaps the only similarity the heroically well-formed statuette before us bears with the long-dead imperial personage it represents. Would Caesar Augustus have become such a celebrity without this reconstructive power of the image, of

Figure 5.11   *Hail Caesar!* (August 2001)

representation, and of the valorization of a lifestyle couched in luxury? Would his memory have so persisted these past two thousand years?

> "Proust was a revolutionary. Death is a memory. Mostly, they say, America has no memory. So perhaps it won't die. Las Vegas isn't America. That's why I came. America is Las Vegas. Look!" She waved her hand into the casino pit. "Mostly, it's the sun." (Kranes 1995b, 160)

NOTES

1. In Dr. Raento's case, this romance with Las Vegas resulted in two postdoctoral research projects, funded by the Academy of Finland (Projects 42380 and 45565, 1998–2001; Project 204377, 2003–2008) and hosted by the Department of Geography of the Universities of Nevada, Reno; Helsinki; and Minnesota.

2. Figure 5.3 and 5.11 by Steven Flusty; all others by Pauliina Raento.

6

Tourist Places and Negotiating Modernity: European Women and Romance Tourism in the Sinai

Jessica Jacobs

The practice and performance of modernity through "traveling" is often seen to represent a masculine subjectivity and, as Soile Veijola notes in this volume, mobility is commonly held as an inherently masculine activity, juxtaposed against the "feminine notion of dwelling and belonging." He wanders at will—he doesn't use charter flights or pack sun tan lotion. Yet, civilization (modernity) itself is often imagined as feminine, "searching for that lost, masculine lover" (Pasztory 2001). In this chapter I explore these ideas of gendered nature of the modern traveling subject and investigate some of the supposed paradoxes of modernity brought out by a specific outcome of travel—the tourist-local encounter, specifically the romantic/sexual encounter. However this is not a study of sex tourism where First World men travel to the "feminized" Third World to buy sex from local women. Instead I focus on tourist-local encounters in the beach resorts of the Sinai desert in Egypt, where the First World tourists are women (mainly from Europe) and the Third World "locals" are (often) Egyptian men, who themselves have traveled from other regions of Egypt to find work.[1] Using material obtained from interviews with women involved in these relationships, I aim to explore some of the tensions and contradictions that arise when European women take on the supposedly masculine subjectivity of travel (and sex tourism).

The paradoxes brought out by these relationships are many and multilayered. For example, I argue that tourist women construct both the landscape and the men of the Sinai as "unmodern," "premodern," and "antimodern" through an Orientalist geographical imagination that depicts the Sinai as a sexually and racially stereotypical Third World holiday destination. By constructing the Sinai as a place somehow "outside" modernity, traveling to the

Sinai fulfils the desire to "escape" from modernity. Yet it is the very technologies and privileges of modernity, acquired to some extent as a result of a
colonial history that is being celebrated and imagined, that allow women in
Europe to travel there in the first place. And it is these privileges of travel inherited from the West's colonial legacy—the sovereign subject status of the
First World traveler/tourist (Urry 1990; Gregory 1999)—that give the women
the confidence to travel, often alone. Furthermore it is the dualistic nature of
modernity that helps to construct a world divided into spaces of work and
leisure, of those who travel and those who are traveled upon, of the modern
developed nations and the undeveloped—that encourages the modern subject
to travel, to go on holiday, and to "get away from it all."

As I mention briefly above, the very act of traveling is considered a masculine activity, while sex tourism is considered even more so. This adoption
and adaptation of a supposedly masculine pursuit is also a very "modern"
mobility, one that gives these women the opportunity for experimentation
with, and the reconstitution of, dominant narratives of sexual and other identities of both the female tourist/traveler and the male local. This, in turn, goes
on to shape and form both their ideas about their relationship with modernity
and their consequent experimentation with identity.

The distinctions between *unmodern, premodern,* and *antimodern* are important. I hope to show that these distinctions travel in different directions,
making a straightforward binary between the modern and its opposite un-
workable; there is instead a range of different alternative "opposite" imaginations of modernity, of antimodernisms at work.

WESTERN EUROPEAN GEOGRAPHICAL
IMAGINATIONS OF THE ORIENT

The west, or Occident, has had a long and complicated relationship with the
Middle East, or Orient.[2] As Said (1978) has argued, the Orient has a special
place in the European experience, acting as a binary opposite for the dominant European identity.[3]

> The Orient is not only adjacent to Europe; it is also the place of Europe's great-
> est and richest and oldest colonies, the source of its deepest and most recurring
> images of the Other. In addition the Orient has helped to define Europe (or the
> West) as its contrasting image, idea, personality, experience. (Said 1978, 1–2)

Much of the strength of this imaginary comes from the very powerful image
of Southwest Asia as a desert, and therefore deserted, located on the margins

of Europe. In the past this desert has been used as a sanctuary for those disaffected with political systems and cultures, and it has been associated with
strong spiritual, metaphysical qualities. However, while an imaginary of the
desert as a place of introspection is a common motif in many cultures, the
"othering" of the desert landscape and people is, according to Beezer (2003,
132), unique to western European sensibilities:

> the desert, as a site conceived as a place on to which to project one's other self
> which is in need of spiritual re-awakening, takes on a quite different political
> resonance when it, along with its associated metaphors of the tent and the no-
> mad, is constructed as the space inhabited by "others" whose sole function is the
> reinvigoration of the jaded Western self.

If anything, with the onset of modernity and ideas of civilization, deserts
and their inhabitants hold a stronger place in the imaginary of the western European and American consciousness than ever. For theorists like Bauman
(1996) and Baudrillard (1988a) its significance goes well beyond that of a
mere geographical area or landscape; the desert represents what Kaplan
(1996, 64) calls "the site of critical and individual emancipation in Euro-
American modernity," while the Bedouin dweller symbolizes "a subject position that offers an idealized model of movement based on perpetual displacement." Bauman (1996, 20), for example, refers to the desert as archetypal
"raw, bare, primal and bottom-line freedom."

> The desert meant putting a distance between oneself and one's duties and obli-
> gations. . . . The desert . . . was a land not yet sliced into places, and for that rea-
> son it was a land of self-creation. (Bauman 1996, 20)

Lindqvist (2000), a self-confessed desert romantic brought up on tales of adventure, heroism, and tragedy in the Sahara, suggests that this imaginary of
the desert as a site of "freedom" from modernity was firmly cemented during
the colonialist history of the region:

> It is doubtful whether the colonies ever produced either the power or the income
> their supporters hoped for and advocated them in expectation of. But in the spir-
> itual life of Europe, the colonies had an important function—as a safety vent, as
> an escape, a place to misbehave. (Lindqvist 2000, 124)

Contemporary tourism, it would seem, has combined elements of this angst-
ridden modernity with an enthusiasm for following in the footsteps of the
very same colonial adventurer explorers who helped to create the powerful
imaginary of the desert in the first place, sometimes literally. According to

Beezer (1993, 123), the tourist genre of "adventure travel," in particular, is a movement between two worlds:

> the western (or modern) world which is the cause of the adventure traveller's malaise, and the world of travel, which is a kind of patchwork, a series of places, an infinite number of locales to be "discovered."[4]

Adventure travel to the Third World offers the modern would-be traveler this experience through the "ethnic encounter"—one of its main selling points. The potential customer is invited to experience the difference and hospitality of other ethnicities as a cure for their malaise. This type of encounter is presented as able to provide the traveler with both physical and spiritual nourishment. As Tomlinson (1991, 122–25) argues, the contemplation of other cultures is "an 'exportation of loss' which allows us the sense of escape from the contradictions inherent in the condition of modernity."

The power of the written word to disseminate Orientalist ideologies and fix particularist representations of "Middle East" in the imagination of colonial cultures has not gone unnoticed (Said 1978, 93): "People, places and experiences can always be described by a book, so much so that the book (or text) acquires a greater authority, and use, even than the actuality it describes." Gregory (1999, 115) has followed up this argument in his study of Victorian traveler/writers in Egypt to show how their literary efforts contributed to the production of colonial and contemporary travel and tourism in a process he calls "scripting."[5] Tourist brochures selling holidays in the Middle East today offer up itineraries that often involve an attempt to capture the experiences of a late colonial traveler's desert romance by visiting locations they wrote about and re-tracing their steps or camel journey (see Wang, this volume).

Today "scripting" of the Orient is no longer confined to the literary output of the Victorian adventurers, and places can gain popularity and meaning for the European visitor simply because they have been used as locations by influential movies, such as Petra in Jordan (used in Steven Spielberg's 1989 *Indiana Jones and the Last Crusade*). The desert, in particular, is not only the site of contemplation on the nature of freedom for such modern theorists as Baudrillard and Bauman, but it is also inextricably embedded in the western public consciousness through the powerful imagery of romantic cinematic interpretations in such "epics" as David Lean's *Lawrence of Arabia* (1962) and David Robbins's *The English Patient* (1996) (see Beezer 2003). The road movie, especially those filmed in Mexico and the United States, but even Australian versions like *Priscilla, Queen of the Desert,* also utilizes the supposed emptiness of the desert to highlight the protagonists' journey and identity search. Popular media filters and repeats these images so it is no longer necessary to have actually read the book or seen the film to be affected, while travel brochures often refer to these filmic imageries as a major selling point, offering a way in to experiencing a place that might otherwise just appear to be a wide expanse of sand and rock.

WOMEN AND TRAVEL

Just how heavily gendered the concept of travel is in western Europe can be seen in the perceived differences in the literary output of Victorian men travelers to their female counterparts. In contrast to the close association of male adventurer explorers with the production and dissemination of colonialist ideologies, Victorian women travel writers have often been celebrated as protofeminist heroines (Russell 1988; Birkett 1989). Others, such as Mills (1991), McEwan (2000), Pratt (1992), and Blunt (1994), have been more circumspect, noting the women's ambivalence toward the colonial project compared to their male counterparts. Several have commented on the opportunities the desert gave colonial travelers, both men and women, to cross-dress and experiment with their sexual identities by adopting the "costume" of the Arabs and Bedouins.[6] In the European imaginary, then, the desert as a stable, neverchanging site that is supposedly a place of emptiness has allowed for the placing of all sorts of imaginaries upon it—especially those of gender and race. Racial and sexual identities can be written and re-written. Its role as a place to "escape to" has never been more pertinent.

Sinai Ladies

The Sinai desert extends over approximately 61,000km^2 from the Mediterranean in the north to the Red Sea in the south. At the southern end of the peninsula the Red Sea divides into the relatively shallow (80–90m) Gulf of Suez to the west and the much deeper (1240–1260m) and coral-rich Gulf of Aqaba in the east, part of the Syrio-African Rift Valley. Most western tourism, concentrated along the 250km coastline of the Gulf of Aqaba, developed during the Israeli occupation of the peninsula between 1967 and 1982. However, while the resorts of Dahab and Nuweiba have grown up around resident Bedouin communities, the bigger and brasher resort of Sharm El Sheikh has never had a reliable source of fresh water so was not settled by Bedouins, until the late 1960s, when the Israelis built a military outpost and settlement called Ophira. Until Sinai was handed over to Egypt, Ophira's tourism facilities were limited to two hotels and some basic camping accommodation (see figure 6.2a). Since Egypt took over control of the Sinai,[7] tourism development has rapidly expanded and the re-named Sharm

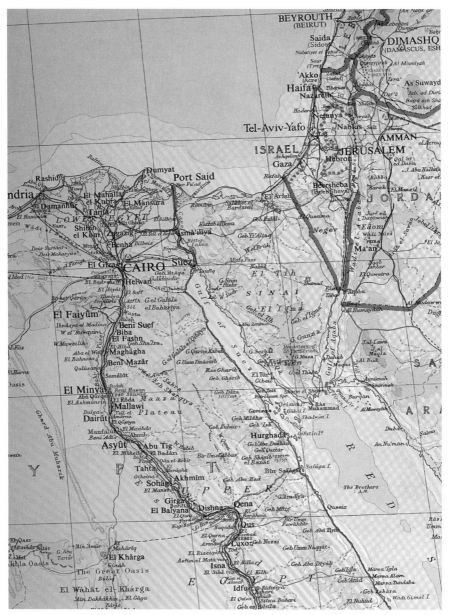

Figure 6.1   Map of Sinai. Reprinted by permission of HarperCollins Publishers Ltd ©
Bartholomew 1996.

Figure 6.2a,b   Before and After: Sharm El Sheikh's Na'ama Bay Circa 1987 (a) and in 2001 (b) after 14 Years of Intensive Tourism Development

El Sheikh now has approximately 150 mostly "luxury" hotels run by Egyptian businesses in conjunction with such global hotel chains as the Hilton, Marriott, Intercontinental, Sheraton, Hyatt, Novotel, and others (see figure 6.2b). In the early 1990s most tourists were northern Europeans who came for the scuba diving and desert safaris. While this is still an important component of tourism in Sinai, especially in Dahab and Nuweiba, much of the recent expansion in Sharm El Sheikh (and Taba in the north) has been focused around large numbers of mostly northern European, Italian, and Russian tourists coming to enjoy beach and hotel-based holidays, with the odd ethnic Bedouin encounter and desert day trip thrown in. Sinai's relatively recent reincorporation into Egypt, its high prices and a general lack of facilities other than those for tourists—especially affordable housing—means it does not yet have a very large permanent Egyptian resident community and it is not considered a very family friendly place for most Egyptians who work there. Thus the "locals" that the tourist encounters are mostly men, who commute from towns and cities in Egypt, working a shift pattern with spells back in their hometown.[8]

Nowadays, while backpackers might still arrive by bus from Cairo, or via kibbutzim in Israel, the majority of visitors to the Sinai—over 1.5 million tourists in 2002—arrive by charter plane via Sharm El Sheikh's international airport before being transferred to their hotel accommodation. A significant proportion of these tourists are European women who engage in romantic encounters with "local" men.

Discourses that utilize the metaphor of the desert to signify displacement and a search for identity have tended to be written by men, and the archetypal desert is often depicted by images of the sand dunes of the Sahara. Yet it is predominantly women from Europe who are actively seeking out the desert through the modern industry of tourism in the Sinai. It would seem that the western woman is just as disaffected with modernity and seeking displacement, and she too is looking for a means of escape. But her quest is more reliant on the package tourist industry, which is more literal and involves more physical engagement, not only with the place, but also with the people.

Kaplan (1996, 73) argues the male theorists on the desert assume a male subjectivity when using their metaphors:

> "Man" can only be inferred as the one who has the right to the point of view, to the acts of theorizing and writing, and, of course the seeking of ecstasy through travel. This "man" could also be seen as a construction of Euro-American prerogatives: "central," he visits the margins; "empty," he recreates emptiness in the world around him; "modern," he looks for an escape from modernity.

The lone male at one with the wilderness of the desert is very different than the desert of the Sinai with its large hotel development and hundreds of charter flights from Europe. If a European woman is just as disaffected with modernity and seeking displacement, if she too is looking for a means of escape, she need look no further than the Sinai.

As a tourist destination, however, the Sinai holds another card that appeals to women, perhaps more than to men. Not only is it a desert, it is also a beach.[9] The date palm of the oasis doubles up as the coconut palm of the paradisial[10] *Bounty Bar* beach. In the European geographical imagination the location of paradise is important (see Löfgren 1999; Littlewood 2001). Like the desert it has to be isolated, on the periphery. And as Third World destinations the Sinai and Egypt are heavily loaded with a geographical imagination of colonial encounters with "natives." These and other more globalized images, such as the luxury hotel, swimming pool, water sports, the climate, the body beautiful, and the suntan, are used to sell and experience the Sinai as a tourist destination.

MODERNITY AND ITS OPPOSITES

From the interviews I conducted with (mostly) European women tourists[11] in the Sinai, I found that these women have incorporated the western imaginary of the desert as metaphor: a site of angst, loss, solitude and displacement; being at one with nature; a demarcation of a boundary defining Europe, European identity, and other boundaries, including geographical, social, racial, sexual, gendered. The desert was a site of adventure for many women, a place to search for identity, experiment with identity, and forge identities. And these imaginaries were bound up in the Sinai's role as site for sexual and romantic relationships where the idea of love and "romance" was based on Orientalist geographical imaginations along with such connected notions as nostalgia, purity of nature, and its concomitant escape from modernity.

Despite the Sinai being a relatively small desert, filled with hotels, airports, and roads, the imaginary of the desert was still one of a vast empty space, devoid of life and full of sand dunes. Like Kaplan's disillusioned modernists, the women are traveling to the desert to "escape from modernity." However these women aren't theorizing about modernity; they are using its technologies and infrastructure, its airports and airplanes, as well as the privileges of economic and cultural capital gained from living in the "modern" First World, to physically travel to a desert. And although many would like to be, and some try to be, more like the archetypal male modern traveling subject—traveling alone on a seemingly endless quest—such practicalities as annual holiday entitlement and marriage and family commitments often cause them to be more pragmatic, and they arrive in the Sinai rather than the Sahara, they fly on charter flights and book package tours— they consume the place through the facility of the vacation.

Geographical imaginations of the sexually adventuring European female tourist, like her colonial predecessors, are based on binaries that juxtapose Europe with the desert landscapes of the Middle East—where both its people and place are positioned as different and "othered" (Bhabha 1994). Although the comparisons made by women tourists between Europe and the Sinai focused on modernity versus various states of unmodernity, they were still reduced to binaries, lumped together as "opposites" to Europe and the modern. Associations with the places and people of Europe and Egypt

(Sinai) were split by the women along such lines as technological First World modernity versus "culture and ethnicity"; city versus nature and "city sophisticate" versus "naïve nature boy"; corrupt western system versus pure, simple life; and "busy and stressful" versus "quiet, laid-back and stress-free" (see Fabian 1983).

These binaries were often articulated by the women I interviewed who stayed in four- and five-star hotels of the resort of Sharm El Sheikh, but were even more strongly voiced by those who rejected the "touristy" Sharm El Sheikh and instead headed straight for the desert and beaches of the smaller, quieter Nuweiba and Dahab resorts, where they stayed in simpler, more "natural" accommodation with their predominantly Bedouin hosts. For the purposes of this section I have separated these binaries into three broad categories: the unmodern, premodern, and antimodern, although in practice they were far more entangled, incorporating elements of each other in their articulations.

The Unmodern

In many ways the "unmodern" was conceptualized by the women I spoke to simply as an absence of development that was seen as common to all Third World geographies on the tourist itinerary. Responses to this perceived state of "unmodernity" were varied and revealed a large degree of confusion around what holiday destinations should be. One definition offered was its lack of adequate infrastructure in comparison to Europe. This imaginary of the "unmodern" was often welcomed and criticized at the same time by European female visitors. For example, the relative absence of roads and traffic in the Sinai was both enthusiastically received as a sign of being close to nature and being away from normal city life and disapproved of because the lack of roads and their general condition were not up to European standards and could impede their travel plans.

While Egyptians look upon Sinai as a symbol of their country's embrace of modernity, epitomized by its beach resorts, the same resorts have problematized Egypt's perceived lack of modernity in the European geographical imagination of the region. In all the tourist literature on the region it is only the Egyptian Tourist Authority that refers to the Sinai as "ultra-modern."[12] British tour operators, for example, prefer to concentrate on the permanent, unchanging history and traditions of the region. The facilities of the Red Sea resorts, such as diving centers and hotels, are referred to as "modern" in the brochures, but perhaps because this "modernity" is seen as exclusively designed for (mostly) western tourists rather than Egyptians, this "modernity" is also seen as western rather than Egyptian. Among the women I interviewed the biggest and brashest of the three resorts, Sharm El Sheikh, was either praised or vili-

fied for this "modernity." For some women the "modern" five-star hotel resorts were a reassuring refuge of modernity in an unknown "unmodern" country; for others their "ultra-modern" facilities were exactly what they had come
to Sinai to escape from. Gertrude and Caroline[13] were both in their fifties and
had come to Sharm El Sheikh for the first time on a two-week package from
their native Germany. I met them on their hotel beach with two "local" men
in their thirties who they had befriended; one was the receptionist at the hotel,
the other worked in air traffic control. They told me how they were flicking
through travel brochures at home when they spotted a photo of a hotel on a
cliff top with a lift built into the cliff that took guests to the beach below. It
was this lift, they said, that made them choose to come to Sharm El Sheikh—
a reassuring emblem of modernity in an unknown "unmodern" country:

> JJ: The first time you came to the Sinai, what made you decide to come? What
> was the . . . ?
>
> *Gertrude: It's a nice story. We wanted to go to Sri Lanka, but we look in the cat-*
> *alogue and then I say "Ah we can go to the Sinai," and then we don't know a*
> *nice place, then we see one nice with the elevator here and then I think of course*
> *I read it was Hilton before and I think when there was Hilton before it's a nice*
> *place, very nice looking and then I see this elevator and I say come let's try Car-*
> *oline. We'll go there and we'll take this hotel. So we be right!*[14]

Another aspect of imagining Sinai as "unmodern" was its cheapness in relation to Europe. As I discuss later in the section on the privileges of travel,
Sinai was imagined as a cheap destination, whether than meant bargain luxury hotel packages or budget backpacker camping. Sharm El Sheikh was attractive because it was seen to combine a cheap holiday—due to the "unmodern" nature of the Third World—with "luxury" facilities promised by the
international First World standards of a Hilton (or at least a former Hilton).
However, the tourist's conceptualization of Sinai as a convenient combination
of the "unmodern" and "modern" led to tensions and disappointment. The
same women found other aspects of modernity displeasing and out of place
in their expectations of Egypt and Sinai, especially when it came to cost. The
"unmodern" was supposed to be cheaper than the "modern." Gertrude and her
friend were particularly indignant at the price of alcohol, which was on a par
with the price they would pay at a hotel in Europe. "Really the price of drinks
here are too expensive! . . . Yes you would pay this in a hotel in Europe, but
this isn't Europe! It's not the same."[15]

This was explained to me as an acceptable assumption because a five-star
hotel in Egypt could not be compared to a hotel in Europe. Modernity, especially its more luxurious elements, is not expected to be cheap, but making

consumer decisions based on price is an integral part of the tourist industry, and most tourists traveling to the Third World expect prices to be significantly lower than in the West. The expectation of cost is split even further along "modern" and "unmodern" lines. The cost of hotel accommodation and the price of scuba diving courses, for example, are expected to be cheaper than if consumed in Europe, but they are still considered western products and are often priced in dollars or Euros to reflect this, as if they are imported goods. However the cost of what are seen to be "local" commodities are expected to be significantly lower.[16] Many visitors to Sinai expect to get the best of both "worlds"—a veneer at least of modernity, at a thoroughly unmodern price.

This conceptualization is maintained despite the relative sophistication of resorts like Sharm El Sheikh, because the infrastructure is tourist infrastructure, designed mostly for Europeans, and as such it represents western modernity, albeit with an "exotic" flavor. It is a little piece of home for the tourist/ traveler to venture out from.

The Premodern

The Sinai, however, is not just a place of unmodernity, signified by the supposed "absence" of modernity; it also represents a state of "premodernity" to many women tourists, a site where it is possible to experience time and space *before* modernity. This "premodernity" can be found not only in the women's connection with the Sinai's religious past and spirituality, but also in their nostalgia and their projection of a supposedly "authentic masculinity" upon its inhabitants. Its desert landscape is a landscape of history— biblical and Pharaonic—but the contemporary inhabitants are also considered to be "premodern" primitives whose supposed ultramasculinity is crucial in facilitating the women's access to this imagination of a Sinai of old. While it has been noted that holidays in the Third World attempt to offer tourists a different "time and place" (Wagner 1977), accompanying these feelings is a strong sense of nostalgia, a desire to experience a time and place *before* modernity began.

The Sinai has many historical religious associations with western Christianity and Judaism; in the Old Testament it is written as the birthplace of monotheism,[17] and in the New Testament Jesus is supposed to have passed through this desert on his "Flight to Egypt." It is also the location, along with Egypt's Eastern desert, of the first desert monastery retreats, and a significant proportion of Sinai tourists are there specifically to climb Mount Sinai, the supposed site of Moses receiving the Ten Commandments, and to visit St. Catherine's Monastery, built in the valley below to commemorate the event. The desert, perhaps like no other landscape, is presented as somehow "frozen in time"—which leads to attempts to read the landscape as still representing a past time, in this case, a spiritual past that existed prior to the onset of modernity and somehow still manages to exist alongside modernity in the landscape of the Sinai and in the lives of its Bedouin inhabitants.

The search for "origins," both physical and metaphysical, has been a major motif of modernity and has given impetus to countless voyages of exploration. That many searches get forgotten only to resurface later in response to political and cultural developments as the reworking of past traditions is in itself a symptom of modernity. The creation of the state of Israel has had a great effect in this regard on the Sinai, influencing and providing tourists (both Christian and Jewish) with religious-themed holidays.

Looking for your homeland or what Veijola (this volume) calls *Heimat* is often an ephemeral affair that suits the practice of tourism precisely because it does not have to be a physical return to the place of your childhood. The practice of tourism itself is often a journey imbued and made meaningful by memories of the geographical imaginations of your childhood exemplified by Lindqvist's (2000) Sahara sojourns. And while you certainly don't have to be a local to look for your homeland, it certainly helps if the locals can embody (and the landscape can reflect) this imagined space for you. For many childhoods the European *Heimat* is precisely here in the Middle East of Southwest Asia, where "our" history and "our" religion began and can still be visited, because it is there in the empty desert landscape and the biblical galabeyas of the Bedouin. Like unmodernity, the idea of a premodern Sinai and its people has become intertwined with the women's romances, but this is no museum.

Katrin, age twenty-six from Switzerland, was a twenty-one-year-old Christian when she first came to the Sinai, drawn by its original significance as the premodern site of the origins of monotheism. Her geographical imagination of the romance of the desert landscape was expressed as a spiritual search, inspired by previous visual encounters with the Sinai:

> I didn't know a lot about Sinai when I was in Switzerland. I saw some films about the monastery of St. Catherine. And it impressed me I remember this now. And I imagined that I would live in this area. But I remember that I saw this film and it impressed me—this area and these mountains and this silence and also this mystic atmosphere, the history also. It was somehow impressive for me because [of] the religion—most of the big religions are here. You meet everyone, you meet people talking about religion. So it was for me a place of secrets and it made me just curious.[18]

Katrin's romantic and religious landscape combined when, on the same trip, she met and fell in love with an Egyptian man, fifteen years her senior, in the backpacker resort of Dahab. After one week of meeting him, she had married and converted to Islam. By combining the two—her Egyptian partner and the landscape of the Sinai—she had achieved her goal of reaching the premodern, the origins, of getting "closer to God."

> Yes, it's nice because when you get really into this religion, you enjoy it. You start to enjoy it—to feel that you have a way to get closer to God. And this was always my aim, because I see this world and I see this nature and I know there must be some power who did all this.[19]

The representation of Sinai as premodern, and to some extent unmodern, was reinforced for many women by a perception of Egyptian and Bedouin men as "real" men, conforming to traditional stereotypes of masculinity. It was explained to me by several women I interviewed that, because their men were ultra "masculine," this made them feel like "real women." Consequently this allowed the women to perform a version of femininity in response, something they felt they could not do in Europe. Heike, a thirty-nine-year-old special needs teacher from Germany, claimed after coming to the Sinai she had lost interest in German men completely. She explained to me:

> They are more man. I mean they are *real* man. . . . They know how things are going. They know what they want or what they . . . the way they are. It's more clear, they are more clear. In Germany everything is more in between, so it's also more easy to be a woman, when you are with a man in the Sinai. . . . When I start to come here, my interest in German men stopped, khallas. [Arabic for finished/enough][20]

Katrin echoed Heike's comments:

> I'm very happy that I have a man from this area because I can't talk for all of them, but I feel that they are romantic and they can give a woman a lot. Because they are—I don't know—it sounds maybe difficult to understand—they are more male. They are more men. In their way. With their pride and their way how to behave in this society. They—as a woman they give you the feeling that they are strong.[21]

For many women the men's authenticity, their credentials as representing the unmodern, and belonging to the landscape of un- and premodernity, were borne out through their costume and dress. Phillips (1999), O'Connell Davidson and Sanchez Taylor (1999), Sanchez Taylor (2001), and others (Press 1978; Karch and Dann 1981; Albuquerque 1998) argue that female "sex tourism" consists of racial and sexual fantasies about "natives" and is an activity that takes place within the inequality of contemporary First World–Third World relations. As Phillips (1999, 183) notes, "This quest is structured along racial and gendered lines, where the white emancipated Western female goes in search of the quin-tessential hypersexual black male in the center of the Other."

However, in the Sinai at least, it is impossible to separate this racial and gendered "othering" among the women from their imaginations of modernity (see also Frankenberg 1993). When I asked Ulrike, fifty-seven, from Switzerland, why she came to the Sinai, she told me:

> I tell you something, you can put me [in front of] 100 naked Caribbean men, nothing with me. A nice body. And here you can put one man in a galabaya [a traditional Bedouin/Arab dress] and everything in my face change. Not a naked man. They [the Bedouin] are one with the nature and most of them are one with God.[22]

The "modern" European man was constantly compared to a "local" man, with different ideas of modernity—as well as stereotypical Orientalist notions—helping to bipolarize them into two different types of stereotypical masculinity. This placed the nonwesterner male as a real man because, as his clothing proved, he was closer to nature and therefore further away from modernity. He doesn't just give her sex, but through his connection to "nature" and "religion" she can also connect to a time gone by, a time and place no longer found in "modern" Europe.

Ideas held by the women about premodernity and unmodernity gave them different senses of time when they were in the Sinai. An idea that Sinai represents premodernity allows the holder to experience the persistence of an old time in the present, and facilitates the finding and creating of a space for difference by bringing older time into the present. The idea of a different "time" in Sinai applies to the sense of history that it evokes, especially among the geographical imaginations of the European visitor. It is premodern in this sense but also in the rhythm of life of the people who live there. The Sinai is seen to offer the tourist/traveler a different time to that of the west, a time out from the stress of the city and modern life. For Lena, a fifty-year-old German woman who ran a camp and diving center in Dahab, it was the different rhythms of time that contributed to her losing her "heart" in the Sinai, that gave her the sense she had left modernity for another "time" populated by a "premodern" group of inhabitants—the Bedouin.

> Also I have a feeling like . . . I don't know how to explain, but my heart opened you know. It was like—actually I'd run away from the stress and from too much work in Germany you know . . . I see the Bedouins—these people that live long time here—but I doesn't talk one word Arabic in this time. I don't want, you know, I just want to enjoy my time. To relax from Germany you know. And the life, it was . . . I mean it's hard life sometimes here, of course, when you have

business you know. But in the same time it goes everything a step slower you
know from the rush that we know.[23]

Modernity, then, is fast moving, stressful, and focuses on work, while premodernity involves a much slower, more relaxed tempo. You can fly to the
Sinai in a matter of hours, but once you are there, you can sit in a café and
wait the same amount of time for a cup of tea.

The Antimodern

For some women, such as Lena, conceiving Sinai as premodern and unmodern, of a different time, led to tensions between their conception of Sinai as
timeless and time rich and its position in developing modernity. Many women
voiced strong opposition to what was felt to be the encroachment of modernity
in Sinai, mostly in the form of tourist development. This "antimodernity" was
felt particularly keenly by women who lived in or visited the less-developed
Bedouin resorts of Dahab and Nuweiba or lived with Bedouin in their communities; women who were attracted to the lifestyle of the Bedouin, which
was perceived as free from the trappings of "modernity."

The antimodern but positive association with Sinai and its Bedouin inhabitants with the "premodern" has elements of what Pasztory (2001) calls "nostalgia for mud," which she defines as "ascribing higher spiritual values to
people and cultures considered lower than oneself, the romanticisation of the
faraway primitive." The antimodern woman not only felt that the landscape
and Bedouin people were closer to "nature" and therefore closer to God, or
spirituality, but she presented this as preferable to a life of modernity in Europe. This was another manufactured binary that tended to disintegrate upon
closer inspection. For example, Egyptian men, unless they had adopted a similar way of life among Bedouin-dominated communities, sat uneasily in this
geographical imagination, being neither "native" enough nor sufficiently
western to fit comfortably in either camp. Unlike the women tourists enjoy-
ing the eclectic combination of modernity and unmodernity in Sharm El
Sheikh and feeling they were experiencing an Oriental Egypt, the antimodern
women in the more remote and basic resorts distinguished between Egyptian
space and Bedouin space, associating the former with an oppressive, colonizing modernity and the latter with a way of life that was considered to be simple, natural, and therefore more "pure." For most of them, they weren't in
Egypt, but in the Sinai. This did not stop them from getting romantically involved with Egyptian men, as long as they too were "escaping from modernity" by going to live a Bedouin-inspired life in Nuweiba and Dahab. Some
women took this even further by leaving their western lifestyles altogether to
live in the Sinai with their Bedouin husbands, as Bedouin women.

Western women going "native" can be traced at least as far back as the colonial period when such women as Isabelle Eberhardt and Gertrude Bell "discovered" the advantages of covering up by adopting local dress and customs. However, the European female tourist as "native" was first noted in the Sinai in the 1970s. Today there are around a dozen "Queens of the Desert"—European women who have married into Bedouin communities and adopted the dress and customs of Bedouin life; they are mostly young women from the smaller provincial cities and towns of northern Europe.

Meike, now thirty-four, was a twenty-two-year-old trainee nurse from a small town in Switzerland when she first came to the Sinai in the early 1990s. While on a fortnight's holiday with a group of friends, she met and fell in love with a Bedouin man called Jamia from the Tarrabin tribe. Although she returned to Switzerland at the end of the holiday it was only to arrange her affairs there so she could return to live with him in the Sinai. For the first few months she continued to wear western clothing in her husband's village "in the mountains" (away from the tourist coast), but gradually she stopped dressing as a European, learned the Bedouin Arabic dialect, and adopted the clothes and customs of a Bedouin woman, as taught to her by his mother. Later the couple left the village and moved to a small hut on an isolated part of the coast near Nuweiba, where she now lives with her three sons. She cooks solely on a fire, uses no electricity, and brings up her children as Bedouins while her husband works as a guide for tourists, many of whom are friends of hers, or friends of friends from Switzerland.

For Meike and others adopting similar lifestyles, the perceived difficulty of the natural life seems to be a major part of the attraction and proof of its authenticity. Here modernity might be stressful and complex, but Bedouin life is simple and pure. Leaving modernity was deliberate.

"I'm very glad I'm out of it, of the system what we . . . how I was living. I live in another kind of system, but it's not so tight. It's less tight."[24]

To the antimodern woman the large-scale tourist development, the schools, roads, hospitals, bus networks, hotels, construction, electricity pylons; all the paraphernalia of "civilization" that has recently turned up in Sinai, is viewed as the enemy. They hark back to a "golden age" when only people like them visited, people who "understood" the Sinai, who loved and respected it. This is a different nostalgia from the yearning for the premodern, however, in that the "golden age" that is being referred to is one that took place in the women's lifetimes and can be narrowed down to the period between 1980 and 1995, before tourist development really took off. Modernity is ever changing and developing, but un- and premodernity is mostly viewed as fixed and unchanging. Meike and other women who have made Sinai their second or first home passionately believe the Sinai should not change, but remain a wilderness, a paradise for the people who imagine it as such and want to enjoy it as such. Other people are not welcome. There is an appropriate place for electricity and development—Switzerland, Cairo perhaps—but not Sinai because, for women like Meike, it was originally experienced as "empty."

> And how they treat the place it's very sad, very sad. They don't care about it. They don't know where they stay. Where they are. When we start to put light, we close the light [if people use electricity you cannot see the natural light from the moon and stars]. [As we talk there is the noise of the generator starting up in the background from a nearby Egyptian camp]. It's so disturbing.[25]

Of course the Egyptian government and package holidaymakers see things very differently, but here Meike is constructing an "Us" and "Them," which isn't based on nationality, race, culture, or gender, but on attachment to land and on different, and conflicting, geographical imaginations of this land. Here "they" refers to the Egyptian government and big-business Egyptian entre-preneurs who come to Sinai to set up tourist businesses and package tourists. Yet Egyptians who have come to set up businesses sympathetic with and sim-ilar to Bedouin enterprises are mostly accepted.

The strong sense of nostalgia was most keenly felt by women who had spent a long time in the Sinai and who could remember their first experience of the desert—in the 1980s perhaps when it was equated with the good old days of Israeli occupation or the early 1990s before Egyptian expansion re-ally took off—as a time when they felt they could imagine and experience the Sinai as premodern and unmodern and relatively undisturbed.

> [Sinai] was a natural place where the people lives with the nature and the Bedouins you know. I mean. What's going on now with all the Egyptian come and try to take land and everything. Just to find money here in Sinai—I mean, they sell the land you know. They throw away a lot of palm trees and they don't care about the nature, you know. So this is the problem which we have now. Just looking for money. But when I came it was real Bedouin village you know. So the people walk out in the desert with their goats you know. A simple life, very simple. They have no electricity. Somehow a little bit. The life was not so easy like now. You have to carry water from the well but the people live happy there you know. And these few tourists what's coming, they come to enjoy it, this kind of life.[26]

This perspective also throws up paradoxical attitudes toward the modern and its longed-for opposites. For while Lena's imagined "premodern" and "unmodern" Sinai is authentic because it is a "real" and "natural place where the people lives with the nature and the Bedouins," the "modern" economic entity that is Sinai today is positioned as "unreal" and therefore fake because "they" (modern Egyptians) "don't care about the nature" and "sell the land." In addition Lena's idea of authenticity is one where one form of "fake" modernity—the mobile modern European woman—is permitted to impose itself upon the "natural" Bedouin way of life, without supposedly affecting the authentic naturalness of the scene. Karen, a photographer in her forties, was more practically nostalgic. Having divided her time between the modernity of New York and pre/unmodern Sinai for the last twenty years, she makes her living from selling photographs of Bedouins in traditional dress to a wealthy western clientele. However, her work is now threatened by the Bedouins' adaptation to "modernity" exemplified by their preference for denim jeans and Nike baseball caps while her profit margins are being eroded through their increasing requests to be paid for being photographed. Her ability to sell a representation of authenticity in the form of a traditionally dressed Bedouin reflecting their purity and closeness to nature was being eroded by the effect of the Bedouin's supposedly "fake" encounter with modernity.

> They were so pure in their thinking, so naïve, like children, not knowing that something would harm them. At the same time a bit hostile, a bit violent because that was in their nature.[27]

The "premodern" here is a paradisial image of purity, nature, and the traditional. Modernity is what comes after. This depiction of a "pure" Bedouin, untouched and unsullied by the corruption of modernity, is only made through the association of the Bedouin with the "natural" and heavily gendered landscape of the desert that surrounds them. Here the masculinity is emphasized—a masculinity that is, strangely enough, compared to that of a child—yet its parallel with nature, its "supposed hostility and violence," is also stressed. The childlike qualities they are associated with are important. This enables the women to experience the Bedouin as violent, but to do so without any fear. After all, Karen is positioning herself in a powerful place here; the Bedouin are simply children, their violence is not directed at her—she can even control and channel it. Or at least she could.

ESCAPE FROM MODERNITY

The Orientalist and other geographical imaginations at work among European women tourists and travelers engaging in relationships in the Sinai help to perpetuate a narrative where Europe, its urban centers and its people, represent "modernity" while the Sinai, its landscape and people, are constructed as "unmodern," "premodern," or "antimodern." The construction of the Sinai as an ancient and timeless place and people positioned on the margins of civilized Europe makes the tourist resorts of the Sinai suitable for tourist women's expression of anxiety about modernity and their accompanying nostalgia for pre/unmodernity both in the near and far past. By staying in one of the three different resorts on offer, the women have the opportunity to experience the "freedom" they seek through the landscape and through the "local" men who are seen to embody this condition of un/pre/antimodernity. Entering into relationships with "local" men allows the women to experience or consume this state.

Mobility is an essential component of this conceptualization of modernity. Modern cultures travel (Rojek and Urry 1997b). Traveling to a desert or beach location on the margins of Europe is seen as a movement from the modern to the "unmodern" or "premodern."[28] Modernity is all about travel and the modern European woman believes travel allows her to "cross" over to an absence of modernity. Engaging in relationships with "local" men is therefore very much a "way in" to this condition—a way to not only become local and to feel they belong, but to express feelings of antimodernity and access/experience the landscape and culture/ethnicity of their geographical imaginations, a way to escape the perceived superficiality of the modern tourist experience. Yet, although the modern woman might well believe she can travel unaffected to a place where it does not exist, a place seen as fixed and unchanging, the crossings of these boundaries are really blurrings of the boundaries. As I mention above, this is no simple binary at work—there is more than one "opposite" to modernity, and these alternatives to modernity themselves "travel."

PRACTICAL PRIVILEGES

The geographical position of Sinai in relation to Europe is crucial to both its place in the European imaginary and its convenience as a holiday destination. A trip to the Sinai fits into dominant working patterns in Europe, where most people in employment have just a few weeks off every year. Sinai is just a few hours flight away—no long-haul flight is necessary in order to feel you have left Europe and "modernity." This proximity to Europe combined with the cultural privileges of being a western European means it is very simple to just hop on a plane and go. It is also very easy to organize the trip. Cheap flights and one- or two-week packages are easily available from a variety of tour operators who are only a telephone call away. Return charter flights from most European cities cost between €150–400 depending on the time of year. Packages including hotel accommodation can be obtained for almost the same price outside such peak times as school holidays, Christmas, and Easter. Booking online or over the phone ensures that a flight or hotel package can be arranged in a matter of minutes. Visas are automatically issued to Europeans on arrival, so the tourist traveler only needs to pack her bag and get to the airport; the rest is taken care of. Even frequent and long-stay visitors like Lena can buy one-way tickets in Europe, then get a flight back from one of the travel agent's representatives in Sharm El Sheikh at a day or two's notice:

> It's good for me, from Germany, it's just four hours by flight you know . . . it's a good feeling if you know you can be one day, two days at home.[29]

Yet the modernity the women imagine they are escaping from does not remain in Europe; it comes with them. An airplane needs an airport to land in (and one of a comparable standard to the one it left) and tourists, even those who want to get close to "nature," require a relatively sophisticated infrastructure. Without lorries bringing food and thousands of bottles of mineral water, for example, Sinai wouldn't be quite such a hospitable environment.

The relative cheapness of Sinai does not stop at the cost of getting there. Despite being far more expensive than the rest of Egypt, prices still compare favorably to those in Europe, especially with a weak Egyptian pound. Anja, twenty-six, from Germany, was on her second visit to Dahab on a six-week diving holiday, which included a lot of time sitting in the beach cafés people-watching. She thought the favorable exchange rate afforded women travelers an instant elevated advantage from the "locals."

> And the money system of course. You know the difference between Egyptian pounds and German marks gives you privilege here.[30]

Here privilege entails, among other things, having more money than many of the locals—most of whom are men. This positions tourist women in the (still) relatively unusual situation of being financially better off than many men in the area. And in Egypt, this often means substantially better off. Of course this has a variety of impacts on the relationships that occur. Privilege is inherent in the women's ability to exploit their greater economic and cultural capital, gained through the process of travel, through their mobility, to choose men. If the search is on for "real" men, men as they used to be, this search is only possible because of the impact of feminism in modernity on women's mobility in the west. Change in the economic and social position of women has enabled more and more women to travel, to have a mobility that allows them to "experience" men and an alternative to their modernity in different societies around the world.

When I asked Anja if she thought European women had other privileges, she couldn't help but comment on the difference between her fellow women travelers' social status in Germany—a status other non-German travelers and "locals" were mostly unaware of—and the more elevated status they achieved in Sinai:

> Yes, many. Even if you take the silliest woman from the smallest town in Germany, [laughs], it's just because they are European. With the behavior [attitude of the local men] you get that.[31]

The privilege Anja is referring to here represents another form of mobility present in these women's traveling: an upward mobility of social status/class.

This change in circumstance through mobility was most keenly felt by women who did not consider themselves to be wealthy or sexually desirable in the modernity of Europe. Older women found they could pick and choose from a selection of much younger men. By being able to stay in four- or five-star hotels in Egypt, when the option doesn't even get considered in Europe, students, backpackers, and women in relatively low-paid jobs were instantly elevated to another social and financial status. Or perhaps this status came through finding that a week's worth of money in Europe could last for months if they opted for the more budget-oriented destinations, such as Dahab; a destination that was recommended to Katrin, twenty-six, from Switzerland, by other backpackers she met in Cairo:

> I heard about Dahab, that it's nice and special and everyone says it's very cheap.[32]

Financial and social privileges from being a First Worlder and a woman could also accrue in more unexpected ways. Being an industry based upon hospitality, tourism often stresses the welcoming nature of "natives" in developing countries; a hospitality that can easily be taken advantage of. The photographer Karen, who divided her time between Europe, America, and the Sinai, had set up a home from home in the backpacker resort of Dahab, and constantly marveled at her ability to live off the generosity of the Bedouin.

> I came here with $100 you know, and I stayed a few years.[33]

This position of elevated social status is often held as a temporary state, however; while the new position is enjoyed, self-perception as relatively poor is maintained. Instead of crossing financial barriers and leaving behind socio-economic status held in Europe, in modernity, this perception tends to tag along and mix uneasily with the newly found elevated position. Hence the bewilderment and automatic denial that often accompanies tourists when they are seen by the toured as "rich."

Many women traveled with the purpose and aim to escape modernity's stresses and structures. For Lena, her first visit to Sinai was an "escape," like many holidays are:

> Actually I'd run away from the stress and from too much work in Germany you know. . . . I just wanted to enjoy my time, to relax from Germany.

When European women use this First World mobility to actively move from a place conceived as modern to another pre/un/antimodern place, not being of that place releases them from their normal routine, giving them greater freedom to move in and out of tourist scenarios, at will. Sylvia, thirty-seven, from Germany, relished the lack of routine available to her in Dahab, where she could follow her whims:

> The life here is still very simple. You can concentrate on a thing, you know what I mean. Also you have nothing to do. You don't have to wake up at seven or doing things like this. You eat when you like to eat, you wake up you don't know what the day will bring you—you wake up and you meet this person. You're more open, you . . . yes you really do what you like to do more.[34]

The photographer Karen saw freedom, whether sexual or not, as the major attraction and one of the main differences between her life in modernity and her life in the un/premodern Sinai.

> There's no such thing as total freedom, but it's about as total as it gets in Sinai.[35]

The Sinai "embodies" freedom, through its desert and beach landscape and through its people—a freedom based on an idea of the Bedouin's and the Sinai's lack of civilization, lack of modernity, yet a freedom conceptualized from and based upon a completely modern way of thinking:

> Freedom is the really big issue, like Sinai and freedom are two interlocking concepts. Sinai is important because it embodies freedom. The fact that it had no roads, that it's not civilized. A wilderness, but one that you can walk into and still come out alive. It's kind of an accessible wilderness you know. For me that was the attraction. I love the wilderness, but as a single woman I can't approach it. So for me Sinai was the approachable wilderness. Sinai itself has come to mean to me a symbol of freedom. And just the way of the Bedouin's lifestyle as well. They see the serenity as an activity. Just sitting somewhere quietly.[36]

Figure 6.3   **Bedouins are often imagined as somehow existing in a separate, fixed space apart from "modernity." The text on the reverse of this Israeli postcard circa 1980 depicting the tourist haunt of Asilah in Dahab states: "Dahav-Di-Zahav—An oasis on the shore of the Gulf of Eilat inhabited by Bedouin who live off dates and fish." Even at this time there were far more foodstuffs available, and Bedouin regularly traveled to north Sinai and Israel as migrant workers.**

Freedom here is one of not having any ties, a kind of freedom associated with and celebrated within modernity, yet paradoxically it is being attached to a people and landscape of "tradition" with fixed rules, customs, and family ties. It is a very "modern" idea of freedom that is unlikely to be shared by the Bedouins although it is very much based upon identification with them. It is also a freedom obtained through modernity's introduction of accessibility. After all, the Sinai is "an approachable wilderness."

MODERNITY, MOBILITY, AND SEXUAL IDENTITY

This notion of freedom that the women associate with the Sinai and the Bedouin is also a very heavily gendered (masculine) freedom; after all, they are certainly not referring to the freedom of the Bedouin women. It has been suggested that the modern female "sex tourist" is experimenting with her gender identity (Pruitt and La Font 1995) and that, by rewriting her "gender script," she is contesting "the constraints of conventional gender identity" present in her own culture. In the Sinai, despite many European tourist women's claims that "local" men are "real men" and make them feel like women, the women are often in relationships where the rewriting of the gender script involves borrowing some traits normally associated with masculinity. By these traits I mean the women's use of the "modern" world, their First World status, their economic and cultural capital, *and* their ability to travel freely back and forth between the two different spaces—the space of modernity in Europe from whence they obtain their privileged position and the [mostly geographically imagined] space of the unmodern, premodern, and antimodern Sinai where they exhibit their privileges and where their privileges became exaggerated and worth more in the local currency.

In their interviews women tourists often juxtaposed "local" men with their European counterparts, effectively bi-polarizing them into two different types of masculinity, with the non-westerners coming out on top, being real men, because they were closer to nature and therefore further away from modernity.

The paradoxes and contradictions loom large. Women are appropriating what western society perceives to be "masculine" forms of behavior and lifestyle—travel, holidays, tourist sex, independent mobility—along with their masculine colonial geographical imaginations—in order to feel more like "real women," in order to experience their femaleness. They are using the trappings and technologies of modernity—the privileges of life in the West—in order to escape it, again by adopting masculine colonial geographical imaginations—stereotypes of race and gender and very "modern" masculine notions of "freedom" linked to nostalgic stereotypes of primitivism. Yet it is the men's "hyper" masculinity that attracts them, a supposedly paradoxical situation that, in effect, undermines the modernist support for the dualism of masculine-feminine. Unequal power relations between the First and Third Worlds means that European women can exercise more control over their relationship with "masculinity" in the Sinai than they can in modern Europe. They travel to the Sinai—they escape from modernity—to experience a more satisfying ideal of femininity because they can do so relatively safely; the masculinity on offer is being "experienced" within a framework where the women can expect to stay in control thanks to their greater economic and cultural capital and the privileges of being a modern European. And if it doesn't work out, or they get bored, they can always get on a plane and return to their modern lives.

Happiness and simplicity are strongly bound together in European women tourists' ideas of antimodernity, a notion that needs to be fixed, stable, and unchanging, while their complex life in modern Europe—linked to stress and misery but also to income and privilege—is ever mobile and dynamic.

A postcard first produced during the Israeli occupation of the Sinai but that can still be bought today in tourist bazaars shows an early Dahab that is more palm-treed oasis than backpacker resort of bazaars and camps. The text on the back informs the tourist that Bedouins "live on dates and fish" (see figure 6.3). This construction of the Bedouin as a "simple" people, living outside the global economy on what grows around them, is still largely believed despite the complexity of their lives as they attempt to survive the impact of the Egyptian state and tourist development along the coast. Nevertheless, for the purposes of the weary western European looking for an alternative to her modernity, the Bedouin, their home and their lifestyle provide a fitting back-drop to experience the absence, negation, and antithesis of modernity. That their community is not fixed, does not stay the same but adjusts and is mo-bile, is one of the many tensions in the construction of modernity as "West-ern," that, arguably, all tourists experience on their travels.

For Lena, and many others, these paradoxes of modernity are now ex-pressing themselves in a variety of ways. Keeping "modernity" with its mo-bility separate from a notion of a fixed, unchanging, antimodernity is increas-ingly difficult as the geographically imagined boundaries get increasingly blurred (not that they ever existed) when they are crossed. Sinai's authentic-ity and therefore its commercial appeal is based on an imaginary of emptiness, an absence of civilization. With the ongoing tourist development on the coast—the encroaching modernity—accessing this particular imagination of the Sinai has become more difficult. It is no longer immediately outside the front door, but a drive away, away from the people [modernity, civilization] and *in*to the desert (emptiness, pre/un/antimodernity). This creates another tension in the modernity versus antimodernity discourse expressed by many of the women I interviewed. Like countless other women, Lena described the Sinai as "very romantic." But Dahab, formerly included, has become the point from which the romance of the desert is reached—it is no longer the desert. Like Europe, which is four or five hours away, Dahab is "twenty minutes" away. The romance of un/pre/antimodernity is measured in distance from "modernity," whether that is where the women used to live, or where they are now earning their living and creating modernity around them:

> For me, the sunset you know. Some days the mountain comes totally red. And the sea of course . . . just the nature. It's very quiet. And romantic . . . just twenty minutes [from Dahab] and you can go in the desert you know. I can relax totally in my head and everything.[37]

When a place is sullied by the presence of modernity, there is very little op-tion left but to move on. Modern women escaping modernity fail, as moder-nity inevitably follows. Heike, the thirty-nine-year-old teacher from Germany, had been visiting the Sinai for many years and had several different male partners there. Her solution was to leave Sinai altogether and move further south, to the Sudan with her new Sudanese boyfriend.

> It changed. It's not like before. I mean before it was really nobody was thinking too much about money. In the beginning, in the first years when I start to come, everybody had time to drink tea, to talk, to be together. . . . But with normal tourists now, it's not the same. The atmosphere.[38]

CONCLUSION

Geographical and historical imaginations of "tropical island paradise" and "desert" are crucial to tourist imaginations of the Sinai and its Red Sea coast. However, this imagination is not just based on a difference in climate and landscape, but on a spatial and temporal difference, and the Victorian colonial Orientalist elements of these imaginations mean that a journey to the Sinai is presented not only as a journey through space, but also time. And it is through these geographical imaginations that binaries are constructed, with the western European cities and civilization of "modernity"—and their modern traveling representatives—on one side and the ancient, traditional nature and wilderness of the Sinai and its people, their supposed opposites, on the other. While access to these geographical imaginations as a tourist can be all too brief and feel very superficial and inauthentic, a romantic and/or sexual encounter with a "local" man can be seen as a way "in" to connect, another means of travel where the residents of Sinai are implicated in these geographical imaginations and, through racial and sexual stereotyping, are seen to embody ideas of a masculinity associated with an absence of modernity and a presence of nature, history, and wilderness. The idea of the desert as a "transparent space," a place of emptiness, lends itself readily to the modern woman's desire to escape modernity and oneself especially regarding restrictions of gender. Yet paradoxically it is tourist resorts and the inhabitants, the men who live in this supposedly empty place, that are the "way in." The journey in mind for the modern tourist is to leave behind modernity, yet it is modernity—its privileges and technologies—that gives us this idea in the first place and enables and encourages the modern tourist to do this.

Traveling women are adopting what have been seen to be "masculine" imaginations, more usually reflected in discourses of displacement and exile in literature on the modern traveling subject and tied up with colonial geographies and notions of the tourist as sovereign subject, the bearer of the steely tourist/male gaze. They would also seem to be incorporating supposedly "masculine" forms of behavior and lifestyle—especially those associated with mobility in general and sex tourism in particular. Yet this is supposedly all done in order to feel more like "real women," in order to experience their femaleness.

Yet disappointment looms. The desire to escape modernity is difficult to maintain when tourists require a relatively sophisticated "modern" infrastructure when they travel. We all know the problem with traveling is that your destination is sullied by your presence and you can't help but bring "modernity" with you even if you displace this activity onto other tourists. Sinai has to be many things—"unmodern," "premodern," and "antimodern"—ideas that often conflict and travel in different directions. And the crossing isn't straightforward; as the borders are traversed, they also get blurred. Inevitably the Sinai, its resorts, and its male residents will fail in this impossible task of representing the past, hypermasculinity, and the unmodern in order to provide women tourists with a temporary refuge from "modernity." At the same time such tourist spaces as those in the Sinai seem to be able to represent a myriad of meanings and modernities and continue to be able to do so, despite the glaring inconsistencies and impossibilities of being so many different times and spaces. Interactions and negotiations within these points of contact allow for the playing out of tensions and potential conflicts between the opposing but simultaneously occurring geographical imaginations. Tourist places are spaces where "modernity" meets itself in many shapes and forms; they are places of possibility where roles are changed and identities are experimented with.

NOTES

1. Other men in my study are Bedouin who live in the Sinai. However, they also often travel from other parts of the Sinai to work in the tourist resorts.

2. The name *Middle East* is itself a product of the colonial period, when the countries of North Africa and Southwest Asia were perceived in relation to British and French interests in the "East" (Asia). See Lewis and Wigen (1997).

3. For a gendered perspective on Orientalism, see Lewis (1995).

4. Beezer argues that it is often women and nature, condensed into a single figure, which are made into representatives of the "otherness" the western traveler seeks. My study of course, deals with women as western travelers.

5. Gregory (1999, 115) defines scripting as a "developing series of steps and signals, part structured and part improvised, that produces a narrativized sequence of interactions through which roles are made and remade by soliciting responses and responding to cues."

6. Cross-dressing, disguising yourself as a native woman or man, is a motif of many films and books based in the Middle East, from Carry On films to romantic novels like Ahdaf Soueif's 1999 Booker-nominated novel *The Map of Love* (London: Bloomsbury).

7. When Egypt took over the Sinai from Israel in 1982, they agreed to suspend major development for five years until 1987.

8. Sinai's relatively recent reincorporation into Egypt, its high prices, and general lack of non-tourist infrastructure have meant many wives and children of men who work in the Sinai are unwilling or unable to move there. Money is sent back to the family home. Egyptian women are less likely to work in the resorts of Sinai than men, unless it is in a large reputable hotel with a good level of accommodation.

9. The beach, and the suntan achieved from spending large amounts of time there, are important constituents in experimenting with sexual and racial identities.

10. Although "paradise" has previously been more closely associated with religious concepts, its literal Greek definition—a "walled enclosure"—makes it an appropriate metaphor for much of modern tourism, taking place as it does within the walled enclosures of hotels.

11. For my fieldwork I spent approximately four months (in two periods of two months in 2000) in the Sinai resorts and carried out in-depth interviews with fifty-seven people: twenty-one "local" men and thirty-six tourist women. I myself have been a frequent visitor to the region since 1985, and since 1994 I have worked for the Rough Guides producing the chapters on the Sinai, Red Sea coast, and the Canal cities for their Egypt guidebook.

12. "From Cleopatra's Alexandria to the ultramodern resorts of Sinai and the Red Sea, Egypt is an unmatchable holiday destination" (advertisement from the Egyptian Tourist Authority in *Observer* magazine, 2002).

13. All the names of the people I interviewed have been changed.

14. Gertrude, fifty-eight, from Germany, interview with author, Sharm El Sheikh, April 2000.

15. Gertrude, as above.

16. I have seen tourists, especially "budget backpackers," pay a diving center over €300 for a diving course without blinking or bargaining, then argue with a taxi driver over a fare of 9LE (Egyptian pounds equivalent to €1.50), or haggle over the price of a 6LE (€1) pair of trousers or a 30LE (€5) hotel room.

17. Monotheism is often put forward as one of the founding principles of modernity, and in some ways a visit to the Sinai can be seen as a physical journey to the birthplace of modernity.

18. Katrin, twenty-six, from Switzerland, interviewed with author, Dahab, September 2000.

19. Katrin, as above.

20. Heike, thirty-nine, from Germany, interview with author, Nuweiba (Tarrabin), September 2000.

21. Katrin, as above.

22. Ulrike, fifty-seven, from Switzerland, interviewed with author, Nuweiba, September 2000.

23. Lena, fifty, from Germany, interviewed with author, Dahab, September 2000.

24. Meike, thirty-four, interview with author, Nuweiba, April 2000.

25. Meike, as above.

26. Lena, as above.

27. Karen, forty, from the United States, interview with author, Dahab, April and September 2000.

28. It is important to note on any discussion around concepts of modernity that it is not just a construct of a geographical imagination but a hard-edged technological economic and cultural entity affording women the freedoms, means, and opportunities to travel in ever increasing numbers.

29. Lena, as above.

30. Anja, twenty-six, from Germany, interview with author, Dahab, September 2000 (before the Euro was introduced).

31. Anja, as above.

32. Katrin, as above.

33. Karen, as above.

34. Sylvia, thirty-seven, from Germany, interview with author, Dahab, September 2000.

35. Karen, as above.

36. Karen, as above.

37. Lena, as above.

38. Heike, as above.

7

Re-inventing the "Square": Postcolonial Geographies and Tourist Narratives in Jamaa el Fna, Marrakech

Claudio Minca

It is the storytellers who have the biggest following. It is around them that the crowd is the thickest, most curious. Their performances last a while: the spectators crouched on the ground before them form a first, attentive circle, showing no visible hurry to move on and let others take their place. Others, standing, form a second circle around them: these on-lookers too are practically immobile, hanging on the story-teller's every word and gesture. Sometimes, two men will take turns reciting the story. Their words come from afar; they remain suspended in the air longer than the words of mere mortals. . . . For me, these words proclaimed forcefully, with passion, were without meaning; for their owner they were precious, he was proud of his words. . . . The spectators were gripped in a feverish atmosphere; and even one such as myself, with my limited understanding, could feel the life pulsating in the minds of those who were listening.

As though in honour of their words, the story-tellers were dressed in flamboyant fashion. Their clothes clearly distinguished them from their spectators. They favoured, above all, rich fabrics. . . . They looked like dignitaries who had stepped out of a fairy tale. . . . Naturally, the story-teller had noticed me, but within his magical circle I was simply a stranger, since I could not understand him.

. . . At the same time, I was glad not to be able to understand. They remained for me an enclave of an older, intact life. . . . Words were their nourishment and no one could induce them to trade that nourishment for another recompense.

. . . Just a few steps away from the story-tellers sat the scribes. Their place was a place of great peace, the most peaceful corner of the Jamaa al Fna. . . . They were almost invisible, only one thing mattered here: the silent dignity of the parchment.

—Elias Canetti, *Le voci di Marrakech*
(1989, 93–126, translation by the author)

Jamaa al Fna is a perfect distillate of exotic orientalism. It is the sum total of all the characteristics attributed to Morocco in the European imaginary. Jamaa al Fna is the "magical square" that "seduces" Westerners—symbolic of the "perpetual seduction" of Marrakech as a whole (to cite *Condè Nast Traveller* magazine).

In 1997, Spanish writer Juan Guytisolo forwarded a proposal to UNESCO to include the Jamaa al Fna in the list of world heritage sites. The square and its performers, Guytisolo argued, should be preserved above all as symbolic of a *universal oral heritage*. The very possibility of preserving an *oral* heritage—in particular, through its association with a specific place—is certainly debatable. It is not my goal here to address this question that nevertheless merits discussion. What I would like to remark, however, is how the very ideal of the preservation of "traditional cultures" is indelibly tied to the modern colonial project (Mitchell 2000a; 2000b). Postcolonial critiques articulated in recent years have, indeed, attempted to question this vision, highlighting the relations of power between colonizer and colonized implicit within the ideal of heritage. Patricia Morton (2000, 93), for one, has noted the ways in which "the fossilization of indigenous civilization into 'unchanging' and 'timeless' cultures and societies" was a fundamental part of "the process of inventing traditions under colonization." In the pages that follow, I attempt to demonstrate how the present-day tourist fascination for the Jamaa el Fna continues to be informed by colonial readings that first "recognized" this place as a square and as the symbol of a "Moroccan essence" to be valorized and preserved at all costs.

The so-called discovery of Jamaa el Fna and its first codification as a cultural heritage site can be traced back to the years of the French Protectorate and, in particular, to the efforts of then-Governor General, Maréchal Hubert Lyautey. Within this chapter, I try to show how the narratives that inscribe and shape the square today (both those articulated by the Moroccan authorities, as well as those of the tourists), are marked by Lyautey's colonial vision. Tourist narratives on the Jamaa el Fna are, increasingly, a vital factor in the symbolic definition of the square, but also within the construction of a Moroccan national identity where the imaginary of the square plays a crucial role. In my analysis, I look to the role of the colonial legacy in contemporary tourist and cultural interpretations of this unique place, noting how the Jamaa el Fna has progressively become a hybrid and ambivalent context, despite official and unofficial attempts to represent it as *the pure essence of Moroccan heritage*, to be preserved and frozen in a museumlike framework.

Much has been written about the ways in which the revalorization and spectacularization of urban landscapes is not only an economic but also a cultural and identitary project, which can play a fundamental role in the redefinition of local—as well as national—identities (see, among many others, Atkinson and Cosgrove 1998; Edensor 1998; Graham, Ashworth and Tunbridge 2000; Jacobs 1996; Johnson 1995). The multiple meanings that come together on the Jamaa el Fna today have given life to a genuinely postcolonial place, where diverse (and seemingly contradictory) performances and identitary strategies intersect, initiating processes of hybridization between the various subjects that create this square-event in practice. Here, in the most "Moroccan" of tourist places, traces of the colonial project are interwoven with tourist performances and ever-new local reinterpretations of the very concepts of "heritage" and "cultural identity."

LYAUTEY'S VISION AND THE ASSOCIATION THEORY

> That of which I dream, that of which many among you dream with me, is that *amid much disorder which disturbs the world* . . . there should begin to develop steadily in Morocco a strong edifice, ordered and harmonious, which could offer to the world the spectacle of a congregation of humanity where men, so unlike in origins, dress, occupations, and race, continue, without advocating any of their individual conceptions, their search for a common ideal, a common reason to live. Yes, I would dream that *Morocco appeared as one of the most solid bastions of order* against the mounting tides of anarchy.
>
> —Lyautey (1927, in Abu-Lughod 1980, 142, italics added)

According to Paul Rabinow (1989), French rule in Morocco was, among many other things, also an attempt to realize a laboratory for social modernity. The creation of the Protectorate in 1912 did not, indeed, merely mark the informal incorporation of Morocco into the French colonial empire; it was also the start of a grandiose experiment in social engineering. It is in Morocco that the techniques and sociocultural categories elaborated in the Metropole would first be put into practice, in the attempt to realize in these territories the project of social pacification that was finding so many obstacles in France.

The experiment centered around three key concepts: the ideal of the "*association,*" that of the "dual city," and that of the "valorization and respect" of the political system and cultural traditions of the "protected" country. Indeed, the legitimacy of the Protectorate was based within the application of these three concepts and I analyze each of them in detail in the pages to follow. It is also important to note, however, that even present-day tourist readings of Moroccan cultural space continue to be marked by the legacy of the Protectorate and its ideals, while the focus of the tourist economy on the country's "heritage" can also be traced back to the strategies of the French colonial administration.

To fully understand the influence of the Protectorate on Marrakech and its most famous square, it is useful to say something more about the creator and chief protagonist of these strategies: Maréchal Lyautey (see, among others, Hoisington 1995; Le Révérend 1983; Maurois 1931; Pennell 2000; Rivet 1988; Scham 1970; Usborne 1936; Venier 1997). Lyautey was strongly influenced by a group of French intellectuals gathered in those years around the Musée Social. Drawing on the theorizations of these thinkers, the Maréchal believed that in the colonial context an inverse ratio existed between the welfare of a society and its dependency on overt forces of order. Order achieved by force was, indeed, less desirable and more costly than a "well-tempered social regulation," a vision that Lyautey would promote in many of his speeches. This ideal of "*pacification*" had strongly influenced his previous colonial experiences in Indochina and Madagascar, bound to an attempt to identify the "scientific" and cultural bases of a "durable and harmonious social order." In Lyautey's vision, colonized peoples were to be incorporated not by force but, rather, by assuring their full adhesion to the civilizing mission of "*la plus grande France*" (for a fuller discussion, see Rabinow 1989).

In her book *Hybrid Modernities*, Patricia Morton (2000, 188) recalls how Albert Sarraut, a prominent advocate of the *association* principle and former minister of the colonies, summarized the relation of the colonies to France as that of pupils to their teacher:

> Instead of adapting all our proteges by force to the conditions of the Metropole, according to the old assimilationist error, it must be understood that, under our tutelage, their evolution should be pursued in keeping with their civilization, their traditions, their milieu, their social life, their secular institutions.

It was in these very years, too, that the principle of *assimilation* that had guided French colonial politics thus far was being seriously questioned. Problematic, above all, was its inherent contradiction: France justified its presumed superiority over the colonized cultures by appeal to a set of universal values that guided its *mission civilisatrice*—a set of democratic and egalitarian values that were to bring progress and justice to the peoples under its rule. Yet once colonial subjects achieved these ideals, France's mission would have exhausted its declared aims—thus depriving the colonial project of its legitimizing rhetoric. New justifications for French colonial rule would therefore have to be formulated. As Morton (2000, 204) and others have noted, in the "late colonial order," the claim to authority made by the colonizers was dependent on the relative superiority of metropolitan culture rather than the innate right of Europeans to colonise other peoples. The change in French policy from *assimilation* (the prerogative of colonisers to colonise based on their absolute superiority) to *association* (predicated on the contingent, if definitive, superiority of colonisers) clearly delineated this shift from innate right to relative order. Preservation of this order of things was based on visual classification of the colonial landscape, etiquette, body language, architecture, clothing, and other outward signs of authority.

In response to the new theories of race and evolution elaborated in those years and conditioned by the negative results of assimilationist policy in the colonies, the French elites embraced the new "native" policy of *association*. This policy was to be grounded in a strict physical, political, and cultural segregation of natives from the French population: the ideal of the *association* was predicated, indeed, on the precise and subtle differentiation and division of peoples, societies, and cultures into race-based hierarchies. As Morton (2000, 7) notes, "the colonised peoples had to be proved barbarous to justify their colonisation, but the *mission civilisatrice* required that they be raised above this savagery. If the colonised peoples acquired too much civilization and became truly assimilated to France, colonisation could no longer be defended, having fulfilled its mission." They would also cease to be exotic objects of interest—a theme to which I return in subsequent paragraphs.

The principles of the French colonial doctrine of *association* were to be most fully enacted by the Moroccan Protectorate, under Maréchal Lyautey's vigilant guidance. Lyautey believed that by preserving local ways of life, *association* could sponsor the renewal of indigenous culture and the creation of a modern, prosperous colonial state. His so-called *politique indigène* left existing Moroccan cities intact and built new European cities alongside; retained the traditional Moroccan government, although under indirect French control; and encouraged indigenous arts and crafts through schools and workshops set up by the French. According to Harmand, one of the key theorists of the *association* principle, colonial policies were to allow "indigenous peoples" to "evolve in autonomous fashion" by "keeping everyone in his proper place, appropriate to his role in society." "Native" traditions and habits were thus to be influenced light-handedly, "sufficiently" to assure the maintenance of social order (see the discussion in Hoisington 1995).

Janet Abu-Lughod, in her critical analysis of the creation of the Protectorate, suggests that the French authorities favored such policies for two associated sets of strategic reasons. On the one hand, the French felt it necessary to maintain the fiction of Moroccan sovereignty to "facilitate control over the 'natives' by endowing 'French will' with religious legitimacy, since the Sultan's descent assured respect" (Abu-Lughod 1980, 137). On the other, however, this fiction was also highly functional in two other arenas: first, in inscribing the contest between the Resident General and the French government in the Metropole, and second, in justifying the French position vis-à-vis the other European powers. The colonial policies were thus elaborated with an eye toward a plural set of referents, both at home as well as "abroad" (Hoisington 1995).

What I would like to focus on, however, is the theoretical-scientific framework that sustained the principle of *association*—and its accordant elaboration of an entirely new colonial strategy based on a renovated vision of the Other. This strategy found its most striking application in the "dual city system" and in the new cultural policies regarding the preservation and the regulation of Moroccan heritage. The present-day shape and meaning of the Jamaa el Fna, as we see in the paragraphs that follow, pay a high price to the legacy of this vision.

YES, IN MOROCCO, WE CONSERVE

> Yes, in Morocco, and it is to our honour, we conserve. I would go a step further, we rescue. We wish to conserve in Morocco Beauty—and it is not a negligible thing. Beauty—as well as everything which is respectable and solid in the institutions of the country . . . all of your researchers conserve and save, whether it be a question of antiquities, fine arts, folklore, history, or linguistics. We found here the vestiges of an admirable civilization, of a great past. You are restoring its foundations.
>
> —Lyautey (1927, in Abu-Lughod 1980, 142)

Lyautey's urban politics was based, above all, upon the ideal of the "dual city": that is, upon the assumption that social *pacification* and the respect of the cultural differences between Europeans and Moroccans was best assured by a *doubling* of the city into a *ville nouvelle* and the *medina*. Lyautey's urban planning visions were strongly influenced by debates raging in France in those years surrounding the application of scientific principles of social analysis to the management of French colonial possessions and, above all, their utility in assuring a peaceful integration of the colonizers and colonized. The key concern in such debates was the ideal of *order*: the use of scientific principles to construct a determinate social order able to assure social harmony. Such an "ordered" society, it was believed, could be assured through specific spatial strategies and the construction of an appropriate physical and social milieu.

Henri Prost, the chief architect called by Lyautey to Morocco to plan the new cities, was a firm believer in this vision. In his official declarations, he sustained that urbanism was a "visual art which directs itself to our senses; a beautiful city which we love is one where the edifices have a noble beauty, the promenades are agreeable, and where our everyday life is surrounded by an agreeable décor producing in us a sentiment of profound harmony" (Rabinow 1989, 235–36). He argued that the modern urbanist had to understand that the wishes and needs of the people who were to live in the newly reconstructed cities counted more than "pure conceptions of the future which despised the population's attachment to the past." There was one catch in this reasoning, however. As Abu-Lughod (1980, 175) points out, "in Morocco the French could not claim, as they had in Algeria and Tunisia, that indigenous urban centres lacked a system of municipal governance and administration." The Protectorate, in fact, found itself in the presence of large urban agglomerations with no "proper" municipal life to speak of, but with a long tradition of local administration of which they were proud. Prost's plans, therefore, had to contend with this legacy, and indeed one of the centerpieces of the architect's conception of city and regional planning in Morocco was to become the juxtaposition of old and new within the Protectorate's cities.

The "dual city" ideal had three key foci: the preservation and protection of the "traditional" Moroccan areas; the creation of a greenbelt around these "native reservations" (as they are defined by Abu-Lughod 1980); and the design and construction *ex nihilo* of an efficient and elegant *ville nouvelle* conceived for the resident European population. The philosophy of the dual city system was also based, however, on a fundamental cultural assumption: that is, that "European" cities in Morocco should be built "close enough for contact, but not so close to absorb the native city. Deciding how this should be accomplished required the art of the urbanist, who was called upon to integrate adroitly local social realities" (Rabinow 1989, 294).

The Moroccan dual city was thus born of a complex set of understandings regarding the meaning—and proper place—of local/indigenous culture. It was an entirely novel way of looking at the "Other," couched in an apparent attempt to understand (and thus "respect") the differences between the diverse urban contexts. As Patricia Morton (2000, 147) suggests, this "respect" was fully part of the rhetoric of French urbanists: the practice of constructing new European districts outside—and separate from—traditional cities was justified by the argument for the preservation of "native cities" as "the sites of cultures, that, although inferior to European culture, should be respected."

The search for an understanding of "native" history and culture would form the focus of a number of European intellectual circles of the period. The colonies were also seen, however, as the ideal site for the implementation of social and urban planning. Robert de Souza, one of the members of the aforementioned Parisian Musée Social, asserted that it was in "the colonial lands especially, the very old and the very new, outside of all civilization, or in conflict with our own by reason of its overly archaic and inassimilable civilization" that "the solution [could be identified] that will satisfy both modern, progress and the picturesque" (de Souza 1913, cited in Rabinow 1989, 273). This assemblage of the "picturesque," "progress," and "civilization" as the constituent elements of modernity was characteristic of such Beaux-Arts reformers of the period.

It is interesting to note, however, how this interpretation of the cultural and historical condition of "non-European peoples" would also influence tourist imaginaries in the decades to follow. Indeed, the perspectives elaborated by de Souza and others at the beginning of this century continue to inform even the visions of present-day amateur "explorers" of Moroccan medinas. The connection is not at all remote; already Maréchal Lyautey understood the importance of "cultural heritage" for the development of tourism:

> Nothing has been more deadly to the originality and the charm of Algerian cities, of so many oriental cities, than their penetration by modern European installations. . . . The preservation of the native towns is not only a question of aesthetic satisfaction . . . but a duty of the state. Since the development . . . of tourism on a large scale, the preservation of the beauty of the country has taken on an economic interest of the first order. (Lyautey 1927, in Abu-Lughod 1980, 143)

The effects of this strategy continued to be evident many years after the end of the Protectorate—and are still, to some extent, visible in today's tourist narratives marking out "authentic" Moroccan cultures and landscapes. Writing in his influential *Reflections on Fieldwork in Morocco*, Paul Rabinow noted how even as late as 1977, cities like Fez and Sefrou still had no automobiles in the medina, giving the impression of two civilizations living side by side although epochs apart (Rabinow 1977, 21). What I attempt to demonstrate in my analysis of the Jamaa el Fna, however, is that the idealized "pure" Moroccan space imagined within the dual city structure was never fully accomplished—not during the colonial period (as Janet Abu-Lughod [1980] has forcefully argued), and certainly even less so today, despite the attempts of the tourist industry to trace its confines. The order imagined by Lyautey was never accomplished; it did provide, nonetheless, a formidable rhetorical tool that allowed for the mobilization of powerful processes of *social ordering*.

Lyautey's philosophical considerations regarding the value of preservation (cited above) became, indeed, the accepted guidelines for the management of a now-universal historical patrimony. Timothy Mitchell's account (1988, 163) of the visit of a group of French "experts" to Cairo in this very same period notes the discussion that developed between the participants of the outing surrounding the aesthetic of the city's modern quarters—and their relation to the older parts of the city. One of the invited guests was writer André Maurois. Maurois was especially struck by the insistence with which it was asserted that "there could not be reorganisation of the older part, and if anything were to be rebuilt there, they said, it must be Oriental" (1931, 252–53, in Mitchell 1988). Thus, although the new order appeared at first sight to exclude the Arab town, in a broader sense, it included it. Colonialism, as Mitchell (1988, 163) stresses, did not ignore *any* part of the city; rather, it divided the city in two—"one part becoming an exhibition and the other, in the same spirit, a museum." Indeed, (as Janet Abu-Lughod [1980] points out), the administrative body responsible for keeping the Europeans out of the medinas was the *Service des Beaux Arts*, whose ostensible charge was to preserve the architectural and historic heritage of the country.

The representation of the "natives" within the logic of the exhibition was a typical expression of colonial modernity (Mitchell 2000a; 2000b): an attempt to conceal the contradictions inherent in a vision that advocated a progressive ideology in domestic affairs while relying on imperialist expansion in its geopolitical strategies. The urban experiment undertaken in Morocco was its perfect embodiment, a direct heir to the colonial exhibitions promoted by the French state in those very years. The most famous of these "Expositions Coloniales," which took place in Paris in 1931, was organized by none other than Lyautey himself. The rhetoric of the "world-as-exhibition" (Mitchell 1988) promoted in these events was fundamental in reconciling the contradictions of colonial geopolitics and the modern state. Lyautey's project was, in many ways, above all an attempt to overcome the ambivalence of modernity's fascination for alterity, the search for ways in which "other" cultures could be adopted as a "background" against which European and French identity could be defined. In the Moroccan "traditional culture" for which he cared so much, Lyautey found that sense of "wholeness" that he considered missing in European modernity. The Maréchal was faced with a fundamental "theoretical" problem in creating and managing the Protectorate, however. How could the colony and colonization be "accurately" (i.e., scientifically) understood (and thus managed) without recourse to the suspect and often carnivalesque images that had circumscribed past relationships between the Orient and Occident? Or, as Patricia Morton (2000, 4) aptly describes, "how to avoid exoticism and inauthenticity and still refer to the plethora of images created by colonialism, through which most Westerners understood the rest of the world?" This, in many ways, is still the dilemma faced by tourist operators and authorities in Morocco today. Timothy Mitchell (1988) has argued forcefully that modern colonial strategies of conquest and incorporation of the "Other" relied on the adoption of what he terms the "metaphysics of representation": a binary vision framing not only all relations between "us" and "the Other" but also those between representation and the object represented (Minca 2001). The dilemmas of Lyautey's strategies of *association* could thus only be resolved within a "proper" management of an "authentic" system of representations.

Both Patricia Morton (2000) as well as Paul Rabinow (1989) have written extensively on the ways in which the preservation of "native cultures" within colonial exhibitions formed part of a much broader vision based within an interesting compromise between the "scientificity" of the representations within which "other cultures" were circumscribed according to determinate rules, and a fascination for the exoticism that only direct contact with the "real" representatives of these same cultures could guarantee. The scientific rigor of colonial exhibitions was assured by recourse to models elaborated within the natural history museums and ethnographic collections of the period, such as those developed by Paul Rivet and Georges-Henri Riviere at the Trocadero Museum. Rivet and Riviere approached museology through a contextualization of objects based on extensive ethnographic documentation. In their vision, the museum's scientific role consisted of "promoting technical and sociological studies of objects and peoples cast broadly within a Maussian *fait total* perspective in which each object was illuminated by—and metonymic of—a whole society. Each society was juxtaposed with neighbouring regions and areas; the sum of these represented the whole world" (Rabinow 1989, 353).

This theoretical perspective would also be applied in the management of the colonies—and their peoples. According to this logic, the colonial exhibitions of different "cultural wholes" (just like tourist images today) were based upon a theoretical—and thus spatial and practical—separation between the colonizer and the colonized. The *Expositions* also highlighted a contrast between the colonies as "the Orient"—the site of rampant sensuality, irrationality, and decadence—and the colonies as the laboratories of Western rationality.

This conceptual shift, as Morton (2000) suggests, was achieved through a process of scientific "certification" of the authenticity of specific images, contrasted with the carnivalesque tenor of other, more "metaphysical" and exotic ones. This distinction between the image and the "thing itself" was most forcibly enforced through the use of real persons within the exhibition, depicted engaging in their daily tasks and representing, in a sense, themselves:

> The most efficacious means for reinforcing the apparent authenticity of the pavilions was the native, engaged in his or her "primitive" crafts, rituals and performances. Natives inhabited the pavilions and performed daily activities, expurgated of European habits, clothing, and technology; as if they were in fact occupying authentic reproductions of indigenous buildings in a precolonial pastoral. (Morton 2000, 207)

Such a display of people was, of course, also a display of power. The exhibition of "natives" within the *Exposition* was also a symbolic performance marking relationships of power between exhibitor and exhibited. What is important to note, moreover, was that the relationships displayed also presented a fictitious unity of "colonial peoples," within which persons differing vastly in cultural traditions and aspirations were made to appear as one within the colonial project.

Although the French colonial project was in many ways contradictory in its political as well as cultural intents (as I have tried to suggest, above), this in no way hampered its efficacy in fundamentally transforming Moroccan cities within the space of a few years—as well as in assuring the loyalty of some key colonial subjects. The exhibitions organized by Lyautey in Morocco during those years enjoyed, indeed, the support of a large part of the Moroccan elite as well.

The present day valorization of the cultural heritage of the Jamaa el Fna cannot be divorced from this legacy, albeit its discourses and strategies may differ significantly from similar colonial attempts. Moroccan culture and the places selected to represent it must still be "preserved" according to the perverse logic of the museum. In the tourist imaginary, Moroccan culture becomes an object, a whole to be narrated, interpreted, and essentialized within a set of performances and places. Certainly, tourists' awareness of the "artificiality" of such performances might disrupt the supposed "purity" of the representations. Yet the game continues nonetheless, with the willing participation of both "spectators" and "actors." The places of these performances become the key nodes of these strategies, but also the places within which such performances create ever-changing postcolonial geographies, open to hybridization and to continual disruption of the presumed order.

It is within these encounters that we can identify the ideologies driving the preservation of cultural and archaeological heritage (including even the preservation of a supposed "oral heritage," as in the case of the Jamaa el Fna) by a cadre of "international experts" and organizations. The assumption driving such attempts is a simple one: the present-day inhabitants ("natives") of the places that contain such priceless testimonies of past civilizations are not able—for economic, political, or "cultural" reasons—to guarantee the proper preservation and valorization of the treasures of their ancestors. They must, therefore, be taught how to do it—or, better yet, they must be stripped of their exclusive claim to these vestiges, by rendering their inheritance part of a "universal cultural heritage" (McAlister 2001, 125–54). This loss of sovereignty is legitimized and decreed through the "adoption" of the place by an international agency, such as UNESCO, and through its "sacralization" within the tourist imaginary. Such expropriation, carried out in the name of a higher "common interest," reaches also the culture of the present, as in the case of the Jamaa el Fna, aiming to "protect" its oral heritage from . . . the Moroccans themselves.

Such strategies are the fruit of a exquisitely modern compromise between the need to classify all cultures within grand universal schemes and the concurrent search for difference, as well as the equally pressing need to mark the potential dangers posed by contamination (between peoples, cultures, etc.) and ambivalence. The battle waged against vendors hawking plastic toys or cheap souvenirs within "traditional places" is but one expression of such spatial strategies of "purification." The cartographic logic that guides the tourist narratives on the Jamaa el Fna is another.

RE-ORIENTING MARRAKECH:
THE COLONIAL GAZE OVER THE JAMAA EL FNA

> When you walk through a town like this—two hundred thousand inhabitants, of whom at least twenty thousand own literally nothing except the rags they stand up in—when you see how the people live, and still more, how easily they die, it is always difficult to believe that you are walking among human beings. All colonial empires are in reality founded upon that fact. The people have brown faces—besides they have so many of them! Are they really the same flesh as yourself? Do they even have names? Or are they merely a kind of undifferentiated brown stuff, about as individual as bees or coral insects? They rise out of the earth, they sweat and starve for a few years, and then they sink back into the nameless mounds of the graveyard and nobody notices that they are gone.
>
> —Orwell (1954, 187, cited in Said 1978, 265)

The Jamaa el Fna is, in many ways, Lyautey's invention. As part of his project for the "inscription of local cultures," the Maréchal commissioned a systematic study of Moroccan history, relying upon "Western" historiography and methods (on this topic, also see Laroui 1995). This study was to allow the French administration to map and codify a series of key sites whose historical significance was "revealed" by the research undertaken. Jamaa el Fna was one of these places—its significance rediscovered within the new criteria of that whole which we could here define as "Moroccanness."

Before the establishment of the Protectorate, there were no clear borders binding the space of the Jamaa el Fna. It was simply an empty expanse lying at the heart of Marrakech. It was Lyautey who first decided to measure the perimeter of this space and to map its confines. Thus inscribed, Jamaa el Fna became a "square" and also a piece of Moroccan heritage—chosen by the Maréchal as a representative site of Moroccan heritage and culture, and therefore a place to protect and preserve.

Prior to Lyautey's "discovery" of the square and his fascination for its "liveliness," no one (excluding some European travelers) had ever considered that segment of urban space as a singular place to be protected and preserved within a determinate shape and form. It is interesting to note, indeed, the almost total lack of references to the square within modern Arab-language Moroccan literature (where the Jamaa el Fna, if mentioned, is described exclusively with negative connotations). It is European and French-language Moroccan writers who began to grant increasing importance to the Jamaa el Fna in their narratives (Minca and Borghi, forthcoming), creating the myth of the "magic" of the square that is by now a commonplace in all tourist brochures.

It should be stressed that the Jamaa el Fna today is considered by Moroccan authorities—as well as by countless preservation associations that have mushroomed in recent years around it—a central part of the national historical and cultural heritage. The rhetoric that inscribes it draws fundamental inspiration from Lyautey's vision: the square is codified, above all, through its oral tradition that so fascinated the Maréchal. This tradition—seen as the manifestation of a "deeper" underlying "cultural essence"—is to be preserved and protected from every contamination, a pure cultural expression to be saved from "modernity." Within such strategies, the "world-as-exhibition" vision is alive and well—with all its inherent contradictions.

On 21 July 1921, Lyautey signed an *arrete viziriel*, calling for a survey that would allow for the classification of a delimited space corresponding to the perimeter of the Jamaa el Fna. Exactly a year afterward, a series of decrees were promulgated in response to the planning survey commissioned (Borghi 2002). The decrees ordained that:

1. The "center" of the square (identified as such by the survey) would be exempt from further construction.
2. The facades of the buildings surrounding the square could not, from that moment on, be modified in any way without the prior authorization of the competent authorities (the office of the *Beaux-Arts*).
3. Only "natives" could own or rent buildings comprised within the determined perimeter. (translation by the author)

Subsequently, another *arrete viziriel* was signed in order to assure the protection of the entire city of Marrakech's artistic and cultural heritage. This document quite clearly reflects Lyautey's urban vision—as well as his conception of heritage preservation. The opening lines of the decree confirm that the purpose of the new regulations was to "prevent European constructions from compromising the picturesque character of urban quarters inhabited by the indigenous population." The text embodies, indeed, all the principles implicit in the urban ideals of the *association*: the "dual city," conservation, and a spatial order based upon a clear segregation of Europeans and natives. In his attempt to "preserve" Marrakech, Lyautey mapped out not only the places that, to his mind, required a special "regime of protection," but also specified the "proper" characteristics of single buildings and of the activities assigned to specific zones. Each function, each person, each culture would be collocated in the "right place," as in the colonial exhibitions that the Maréchal had directed:

> These laws will serve to maintain the city of Marrakech in *its original state*, obliging the inhabitants not to restore their houses or build new ones if not within the specific guidelines established; guidelines that will respect the harmony and décor of this entire urban agglomeration. (Article 1, translation by the author, italics added)

The above lines express Lyautey's preoccupation with the preservation of the medina and, especially, with the conservation of the "harmony" of the Arab part of the city, a harmony that, in the author's Orientalist view, was intrinsic to Arab culture and its urban expressions. The document follows up with another interesting observation:

> [these preservation edicts] will also assure that the medina reaps the benefits of tourism, as people flock to observe the wonders for which it is universally admired. (translation by the author)

As we can see, the tourist gaze (see Urry 2002b) was already then implicit within the reflections on the value of heritage and universal recognition and patronage.

The arrival of the French and the early years of the Protectorate fundamentally transformed Marrakech and the Jamaa el Fna—paradoxically enough, precisely in the name of the preservation of the past (Minca and Borghi, forthcoming). While on the northern and eastern sides of the square the buildings housing cafés, restaurants, and a variety of artisans were left intact, the southern side of the Jamaa el Fna was entirely reconstructed in order to open up a series of new access ways toward the Koutoubia mosque (the symbol of Marrakech) and the new quarters of Guéliz, Marrakech's *ville nouvelle* (Borghi 2002). The square was transformed into the nodal point of the city's transport network: the place where the "new world" and the "traditional

Figure 7.1   French Café with Terrace That Dominates the Square

city" met (all proclamations regarding the "preservation of its authentic land-scape" to the contrary). Piece by piece, new shops and cafés replaced the old walls in *pisé* that once formed the only façade of the square. The new buildings gradually grew in height, in order to offer even better views unto the square to the clients of their roof-top cafés (Wilbaux 2000).

Jamaa al Fna thus became the "meeting point," the "buffer zone" between the two cities that make up Marrakech today: between Guéliz and all the *extra-muros* extensions of the old city, and the *ancienne medina* (Berdai 2000, see also Borghi 2002). It became a space of mediation but also a symbolic and functional border between the "modern" city structured around wide avenues conceived for automobile traffic, and the "traditional" city made up of intricate passageways designed for pedestrians and animals but certainly not for motorized vehicles. The Jamaa el Fna is also, however, an important node *within* the medina. It is here that all the roads leading to the medina's principal *souq* converge. The square lies, indeed, at the crossroads of two economic "worlds." To the north is the medina and its markets, a sphere of "informal" traffics and activities; on the southern extremity of the square, on the other hand, are positioned the formal colonial edifices of the city Post Office, the Banque al Maghrib, the Police Headquarters, and the offices of the *Arrondissement*.

But the Jamaa el Fna is also a space of spectacle: the stage *par excellence* for the materialization and exhibition of Moroccan culture. It is a spectacle

Figure 7.2   *La Poste*: An Example of Colonial Architecture in Jamaa el Fna

that captures visitors to this day, creating ever-new interactions between the star-struck observers and the "actors" *en scene* that try to draw them into this itinerant carnival. The numerous *halqa* that compete for the attention of passersby offer everything: from storytelling to magic potions and advice on sexual problems, henne designs and fortune-telling, the performances of acrobats, fire-eaters, and snake-charmers. In the language of the tourist brochures that describe it, the Jamaa el Fna is also "the place where modernity and tradition meet." It is a place of lights and sound that fills up each evening with steaming carts offering hundreds of enticing dishes; it is the entrance into an urban labyrinth that evokes all those images, smells, and sounds that the colonial rhetoric has taught us to seek out in every medina and every *souq*. The square thus becomes the very representation of the "essence" of Morocco. But it is also a liminal space, framed by uncertain confines and characterized by an ever-changing spectacle. It is an exhibition, a spectacle that gives rise to ever-new hybridizations of meaning—and a fascinating set of performances that I will attempt to comment on in the paragraphs to follow.

POSTCOLONIAL VISIONS AND TOURIST NARRATIVES

Eternal as the snow of the tallest peaks, imposing as the mountains of the Atlas, rooted in the past as the palms of its red earth, Marrakech is the crowning jewel of a picture of ever-lasting beauty.

Figure 7.3   Young Tourist Being Entertained by Snake Charmers

Contended by the greatest of kings and home to countless noble families. For centuries, sages, artisans, architects, painters and sculptors have flocked here to build its princely palaces, mosques, gardens and *medersa* . . .

Marrakech: the imperial city that gave Morocco its name.

Berbers and Arabs come together within its walls, nomads and mountain dwellers converge in its markets, artisans flourish: it is the paradise of all trades.

For its thousands of riches accumulated over a thousand years, for the delight of your senses, don't miss Marrakech.

—Promotional brochure of the
Moroccan Tourist Office (translated by the author)

Marrakech is, by far, the most important tourist destination in Morocco, with over one-quarter of all national arrivals. With the increasing importance granted tourism as a key economic resource, the importance of Marrakech is sure to grow as well. Marrakech is not only, however, a key reference point for international tourism. A growing number of Moroccans themselves are also choosing the city as a vacation destination, encouraged by a growing campaign to transform Marrakech into the symbolic site of national identity. The city is, above all, however, the chosen destination of those seeking out an "authentic" experience of Moroccan culture and heritage (promoted by the countless European package tours that "do" the "Imperial Cities"). Jamaa el Fna lies at the heart of this search; it is the stage upon which Lyautey's colonial politics have been transformed into a postcolonial reinterpretation of culture, identity, and heritage by both tourist operators as well as the Moroccan authorities.

Today's tourists on the Jamaa el Fna follow the lines laid down by the Orientalist aesthetic that first codified the preservation of the square's "cultural heritage." Edward Said, writing on the attitudes of the first Orientalists toward their "research subjects," notes that:

> Since it was commonly believed that the whole Orient hung together in some profoundly organic way, it made perfectly good hermeneutical sense for the Orientalist scholar to regard the material evidence he dealt with as ultimately leading to a better understanding of such things as the Oriental character, mind, ethos, of world-spirit. (Said 1978, 254)

It is this very same "Oriental character" that many tourists seek out on the "stage" of the square and within the *souq* that surround it. It is a "character" that is timeless and unchanging, according to the numerous glossy tourist publications dedicated to the square. The excerpt below comes from the Italian edition of the *Condé Nast Traveller*:

> [the Jamaa el Fna] is the wildest stage in Morocco. Snake charmers enticing arching cobras, an endless spectacle of street artists. Acrobats, dancers and medicine men that everyday pull in hundreds of curious passersby, fascinated by these spectacles that *have remained unchanged for centuries*. (Ducci 2000, 109, translation by the author, italics added)

The promise that entices potential visitors, then, is the hope of taking part in an event that has been repeating itself for centuries. Spectacle and spontaneity—yet bound within a timeless tradition: a contradictory vision, perhaps, but one that perfectly reflects the Orientalist tradition I describe in the preceding sections. What is more, however, the present-day tourist narratives on the Jamaa el Fna replicate another aspect of the Orientalist view highlighted by Said (1978): the strong individualism of the "explorers" of the Orient and the equally strong identification with the "object of discovery," often expressed in almost "missionary" zeal. For the latter-day explorers, the Orient was their direct experience of it. So, too, today's tourist-explorers are encouraged to "enter" the Orient through their experience of its "essence" in the spectacle of the Jamaa el Fna. Let me turn again to the above cited *Traveller*

Figure 7.4   Exploring the Square and Becoming Part of the Spectacle

magazine. The article on Marrakech features a brief citation from Elias Canetti as a prelude to the "promise" of the city:

> "I did not want to leave . . . I had already been here hundreds of years ago, but I had forgotten this place . . . " wrote Elias Canetti in his collection of essays entitled *Voci da Marrakech* in which he recounts his encounter with the city — still today the chosen destination of all those fleeing a mundane existence and seeking a simpler life. His words express in poetic fashion the love affair that has bound Western travellers to Marrakech from the 19th to the 21st centuries. (Ducci 2000, 109, translation by the author)

We could similarly turn to passages from the work of turn-of-the-century traveler Pierre Loti, or the images of Delacroix (Turco 1995) in order to analyze how the tourist experience of the Jamaa el Fna draws its roots within the visions and discourses of European Orientalists. *Traveller* again:

> Seductive, solar, enticing, sensual. Even better yet: magical. It is impossible to capture with just one adjective the atmosphere of Marrakech. . . . Marrakech

may be but one of Morocco's Imperial Cities, but it is here that the culture and
the traditions of the country find their most vivid expression. (Ducci 2000, 110,
translation by the author)

Morocco thus becomes something ephemeral, an idea, an "atmosphere," a
"category of the spirit." The Moroccans on the country's most renowned
square are actors in this grand spectacle of "universal heritage," while the
tourists are the fortunate spectators, witnesses to a magical event that could
disappear at any moment—and should thus be protected, preserved, and cat-
alogued (by UNESCO, for example).

Marrakech, the city of spectacle.
   Carts brimming with oranges and roasted wheat, women who have travelled
down from the Atlas to sell baskets, story-tellers, musicians, dancers, old scribes
shielded from the sun by black umbrellas, fortune-tellers, potion-sellers, healers,
spice merchants . . . everyone takes part in this daily spectacle.
   As the hour grows late, the acrobats move on to yield their place to the restau-
ranteurs. The kerosene lamps light up one by one. In the starry night, the moon
becomes just another of the infinite number of lanterns illuminating the Jamaa el
Fna. (Brochure of the National Moroccan Tourist Office, translation by the author)

The language of today's official narratives of the square—as well as the
perspective adopted—is not far from that of the colonial *Expositions* of some
seventy years ago. As Patricia Morton (2000, 91) notes, the *Exposition* "fixed
the colonies so that they could be understood as if they had remained unal-
tered by the changes created by colonisation and were frozen at a low level
of evolution. . . . Unlike the real colonies, the *Exposition* was populated by
docile, productive natives who lived in sanitized versions of indigenous
buildings and who practiced their "primitive" occupations for the delectation
of the visitors" (Morton 2000, 91). The "primitive" Moroccans who exhibit
themselves daily on the Jamaa el Fna in an immutable yet spontaneous "performance of Moroccanness" do so playing to tourists' continuing thirst for
exoticism and authenticity:

The governing word is show, which here gives us to understand that the Arabs
display themselves (willingly or unwillingly) to and for expert scrutiny. The
number of attributes ascribed to them, by its crowded set of sheer oppositions,
causes "the Arabs" to acquire a sort of existential weightlessness; thereby "the
Arabs" are made to rejoin the very broad designation, common to modern anthropological thought, of "the childish primitive." (Said 1978, 247)

It is important to note that the power of this system of representation
comes from the naturalization of the perspective described by Said. It is

Figure 7.5 "Alternative" European Traveler Interacting with "Traditional" Moroccan Women

also a perspective, however, that has been adopted by the Moroccan authorities, concerned with the preservation and valorization of the square, as well as by a large part of the "performers" themselves, perfectly aware of being objects-of-observation-that-represent-something-else, but also of the fact that the "heritage" that they embody with their presence and actions *needs them to believe in that very project.*

Over the past years, numerous associations have sprung up centered upon the protection of the square and its heritage. The most important of these is the *Association Place Jema' el Fna*. Its founder and president is, unsurprisingly, a European: the Spanish writer Juan Guytisolo. As I note at the outset of this piece, it was Guytisolo who, in 1997, proposed that the square be designated by UNESCO as part of a "universal oral heritage": the first time that the category of "oral heritage" enters into UNESCO's vocabulary. Guytisolo's action galvanized a lot of national attention as well. From that moment on, the square became the focus of a concerted campaign to mark not only its symbolic role for the country, but also to signify its place in the affirmation of Moroccan national identity (which, according to dominant interpretations, has its roots precisely in Marrakech, seen as the birthplace of the history and culture of Morocco):

> No one can deny today that this square, upon whose future we are called to reflect, is not only a place where countless foreign and domestic tourists converge. It is also a place of memory and of the legacy of a universal heritage that, *by definition*, must be preserved. (Minister for Tourism 2000, 2, translation by the author, italics added)

The tourist industry has been fast to jump on the bandwagon and in recent years has promoted this very image to the inhabitants of Morocco's more "Europeanized" cities, such as Casablanca or Rabat, enticing them to come and spend their vacations in Marrakech "re-discovering authentic Moroccan culture." Since 1998, the Marrakech Municipality in collaboration with the Ministry of Culture and the Cultural Delegation has organized an annual week-long festival in the city designed to promote to the internal tourist market the "variety of national cultural traditions" that risk "extinction" (Borghi 2002).

The Marrakech Municipality has also financed numerous studies of the medina and projects designed to protect and preserve the Jamaa el Fna from real estate speculation and the degeneration of its built environment. In February 2000, a meeting was organized in order to present the work of the urban planners and architects who had been working on the square's conservation plans. The encounter also included scholars of the Jamaa el Fna's folk culture and its oral traditions. The document that emerged from the conference reflected this dual focus, affirming that "the importance of the Jamaa el Fna is not *only architectural, but also cultural*. It is this latter that represents its most authentic manifestation" (Nabil and Abdelilah 2000, 1, translated by the author, italics added). Moreover, the document argued, local citizens should, at all costs, be "made aware of their heritage and culture," and to strive "to better understand this heritage, in order to save it and fully valorise it" (Touri 2000, 5, translation by the author). The document also recalled Lyautey's *arret viziriel* from 1921, noting the numerous violations of the law that had occurred over the decades that followed: a flagrant demonstration, it was argued, of the fact that the preservation of the "integrity" of this "exceptional heritage" had obviously not been a key priority of subsequent urban development plans:

> What has become evident over the past decades is that the law on the protection of heritage has not been respected as we had hoped. On the one hand, there was the absence of specific regulations for various parts of the national territory. On the other, an emphasis on other priorities had prevailed, quite understandably in many cases. We have been faced with poverty, demographic pressures, and the need for new real estate — what has been most deleterious, however, was the lack of an understanding of the importance of heritage. (Touri 2000, 5, translation by the author)

In recent years, there have in fact been numerous violations of the rules established by the *arret*: additional floors were added to several of the cafés, exceeding the established height limits; "traditional" wooden doors (prescribed by the edict) were substituted by metal ones; many stores now sport neon signs that violate all previously established norms and that, according to Touri (2000) and others, constitute a form of "visual pollution"; automobile traffic has increased to levels that render pedestrian movements in and around the square rather difficult and that threaten to severally impact the surrounding architecture with the effects of the growing clouds of exhaust (Borghi 2002).

The "threats" to the Jamaa el Fna are many, and public opinion has increasingly begun to support measures that will, in some way, "protect the square" and its cultural heritage. Alongside efforts to "sensibilize" the local population to the needs of preservation, such as the planned creation of a "museum of oral heritage" (Bilkasis 2000; see also Borghi 2002; Minca and Borghi forthcoming), the Marrakech Municipality has also championed new initiatives to stop illegal modifications to the buildings that ring the square and has attempted to limit car traffic in order to give more space to the *halqa* and artisans. It has also proclaimed that these latter would be favored over commercial activities, which should be strictly limited within and around the square (Borghi 2002). The municipality's actions speak to an explicit effort

Figure 7.6   Moroccan Tourists Experiencing "the Square"

aimed at codifying and regulating a place whose very complexity and unpredictability are what make it appealing. The contradictions of colonial modernity are thus still present within present-day efforts at the preservation of the square's—and Morocco's—cultural heritage.

In the tourist experience of the Jamaa el Fna, such contradictions are bridged within an ever-shifting dialectic between observation and participation, segregation and contamination. Tourist narratives materialize this contradiction within the idea(l) of "collection." Patricia Morton (2000, 11) has argued that "every collection creates its own time—through a temporal vision that edits history on the basis of predetermined criteria—and its space—the territory within which the collection is coherent and self-contained." The ordering of the square within tourist narratives proceeds through the evocation of a self-contained spatial and temporal condition, an epistemological "closed" space, where all these contractions are resolved and all its various fragments united.

Tourist narratives have, indeed, the power to enact two types of "translations." The first is the reduction of the individual observed to a stereotype: as Said (1978) has forcefully argued, the power of generalizations about the Orient has always derived from their efficacy in "rendering paradigmatic" every Oriental "thing." Every atom of the Orient was thus saturated with "oriental" attributes. Every inhabitant of the Orient was, above all, "oriental"—and only then a human being. Similarly, in the official tourist rhetoric, the protagonists of the daily spectacle on the Jamaa el Fna are presented, above all, as "typical traditional Moroccans"—and only then individuals with whom interaction may be possible. The panorama of the square as viewed from the rooftops of its cafés is, in this sense, ideal, canonizing a (post)colonial detachment and the transformation of life into object (of observation).

The second "translation" regards the heritage that these natives both represent and *perform* at the same time. Observing them as the representatives of an "Arab" and "Moroccan" essence, the tourist discourse conveniently naturalizes the ontological stance that positions the different subjects *en scene* and is based on a sort of transcendental distance between the tourist and the Moroccans *in place*, also thanks to the immediacy and naturalness with which the object of observation is codified within the logic of the "collection" (see Morton 2000 above). The performances and interactions in place are thus presented as "fully authentic" (insofar as experienced on the square), but also representable within photographs, reduced into text, cataloged. What is required of the natives is simply to "be themselves," to embody the Arab, the Moroccan, the witness of an "age-old heritage."

Once again, we are faced with the static stereotype of the Oriental—counterposed to the progress and rapid change of Western modernity. This elaborate albeit contradictory semantic architecture is possible, however, only within the self-referential spaces of the tourist experience. And yet the tourist experience, as the archetypal modern experience, needs to reach beyond these closed spaces; it needs to draw upon its "exterior," to reach out to the "real" Moroccans on the Jamaa el Fna—who, in turn, reinterpret themselves and turn *their* gaze upon the tourists. They watch aware of being watched, and in so doing challenge the very same separation between them and Orwell's "thousand others" that, with their presence, they should embody.

THERE IS A HOLE IN THE TOURIST "WHOLE"

To allow for first impressions, the *Guide Bleu* recommends that we climb to the terrace of one of the cafés at dusk, when the last rays of sun light up the urban landscape and make all its magnificence a feast for the eyes. . . .
All guides are wrong.
You cannot capture this spectacle in any way.

—Juan Goytisolo, *Makbara* (1982, 171–90,
in Minca and Borghi forthcoming, translation by the author)

Within the tourist discourse, the spaces of the Jamaa el Fna are reelaborated, captured, acquired. This discourse enacts a new colonization of the square and, inevitably, gives rise to new power dynamics between the diverse sub-jects that take part in the spectacle and spectacularization of the "Moroccan heritage." The Jamaa el Fna, Morocco, the Arab World, the Orient thus be-come an unordered archive of cultures, just as for the colonizers the colonies appeared "to form an unordered archive of history from primitive to advanced civilizations" (Morton 2000, 10). The tourist discourse grants the means to impose some sense of order on these worlds; an order within which each cul-ture and each people has *its proper place*. Cultural tourism thus becomes a discipline of the spirit, a way to frame Others and ourselves.

The Moroccans on the Jamaa el Fna are thus envisioned—and experienced—not only as real, living human beings, but also as monuments to the past. This double perspective encourages a sort of structured irony, very similar in its na-ture to the one attributed by Said (1978) to the Orientalist perspective. On the one hand, the performers are changing and complex social actors; on the other, as the subjects of observation and entertainment, they are "the Moroccans." The discrepancy between these two positionings is only reconcilable within the tourist "whole-world vision."

The modern fascination for the "ordered disorder" of exotic places reveals here the paradoxical nature of contemporary traveling. The order dreamed of by Lyautey is not that different from the order that guides contemporary tourists through/in the Jamaa el Fna: both rely on binary epistemologies and, therefore, on the clear (and unquestioned) separation between (observed) ob-jects and (observing and, presumably, authoritative) subjects. And yet this process of ordering is always incomplete; the need for order is never entirely satisfied—nor could it ever be. The search for ordered disorder inevitably be-comes entangled within the experience of place and within its inescapable paradoxes, within the "placed" (con)fusion between the objective and the subjective, within the ambivalence of positionings *in place*, within the game of presence and absence that makes *this* place so attractive (for the European eye), within the endless negotiations of its meanings.

It is precisely within this *negotiation in place* that the process of social or-dering occurs: producing, in the everyday, the subjectivities and the related positionings of the people involved. It is an ambivalent process, a process governed by paradox because *it takes place in place*, because it is the prod-uct of the contradictory experience of a square like Jamaa el Fna. It is, nonetheless, an empowering process that conjures diverse hierarchies and un-equal spaces of negotiation. It is also a process that may evolve in very dif-ferent directions from the binaries that are often adopted to represent it—and yet, at the same time, strongly influenced by the constraints imposed upon it by those very binaries, by an order that is always incomplete but, neverthe-less, endlessly in the making.

Figure 7.7   Performing in Jamaa el Fna

Figure 7.8   Tourists and "Locals" Negotiating the Square's Meanings by Gazing, Inter-acting, and Performing *in Place*

What can we surmise from the above considerations? In the preceding pages, I have tried to demonstrate the ways in which the management of the Jamaa el Fna and the interpretation of its role within both local and Moroccan national culture have been heavily influenced by the colonial legacy and, in particular, by the *association* policies of Maréchal Lyautey. Within the square today we can see the rhetoric of late French colonialism materialized: an urban order based upon a strict spatial separation of "natives" and Europeans, the conception of the "dual city," and the valorization of the colony's cultural and historical heritage. In many ways, the Jamaa el Fna is *still* the product of the Protectorate.

And yet, despite its capture within the tourist imaginary and the laws that attempt to regiment its actors and spaces, the square remains a liminal space, an unfinished project—not only because it forms a vital symbolic and functional node between the "two cities" of Marrakech, but also because it is a place of endless cultural hybridization. It is a liminal space that everyday plays host to the tourist encounter, giving life to endless reinterpretations of the "special effect" created by Lyautey, and to endless contaminations (all the while the performers enact their "age-old" and "unchanging" roles . . .).

We can trace a direct connection between the Parisian colonial *Exposition* and today's daily postcolonial exhibition on Marrakech's most famous square. The connection is not merely a conceptual one, however. In July 1999, almost a hundred artisans and performers were brought from the Jamaa el Fna to the gardens of the Tuileries in Paris, in an itinerant spectacle of "Moroccan culture" (Borghi 2003): a spectacle, a text, that is by now an infinite reproduction of itself—even elsewhere. The spectacle maintains, nonetheless, "every people in its right place"—in this case, on stage.

Postcolonial—just as colonial—power continues to rely on the absolute visibility of its hierarchies. For the representative of "Moroccanness" in the Jamaa el Fna to know her/his place, the world must be completely ordered and legible, just as it is within the cosmology of the world-as-a-whole-full-of-fragments produced by the tourist discourse, separated into that which belongs to the tourist, and that assigned to the "Moroccan." But this separation is ambivalently re-enacted as well as disrupted by the tourist encounters in the Jamaa el Fna. In fact, the tourist encounters that take place everyday on the square are *also* processes of intersubjective construction of liminal modes of communication, for the subjects involved do not *fully* share common sets of concepts, experiences, and traditions. They merely share a colonial vision that each subject reinterprets in a process of hybrid constructions of meanings and identities. It is this hybridity that exposes the paradoxes in the postcolonial tourist narratives on the Jamaa el Fna.

The very idea of preserving the oral heritage of the Jamaa el Fna reveals all the contradictions already inherent in the colonial vision. The conviction that "material culture" is the expression of a people's identity and thus the proper "tool" for its narration and classification clashes visibly with the impossibility of translating such culture into text, into its "museumification," into binaries. The codification of the square as the embodiment of a "universal oral heritage" amounts to an attempt to reconcile the irreconcilable: an attempt to freeze into immutable text an endlessly shifting daily dialectic.

The result of such attempts are hybrid forms that bridge the fixity of the (cultural) text and the inevitable fluidity of oral communication and personal interaction in place. As Homi Bhabha (1986) has argued, the hybrid was always one of colonialism's unintended consequences—the product of "crossbreeding" between the "metropolitan" (read: tourist) and the "colonial" (read: native). But the hybrid was not—and is not—simply the product of colonial and postcolonial migrations and diasporas: "it is integral to colonial contact and is, in fact, the result of colonialism's institutions and systems" (Morton 2000, 13). The tourists on the Jamaa el Fna observe—and are observed—by the representatives of "Moroccanness." These latter interact with those who observe them—and try to adapt their behavior to the codes of the tourist gaze.

However, the tourist *too* comes into contact with the ambivalent nature of the place and within this encounter is forced to momentarily suspend the system of representation (and beliefs) that reduces the square to a museum, to an archive of culture, giving birth to cultural hybrids that s(he) often (paradoxically) considers the most "precious" of experiences—encounters with a "contaminated," "disordered" place that does not always conform to the rigid hierarchies that orient the order presumably imposed by tourist narratives.

Pierre Bourdieu (1977, 165), in his description of anthropological fieldwork, draws a useful distinction between the role of the "informant" and that of the researcher. We can use this distinction to probe into the role of the "native" on the Jamaa el Fna. What does the "native" do when she/he performs, for the pleasure of the tourist, a representation of her/his own world? It is a performance within which, after all, several structures of meaning converge. The Jamaa el Fna is a place where tourists' need to unify the world-as-a-whole encounters the allure of the diversity of the "inhabitants" who lie beyond any facile categorization or stereotype. The tourist experience of the square—and the construction of its meanings—is thus a typical process of hybridization: a "mutation" that is "an unintentional effect of colonial power" (Bhabha, 1986), producing a division between the authoritative, ordered tourist mappings and its "actual" ambivalent performance within the spaces of the square. If, as Bhabha (1986) notes, hybrids were essential to the functioning of colonial power, acting as mediators between the colonizer and colonized, they are crucial in the constitution of *post*colonial tourist places as well, places where the tourists meet their object of desire and fascination, and where their colonial discourse not only tries to freeze the Other into pre-established hierarchical categories, but it is itself open to alteration and reinterpretation within endless cultural combinations.

I would like to close by turning, once again, to the work of Patricia Morton (2000, 321), who notes that "despite Lyautey's efforts to create a unified, unambiguous lesson of European superiority and colonial inferiority, the *Exposition* was one of those places where colonized and colonizer danced in a fascinating, ambivalent embrace." So too, I would argue, do the tourist and the "native," despite their preordained roles and assigned "places" within the postcolonial rhetoric: in the liminal spaces of the Jamaa el Fna, they meet daily "in a fascinating and ambivalent embrace"; an embrace which is also a struggle for the control of the ongoing process of production of social ordering—and thus the practices that it inscribes. The new "saviors" of the Jamaa el Fna and its "heritage" are key actors in this process of ordering and control, just as the French colonial administration was in years past, albeit with a *post*colonial reinterpretation of the colonial ideal: to protect the square from the paradoxical "special effects" of tourism *and* modernity.

8

Portable Autonomous Zones: Tourism and the Travels of Dissent

Steven Flusty

This is a simple story about a simple thing, a little homespun doll that traveled from southern Mexico to me. These dolls are among tourists' most preferred souvenirs from the Mayan margins of Mexico, the incidental offspring of countless back-strap looms whose shuttles travel back and forth, to and fro between the taut-stretched warp of fabrics in formation. Once complete, such fabrics (like the elaborately polychromatic *huipile* smocks they often become) are maps of the cosmos within which nestle corn-growing peoples who at some level know themselves to have, long ago, grown from corn.

But at the same time, neither this story nor the doll it revolves around are at all simple. Seen from another angle, the dolls are a cottage industry subsidiary to a traditional (or, less respectfully, backward) agrarian economy desperately in need of modernization and, more specifically, marketization. Modern markets, after all, create and diffuse wealth, liberate resources for their "highest and best" use, and free persons to act in their own best interests while providing them the wherewithal to do so.

This latter, devalorizing view of the modern Mayan world is consonant with dominant thinking about the world at large, a kind of thinking that maps a very different cosmos predicated upon a very different human nature. If free markets make for free people and wealth distributed freely, then a global free market necessarily improves material living standards globally, producing and distributing wealth planetwide through the competitive transference of goods and know-how (Dunning 1993). This is not a modernization that comes painlessly. This kind of progress in living standards results from economic change through new innovations that weed out old processes, products, and economically "unproductive" sectors (Caballero and Hammour 2000). Such Schumpeterian "creative destruction" (see Metcalfe 1998), however, ultimately ensures not only prosperity but peace and freedom as well, given that markets depend on both stability and choice to operate. By corollary, the global rights of capital must be guaranteed to assure prosperity, meritocratic equity, and amity (see Friedman 1992) for all the planet's inhabitants. This is what globalization *is*, like it or not, and the people of southern Mexico are no exception.

Weeding out, however, extends to the removal of obstacles to creative destruction itself, most visibly such "impediment[s] to a well-functioning creative destruction process" (Greider 2001) as less economically profitable ways of life, their "politicized institutions" (Greider 2001), and thus established mechanisms of popular political representation. In the absence of such obstacles, political expression is delimited to the realm of consumer choice—collective social aspirations are conflated with a person's presumptive entitlement to select from a determined range of proffered commodities. In the process, citizenship becomes consumership and public accountability is reduced to accountancy, wherein one is entitled to as much influence as one can purchase.

Hypothetically, those with shallower pockets and less economically productive ways of living should eventually find that this unraveling of their emplaced social relations will enrich them sufficiently to claim a voice in such a "daily plebiscite of the penny" (von Mises in Barber 1996, 243). Yet as creative destruction weeds out the lives it strives to enrich, the paradox becomes ineluctable. For very, very many, creative destruction yields not prosperity but widespread and stubbornly persistent disruption, dislocation, and disempowerment, curdling promises of peace and freedom into the material practices of enforced pacification and carefully concealed constraint that underpin the emergence of an intensely plutocratic globality.

And on midnight of January 1, 1994, those southern Mexicans declared that they had been on the receiving end of this conundrum long enough. Amid chants of "¡*Ya Basta!*" (roughly, "Enough Already!"), the Zapatistas appeared as if out of nowhere in the central plaza of the centuries-old colonial city of San Cristóbal de las Casas, Chiapas State. Clad in black ski masks, fatigues, embroidered smocks, and beribboned hats, some carrying rifles and others sticks carved to look like rifles, they raided the town hall, issued a declaration of principles from the government palace, blanketed the city with broadsheets, and attacked a military base on the way out.

This initiated two weeks of skirmishes against the civilian population by local police, and by the Mexican army and air force. Despite this, the network of Zapatista base communities scattered throughout Chiapas's Lacandón rainforest remained intact, then expanded throughout the state and into adjacent regions. Technically, the mobilization of this network constitutes an uprising by the impoverished indigenous peoples of the region, predominantly Western Mayans of the Tzotzil, Tzetal, Tojolabal, and Chol linguistic subgroups. But in the timing of the raid on San Cristóbal, at precisely the moment NAFTA went into effect, it is also a flip of the proverbial finger at the imposition of marketized modernization processes. It is a flip that helped catalyze the *coyuntura*, the resistant convergence or "'coming together' of distinct social and cultural movements" (Ross in Marcos 1995, 9) throughout Mexico. And in its visibility in communications media worldwide it has become the finger flipped around the world, one that has incited a global convergence to germinate some very different globalities.

COMBATING A DISEASE OF THE
HEART THAT ONLY GOD CAN CURE

Of course, the Zapatistas did not come out of nowhere. Broadly, they are a late twentieth-century incarnation of the long-simmering discontent of Mayan agrarian communalists. Southern Mexico in the late seventeenth and early eighteenth centuries was rife with these uprisings, struggles against the colonial appropriation of Mayan agricultural land and the corollary enserfment of the population. More narrowly, the Zapatistas are a continuation of the Mexican Revolution of 1910, led in Mexico's South by the Mayan Emiliano Zapata. This was a struggle against the predominantly Spanish-descended 1 percent of the population who owned 97 percent of the land, leaving 92 percent of the population landless and held in indentured agrarian servitude. This fight for *tierra*, for land/earth, culminated in a recovery of pre-Columbian communal land tenureship through the redistribution of land to peasant farmers under the *ejido* system. Under this system, ensconced via Article 27 of the 1917 Mexican constitution, land is parceled out to persons and families but is nontransferable, held and administered on an institutionalized communal basis (NACEC 2001). The *ejido* system was not fully implemented until 1934, under then-President Lazaro Cardenas, and frequently resulted in marginal parcels of land barely large enough to support a family. Nonetheless, the *ejidos* constituted a significant increase in autonomy for the everyday lives of rural indigenous populations. But most specifically, the Zapatista uprising is a response to the amendment of Article 27 in 1992, under the administration of then-President Carlos Salinas de Gortari. In an effort to expand and stabilize private property rights, realize economies of scale in the rural economy, and so harmonize Mexico with the terms of NAFTA, Salinas sought to de-collectivize agrarian land through three significant legislative changes:

- Peasants could no longer petition for land, nor could land be expropriated from owners.
- Title of existing communal lands would be transferred to their individual occupants, made leaseable, and in many instances transferable through sale.
- Outside investors, and corporations both foreign and domestic, could hold land.

For the Mayans, this "privatization of the countryside" (Foley 1995) was a destructive creation that meant nothing less than the reversal of the 1910 revolution. It raised the specter of losing their land, corn, and lifeways to poverty, outside manipulation, and the competitive superiority of industrial agriculture, and of their becoming either hired hands on newly concentrated landholdings or impoverished migrants to the cities. And ultimately, it impelled the assault on San Cristóbal.

But it has impelled a great deal more as well. Three manifestations of this new struggle are particularly noteworthy. First is a new way of conducting revolution, and a corollary new political practice. The overwhelming rhetoric of the Zapatista uprising has been that it is a rebellion by long-suffering indigenous peoples. Conversely, critics have claimed that this is a public relations ploy intended to conceal a Maoist coup d'etat by the National Liberation Front, a "white dominated Marxist guerrilla group" (Oppenheimer 1996, 22; for a similarly deterministic interpretation from a more sympathetic Marxian perspective see Nugent 1995). Yet others have claimed that in the seeming timidity of its conventional political and territorial claims, this uprising is not a revolution at all (Paz 1994). These characterizations, however, miss the point.

The armed wing of the Zapatistas, the EZLN (Ejercito Zapatista Liberacion Nacional, or Zapatista Army of National Liberation), has been explicit from the beginning that it eschews any and all notion of taking power. Rather, the Zapatistas reject the very notion of power as something to be seized and wielded, believing that in such a taking lay the reproduction of the violences and exclusions they attribute to their enemy. Thus, this is no uprising in the vanguardist Marxist-Leninist mold. Instead, it is one that strives to elide the self-contradictions that have long plagued modernist revolutionary thought, contradictions whereby the seizure of power for libratory ends has time and again resulted in a new boss as keen as the old on conserving the exercise of power.

Rather, the Zapatistas "look at power in a different way" so as to "produce a different way of doing politics" (see Marcos in Libra 1995). This different way does not have "as its premise the objective of power" but instead seeks to construct "space for new political relationships . . . spaces for peace" (Marcos in Libra 1995), spaces in which people may exercise their own power (or "free and democratic 'space'" [in Marcos 1995, 233]). In keeping with this, such spaces are not by and for a single way of seeing. Again the Zapatistas have been explicit on this point. They repeatedly emphasize that their revolt can and must include the divergent perspectives of all professional (and un-, and anti-professional) classifications, all sexes and sexual orientations, all age groups, all religions, and all intellects so long as they are "rebels, dissidents, inconvenient ones, dreamers" (Marcos 1999). In short, this is an uprising that has sought to deploy the different and the othered against their othering—one in which none are asked to surrender their differences in the name of solidarity. To the contrary, such differences—those "characteristics which modernity, in its designs and managerial practices, set about to eliminate and, failing that, tried to conceal" (Bauman 1992, 187–88; also see Latour 1993, on modernism's simultaneous construction and repression of hybrids)—comprise the uprising's principal ammunition against the developmentalist imposition of a marketized modernity.

In this rhetoric of inclusivist spatial metaphors is not just a critique of revolutionary modernism, but also concrete counterproposals—means by which bodies might refuse and resist the arrogated enactment of power through them, and do so proactively by doing differently. The Zapatistas' material practices have been deployed to concretize their metaphorical spaces of liberation as literal terrain as well, politicized and paradoxical spatial "plurilocalities" (Rose 1993, 150–51) carved out of Mexico's authoritative place. Spreading from Chiapas into neighboring states, the EZLN's disordering of state-imposed power relations has supported the emergence of somewhere around three thousand base communities, which in turn have organized into forty-three "autonomous municipalities" (Villafuerte 2001, 17).

Within this terrain of resistance (Routledge 1996), everyday relations are ordered through local assemblies open to all community members over the age of twelve. Larger decisions are addressed through *consultas*, whereby directly chosen delegates (who may be popularly recalled at any time) carry community decisions to municipal assemblages. Similarly, decisions made at the municipal level are, for all intents and purposes, recommendations that must be carried back for community approval, amendment, or rejection. Even the armed force of the EZLN, although hierarchically structured internally, is likewise commanded from below. It takes orders from and issues communiqués by the CCRI (Clandestine Revolutionary Indigenous Committee), which is itself composed of delegates who may be recalled at any time by their communities (Flood 2001).

This system hearkens back to the *ejido* and earlier Mayan modes of popular community rule, but also equalizes social hierarchies so as to mitigate against tendencies toward patriarchal gerontocracy and co-opted *caciques*. This has produced such innovations as the Women's Revolutionary Law mandating gender self-determination and equality in all spheres of everyday life from domestic to military, and youthful mobilizations against such long-standing practices as the payment of marriage dowry. It also has driven negotiators for the Mexican state around the bend, in that any negotiating proposals made by the federal state must be handed down to the Zapatista communities for full discussion and consensus prior to ratification.

Thus the Zapatistas have innovated a practice that recognizes power as nonsovereign and embodied and that proceeds to creatively disrupt the relational order that embodies the monopolistic usufruct of power (see Foucault 1982). In so doing they have opened literal and metaphorical space for self-organization, wherein governance may be popularly reclaimed through an active re-articulation of civil society. It is a proposal and a practice for undermining existing networks of asymmetrical power relations by rejecting high-modern tenets of centralized efficiency entirely, carving out spaces that stave off and starve out power centers to evacuate the center entirely, yet without simultaneously establishing the periphery as a new center in its own right. Zapatismo, then, constitutes a subversion of the modern state that, in its kludging together of cutting-edge autonomism with pre-Columbian forms of protest and rural power apportionment, becomes an alternate modernity (see Gaonkar 2001) in its own right.

The second noteworthy manifestation of the Zapatista uprising is its spokesman, Subcomandante Insurgente Marcos. Commonly known as the "Sup," Marcos has become the recognized face (or more precisely, the blue eyes and big nose poking through a ski mask) of the uprising. According to the Mexican state, behind the ski mask is Rafael Sebastián Guillén Vicente, son of a successful Tampico furniture dealer (Golden 2001). While at University in Mexico City, Vicente joined the NLF and went into the mountains of southern Mexico where, in the course of bringing the locals over to his cause, was no less assimilated into theirs. From this perspective Marcos is a privileged but rurally re-educated white socialist from the Federal District, what might be termed an organicized intellectual. Marcos has not denied this identity, but instead has claimed many others, including that of a Mayan and, in response to counterintelligence campaigns casting aspersions upon his sexuality, a gay waiter from San Francisco.

But in simultaneously concealing the actor in question and heightening his conspicuousness, the mask has come to contain a host of additional meanings in the popular imagination. Mythically, Marcos has become one in a long line of masked Mayan heroes, and a new embodiment of the itinerant prophets of the 1712 and 1868 Mayan revolts (Ross in Marcos 1995, 8–9). In serving as the youthful voice making the case for the radicalized *ejidos*, Marcos has become the Second Coming of Zapata and an irreverent avatar of Ernesto "Che" Guevara (Feinmann 1998) incarnated as the archetypal trickster. Indeed, it is common to see Marcos depicted standing between both. And the mask has in turn become emblematic of the uprising as a whole, with participants donning ski masks, kerchiefs, and even the artisanal masks of the region. Practically, this serves as a means of concealing participants' identities and thus shields them from retribution. These are not, however, the metaphorical masks Mexicans allegedly don to dissimulate passions and self, "to become invisible, to pass unnoticed without renouncing . . . individuality" (Paz 1982, 42). Rather, such "Mexican masks" (Paz 1982, 42) are performatively satirized in the insurgents' ski masks (see Marcos 1995, 83–86) to become a countervailing proclamation of visibility, a statement that anybody in any place may be a Zapatista and that all participants are Marcos.

Equally significant are the writings and speeches that emerge from behind Marcos's ski mask. These words are directly confrontational language-acts regularly attached as (sometimes endless) postscripts to the pronouncements and press releases of the CCRI. They are also circulated as independently released parables, biographies, and folktales. Invariably, they are discursive assaults upon the totalizing and exclusionary economic logic of plutocratic globality's marketized modernity. But most significantly, these words are couched in literary and poetic forms that are alternatively (and sometimes simultaneously) playful, heart-wrenching, obscure, magical-realist, and hugely anti-authoritarian. They have earned Marcos specifically, and the Zapatistas in general, a tremendous readership.

Finally, the third element to have emerged from the uprising is those aforementioned dolls, *muñecas Zapatistas* (Zapatista dolls), the most prominent artifact within the proliferating commodity landscape of Zapatista tie-in merchandise. There is a long history of subsistence weaving among Mexico's Mayan women, and an equally long history of small human figurines assembled from the remnant textile scraps. First appearing in 1994, the muñeca Zapatista is much like these dolls in form and size, but with important modifications: the dolls are dressed in black homespun ski masks and ponchos with woven bandoleers. Some carry rifles made of blackened wood but, on others, the wood is left natural, much like the carved dummy guns first carried into San Cristobál.

In its most common version the doll is stitched with blue eyes like those of Marcos himself. But almost as common are the Comandante Ramona dolls, similarly topped by a ski mask but with long protruding pigtails braided with polychromed yarn. These dolls are dressed in the elaborately woven *huipiles* that signify Mayan identities (Ramona herself is a Tzotzil), and are invariably accompanied by baby Zapatistas dolls with blue eyes. This latter is on one level a joking allusion to a Ramona/Marcos liaison. But on another, it is a celebration of the role of women in the uprising. Roughly one-third of EZLN combatants are female. The size and position of the tiny Marcos on Ramona's back further points to the fact that, true to his rank-title, Marcos is a subordinate commander in the ranks of the EZLN. As a comandante and a member of the CCRI, until her exile in Spain Ramona was among those who issued orders to Marcos (and was also one of the principal draftspersons of the Women's Revolutionary Law; see Wolfwood 1997). But in addition to fighting, female Zapatistas simultaneously reproduce the uprising's combatants. Thus, the tiny Marcos (or, in some cases, Marcoses) clinging to the Ramona doll announces that "all our children are Marcos." Further, such dolls are traditional elements of children's play in the region, a toy that is no less a tool for imaginatively trying out adult roles. So these muñecas afford children the opportunity to play at the role of Zapatista. In so doing, both the dolls themselves and their makers play a part in reproducing the uprising through making the children Marcos. (In what might be regarded as a case of cottage-industrial just-in-time flexible specialization, these same baby Marcoses repeatedly turn up as hair clips, atop miniature horses, and loaded into the backs of rough-hewn wooden toy trucks.)

A full account of the Zapatistas' trajectory since 1994 would require many chapters, even many volumes. In some ways, it has taken the form of a war of attrition so endemic that for many it has become a scarcely noted fixture of Mexico's overall political landscape. It has entailed on-again-off-again negotiations over cessation of hostilities and indigenous rights. For its part, the Mexican government has stayed a traditional course: deploy twenty-five thousand soldiers to spatially quarantine and occasionally occupy Zapatista base communities while hired "white guard" paramilitaries pressure the restive population. (Pressure, however, is a grotesquely polite euphemism given the 1997 massacre of forty-five peasants at Acteal, see Villafuerte 2001, 17.) The persistence of this strategy, reinforced by a general absence of armed response or expansionist territorial offensives by the EZLN, has led to periodic but frequent pronouncements of the uprising's imminent demise.

But the dolls tell another story. From 1995 onward, the muñecas Zapatistas began following established circuits of domestic Mexican travel, turning up across regions of southern and central Mexico most sympathetic to the uprising. And even more telling than these travels of the Mayan-made dolls out from Chiapas was their appearance in new forms clearly native to their regions. In Oaxaca, muñecas Zapatistas were crafted out of ceramic, and in other instances took the form of clay or papier-maché skeletons (sometimes assembled in vignettes about a coffin labeled "PRI," the acronym of the then-ruling party). In Michoacan, terra cotta figurines appeared that matched the Mayan dolls in size, armaments, and, of course, ski masks crowned with earthenware pompoms. And at the swelling edges of the Federal District of Mexico City, muñecas Zapatistas were fabricated by squatters who were, in many instances, themselves recent migrants from the rural south. Kludged together from factory-made materials and salvaged industrial detritus, these dolls were commonly injection-molded action figures carefully rebuilt in the image of Marcos, complete with miniatures of his be-starred dungaree cap, blue eyes, and signature pipe.

During the late 1990s, this recasting of the muñecas Zapatistas into new materials commonplace to their expanding locales of production replicated the extent to which the rebellion was itself being recast to fit new contexts. Throughout the period the Zapatistas reformulated and extended their battle to *not* seize power, and they did so by de-emphasizing armed struggle in favor of a different sort of weapon: the word. The insurgency had become "a war of ink, of written word, a war on the Internet" (Foreign Minister Gurría in Montes 1995, unpaginated). Written, the Zapatistas' words (and especially their formulation by Marcos) were disseminated through the Spanish language press, sometimes as often as two to three times per week, and broadly spread over the Internet. Spoken, these words served as centerpieces to nationally telemediated mass events like rallies, peace negotiations, and the coalition-building *encuentros*. These latter became a hallmark of Zapatista praxis, large-scale hybrids of the teach-in, the professional conference, the diplomatic summit, and the late-1960s style "happening." Through these encuentros, already well-established coalitions of the poor, the socially marginalized, the dissident, and the radicalized came together in base community-style assemblies to civilianize the EZLN into "a space of convergence for various thoughts and intentions" wherein, again in pointedly anti-vanguardist fashion, "they who lead, do so by obeying" (FZLN 1996, unpaginated).

Through the strategic deployment and mobilizing capacity of their words, the Zapatistas repeatedly breached, more or less at will, the cordons surrounding their base communities. In the process they galvanized popular pressure to ratchet down the state's military anti-insurgency operations in

Chiapas so as to preserve their spaces for the exercise of de-centered power from being definitively rolled over by the war machine of the Mexican state. But more significant for the long term, the words of the Zapatistas simultaneously established a sociopolitical vector furthering the articulation of resistance movements, opposition groups, and NGOs nationwide. Thus the Zapatistas became an experiment in exporting and scaling up spaces for peace and new political relationships in collaboration with pre-existing and expanding sectors of Mexican civil society.

Further, this is an experiment that has not only been exported, but has toured as well, and in so doing became a festive pop-cultural event in its own right. The Zapatistas have periodically embodied their "spaces for peace" as a portable Temporary Autonomous Zone (or TAZ; see Bey 1991) and, to much fanfare, taken it on the road. The most recent and dramatic instance, one that simultaneously countered persistent prognostications of the uprising's impending irrelevance (see Ronfeldt et al. 1998), was in March 2001. Preparatory to a congressional vote on legislation guaranteeing indigenous autonomy, a Zapatista caravan set out on a sixteen-day, twenty-one-hundred-mile tour through twelve Mexican states. Their ultimate destination was Mexico City's central plaza, the Zócalo. Officially christened the "Caravan for Indian Dignity" but quickly renamed the "Zapatour" by the Mexican press, this march to the capital consisted of fifteen buses and hundreds of additional vehicles carrying, among others, twenty-three Zapatista comandantes, Subcomandante Marcos, rank-and-file supporters, observers, journalists, and police (AP 2001).

Throughout the tour the Zapatistas held rallies, conducted encuentros, and participated in the congresses of coalition organizations like the National Indigenous Congress (*Report from Nurío* 2001). The arrival in Mexico City, however, was particularly spectacular. It brought out from 100,000 (Romney and Smith 2001) to over 150,000 people (Robles 2001), including numerous rock bands, dance troupes of urban neo-Aztec *concheros*, and more than a few giant puppets. In the process, the Zócalo's roles as Mexico's "political heart," as the hearth of the Federal District, and as a popular tourist destination in its own right ensured its conversion, however briefly, into an ideal stage upon which to perform an emotive de-control of control and comically deride the disorder of the established order (compare with Edensor in Minca and Oakes, this volume). Encamped as a traveling carnival of resistance in the public center of the country—directly between the Cathedral, the National Palace, and the excavated ruins of Tenochtitlan's highest temple—this portable TAZ ensured that Zapatismo's travels would weave it ever more inextricably into new social contexts. These contexts, in turn, invested Zapatismo with a range of meanings that enlarged from the privatization of indigenous ejidos to encompass everything from ruling party corruption and egregious human rights violations to bioregionalist critiques of ecological despoliation.

Of course, the Zapatour arrived with more than just masses and manifestoes. It also came with merch tables selling black ski masks, CDs of rebel music, "Zappo" lighters (AP 2001), and bunches of black balloons imprinted with a flesh-tone strip of Marcos' eyes and nose bridge. And, of course, the ubiquitous muñecas Zapatistas, most prominently the Mayan textile version. But other muñecas came along for the ride as well, among them a plastic doll of the architect of Mexican neoliberalization, ex-president Carlos Salinas de Gortari, now in de-facto exile over alleged ties to official corruption and political homicide. These dolls constituted a particularly carnivalesque touch — they carried large bags of loot in one hand and, when their heads were pressed down upon, exposed enormous erections out from under their black-and-white striped prisoner's smocks.

But such merchandise wasn't the most exotic element to accompany the caravan. The Zapatour included legions of foreigners from the United States, Canada, and Europe, most notably some six hundred Italians. And some of these Italians were exotic indeed, dressed in white jumpsuits and padded rubber armor. These were the "white monkeys" (aka *monos blancos* or *tutte bianchi*), an auxiliary security force organized midway through the tour by the Zapatista comandantes in response to persistent death threats. Their presence points to the fact that the Zapatista uprising has traveled not only nationally, but globally as well. In the process, the continual and disorderly refashioning of its meanings in ever more distant locales has played an inarguable role in inspiring the global convergence of a distinctly Zapatista-esque, indirectly direct assault on the modernizing prescriptions that give rise to plutocratic globality. It has, in short, inspired a global movement for the deconcentration and reorientation of power via the circuits of travel that constitute globalization itself.

FORWARD IN ALL DIRECTIONS![1]

I have had many encuentros of my own with muñecas Zapatistas, but most have not occurred inside Mexico. Commonly, they have been in small shops scattered throughout the metropolitan centers of Europe and the United States. Most of these shops have been cultural spaces, generally run by non-Mexican Zapatista sympathizers who travel intermittently to southern Mexico. Perhaps the most representative of these spaces is the cleverly (and tellingly) named Espresso Mi Cultura, a coffeehouse performance space at the eastern end of

Hollywood. Here, the dolls sit among volumes of the Sup's writings, portraits of Cesar Chavez and the Virgin of Guadalupe, refrigerator magnets bearing the visage of Che Guevara, and leaflets for the self-rechristened Olin Tez-catlipoca's Aztec-revivalist Mexica movement.

The pervasiveness of this outside support for the Zapatistas became particularly visceral for me in late 1998, when I entered Mexico hot on the trail of the muñeca Zapatistas commodity chain. Upon arrival, I discovered that none of my local colleagues could arrange me safe passage into Chiapas. Hundreds of visitors traveling on U.S. and E.U. visas had just been ejected from the area, an attempt by the Mexican state to remove the "infestation of foreign activists who stir up and manipulate many indigenous groups contrary to constitutional order" (*Expreso Chiapas* 1998, 8). Given that this infestation consisted largely of human rights observers hunkered down in "civil peace camps" within Zapatista terrain, the claim of outside agitation would seem to have been targeted toward two ends: discursively delegitimizing the uprising as an alien intervention, and physically enabling anti-insurgency campaigns to proceed unobserved. Nonetheless, the fact of my being denied access was as revealing as anything I may have found in Chiapas itself. The Zapatistas had so successfully rallied support across the Americas and Europe that anyone traveling from those areas was now regarded as a potential sympathizer.

Chiapas is the poorest state in Mexico, but also one of the most stereotypically picturesque and archaeologically significant. Thus, it receives a sizeable portion of its income from tourism. Given the EZLN's emphasis on discursive combat and its care in leaving noncombatants unharmed, the uprising has only served to enlarge Chiapas's appeal as a tourist destination. In this context the dolls are more than a toy and a popular expression of dissident sentiment. The prodigious volume of the dolls' production attests to the fact that the overwhelming majority is not likely to be consumed locally, whether as playthings or not (as is the case with woven Mayan dolls in general). They are also souvenirs and a source of tourist income. As such, they have taken a canonical form that is produced by the thousands, stacked like cordwood at open-air markets for sale to visitors, and diffused to the most travel-affluent corners of the globe.

The dolls' mass-cottage-production implies an asymmetrical disjunction between their roles as popular expressions and as commodities, a dichotomy in which the significance of the tiny Zapatistas is rendered as they become just so much more grist for the tourism engines that grind local specificities into readily comestible exotica. Certainly the unwitting model for the dolls himself, Marcos, initially harbored this sensibility and criticized the dolls' mass-cottage-production and sale as disrespectful of fallen rebels. But upon realizing that those buying the dolls supported the movement, and given that many of the dolls are produced by Zapatistas and even by members of the EZLN, he let the matter drop (Watson 2001). So both materially and symbolically, this dichotomy between the dolls' authenticity and commodityhood is a false one. Chiapas's cities, villages, and Zapatista base communities share memberships, and engage heavily in exchange with one another. As a result, when the dolls function as a fungible tourist commodity they transfer wealth from tourists to the Zapatistas' indigenous supporters. Nor need this exchange entail a loss of meaning on either end. From the producer's perspective, as one Michoacaño ceramicist told me, "I make these to sell and get money, I am very poor. But it is because I am poor that I am proud to make Marcos, to show that I too am Zapatista" (Flusty 1999). And on the receiving end, the dolls have a marked tendency to turn up in cultural spaces with strong leanings toward autonomism and, in the southwestern U.S. case, Chicanismo.

The muñecas Zapatistas, then, do not suffer some enervating transformation whereby tourism vampirically reduces them to commodified shells purged of their vital significations. Rather, the muñecas briefly enter into a commodity state as they transit from the meaning-full context (or "regime of value," see Appadurai 1986) of their Chiapan makers to that of the purchasing tourist. And, in so far as many of these tourists arrive in sympathy with the dolls' makers and the larger Zapatista agenda, the two value regimes are not so discrepant as their cultural and class differences would suggest. As a result, the dolls' brief transit through their state of commodity-ness turns them into one of a number of unconventional methods that transport and translate the uprising into the larger world.

Indeed, the Zapatistas have increasingly relied upon such unconventional practices of translation. This is implicit in Marcos's innovative use of print and broadcast media to disseminate the uprising's case. Of course, such media are not necessarily accessible. This is most notable in the United States, where the major television news outlets have consistently paid scant attention to the uprising (including the otherwise celebrated Zapatour, with U.S. journalists noteworthy for their absence from the caravan's international press contingent). It is debatable to what extent this is a product of the United States' long-standing status as the beneficiary of wildly asymmetrical economic relations with its southern neighbor, relations that are no less beneficial to the handful of TNCs in possession of those major television news outlets. Regardless, the Zapatistas have largely overcome this obstacle, making extensive use of the Internet to disseminate their declarations, the CCRI's communiqués, and Marcos's postscripts (Gray 1997, 5–6, see also www.ezln.org), a precedent-setting instance of arguably effective "netwar" (Ronfeldt et al. 1998). Zapatismo's autonomist practices have thus been translated into the globally diffuse space of the Internet as well. Such translation has resonated with particular strength among educated youth of a more disaffected bent throughout the postindustrialized world, and has created a worldwide visibility that renders state assaults on Zapatista territory "politically inadvisable" (Ronfeldt et al. 1998, 86).

So thousands of tourists, observers, and sympathizers from the outside have been drawn in to the otherwise isolated mountains of southern Mexico. In the process, many of these visitors have become participants in the "Intercontinental Encuentros for Humanity and Against Neoliberalism," globally hyperextended assemblies and consultas intended to produce an "intercontinental network of resistance" and an "intercontinental network of alternative communication" (Zapatistas 1998, 52–53). While these meetings have more often than not produced unenthusiastically unresolved resolutions, they have also served as workshops for facilitators of the subsequent "anti-capitalist mass demonstrations of London J18, Seattle N30 and those that followed in 2000 including A16 Washington and S26 Prague" (Flood 2001, 3).

In their varied efforts to travel at will through Chiapas's military cordons, the Zapatistas have transported new methods for organizing the performance of dissent, drawn in organizers to carry those methods "intercontinentally," and entrained in their wake causes like freedom for political prisoners, Third World debt forgiveness, immigrant rights, and opposition to transgenic foods. Nor is this a happenstance occurrence; such linkages have been actively formulated and popularized by particular travelers to Chiapas. The members of the now-defunct LA-based rock band Rage Against the Machine were one clear example. On CDs and cassette tapes, and at sold-out concerts, this band's hybrid of hip-hop and heavy metal accompanied lyrics that, not unlike Marcos's own writings, deployed violent indignation, principled proclamations, pedagogic analysis, and poetic magical realism to insist upon the reclamation of power through direct practices in the here and now. Concrete methods and established activist networks toward these ends were provided on the band's website (www.ratm.com). Further, the themes were carried through in the band's home-grown merchandising contributions to the commodity landscape of Zapatismo, like T-Shirts emblazoned with the hyperpatriotic slogan "We Support Our Troops" in stars-and-stripes spangled red, white, and blue, subversively juxtaposed with a portrait of four EZLN insurgents.

Beyond this one band, the visages of Marcos, Zapata, and Che have traveled to CD and book covers, T-Shirts, and posters across the planet. The pipe-studded ski mask has even turned up in primitivist illustrations for a readily available children's picture book (Marcos and Domínguez 1996), penned by the Sup himself (and from which, upon realizing the identity of the author, the U.S. National Endowment for the Arts withdrew previously committed funding). Thus, as the uprising has repeatedly moved in and out of a commodity form, it has spread ever further afield. In so doing it has seesawed erratically between, its meaning has undergone varied degrees of slippage through adaptation to a growing range of social contexts and political causes. But in the process Zapatismo has come to play a considerable role in integrating these contexts and causes, a subversive commodity masked as a safely commodified subversion (Minca and Oakes, this volume) that has tiptoed into evermore distant settings and then unexpectedly popped up at the heart of a succession of far-flung mass-actions.

This is not to imply, however, that Zapatismo has consistently avoided wandering into other regimes of value that would leave it suspended in a very voided commodity state indeed. This has been particularly evident in social contexts where the enhancement of sales to youth target-markets is of concern. As early as 1995, the Italian clothing company Benetton, famous for its deployment of controversial causes in advertising, offered Marcos a reportedly lucrative modeling contract (Watson 2001). In itself, this is nothing new. In 1914, Pancho Villa accepted $25,000 from the Mutual Films Company to allow its documentarians at his battles, and went so far as to fight during daylight hours and delay his assault on the city of Ojinaga out of consideration for Mutual's film crew (see Bennett 2000). But unlike his predecessor, Marcos tacitly refused the offer by neglecting to answer it. Spurned, Benetton turned to the Middle East and ultimately produced a catalog featuring the portraits and biographies of Israelis and Palestinians in amicable (albeit sometimes ambivalent) everyday interactions, with all depicted parties conspicuously clad in the company's garments (UCB 1998).

While Marcos may not have been available for licensing, the corollary upsurge in revolutionary chic was public domain, most notably in the person of Che Guevara. In the more informal sectors of the U.S. Southwest's economy, by way of example, this took such forms as the sale of banners bearing Andy Warhol's iconic black-and-red graphic of (Alberto "Korda" Diaz Gutierrez's photograph of) Che Guevara from off the chain-link fences of vacant lots. On the opposite scalar end of the business spectrum, a similar portrait appeared on the face of the Swiss SMH (Societe de Microelectronique et d'Horlorgerie) corporation's "Revolucion" model Swatch watches. Somewhere in between were the relatively spendy Italian-made scarves printed, yet again, with the same image. The most extreme example, however, is another doll, the most perversely distaff form of the muñeca Zapatista to date. Roughly the same size as the Mayan dolls, this one was factory produced in the People's Republic of China. It takes the form of a Chihuahua clad in Che's signature black beret. The beret is adorned on front with a red flag which, upon closer inspection, is the logo of Yum! Brands' (and ex-PepsiCo's subsidiary) Taco Bell restaurant. When pressed on the belly, this plush Che-huahua heroically intones "¡Viva Gorditas!"

Introduced in 1999, this doll was part of a campaign conceived by advertising firm TBWA\Chiat\Day's Los Angeles office. The campaign played upon then-wildly-popular ads in which a talking Chihuahua proclaimed "Yo quiero Taco Bell." But it went further, fusing the dog with antiquated tropes of Latin American revolutionary machismo as a means of introducing gorditas tacos to the fast-food market. Taco Bell restaurants flew red flags emblazoned with the beret-clad animal. Car antennae sprouted red pennants, again adorned with the canine Che. And in heavily run television spots, on a churrigueresque balcony high above the throngs of a dusty colonial city, the "Che-huahua" appeared at a bank of ancient oversized microphones. Upon the dog's intonation of an echoing "¡Viva Gorditas!" adoring throngs chanted and sang in unison as giant red banners unfurled across the sides of buildings, each emblazoned with a massive arm holding a taco aloft. And throughout the campaign, the gorditas slogan was endlessly repeated: "The Revolutionary Taco."

WHITE MONKEYS, BLACK BLOCKS

So, has the revolution been commoditized? There is no definitive answer. Certainly, Taco Bell's spokescanine provides one tacit answer. Conversely, by mid-2000, the Che-huahua partisan of the "revolutionary taco" had been put to sleep. Sales had fallen, accumulation went off, the Chihuahua had transitioned from popular to passé, and TBWA\Chiat\Day lost the Taco Bell account. The commodity, then, is an unstable thing even in its most static forms.

And it becomes all the more so when it takes to the road. The same period that saw the demise of the revolutionary taco also witnessed the sudden appearance of mass actions against the conclaves at which plutocratic globality is administered and imposed. The prototype of these was the "Battle in Seattle." From November 29–December 2, 1999, Seattle was to be the place for the World Trade Organization's ceremonial ratification of the Multilateral Agreement on Investment (or MAI), an unprecedented claim to the absolute sovereignty of capital. Or so it would have been, had not the text of the MAI leaked. In response, activists coordinated worldwide over the Internet (Ronfeldt et al. 1998, 115) to arrange that the WTO functionaries be greeted by approximately fifty thousand dissidents.

What was particularly notable about this protest, however, was not just its size or electronic coordination, but the persistent diversity of its participants and practices. They shipped in from locales as disparate as Atlanta, Turin, Jakarta, and Seoul; represented everything from the most hierarchical church organizations to massing hordes of Black Bloc-ed anarchists; and deployed such diverse tactics as multiple-thousand person marches, tossed brickbats, two-story-tall puppet shows, and even the blockade of a WTO delegates' hotel by arm-in-arm bell-ringing Santas.

This "battle" announced the emergence of an alternate globality dedicated to revealing the contradictory absurdities of its institutionally legitimized, plutocratic other. It demonstrated new practices of resistance centered upon the highly creative and generally playful intrusion of the body into commonplace spatial infrastructure (a practice some participants now refer to as "voting"). And it accomplished all this through the popular production of an environment most closely resembling a gigantic circus. Or, more to the point, a traveling carnival.

In speaking of such events as carnival, I intend no disparagement. In his definition of carnival, Mikhail Bakhtin (1984, chap. 3) characterizes it as the classic Temporary Autonomous Zone, an event mobile in time, space, or both that clears space and time for the practice of the popular-festive form. Carnival marks the inevitable passages of time, the death of the old and the corollary renewal of the world, made concrete in a celebration the people give to themselves. At carnival time, decrepit truths and the humorless authority figures they reinforce are beaten down and mocked with blows that are painful but "gay, melodious and festive" (Bakhtin 1984, 207). Thus, the high is abased and destroyed in the service of low bodily renewal. In the process, the "carnivalesque crowd" organizes itself in its own way, "outside of and contrary to all existing forms of the coercive socioeconomic and political organization" (Bakhtin 1984, 255). In short, carnival is a collective and emplaced bodily practice that playfully dismembers the authorially imposed body politic.

The "battles" in Seattle and beyond, in their loosely collaborative horizontal organization, spontaneity, deployment of violently playful confrontation, and even in such seemingly superficial trappings as their use of costume masks, constitute a hearty resurgence of Bakhtinian festival to bring plutocratic globality down from on high, humiliate its authority, and subordinate it to the body. Such battles are Temporary Autonomous Zones that, in the loosely systematized itineracy of their participants, have become more of a widely portable Permanent Autonomous Zone (a PAZ, perhaps?), a carnivalesque globality that recovers the popular-festive form to hurl its merrily destructive creations against the gray, grim, and self-seriously opaque global administration of creative destruction.

This continuing carnival bears strong isomorphisms with that of March 2001 in Mexico City's Zócalo. Further, it is suggestive that it emerges in conjunction with the Zapatistas' Intercontinental Encuentros. Of course, there are some significant differences, most notably the fact that carnivalesque globality's anarchist bent is at odds with the Zapatistas' support of the nation-state and openness to capitalism. But despite these distinctions, it would seem that the Zapatistas have indeed "inspired and stimulated a wide variety of grass-roots political efforts in many other countries" (Cleaver in Ronfeldt et al. 1998, 115).

The evidence for this "Zapatista Effect" (Cleaver 1998) is to be found in the persons and practices of the protesters themselves. Attendees of the Ruckus Society's Democracy Action Camps are one instance of this. This camp is a traveling emplacement founded in 1995, devoted to training would-be resisters in "nonviolent direct actions" ranging from forming bodily block-ades to rappelling down the sides of building while unfurling unauthorized banners. Consistently, Ruckus participants cite the Zapatistas as their inspira-tion, and many identify their own experiences as tourists in Chiapas as the trigger for their subsequent civilly disobedient practices upon their return home (see Lewis 2000).

An even stronger case is made by those White Monkeys. They are a divi-sion of the Italian (although now multinational) Ya Basta! Association, founded by young urban autonomists in 1996 as a foreign Zapatista support group. Dozens of them were among the "foreign infestation" ejected from Chiapas in 1998. They have pioneered many of the new carnivalesque tactics of a "rebellion of the body" by interposing their own highly visible and well-padded bodies (dressed in white, in day-glo hues, or in nothing at all, taped into foam rubber suits, strapped into nets full of brightly colored balloons, car-rying garbage can lids) where authority wants them least. They tie these prac-tices explicitly to Foucault's ideas of bio-power, arguing that only through the disorderly rebelliousness of bodies can the state's exercise of power through the ordering and silencing of bodies be countered. And they have personally ported these theories and practices with them on their travels to mass protests from the West Coast of North America to the Yucatan and Europe's eastern fringes. But ultimately the White Monkeys cite their experiences and first-hand observations of the Zapatistas' bodily resistance as their principal source, especially the combatants armed with dummy guns and the Zapatista women who have massed unarmed around Mexican soldiers to prevent them entering Mayan villages (see Ramírez Cuevas 2000; Ya Basta! 2001).

The White Monkeys, then, constitute a concretely identifiable link by which Zapatismo's theory and praxis have themselves gone traveling, and traveled so widely as to become an axis of articulation for a carnivalesque al-ternate globality. Further, the White Monkey's particular translation of Zap-atismo has itself been exported as a replicable new paradigm of not-so-passive resistance, informing highly visible direct-action organizations like the United Kingdom's WOMBLES (White Overalls Movement Building Lib-ertarian Effective Struggles) and Australia's WOMBATS (White Overall Mobile Buffer Against Truncheon Strikes).

THE CLASH OF GLOBALIZATIONS

Carnival, of course, is not all fun and play. Carnivalesque globality is similarly a deadly serious production, one that wields like a cudgel the vast contradictions between modernization's promises and demonstrable effects to leave plutocratic globality bruisedblueandcontused (Rabelais 1955, 483). Plutocratic globality in turn has mobilized an ever-expanding arsenal of chain-link fencing, concrete barricades, and multi-million dollar phalanxes of public/private police armed with chemical agents, bean-bag rounds, and rubber bullets to leave its carnivalesque other gassedstunnedshotzappeddousedanddisappeared (see, for example, Garcia 2000; Morales 2001, 11; Kuiper 2001a; *The Economist* 2001; BBC News 2001a, 2001b; and Nordland and Dickey 2001 for a more selectively disinformative presentation of the events at Genoa). Along this trajectory, play assumes a hard, dark edge wherein the carnival mask gives way to the gas mask, and cities that play host to globalist summits become trigger-happy police-citystates (Kuiper 2001b; Flecker 2003) sited in locales as noteworthy for their relative inaccessibility as for their celebrity (MacKinnon 2001).

This hardening could be regarded as a resounding defeat for the resistance of those whose lives are at risk for being creatively destroyed without their informed consent. Then again, the militarization and geographical peripheralization of supranational state summits speaks to the newfound power that travel affords resistance, power sufficient to turn triumphalist transnational conclaves into costly and disruptive menaces regarded by prospective host cities as events best held somewhere else, *anywhere* else but *here*. Through their travels, then, the peripheralized now intermittently peripheralize the center, concretely evicting it to the ends of the earth.

Such displacement in turn viscerally reminds us that time-space does not compress automagically (see Harvey 1989), modernity is not a predestined utopia at the terminal plateau of some teleological timeline, and globalization is not a disembodied and omnipresent juggernaut traveling overhead at warpspeed with nobody identifiable at the helm. Rather, they are all "totalizing locals" with pretensions to universality (Shiva 1993), the generalized outcomes of specific and localizable hegemonic ideologies, valorized personages, and branded commodities that circulate among particular places. Conjointly these actors may well take on the appearance of a "competitive globalization, the globalization of inequalities, the globalization of security and plenty for a few, of the illusion of an eternally happy present for those who can 'consume,' and of oppression, subordination or exclusion for the majority" (Arruda 1996). But this effect is necessarily underpinned by the travels of the personnel comprising the transnational corporations and supranational regulatory institutions that enact such administrative rubrics as "deregulation" and "privatization," of foreign direct investors, of fiscal policy advisors and, when the going gets particularly rough (for instance, see Walton and Seddon 1994), of rapidly deployed troop formations and depleted uranium rounds.

Plutocratic globality's emplacement, embodiment, and enactment in transit are precisely why a muñeca Zapatista traveling across the would-be Free Trade Area of the Americas, or a brick traveling through the window of a chain mega-retailer for that matter, can exert countervailing material impacts. And while such impacts will in time fade, they may also in the interim constitute terrains of resistance "both metaphoric and literal" (Routledge 1996, 517), the warp across which any number of alternate globalities can be woven.

Similarly, the Zapatista uprising itself may no longer be so dramatic, so novel, so sexily telegenic, nor even so locally effectual as was once the case. Indeed, it is possible that, in the Zócalo sometime in the foreseeable future, there will be an enthusiastic trade in priapic black-and-white striped dolls of Marcos. Carnival, after all, is the cyclical business of debasing last year's king. But through its travels into the wuzmoderne timespaces of the asymmetrically overdeveloped (Anton 1995) world, the alternate modernity that is Zapatismo has already done its bit—it has kludged together a terrain from whence we can refuse the imposition of a unitary, creatively destructive modernization and reject the forcible reduction of the global to a single authoritative vision.

NOTES

This chapter is adapted from *De-Coca-Colonization: Making the Globe from the Inside Out*. New York, London: Routledge, 2004.

1. 3 Mustaphas 3 1989.

9

Terror and Tourism: Charting the Ambivalent Allure of the Urban Jungle

Kathleen M. Adams

In the early 1960s *National Geographic Magazine* commissioned a series of articles from a California couple exploring the roadways and waterways of Asia on *Tortuga II*, an amphibious jeep purchased from a World War II surplus depot. The couple's first installment recounts their floating and roading adventures on and along the Ganges, where *Tortuga* would sometimes carry them "to venerable cities and princely palaces" and other times serve as their "campsite in the countryside, where the only wealth was in the stars" (Schreider and Schreider 1960, 445). Their next installment, published in May 1961, chronicles the couple's travels through Indonesia. As the article's subtitle heralds, this leg of their *Tortuga* adventure transpires in a "young and troubled island nation." Their essay opens dramatically, with their arrival in the capital city of Jakarta, a little over a decade after Indonesia's independence from the Netherlands:

> Djakarta's traffic swarmed around us: I made my turn with more than usual caution. Crack! A rifle flashed close by, and a cordon of soldiers materialized. In minutes we stood in the office of an army commandant. "But all I did was make a wrong turn," I protested. "Your sentry could have blown his whistle—he didn't have to shoot!"
> The commandant smiled in apology.
> "Forgive us," he said, "but Indonesia is in a state of emergency. Even here in the capital, one sometimes shoots first and asks later." (Schreider and Schreider 1961, 579)

Encapsulated in the opening paragraph of this Indonesia travelogue is a theme central to this chapter, namely, the imaging in global travel media of certain insular Southeast Asian locales as danger zones, inspiring aversion and allure for armchair travelers and intrepid adventurers. This chapter is broadly concerned with danger-zone travel to insular Southeast Asian cities. Whereas safaris to untamed wildernesses caught the fancy of elite thrill-seekers in colonial times, in the contemporary postcolonial era "urban jungles" are developing a new allure for a certain breed of Euro-American adventurers. In the pages that follow, I examine the touristic imagery and cybercelebrity of these postcolonial urban jungles. Through this exploration, I seek to highlight some of the ways in which danger-zone tourism embodies an array of paradoxes that are illustrative of the experience and dynamics of modernity. Most prominent among these is how danger-zone tourism paradoxically marks locales like Dili as both global metropoles and untamed urban jungles.

Much has been written on the ways in which Southeast Asian cities have been undergoing touristic (re-)imagining, (re-)structuring, and (re-)framing in the postcolonial era, as nations once relegated to the fringes of Euro-American consciousness now pursue a dual quest for foreign capital and global celebrity (cf. Cartier 1998; Chang 1997; Kahn 1997). With such cities as Paris, London, and New York hailed as central nodes in transnational economic, technological, and media networks, some Southeast Asian governments have begun strategizing to add their capitals to the list of "preeminent global cities," with the aim of thereby infusing these capitals with a different sort of capital. As governments and planners strive to transform their Southeast Asian cities into international "command posts" for finance, technology, markets, media, and creative genius, a relatively consistent theme has been the re-imaging and touristic promotion of these cities. Paradoxically, for a number of Southeast Asian cities, becoming a destination for international tourists appears to simultaneously contribute to and underscore one's status as a so-called "global city." Witness Singapore's recent campaign to reinvent itself as a "Global City for the Arts," capable of attracting and retaining foreign businesses as well as international tourists (cf. Adams 2003b; Chang 2000b). Likewise, Indon.com's (a leading Internet company representing Indonesia in the international Internet community) "Welcome to Jakarta" Web page celebrates Indonesia's capital as follows:

> Home to over 10 million people, Jakarta is always bustling, from the sound of the wheel of government turning to the sight of the economy churning. Skyscrapers, single story residential houses, modern apartment complexes, survivalists' shanties—all coexist in this city. So why should you visit Jakarta? Well, for the same reasons you would visit New York, or London, or Paris, or Singapore or any other big city. Because you can find everything there! (www.indo.com/jakarta/tourism.html, downloaded 20 December 2001)

In short, for some, a city's touristic magnetism underscores its status as a so-called "global city," worthy of joining the ranks of New York, London, or other global cities. That is, the ability to transmit an alluring image as a cultural center and draw international tourists can be seen as an accoutrement of a global city. But what of the dynamics in tumultuous times, when images of these cities as sites of rioting and violence are projected around the globe on nightly CNN reports? How do mayhem and the threat of urban violence unsettle conventional assumptions about the trajectory to "global city" status?

There is a growing literature on the effects of political instability and violence on tourism to urban Asian destinations (cf. Gartner and Shen 1992; Richter 1992; Parnwell 1998; Bishop and Robinson 1998). To date, the predominant focus of research on tourism and political instability has examined political unrest in destination cities in terms of tourist flows, economic impact, or image management (cf. Pizam and Mansfield 1996; Wilson 1993; Gartner and Shen 1992). However, surprisingly little scholarly attention has been directed to the ironic ways in which urban violence rearticulates touristic images, conceptions, and fantasies about postcolonial Southeast Asian cities. Moreover, the forms of urban tourism that thrive in tumultuous times have been largely ignored. This chapter explores these themes in Indonesia and East Timor, drawing on ethnographic data collected in Indonesia in the 1990s, interviews with returning "danger-zone tourists" encountered in Singapore and the United States, analysis of blogs, and postings to travel-oriented Internet sites. I suggest that this underexplored genre of tourism has the potential to reconfigure perceptions of Southeast Asian cities in paradoxical ways: danger-zone travelers are not merely innocuous observers of political clashes but can play a role in the reshaping of sensibilities about distant urban sites. I argue that the narratives and electromagnetic images produced by urban danger-zone travelers ironically both inscribe such cities as Dili and Jakarta as global metropoles and simultaneously mark them as wild urban jungles. Tracing the specific historicity of travelers' images of Dili underscores the centrality of the electromagnetic sphere in concomitantly globalizing *and* disenfranchising Dili as a ruinous city scarred by its legacy of violence. I also suggest that urban danger-zone travel offers a lens for understanding Dili and other tumultuous urban Southeast Asian destinations as "futural cities," harbingers of the total urban mobilization depicted by Armitage and Roberts (2003). In short, the dynamics of danger-zone tourism reveal (post-)modernity's ongoing morphology.

This chapter is organized into four sections. First, I begin by delineating the category of "danger-zone tourist" as a quintessential form of modern tourism, embodying many of the paradoxes of modern subjectivity. Next, I turn to outline the imagery of danger-zone tourism in postcolonial Southeast Asian cities.

Following this section, I examine the context for urban danger-zone tourism in Indonesia and sketch the array of images (both subjective and objective) propelling this genre of tourist. Finally, I focus on the case of the city of Dili, capital of East Timor. As one of the world's newest postcolonial cities, with historic roots in the spice trade, years of Portuguese and Indonesian colonialism and, more recently, as a much-televised urban site of turbulence, suffering, and destruction, Dili offers a unique lens for viewing the interplay between historicity, geopolitics, and global communications networks. Whereas in colonial days, Dili drew traders seeking Timor's sandalwood and offered a stopover for vessels en route to the Spice Islands, today's postcolonial Dili has become an urban magnet for not only reporters and international aid workers, but also a particular breed of danger-zone tourists who chronicle their adventures in this "war-scarred city" on the global electromagnetic stream.

DEFINING DANGER-ZONE TOURISTS

As Malcolm Crick observed, sun, sand, sea, and sex are the four "S"s often perceived as the essence of a developing nation's touristic appeal (Crick 1989, 309). And as Linda Richter added, "a fifth 's' is even more critical: security" (Richter 1992, 36). However, these ingredients tend to be irrelevant or even antithetical to one genre of tourist generally overlooked in the tourism literature. While tumultuous Southeast Asian cities have frightened off many package tourists, they have emerged as alluring destinations for what I term "danger-zone tourists."[1] Danger-zone tourists are travelers who are drawn to areas of political turmoil. Their pilgrimages to strife-torn destinations are not for professional purposes but rather for leisure, although in some cases the professional identities of danger-zone tourists are related to their leisure pursuits.[2] The desire to vacation in an urban riot or war zone may strike some as peculiar to relatively maladjusted individuals, but I would suggest that danger-zone tourism is simply an extreme form of modern tourism. It embodies the epitome of the paradoxical dynamics found in other genres of tourism (as discussed in the introduction of this volume) and offers a unique lens on modernity. Danger-zone tourism is driven by the modern infatuation with authenticity and, as we shall see, entangled with processes of commodification.

The backpacker traveler in Thailand featured in Alex Garland's recent novel, *The Beach*[3] (1996), captures the mind-set of many danger-zone tourists when he reflects,

> I wanted to witness extreme poverty. I saw it as a necessary experience for anyone who wanted to appear worldly and interesting. Of course witnessing poverty

was the first to be ticked off the list. Then I had to graduate to the more obscure stuff. Being in a riot was something I pursued with a truly obsessive zeal, along with being tear-gassed and hearing gunshots fired in anger. Another list item was having a brush with my own death. (Garland 1996, 164)

A similar mentality pervades "Fielding's BlackFlag Café," a website devoted to travelers returning from and planning visits to dangerous places. The site's byline explains its unique orientation:

Looking for fun in all the wrong places? Well you've found the nets [sic] only hangout for hardcore adventurers, travel junkies, DP'ers [dangerous placers] and just about anyone who runs screaming from glossy brochures, backpacker guidebooks and Robin Leach. So let's get busy. Got a tip? Just came back from the Congo, just heading off to Albania? Let us know and don't be surprised if the staff of Fielding, the authors of DP [Dangerous Places] or the CIA drops you a line. (Anon., Fielding's BlackFlag Café Website: www.fieldingtravel.com, downloaded 15 January 2000)

BlackFlag Café frequenters appear to have varying levels of experience with danger-zone travel, though all seem to share an intense interest in adrenalin-rush travel. While some of the BlackFlag Café visitors are arm-chair danger-zone travelers, others are actively engaged in touring the world's hot spots, often beginning with risky off-the-beaten track destinations and working their way up to battlefields and war zones. As one recent BlackFlag Café posting reads,

A traveller in many "soft" DP [dangerous place] countries over the past ten years, I have decided it is time to go for my first war zone. Armed with my clippings, letters of intro and mas bullsh**, where should I go for my first ringside view of armed conflict? Should I dive into the thick of it "Chechnya?" or should I find a good "intro" hotspot? (Andre, "My First War," Fielding's BlackFlag Adventure Forum: www.fieldingtravel.com, posted 10 February 2000)

Among the Asian destinations suggested by repliers were sites of civil strife in Indonesia and the war zone in Afghanistan.

The BlackFlag Café Website is an outgrowth of Robert Young Pelton, Coskun Aral, and Wink Dulles's popular travel guide *Fielding's The World's Most Dangerous Places* (1998). Hailed by *The New York Times* as "one of the oddest and most fascinating travel books to appear in a long time" (Pelton, Aral, and Dulles 1998, cover), the 1998 edition of this volume features chapters on Cambodia, Myanmar, and the Philippines, as well as shorter entries on Indonesia (Timor) and Laos. With its fourth edition published, the book has enjoyed cult popularity among both armchair travelers and American danger-zone tourists. The brisk sales of this and other related guidebooks, as well as the touristic popularity of T-shirts with such slogans as "Danger!! Mines!! Cambodia!!"[4] not only suggest the allure of danger-zone travel but also illustrate the commodification of this emerging genre of travel. The paradoxes of modern tourism are particularly salient in this commodification of desire. These war-zone guidebooks and souvenir apparel celebrating close brushes with peril testify to the danger-zone traveler's need to essentialize and objectify the world (rendering it comprehensible and orderly—the task of guidebooks) while preserving the subjective experience of difference, discovery, and risk.

While the numbers of danger-zone tourists appear to be rising, the allure of touristic forays into politically risky regions has a long history, as do danger-zone travel entrepreneurs. According to Mitchell (1988, 57), as early as 1830, French entrepreneurs were ferrying tourists to North Africa to witness the French bombardment of Algiers. In more contemporary times, educational tour organizers have marketed trips to Indonesia to explore the religious strife between Christians and Muslims in Indonesia and the U.S.-based "Reality Tours" has offered group trips to politically volatile events and destinations in Latin America and Southeast Asia. Likewise, an Italian travel agency has organized groups equipped with doctors, guards, and combat gear to usher tourists to the edges of battle zones in places like Dubrovnik and the south of Lebanon (Phipps 1999, 83, cited in Diller and Scofidio 1994, 136). Such touristic expeditions to "the places shown on the television news" can have hefty price tags: the aforementioned Italian tours were sold at US$25,000 per person (83). While many danger-zone tourists are low-budget travelers, the fact that some are willing to spend extravagant amounts for their travels prompts questions concerning the compelling allure of this genre of travel.

In his exploration of the relationship between tourist discourse and tourist death, Phipps (1999) ponders the appeal of risk travel. Drawing on the work of Albert Camus, he suggests that fear gives value to travel: "[t]his threat of death and danger is something that tourism relishes so as to retain its imaginative power as a space for reconnecting with the 'real' which remains so elusive . . . in this order of highly stratified, regulated and abstracted capitalist postmodern society" (Phipps 1999, 83). While the promise of so-called authentic encounters and experiences is intrinsic to danger-zone tourism, I believe that there are also issues of class and social differentiation at play. Inspired by Bourdieu (1984) and Featherstone (1987), Munt (1994, 102) has suggested that the consumption of unique travel experiences has increasing salience in defining social distinction. Munt argues that, in striving to establish distinction from the touristic practices of classes below them, the new middle classes have embraced a number of new forms of travel (Munt 1994, 119). Travel to Third World destinations, says Munt, is one of the major experiences embraced by the new middle class to establish and maintain social differentiation, a practice that separates these "adventurers" from the masses of package tourists. In writing on the broader topic of risk tourism, Elsrud (2001) makes a related observation. She suggests that risk narratives are a form of traveler's capital; they play into a hierarchical value system positioning travelers vis-à-vis one another and vis-à-vis their stay-at-home friends. The insights of Phipps, Munt, and Elsrud resonate with my perceptions of the appeal of danger-zone travel.

Wayne Pitts is one of the few scholars to have made passing note of this genre of tourists, which he terms "war tourists" (Pitts 1996). In his discussion of the impact of uprisings in Chiapas (Mexico) on the tourist economy, he comments, "Just like drivers on the interstate stretching their necks trying to get a glimpse of 'what happened' at a wreck scene, these individuals [war tourists] wanted to be a part of the action" (Pitts 1996, 221). As Pitts later adds, the "war tourists" in Chiapas were there "to experience the thrill of political violence." One magazine reported a Canadian woman explaining her reasons for visiting Chiapas were "journalism, a tan and a revolution" (cited in Pitts 1996, 224). Likewise, while researching the broader topic of risk creation in travel narratives, Torun Elsrud reports that she has come across interviewees who say they are looking forward to riots in Indonesia, as it is "cool to have seen/been in one."[5] These descriptions hint at some of the varied activities and motivations of the genre of tourist that are drawn to tumultuous urban sites in Southeast Asia.

In spite of the precedent set by Pitts, I prefer to employ the term *danger-zone tourists* instead of *war tourists,* as I believe this particular form of tourism necessitates distinction from the broader category of "war tourism" discussed by Valene Smith (1996). In her exploration of war tourism, Smith focuses on the commemorative dimension of tourism to the sites of *past* wars—battlefields, cemeteries, military re-enactments, monuments, and so forth.[6] My interest here, however, is not tourism pertaining to *past* wars, but rather tourism to tumultuous urban locales, cities that are not necessarily the sites of declared wars but are nevertheless sites of *ongoing* political instability, sites where there is at least an imagined potentiality of violent eruptions. Likewise, I have not adopted the term *risk tourism* embraced by some writers (cf. Elsrud 2001), as this term covers a broader array of activities including such physically challenging hinterland enterprises as whitewater rafting in Sarawak. For these reasons pertaining to precision, in this chapter I adopt the expression *urban danger-zone tourism.* One final point merits underscoring: a wide array of motives and interests fall under the heading "danger-zone tourist"—from humanitarian/activist tourists, to adrenalin-rush pursuers, to those seeking firsthand journalistic experiences—as becomes evident in our discussion of urban danger-zone tourism in Indonesia. In discussing urban danger-zone tourism, I am not arguing for an essentialism of this genre of tourism, but rather advocate the need to attend to the image-trafficking manifest in urban danger-zone travel.

THE IMAGERY OF URBAN SOUTHEAST ASIAN DANGER-ZONE TOURISM

Fielding's The World's Most Dangerous Places, the definitive guidebook for danger-zone tourists, devotes chapters to several Southeast Asian nations and their cities. In the 1998 version of this handbook, as in the corresponding website, Cambodia and Myanmar (Burma) figure prominently. As tourists develop images of their vacation destinations long before they depart, through media images and guidebooks, and as they draw on these glossy images in assessing their experiences in these destinations (Adams 1984), it is apt to begin our discussion with an examination of the urban danger-zone imagery found in such guidebooks and travel advice websites.

In logging onto Fielding's website devoted to dangerous places (www.fieldingtravel.com), one immediately knows one is in a different sort of travel zone. The background wallpaper for pages devoted to Cambodia, Myanmar, and the Philippines features cartoon-like images of rifles, shields, and spears in crossbones positions and dynamite time bombs. Likewise, each chapter of the book version of *Fielding's The World's Most Dangerous Places* (Pelton et al. 1998) is decorated with a comic image of a sunglass-sporting skull toting a baseball cap adorned with the DP logo. The chapters themselves are illustrated with smaller cartoons of exploding demonstrators, bazooka-carrying troops, burning dynamite sticks, and fierce killer bees. These comic images seemingly "tame" the terrors of riots and warfare, offering the subliminal message that dangerous travel can be something entertaining. Even the danger-themed photographs accompanying each chapter have lulling dimensions. The Myanmar chapter, for instance, opens with a shot of artificial limbs dangling decoratively from tropical vegetation. Other images in this chapter include two plump toddlers holding whimsically decorated guns, and troops trotting in front of a thatched-roofed pavilion. While smiling gunmen and helicopters make frequent appearances in the pages of this book, there are no images of corpses or actual warfare. In a paradoxical fashion, this and other similar books render danger-zone travel inviting yet thrilling.

The narrative "Cambodia—In a Dangerous Place" underscores these themes of unpredictable danger for the unaware and excitement for the savvy traveler. As the writers recount,

We went to Cambodia on a lark. These days, Cambodia is not necessarily the most dangerous place in the world, or even a nasty place, but it is an exotic, very inexpensive stop that every traveler to Asia should make. Is it safe? Well, if you stay inside the tourist ruts (literally), don't venture outside the ill-defined "safety" zone and watch where you step, Cambodia can be safe. Cambodia can also be brutal if you pass through the invisible safety barrier and end up in the hands of the Khmer Rouge. Just remember the advice of your first grade teacher, "Don't color outside the lines. . . . One tourist can fly into Phnom Penh and Siem Reap on a modern jet, stay in a five star hotel, and see the temple complex, complete with cold Pepsis, an air-conditioned car and a good meal, followed by an ice-cold beer at one of the many nightclubs the U.N. soldiers used to frequent. Another tourist can find himself kneeling at the edge of a shallow, hastily dug grave, waiting for the rifle butt that will slam into his cortex, ending his brief but adventurous life. The difference between the two scenarios might be 10 km or lingering a few too many minutes along the road. (Pelton et al. 1998, 364)

Southeast Asian cities in Cambodia and Myanmar, in particular, receive dramatic danger-zone profiling in the 1998 edition of Robert Young Pelton's book. In a section of the Cambodia chapter entitled "In a Dangerous Place," Pelton devotes two pages to describing a typical evening in Siem Reap. His narrative could easily have been drawn from the script of a Chuck Norris film, encompassing guns, seedy discotheques, incipient violence, a brutalized police officer, and danger-habituated bar hostesses:

That night back in Siem Reap we go to a nightclub. The sign outside says "no guns or explosives." The music is pure sing-song Khmer played at ear-damaging levels. . . . Wink [Pelton's fellow danger-zone traveler and co-contributor to the volume] decides to get up and jam with the band. The audience is dumbstruck and stares open-mouthed for two songs. The dance floor clears out and the Cambodians don't know if they should clap or cover their ears. Wink finishes up to a round of applause. After Wink sits down, it seems not everyone is thrilled with the impromptu jam session. We are challenged to a fight in a less than sensitive manner. An elbow not once, not twice, but three times in the back—hard. We decide to split. This would not be a John Wayne punch 'em up. But probably a good ole' sloppy burst of gunfire. (Pelton et al. 1998, 368)

They change venues and have yet another close call with the nightly violence of Siem Reap:

Sitting outside to avoid the chilling air conditioning and deafening noise inside, we are interrupted as a Cambodian cop comes flying out of the glass entry doors, followed by shouting, punching and kicking patrons. The girls sitting with us immediately react, jump up and drag us around the corner and down an alley. They plead with us to "Go, go, run! Please, before you are shot! . . . We push past them and are in time to watch the cop being kicked and beaten and slammed unconsciously into the back of a pickup truck. The girls explain that we are lucky (a term we are hearing a lot here). Usually, there is gunfire . . . I laugh . . . The sad look in her eyes tells me I am being far too casual about a very real threat. With a sense of resignation, she says, "This is a dangerous place. You should not be here." (Pelton et al. 1998, 369)

By 2000, Siem Reap has begun to lose its cache for danger-zone travelers. One returnee from a trip to Siem Reap posts his advice on Pelton's BlackFlag Café Website, warning other danger-zone travelers to give Siem Reap a pass, as it had ceased to be a danger-zone destination—it had become a "TOURIST TRAP." As he grumbles, "Its no longer adventurous, dangerous, fun etc. to go there—every tourist in Cambodia goes there. Go to Burma" (Mike "Cambodia" Fieldings' BlackFlag Café, www.fieldingtravel.com. www.zinezone.com/pubbin/login, posted 5 February 2000).

As such postings hint, danger-zone tourism has fickle tendencies: as destinations become perceived to be calmer and draw growing numbers of "ordinary" travelers, danger-zone pilgrims move on to new sites of tumult. Mirroring the paradox of mainstream tourism whereby the presence of other tourist hordes "spoils" the destination, for danger-zone tourists, places like Siem Reap lose their attractiveness by becoming too safe. The various editions of *Fielding's The World's Most Dangerous Places* attest to the rapidity with which destinations move in and out of vogue with this genre of traveler. Dangerous cities spotlighted in one edition are often absent from the next, replaced by new war-torn sites currently featured on CNN reports. When Pelton et al.'s volume includes dangerous destinations that are not active war sites, they are often depicted as camouflaged tinderboxes. For instance, the 1998 edition of Pelton's book devotes copious pages to Burma/Myanmar and includes a lengthy section on the city of Yangon. Here, as elsewhere, we find the theme of superficially "normal" urban scenery masking lurking dangers:

Yangon has a slightly cosmopolitan feel. The sidewalks are packed with a mish-mash of races in the colorful garb denoting their ethnic blueprints: Indian, Burmese, Bangladeshi, Chinese, Shan. They stroll past the washed-out aqua, yellow and pink pastels of apartment buildings and businesses and the restored, grand buildings of British colonial days.

During rush hours, Yangon's streets rival those of any other Southeast Asian capital; traffic crawls at the pace of democratic reforms here. But not at the pace of hotel construction; five-star caravansaries are shooting skyward in all parts of the city like a seismograph in Riverside County, California. . . . The streets of Yangon are clean, curbs freshly painted . . . lawns, parks, and even road medians are meticulously manicured and landscaped. There are few beggars. People dress remarkably well. . . . Comparisons with Singapore come to mind. In fact, a visitor here is struck with an indelible sense of Yangon being a prosperous city-state rather than a Third World capital.

Unless one is accustomed to hanging around dictatorships, the causal visitor won't get it. . . . But dig a little deeper and the observer will be shocked. (Pelton et al. 1998, 613–14)

The contributing author, Wink Dulles, goes on to compare the city of Yangon to a library, where if one talks at all, it is in hushed voices. Noting that the topic of politics will instantly clear a room, he adds, "Ask a shopkeeper in Yangon why barbed-wire barricades have been set up on the street in front of his establishment and he'll answer 'to slow traffic.' Ask what kind of traffic and you'll be asked to leave" (Pelton et al. 1998, 614). Dulles proceeds to chronicle his evening adventures in the streets of Yangon, the time most favored for observing the "'viscera'" of this particular urban danger zone.

I picked a delightful March evening for a stroll through the capital. . . . I first dined on curried roadkill down the street. . . . A troop transport truck rolled up to the corner; a half dozen rifle-toting soldiers jumped to the street and made themselves conspicuous. The rest of the patronage paid their bills. I did so as well and headed in the direction of the mosque, where three other troop transport trucks, packed to the stakes with soldiers, had set up shop for the night. I walked past; the soldiers all wore the same expression—like the way the Green Beret guy with the bloody hands stares at Martin Sheen when he arrives at Col. Kurtz's kingdom in "Apocalypse Now." (614–15)

Eventually Dulles finds himself questioned by a sinister character in charge of the troop movements. He claims to be merely a tourist out for a smoke, and his disbelieving interrogator gruffly sends him back to the confines of his hotel. Noteworthy here, as at the BlackFlag Café Website, is the allusion to Hollywood images as prior texts for processing travelers' adventures in dangerous destinations. Peppering the narratives of some danger-zone travelers are references to *Apocalypse Now*, *The Year of Living Dangerously*, and *The Beach*.

Having briefly surveyed some of the pre-travel Southeast Asian urban imagery offered to budding danger-zone tourists, I turn now to examine danger-zone tourism in the urban Indonesian context. As the Indonesian case illustrates, the range of urban danger-zone tourists is varied, as are the images they produce of Indonesian cities.

URBAN DANGER-ZONE TOURISM IN INDONESIA

Since mid-1998, Indonesian tourism promoters have struggled against mounting negative imagery due to political, economic, ethnic, and religious unrest. As a September 1999 online article headlined "Indonesian Tourism Industry Battered by Images of Violence" reports, "Indonesia has been plagued by image-problems in recent times—from last year's economic crisis and related unrest to this year's militia rampage in East Timor and riots in Jakarta" (Mintier 1999). Likewise, increasing numbers of independent travelers sharing advice on the Web are painting a tableaux of Indonesia as a land of travel traumas, urging fellow travelers to opt for Thailand or Malaysia's more predictably peaceful isles. Such negative imagery has taken its toll: in 1998 the number of foreign visitors to Indonesia shrunk by 18.6 percent (to 14.4 million), with Bali being the sole Indonesian destination to record an increase in foreign visitors. Following the 2002 Bali disco bombing and news reports of Al Qaeda cells throughout Indonesia, tourism has fallen off dramatically in Bali, as well.[7] It is precisely in this sort of context that danger-zone tourism emerges.

Indonesian danger-zone tourism comes in various forms, reflecting the varied orientations and motivations of danger-zone tourists. At one end of the continuum are the independent budget travelers who make their way to cities like Dili and Banda Aceh, priding themselves on slipping into off-limits destinations. At the other end of the spectrum are the "reality tours" packaged by such operations as Global Exchange and even Indonesian travel houses. Interviews with independent travelers, examinations of danger-zone travel narratives, and perusal of advertisements for Indonesia "reality tours" suggest a number of themes in the imagery of urban danger-zone travel. These include the promise of having authentic encounters with grassroots actors, the potential for enhancing one's personal identity as an activist or humanitarian, and the allure of a unique, "exciting" travel experience that will distinguish the traveler from the growing hoards of ethnic and cultural tourists that now voyage to most corners of the globe. Let us turn to examine this imagery.

My awareness of danger-zone group tours to urban destinations in Indonesia was first prompted by a newspaper advertisement for a planned March 1998 "Reality Tour" to Java billed as "Democracy and Culture of Resistance in Indonesia: Suharto's Last Term?" The tour was organized by Global Exchange, a San Francisco–based group. The imagery of authentic grassroots encounters is a recurrent theme in their Web page. As it explains, their "Reality Tours" are designed "to give people in the U.S. a chance to see firsthand how people facing immense challenges are finding grassroots solutions in their daily lives" (Global Exchange 1999, 1). Moreover, "Reality Tours provide North Americans with a true understanding of a country's internal dynamic through socially responsible travel" (Global Exchange 1999, 2). Here, then, we find the image of the politically correct traveler. For US$2,150, tourists were invited to sign on for a group trip to Jakarta to witness the goings-on of the March 1998 pre-elections. The initial itinerary promised conversations with former political prisoners (including as a possibility the celebrated Indonesian writer Pramoedya), factory workers, and human rights activists. The pièce de résistance, however, was to "dialogue with Indonesians and observe the election day atmosphere in the capital." The repeated use of the word "resistance" and the emphasis on the tentative nature of the itinerary "due to circumstances beyond our control" offer a subtle background image of potential danger, as befits this particular special-interest market.

I Gede Ardika, Indonesia's Director General for Tourism, was quick to pick up on this special-interest market. On March 5, 1999, he told reporters that several parties have welcomed the plan to turn the general election into a tourist attraction. For US$200 a day, three Indonesian travel agencies were selling the "general election tourism package," which promised not only the latest update on the national election process, but also a "close look" at the election process (Asia Pulse 1999). Not surprisingly, the theme of danger receded from the Indonesian packaging of the elections tours; however, the theme of accessing an exciting political event to which only few foreigners are privy remained.

The co-mingling of politics, idealism, and the rare opportunity for authentic face-to-face dialogues with Indonesians about potentially explosive issues does not only manifest itself in elections-watch tours to Indonesia's capital city, but also in a religion-focused tour sponsored by the Hartford Seminary. Entitled "With Muslims and Christians in Indonesia," this 1999 tour offered a first-hand experience that would "deepen participants' awareness of the state of Christian-Muslim relations and peace-making in the region by seeing the issues through the eyes of the indigenous communities" (Hartford Seminary 1999, www.hart.sem.edu/macd/events/Default.htm, accessed in July 2000). Addressing recent upheavals in various cities in Indonesia, the Web-page tour advertisement promised that "close attention will be given to the social, economic and ethnic reasons behind the recent unrest, and the role religious communities are playing, especially in relations to dialogue and understanding between Muslims and Christians" (Hartford Seminary 1999). As in the elections watch tours, here, too, we find the imagery of "first-hand" dialogues with local communities. In this case, however, the imagery of humanitarian and spiritual activism is even stronger.

Such "reality tours" to Indonesia's capital, where participants risk close-up encounters with political riots and religious violence, spotlight Jakarta as a member of the matrix of global cities. In essence, these danger tours underscore Jakarta's position as a political center worthy of the world's attention. Moreover, these political and humanitarian tours' Web-based imagery of potential urban violence and lurking unrest project perilous images of Indonesia's capital city. These Internet-propelled images, as well as returning participants' slide shows and travel tales, have the potential to subtly shift Euro-American sensibilities concerning the quality of urban Southeast Asian life.

Ironically, such danger-zone tours both herald Jakarta's arrival as a global city and simultaneously reify it as an unruly urban jungle. Having sketched Jakarta's paradoxical imaging as global city/global jungle, I turn to Southeast Asia's newest postcolonial capital city, Dili (East Timor), where I trace the traffic of danger-zone images of this city.

DILI, EAST TIMOR: A COLLAGE OF
TRAVELER'S IMAGES, FROM INSALUBRIOUS
FEVER TOWN TO SLEEPY OUTPOST TO SCARRED CITY

While Chinese and Javanese traders seeking sandalwood and beeswax visited East Timor from as early as the thirteenth century, travelers' mentions of Dili are scant prior to the era of Portuguese colonialism. Portuguese explorers and traders began visiting the island in the early sixteenth century (around 1515 AD). One of the earliest European maps and accounts of the island derives from Pigafetta, the son of an aristocratic Vicena family who joined Magellan as the chronicler of his voyage (Lach 1965, 163). Following Magellan's demise in the Philippines, Pigafetta sailed to the Timor archipelago with Magellan's successor, Captain J. S. de Elcano. They landed in Amaben (on Timor's north coast) in January 1521, seeking provisions. While Pigafetta recounts learning of Timor's white sandalwood and wax, no mention is made of Dili in this account of their travels. By 1556, a small group of Dominican friars had established Portugal's first outpost at Lifau. It is not until much later, however, that Dili becomes the seat of Portuguese Timor and gains a growing place in the imagery of Eastern Indonesia.

The English naturalist Alfred Russell Wallace offers one of the first images of Dili to be imparted to a wider European readership. Writing of his visit to Dili in the 1860s he conveys a miserable image of a lonely outpost town:

> Delli [Dili] is a most miserable place compared with even the poorest of the Dutch towns. The houses are all of mud and thatch; the fort is only a mud enclosure; and the custom-house and church are built of the same mean materials, with no attempt at decoration or even neatness. The whole aspect of the place is that of a poor native town, and there is no sign of cultivation or civilization round about it. His Excellency the Governor's house is the only one that makes any pretensions to appearance, and that is merely a low whitewashed cottage or bungalow. Yet there is one thing in which civilization exhibits itself—officials in black and white European costume, and officers in gorgeous uniforms abound

in a degree quite disproportionate to the size or appearance of the place. The town being surrounded for some distance by swamps and mudflats is very unhealthy, and a single night often gives a fever to newcomers which not unfrequently proves fatal. (Wallace 1869)

Apparently Wallace's dismal imagery of Dili and Portuguese Timor lodged in the imagination of other nineteenth-century British travelers. From 1878 to 1883 the British naturalist Henry Forbes traveled in Eastern Indonesia and offers his "field notes made during [his own] wanderings to be considered in light of an *addendum* to . . . [Wallace's] model book of travel" (Forbes 1885, 5). As Forbes submits in his preface, his publication represents the first detailed account of the inhabitants of the interior of Timor. Indeed, it offers not only a wealth of early images of the island's inhabitants but of the town of Dili, as well. Accompanied by his wife, Forbes arrives in Dili by steamer in late 1881. His initial impressions are hardly positive:

> Landing [in Dili] later in the day, we perambulated the town, which wanted much before it could be termed neat or clean or other than dilapidated, but when we afterwards came to know how terribly insalubrious it is, we were surprised that the incessant fever and languor which made life on the lowlands an absolute burden left a particle of energy in anybody to care for anything. The supreme evil of Dilly[8] is its having been built on a low morass, when it might have stood far more salubriously on the easily accessible slopes close behind it. (Forbes 1885, 286)

The sapping fever and pestilence of the city are steady themes in Forbes's subsequent commentary on Dili. Upon returning to Dili after a foray to the Moluccas, Forbes is horrified by the emaciated countenances Dili has produced in his European acquaintances.

> In all of them the notorious Dilly fever had killed down the cheerful vivacity, buoyancy of spirit and bright eye with which they had stepped ashore in the month of May. With the utmost kindness commodious apartments were offered to us in the Palace, but it was perfectly evident that if I wished to accomplish any serious work in Timor, it could not be from Dilly as a center, constantly exposed to the pestilence that nightly rises from the marshes surrounding the town. (Forbes 1885, 415)

Forbes's text also offers glimpses into the ways in which his vision of Dili is refracted through Alfred Wallace's prior text:

> The town, though vastly improved since Mr. Wallace's visit, was still disappointing in may respects, and its Hibiscus-lined streets looked poor and uninviting. The lack of money to carry out efficiently the necessary municipal

arrangements was painfully evident. . . . had the necessary resources been at [the local officers'] disposal, Portuguese Timor might have caught the tide of prosperity she had long waited for. (Forbes 1885, 286)

Forbes's recordings convey not only his aversions to the city but also some of its appeal to European naturalist-explorers. He is unabashed in his fascination with the city as a crossroads of peoples, languages, and cultures:

> In going into the various offices and shops I was struck to find all business conducted not, as in the Dutch possessions, in the *lingua* franca of the Archipelago, Malay, but in Portuguese. . . . In the different quarters of the town native police posted in little encampments are always on guard, and during the still nights it was curious to hear from Timorese throats the *Alerto sta!* at the stroke of every hour. Besides the official staff very few Europeans live in Dilly; the entire trade of the island being conducted by Arabs and (chiefly) by Chinamen.
>
> The streets of Dilly itself offer to the traveller a fine studio for ethnological investigation, for a curious mixture of nationalities other than European rub shoulders with each other in the town's narrow limits. . . . Tall, erect indigenes mingle with Negroes from the Portuguese possessions of Mozambique and the coasts of Africa, most of them here in the capacity of soldiers or condemned criminals; tall lithe East Indians from Goa and its neighbourhood; Chinese and Bugis of Makassar, with Arabs and Malays and natives from Allor, Savu, Roti, and Flores; besides a crowd in whose veins the degree of comminglement of blood of all these races would defy the acutest computation. . . . The shop of Ah Ting, Major of the Chinese, was my favorite study-room while in Dilly, for there during the whole day came and went an endless succession of these nationalities for the purpose of barter or simply to lounge. (Forbes 1885, 417–18)

Forbes's sojourn in Portuguese Timor was ultimately cut short. After several months of ornithological and ethnological work, Forbes's wife became violently ill with "Dilly" fever and so, five months after their arrival, they fled Dili on a mail steamer.

For almost a hundred years following Forbes's account, travelers' images of Dili rarely surface in widely viewed media. A 1943 *National Geographic* article profiled Timor as a "key to the Indies" (St. Clair 1943), conveying the perception of the island as being of great strategic importance in World War II. However, it is not until 1962 that American readers are treated to a new set of adventurers' images of the city. This time, the images come via a final *National Geographic* installment of the Schreiders' amphibious jeep trip across the Indonesian archipelago (Schreider and Schreider 1962). The Schreiders arrive in Dili following a harrowing stormy night crossing the sea between Alor and Timor. Eerily, the tone of their danger-laden arrival in Dili and their description of the city with its "scars of war" foreshadow some contemporary danger-zone travel narratives:

> At the end of nine hours we were desperate to reach land. In spite of the ever-growing metallic cadence from the engine, I again increased our speed. Slowly details became distinct through the binoculars: first a lighthouse, then the red roof of a military post, finally the rows of trees marking the road to Dili, capital of Portuguese Timor.
>
> When the last swell pushed *Tortuga* ashore, we knew how Captain Bligh must have felt when he ended his own small boat journey on this same island 173 years ago.
>
> Dili was still rebuilding from World War II. Despite Portugal's neutrality, Timor had been occupied by the Japanese and had suffered heavy bombardment. By the end of the war its sandalwood—long a lure for traders—was gone, its coffee plantations were overgrown, its cattle herds decimated, and most of its white Portuguese population dead of starvation, sickness or reprisals. Only the newly rebuilt residential area, clinic, church and government building gave evidence of what Dili would become. (Schreider and Schreider 1962, 275–76)

In the years until 1974, when images of Dili surface in adventurers' travel accounts, they are generally that of a quiet colonial outpost, or a regional crossroads. It is not until the tumultuous events of the mid-1970s that Dili bursts into global consciousness once again, setting the stage for it to become a magnet city for international danger-zone travelers.

DILI: AN URBAN DESTINATION FOR DANGER-ZONE TOURISTS

Today, as in the post–World War II period, the dominant image of Dili is once again that of a "scarred" city. Following a military coup in Portugal in 1974, East Timor was poised for Independence when Indonesia invaded. An estimated two hundred thousand people perished in the ensuing battle and famine. By July 1976, amid international controversy, East Timor was declared Indonesia's twenty-seventh province and Dili its capital. For most of the twenty-four years that East Timor was occupied by Indonesia, the area was closed to foreign travelers, as Indonesian troops attempted to suppress the Fretilin[9] resistance movement. However, for a brief period in the late 1980s and 1990s, Indonesia opened the city to foreign tourists. During this window period, Dili becomes a featured city in Eastern Indonesian tourist guidebooks and Web-based travel accounts. The imagery of these tour books is notably tame in contrast with travelers' Dili diaries. One officially sanctioned guidebook from this period spotlights Dili as "A Slowly Awakening

Capital City," "super-clean and yet soul-less" (Muller 1995, 230): a city of "ruler-strait one-way streets" boasting the largest cathedral in all of Southeast Asia. Another Web-based guide describes Dili as a

> quiet, clean town with a very colonial feel, the long sea front road is littered with old Portuguese mansions and offices. Many of the streets behind are strewn with old bond houses and sailors' quarters and give a quick idea of the large export business the Chinese and Portuguese ran from here. With its large supermarkets, hip clothes' shops, traffic lights and wide streets it exudes a wealth and sophistication unlike any other city in this part of Indonesia. (members.tripod .com/balloon_2/tdili.htm)

While this Web-based guide to Dili Regency goes on to note the large military and police contingent in Dili, it downplays the theme of touristic danger. Indeed, most Indonesian-government sanctioned guidebooks of this period avoid accentuating that Portuguese colonialism had been replaced by Indonesian colonialism. Instead, the officially approved tour books of the late 1980s and early 1990s touted the colorful vestiges of Dili's Portuguese colonial history, or hailed Dili's recent emergence as an urban hub of Eastern Indonesia. Dili is scarcely linked to danger in the pages of these books. In contrast, a number of banned guidebooks and travelers' Web-based chronicles of their adventures in Dili draw heavily on the imagery of threat and imperilment. For instance, a Canadian's Web journal entry describes his and his wife's trip to Dili as follows:

> At the first road junction we encountered, just before coming into Dili, there was a check point where we had to get out of the bus and go into a police post. The plainclothes man there took down all our particulars. We were on our way back on to the bus when we were called over to the military post on the other side of the road . . . where we were surrounded by soldiers in full battle dress armed with M16s, while they again took down all our particulars. It was a little tense. (www.infomatch.com/~denysm/indon913.htm)

Accompanying this writer's account of this trip are excerpts from *The Jakarta Post* and other newspapers on the violence that had transpired in Dili just weeks before their arrival. The writer's friends at home and other curious Web surfers were thus offered journalistic "proof" of these intrepid travelers' brushes with danger.

A New Zealand traveler's Web-based account of his 1998 visit to Dili paints a similarly militaristic image of the city. Again, as with some of the entries in *Fielding's The World's Most Dangerous Places*, we find the initial imagery of tranquility yielding to that of incipient violence:

It was a beautiful morning as the boat approached the Dili port. The sea was calm. In the distance stood the prominent Motael Church and other old Portuguese buildings visible through the scattered trees. In the background were the browned hills. All of this created a sense of tranquility. Not exactly the feeling I expected to be having on arrival in East Timor. It was short-lived, as on the wharf stood armed uniformed soldiers and a handful of police. Like thistles on a golf course, soldiers nullify a tranquil environment. For the next eleven days spent in East Timor, I observed how thoroughly permeated the Indonesian military and police force are in East Timorese lives. In the main part of Dili there are several barracks. Out towards the airport in Comoro, two large military trucks full of soldiers from Battalion 744—all wearing bullet-proof vests and guns deliberately visible—came thundering down the main road. . . .

The Indonesian government appear [sic] to be promoting tourism in the country, but in reality they don't want foreigners there. More chance of their crimes being exposed. But it is beneficial for East Timorese that more travelers visit their country. . . . It presents an opportunity to disclose their situation to more foreigners. And also it would make it easier for human rights activists and journalists to enter and move around the country. (Sugden 1998)

By the late 1990s, as global pressure for East Timor's independence intensified, and tensions and violence mounted, Indonesia cracked down on tourist visas to the region. It is in this period that urban danger-zone travelers' interest in Dili intensified. The imagery in the narratives of some of these independently traveling danger-zone tourists parallels that found in the elections watch group tours to Jakarta discussed above, where potentially explosive urban destinations commingle with the travelers' self-images as activists, humanitarians, or travelers seeking journalistic first-hand experiences. As one Australian male planning a 1999 adventure in Dili and East Timor explained to me,

The reason that I'm going [there] is as much for the adrenalin as it is for the ethical side that is if I can do something, anything, to help then I'm obligated to. The crew that I'll be traveling with and myself are all environmental activists in Australia and for me that is my full-time job. Living in and touring the forests of Oz in a kind of bourgeois, middle class, pacifist, guerrilla war gives me as much satisfaction for doing "the right thing" as it does for providing me with the rush of doing illegal stuff in the middle of the night in the forest. You see the same crew at the camps all over Australia, most are transients and all do it for the reasons that I have just mentioned. (personal communication, August 30, 1999)

Clearly, the allure of urban danger-zone travel is complex. For some, humanitarianism intermingles with addiction to adrenalin rushes while for others the desire to witness news-in-the-making is paramount. As an American applied social science researcher in his mid-30s told me when he learned of my interest in danger travelers and Dili,

> I went to Dili for a long weekend, just to see what was happening there. That's how I spend my vacations, going to places like Kosovo and the Balkans. For a while, a few years back, I even toyed with the idea of starting a hot-spot travel agency. There are a lot of people like me, interested in experiencing these places . . . and understanding first-hand what is going on. (personal interview, August 25, 1999)

As the news of East Timorese resistance movements became more prominent on the global electromagnetic stream, Dili drew increasing numbers of activists. Their Web-postings further enhanced Dili's appeal to urban danger-zone travelers. An Australian university student's Web-based journal of his early 1998 trip to Dili to meet members of the East Timorese resistance offers a sample of an activist's portrait of the city:

> Thursday. Arrived in Dili. Everything on the ground hot and dry. Taxi driver soothed our jangling nerves with loud Billy Ocean tunes. . . . Stopped in a café for a warm lemonade. Three police armed with automatic rifles sat next to us. Got spooked by the guns and had to leave. Tried to look like bank clerks rather than student activists. . . .
> Friday . . . wandered by the University—the scene only two months ago of the shooting of students during their mid-year exams. Made our first contact with clandestine student operatives. Told to return tomorrow. In the afternoon we climbed Christus Raja, the second largest statue of Christ in the world, kindly donated to the "liberated peoples of East Timor" by Suharto. The statue stands 27 metres high (to symbolize East Timor as "Indonesia's 27th province") on an ocean cliff top facing Jakarta with open arms. (www.geocities.com/CapitolHill/Senate/7112/essay_01.htm)

In other danger-zone travelers' accounts, activist and humanitarian interests take a back seat to the imagery of fearless ventures to a life-imperiling site. As one Australian male who had visited Dili commented in an e-mail to me,

> I've got some friends over there now in a non-work capacity. They had to sneak in as no tourist visas are being offered. The sh** is really going down there now and caucasion [sic] people are being targeted. The scenary [*sic*] is great and ordinary people are cool but unless you are like my friends who are there for an adrenalin rush then your timing sucks. Keep in mind the Indonesian people (yes I know the Timorese are a hugely different ethnic group) invented the word amock [*sic*] ie. Run amock [*sic*] and in Indonesian it means to spontaneously

lose control in a frenzy. I've been around when this has happened before. (Personal e-mail communication, September 2, 1999)

In late August, just days before the above e-mail was sent, an historic election organized by UNAMET (United Nations Mission in East Timor) resulted in 78.5 percent of East Timor's population voting for independence from Indonesia. The celebration was short-lived: within days of the September 4, 1999, announcement of election results, armed militia groups backed by the Indonesian military had tortured and killed tens of thousands of East Timorese and had torched much of the city of Dili. Eventually, UN forces suppressed the slaughter and the Indonesian government agreed to grant autonomy to East Timor. Through much of late 1999, nightly CNN telecasts transmitted images of the ravaged capital of Dili round the globe, and newspapers worldwide featured front-page accounts of the devastation. By October, the United Nations Transitional Administration in East Timor (UNTAET) was established to oversee East Timor's transition to independence. Foreign aid workers and entrepreneurs flooded into the country, and volunteer political observers and still more danger-zone travelers have followed. Their accounts of their harrowing, haunting, frivolous, and daring experiences are prevalent on the Internet, in the form of diaries, reports, and postings to danger-zone Web pages. A sampling of the titles of these postings conveys the predominant themes: "Terror and Fear on the Streets of Dili,"[10] "Dilly Dally,"[11] and "Tempest in Timor."[12] While varied in content, one Australian adventurer's Web journal of his April 2000 visit to Dili conveys a number of salient images and offers a new take on the history, layering, and structuring of the global in newly postcolonial Dili:

We catch a bemo back to Dili. After a ten minute ride I'm in one of the most depressing places I have ever seen. I have never been in a war zone before and the sights are quite shocking. Now all the destructions are on a much larger scale, multi-story buildings are deprived of everything but their outer shell, block after block. Only a couple are repaired, one is a huge white palace-like structure, the governor's or government palace, with big UNTAET signs on it and the roof (corrugated iron) being painted green right now. That's the place that first had Portuguese in it, then the Indonesians, now the UN. To the average Timorese it's perhaps just the change of some meaningless sign anyway. Soon the CNRT will take residence and the big black Volvos will replace the Landrovers. At the moment, Dili has probably the population of Darwin and that's the end of the comparison. . . .

We . . . walk around the town a bit. It is not a pretty sight, although most of the rubble has been cleaned up. There is still the occasional rampaged building with all the debris inside, a couple recently renovated—a hotel a Telstra office, but the overall impression remains. And on top of that there are the vehicles—lots of

4WDs, the ever-present bemos,[13] scooter and bicycles, and occasionally a sedan, usually big ones—Mercedeses, Fords, curiously enough some Lancias, the black Volvos of the CNRT. The plates are a real Babylon, from all over the world, making Dili the most cosmopolitan place to be. If you're a car plate. It's time to go back to the airport. I'm utterly depressed by the sightseeing and just want to get out of here. (Unfolding Timor, www.geocities.com/utimor/7/7.html, downloaded 12 November 2000)

FINAL RUMINATIONS

A pervasive theme in these Internet diaries and in recent danger-zone traveler's images is that of Dili as a shell of a city—a scarred city. In a physical sense, after the destruction of 1999, Dili is an anti-city, a city of spaces where buildings once were. But these spectral memories lend it all the more salience as a postcolonial global entity. Dili's terror scars have drawn the international media and international curiosity seekers. The city's scars are filmed, televised, photographed, and reproduced in newspapers and on the net, transporting the idea of Dili (and independent postcolonial Timor) into living rooms and studies around the world. And yet, ironically, these Dili images circulating through the global electromagnetic stream are only visible in the living rooms of the most privileged of Timorese today. Those Timorese without homes, roofs, or electricity are obliged to haunt actual ruins, rather than view virtual ruins from the comfort of their armchairs.

Meanwhile, entrepreneurs, global marketers, United Nations staff, international consultants, and danger-zone tourists continue to flock to Dili. The wealthiest among them, however, need no longer stay amid the scars of the city: As of October 2000, a deluxe Thai-owned floating hotel has been docked in the Dili Harbor (Anon 2000). The Central Maritime Hotel, a former cruise ship, is outfitted with hundreds of rooms, a swimming pool, speedy Internet connections, and other assorted business and leisure services.[14] In essence, this floating hotel (and the floating offices in the white government palace of Dili) may well be harbingers of the "mobile city of hypermodernity" (see Armitage and Roberts 2003). Dili shares traits of what John Armitage and Joanne Roberts have termed a "gray zone of total mobilization," a city divorced from the temporal and territorial, characterized by "emergency and disintegration," based on a "mentality of total mobilization." In this sense, danger-zone tourism offers a lens for understanding Dili and other Southeast Asian urban-danger destinations as futuristic cities in other ways, as well. In broader terms, danger-zone tourism embodies an array of paradoxes illustrative of the experiences and dynamics of modernity.

Urban danger-zone tourism is very much a product of the global era. (However, as the examination of earlier imagery of Dili suggests, there is a parallel in earlier colonial eras. Then, as today, adventurers harvested new experiences in what they considered exotic outposts and marketed these novel tales back in the homeland.) CNN news coverage of the world's hot spots, worldwide networks of activists, and Internet danger-zone travel sites have fueled the global traffic in images of such postcolonial (and futuristic) "urban jungles" as Dili, facilitating the blossoming of urban danger-zone tourism. Danger-zone tourists are generally fueled by global politics, their itineraries inspired by the imagery of nightly news reports from the world's tumultuous zones. As I suggest in this chapter, urban danger-zone tourism has the potential to subtly shift nontravelers' sensibilities concerning the quality of urban Southeast Asian life. Their adventure tales are recounted, and their Web-based travelogues with images of urban strife zones are read and amplified by cybervoyagers round the globe. Danger-zone travel, then, paradoxically both inscribes such cities as Dili and Jakarta as global metropoles, and simultaneously marks them as wild urban jungles.

NOTES

I wish to thank Peter Sanchez and Ryan Bishop for their encouragement and thoughtful suggestions. The Centre for Advanced Studies at the National University of Singapore and the Singapore Tourism Board provided me with an Isaac Manasseh Meyer Fellowship that facilitated my initial explorations of the topic of danger-zone tourism in Southeast Asia. I am grateful for their support, as well as for thoughtful comments at this earlier stage from colleagues at the National University of Singapore, especially Ryan Bishop and Maribeth Erb. This chapter is a revised version of an article that appeared in *Postcolonial Urbanism: Southeast Asian Cities and Global Processes* (see Adams 2003a). Reproduced by permission of Routledge/Taylor & Francis Books, Inc.

1. For a fuller exposition of this concept, see K. M. Adams (2001).

2. A number of public-policy planners, social science teachers, and activists were also among the danger-zone tourists I interviewed.

3. The film version of *The Beach* was released with great hoopla in early 2000. In this version the British hero of the novel has been transformed into an American backpacker traveler. In both versions, however, the action is set in Thailand and the hero is a young man who deliberately targets dangerous, off-the-beaten-track destinations, believing that risk-packed experiences would make him more worldly and interesting.

4. Torun Elsrud notes that while in Thailand conducting field research, she observed tourists sporting war-related T-shirts with such slogans as "Beware of Mines-Cambodia" or "Saigon" with an image of a gun. As Elsrud comments, "It appeared

quite a few travelers and other tourists took a few weeks in Cambodia or Vietnam and at least some returned to Bangkok with these t-shirts as a symbolic expression of their trip" (personal e-mail communication, 1999).

5. Torun Elsrud, personal e-mail communication (1999).

6. For related explorations of forms of war tourism, also see de Burlo (1989), White (1997), Yoneyama (1995), and Young (1995).

7. According to Mary Hennock (2003), prior to the bombing Bali was receiving approximately 5,000 tourists daily. In the month following the bombing Bali received 800 tourists a day. And six months later, in February 2003, only 2,000 tourists were arriving daily. As she noted, "many of Bali's 35,000 hotels remain shuttered" and, in a reversal of past patterns, hotel workers are relying on their family members to support them.

8. The older orthography of Dili.

9. The Frente Revolucianario de Este Timor Independente (Revolutionary Front for an Independent East Timor).

10. www.geocities.com/CapitalHill/Lobby/9491/pub/etimor/jerald.html

11. www.gonomad.com/caravan/0105/javins_worldtour2.html

12. www.etan.ca/winnipeg/louise.html

13. A minibus often used as a form of public transport in Indonesia and East Timor.

14. As the Lonely Planet Travel News Review notes, the hotel "seems to have a penchant for anchoring luxury tourism in dubious destinations, as it was previously floating in Yangon, Myanmar" (Anon 2000).

10

Get Real! On Being Yourself and Being a Tourist

Tim Oakes

The search for authenticity both generates its antithesis and makes that antithesis unviable, even fatal, in the end.

—Marshall Berman (1970, 264)

The American tourists had come for authenticity. They had grimly suffered the wine-drenched welcoming ceremony as their dues, paid for the privilege of seeing and photographing a picturesque Miao ethnic village deep in the subtropical mountains of southwestern China. I had been staying in this village for several weeks, observing the elaborate reception routine put on by these Miao farmers sometimes twice or three times a day, for visiting tour groups (see Oakes 1998). The visitors were usually Chinese tourists from distant cities, but occasionally they were Japanese or French. Today was the first time I'd seen a group of fellow Americans in the village. The formal reception routine now complete, the Americans were finally free to stroll about the village and enjoy what they had been waiting impatiently for. Their attempts to achieve an unmediated view of the cobbled lanes, weathered wood houses, and colorful strings of fiery red chiles and golden dried corn was being accomplished with considerable difficulty, however. The tourists had just completed the final ceremonial "dance of unity"—in which they had been invited to join the villagers to march around the banging bronze drum behind a phalanx of *lusheng* pipe players. The end of this dance was the village women's cue to grab their baskets of souvenirs and begin the phase of the visit which *they* had been waiting impatiently for. What ensued had become as much a ritual as the welcoming ceremony itself, a frenzy of hawking until the tourists beat a hasty retreat to the safe

Figure 10.1   The Authentic Tourist Experience

confines of their minivan, disappointed and made haggard by the troubling intensity of the commercial spectacle amid such an otherwise "authentic" and beautiful setting (figures 10.1 and 10.2).

I couldn't help but sympathize with the Americans as they tried to steal a couple more photos from the van windows, while the hawking women thrust their wares at them. It had been a difficult visit from the beginning. The villagers had thought it would be fun—this being a group of "my home people"—to dress me up in traditional festival costume and station me at the village gate. I greeted the Americans with a bull horn full of potent rice wine in hand. Here it should be pointed out that all tour groups making their way toward the village gate must walk past several "roadblocks" of wine-proffering villagers, such that they have imbibed as many as twelve times prior to actually entering the village. This was to make them sufficiently tipsy to fully appreciate the sincerity of Miao hospitality. I had been stationed at the final step of this intoxicating gauntlet. If the addition of a grinning American geographer to this "ancient welcome ritual" seemed unceremonious enough to the tourists, it should also be mentioned that the festival costume I wore was a *woman's* dress. The villagers weren't trying to play gender games; they simply thought I should be wearing the most elaborate costume available, and this, naturally, would be a woman's.

The tourists, however, were nonplussed. And any remaining credibility that the site might still have had as an "authentic Miao village" would of course

Figure 10.2   The Indifference of Commerce

soon be dashed by the rampant commercial display that greeted the tourists upon their release to stroll around and take pictures.

As they escaped back down the narrow winding valley in their shiny white Toyota I paused to reflect on what had transpired, and how it seemed that the Americans had, in their pursuit of authenticity, left with a thoroughly unsatisfying experience compared to most of the Chinese groups I had observed undergoing the same treatment. Watching the minivan's dust cloud disperse across the newly transplanted rice fields hugging the riverbanks along the valley floor, I felt a mix of exasperation and sadness. Exasperation because the villagers had so clearly failed to provide the tourists with the kind of cultural experience that they had traveled so far to have. And sadness because I had grown fond of this village and wanted it to succeed. The Americans would by now have made it clear to their guide that she should have arranged a visit to a "real" village, not a tourist trap. She would learn her lesson, and the next group of Americans would be steered well clear of this village in their quest for a more authentic alternative.

The villagers asked me why "my home people" had left so quickly, and I made something up about their busy itinerary. "Americans do everything in a hurry," I said. My lie was less an attempt to save face for the villagers and more an implicit acknowledgement that I wasn't prepared to answer for the odd behavior of my countrymen. Their desire for authenticity would have struck the villagers as nonsense. And rightly so, I felt. So the issue passed. Another group was coming the next day, a Chinese group this time, and I knew they would leave with the satisfaction of having been happily entertained, liquored, and charmed by their "Miao cousins." I continued my fieldwork for several more months, examining other villages in the region as well, and eventually wrote a book on what I thought the villagers were up to when they received and entertained tour groups (Oakes 1998).

But the question of what the tourists themselves thought they were up to has remained with me. Why *did* the Americans leave in such disappointment? There has been no shortage of answers offered, of course. And as already suggested, what I settled upon—with the help of other theorists who have thought about this problem—is the relatively simple idea that they were "seeking authenticity" (see Culler 1981; MacCannell 1989; McIntosh and Prentice 1999; Wang 1999). But I have found that this answer provides little closure. Far from settling the issue, the search for authenticity leads one into a paradox. Authenticity is a phantom of modernity. It answers nothing, but only tempts us with further questions until we forget what we had originally been seeking.

This chapter offers an exploration of why authenticity in tourism is a paradox, and what interpreting it as such can contribute to the way we understand the relationship between tourism and subjectivity. I have come to believe that there is no simple answer to the question of "what the tourists thought they were up to" when they visited the Miao village only to retreat disappointed and unsatisfied. The search for authenticity is perhaps best thought of as a convenient code for something that in fact evaporates under scrutiny and yet remains nevertheless necessary as a framework for understanding the tourist experience. In what follows I do not, therefore, focus on authenticity *per se* but rather on the paradox of modernity signified by the term. As a search for authenticity, tourism represents, among other things, an attempt to negotiate the paradox of modernity, to repair modernity's polarizing and paralyzing dualisms, to absolve the anxiety and ambivalence of the modern experience, and to recover a sense of one's self in the modern world. These questions of experience, of self, ambivalence, and consciousness, then, are the subject of this exploration, and I approach them with the vision of my American compatriots' hasty retreat down the valley hovering over my reflections. I hope to show how the tourism experience marks two intriguing qualities of subject formation. One of these is the often upsetting experience of intersubjective encounter—a readily apparent feature of the Americans' visit to the Miao village. The other is the usually brief but terrifying recognition that authenticity is an abyss, a dream that can never be realized (Berman 1970, 264). Despite the fact that a whole industry has been built around an effort to hide the fact of authenticity's emptiness, tourism is an experience in which that abyss can abruptly reveal itself. We all gingerly step away from the edge, though, convincing ourselves to look elsewhere. Tourism offers all the myths necessary to divert our thoughts from the unsettling prospect. But somehow we know that we've seen the answer already: it is merely a void.

ENCOUNTERING THE VILLAGE—
THE SHOCK OF INTERSUBJECTIVITY

The first order of business upon entering the village and settling down on benches lined up around the village square was a song and dance performance. While they watched, the Americans asked me all sorts of questions about the village. I had been in this position before. As an outsider "marooned among the natives," most tourists saw me as some kind of trustworthy medium through which they could learn the "truth" of the village. Among the village's Chinese and other Asian visitors, it was also assumed that I was an expert on Miao culture and customs, for none of them could really believe that my main interest was in tourism itself. I had been asked about the authenticity of the songs and dances being performed. I had been asked—more often by drivers and guides than tourists themselves — if the Miao were really as sexually promiscuous as they were made out to be. Most of the questions I had been asked by Chinese and other Asian visitors focused in this way on Miao culture and whether or not the village was an accurate representation of the "exotic and primitive" lifeways of the Miao.[1] But the Americans weren't interested in these kinds of questions at all. Instead, they asked about the material conditions of the village, how much money villagers were getting for the performance, and whether tourism was improving their lives. Like me, they were actually interested in tourism itself, and in their questions I heard the anxious subtext of anxiety, guilt, and ambivalence. These tourists were asking not for information but for reassurance. That being "tourists" weighed heavily upon them was clear, for although they wanted to think of themselves more as ambassadors of friendship and development, they were haunted by the indifference of their hosts to such lofty intentions. To the villagers, the Americans were simply tourists. And the Americans knew the truth of this too well to ignore it.

The Americans were the second tour group to visit the village that day. They had been preceded by a Japanese group. The Japanese had brought with them all sorts of dime-store trinkets for the villagers, and candy for the children. They marched around the village with great satisfaction, happily doling out goodies as if the villagers had never seen a key chain before. The Americans, in contrast, brought seeds. Vegetable seeds. Whether this was meant to be a gesture of poverty relief or horticultural exchange I didn't ask, but it illustrated clearly how the Americans wished to be received by the villagers. They wanted badly to feel that their visit was somehow helping the village, and this desire was perhaps even more pressing since life in the village had obviously become so tourist-oriented. They wanted to believe that the village's Faustian bargain with tourism would somehow turn out all right despite what they saw as a disturbing cultural corruption required by such a bargain. And so, the Americans wanted to see themselves as aid workers more than tourists.

In this capacity, they offered advice about how the village could improve its song and dance routine so that it would appear more authentic. One woman suggested that the young dancers could have used some training, and that they should be wearing traditional shoes instead of "modern sneakers." These, she pointed out, clashed with their costumes and wrecked a good photo-opportunity. These suggestions she asked me to convey to the village leadership. While Asian visitors had also felt free to critique the village's song and dance routine, they had never done so on the basis of maintaining a veneer of authenticity. Rather, their criticisms tended to be aimed at improving the contemporary entertainment value of the routine by adding some newer songs to which the visitors could also sing along, or adding karaoke.

The Americans also did their best to make a significant financial contribution to the village. Despite their discomfort with being hounded by the hawking women, they actually bought more than most visitors did: crowns, combs, silver horns, embroidered jackets, *lusheng* pipes, everything. Whether they did this primarily in order to enhance village incomes (I had already told most of them that selling souvenirs was how the village made most of its tourism income) or simply in hopes of earning a reprieve from the hawking wasn't clear. In any case the ease with which they opened their purses and wallets only ratcheted up the determination of the village women to squeeze as much cash out of them as possible. The villagers were clearly indifferent to what the Americans felt was an appropriate set of rules to the game. They would buy two or three things from a couple women, then wave the rest away in exasperation: "I've done my part now, I've done my part!" When it became clear that this approach was merely encouraging more, rather than less, attention, they began retreating to their minivan. As one woman told me, "I would have liked to have walked around the village some, it's so beautiful. But I just can't with all those women thrusting things in front of me." Another, who hadn't actually bought anything, added, "I would actually like to buy some things, but that was like a feeding frenzy. I can't function in situations like that. They push everything in front of you so you can't even look at it."

While the Americans were clearly justified in their discomfort with the disorderly commercialism that engulfed them that day, what they failed to comprehend was how the village's "inauthenticity" was not just the result of some Faustian bargain with the diabolical tourism industry, but was more precisely what Berman termed the "unviable, even fatal" antithesis generated by the search for authenticity itself. For the villagers, the reception's commercialism was simply the logical extension of the whole cultural experience they offered, not its opposite. It is simply what they had learned to do with this new tourist object called culture: sell it.

But what was perhaps, for the Americans, even more disturbing than the cold slap of ethnic commerce was the *indifference* of the villagers toward the tourist's desire to be received as more than just a group of tourists. As MacCannell (1992) has noticed in his viewing of Dennis O'Rourke's stunning film *Cannibal Tours*, the tourists needed to believe that their encounter would be genuine and meaningful for the villagers, that their presence in the village represented more than the cold commercial transaction that it was: we pay you for entertainment, you entertain us, we buy your things, you let us take pictures. The tourists wanted to believe that this was really a "visit," instead of an entertainment purchase. Indeed, the "visit to a Miao village" is marketed by travel agents and tourism officials as an opportunity not to contribute to the economic development of the Miao, but to experience their ancient hospitality, warmth, and friendship. Village leaders themselves—all of them men—expressed precisely these sentiments whenever I asked them what they thought of all the visitors they received. "It makes me so happy," one told me, "to see so many people from all over the world come all this way and endure such hardship just to visit our village. It fills my heart." His wife, however, held a decidedly more practical view. She had no patience for tourists unless they were willing to part with their cash. Indeed, a gendered division of attitudes throughout the village revealed that women were far less concerned with feeling honored by yet another opportunity to host distant strangers than with making sure those strangers left behind some of their money.

For the tourists, then, the dominant experience of the village was one of intersubjective disjuncture, a kind of culture shock which *failed* to confirm expectations of difference. The village women, in particular, refused to play along in the tourists' hapless dream of reciprocity (Burland 1988), a dream that had more to do with the needs of the tourists themselves than those of the villagers. Intersubjective encounters with others, it has been argued, are a fundamental part of how people build a sense of self through travel, mobility, and journeying (Bruner 1991; Neumann 1992; Oakes 2005). As David Patterson (1988, 17) has written, "Encountering the other, I encounter myself as the other and perceive myself through other eyes and ears, thus stepping outside myself, moving elsewhere to gauge my relation to truth. Only by thus placing myself in the position of other can I return to the truth of myself." There is something of this imbedded in the tourist's desire for an authentic experience. But a disjuncture occurs when the tourist's desire to subjectively experience the world of the other is met with indifference. *Indifference* is a particularly appropriate term here, because if the encounter with the other is to produce the desired affect of unsettling the tourist's taken-for-granted world, then the job of the other is to "be different." Clearly, there was much about the village that was exotic, different, and otherworldly for the tourists, but when their visit degenerated into a commercial frenzy, they saw only the warped image of their own selves reflected back on them. The ultimate indifference of the villagers, displayed in their commercial instincts, only reminded the Americans of what they knew they were all along: a group of tourists fantasizing about becoming something else.

This realization, providing a brief glimpse into the true abyss of authenticity, was too shocking to acknowledge. Instead, they rushed off, determined to find a village that had not been spoiled.

FIND YOURSELF—THE DESIRE FOR EXPERIENCE

Why is it that intersubjectivity should yield such ambivalence? To understand this question, we need to consider in greater detail the issue of difference and otherness in tourism encounters, and why the villagers ultimately failed to adequately provide this for the Americans. In the discussion that follows, I hope to develop the argument that tourists who seek an authentic experience of encounter with otherness end up reifying authenticity as that ideal moment when alienation disappears and the fragmented world becomes whole again. Such a reified ideal, however, is necessarily (by definition) forever out of reach, and in fact becomes part of the tourist's reproduction of the world according to the binaries of modern epistemology. The only authentic experience to be had is the experience of the outsider, the experience one has *as the tourist*—rather than as a local—and this only reinforces the distance that authenticity-seeking tourists hope to overcome. This reflects a broader problem of modernity in that our efforts to transcend the binary dualisms of modern epistemology only succeed in reinforcing them.

A significant caveat should be noted at the outset, however. The reader may find that the most interesting question raised by the visit of the American tourists is not why they left dissatisfied, but why their experience struck me as so different from the Asian tourists, particularly the Chinese. This question is, in part, the subject of a different essay (Oakes 2006) and cannot be discussed adequately here. In what follows, I explore the relationship between tourism and subjectivity within a particular cultural context, one that emerged within Western Europe and North America. I seek to understand the tourists' experience within that context, but do not presume this to be a universal experience for all tourists.

As discussed in this volume's introduction, the experience of modernity is articulated through and built upon such fundamental dualisms as subject-object, mind-body, culture-nature, progress-tradition, reason-experience, and masculine-feminine among many others. While the idea of modernity, often in the guise of "modernization," has typically been thought to express one side of these dualisms, it is the dualisms themselves that best capture modernity in all its paradoxical (in)completeness. Thus, modernity does not simply represent a privileging of reason over experience, or a celebration of progress over the death of tradition, but more accurately conveys the ambivalence between reason and experience, and the sense of loss and nostalgia that progress entails. Here, Scott Lash (1999) has developed an argument in which he terms the modernity of Enlightenment "first modernity." This is the cognitive modernity of reason and progress. But, he argues, we must also speak of "another modernity." Agnes Heller (1999, 4) has described this other modernity as that which we more familiarly know as the postmodern, or modernity's "self-reflexive conscience." "It is a kind of modernity," she continues, "that knows itself in a Socratic way. For it (also) knows that it knows very little, if anything at all."

Lash's two modernities express something of what Deleuze and Guattari (1983 and 1987) saw as the schizophrenia of modern subjectivity. Where one modernity is concerned primarily with epistemological questions, the other develops a critical stance toward knowledge and concerns itself more with ontology. And Heller's comment suggests that while the "first" modernity of Enlightenment rationalism is busy building binaries through which to know the world, the "other" modernity seeks to transcend these binaries altogether. Yet this latter pursuit is fraught with ambivalence, for the ontological questions broached have no clear answers; they merely confirm that modernity "knows that it knows very little, if anything at all." As Lash argues in another article (1993), "reflexive monitoring" of the modern experience yields little reassurance as to the actual truth of things. Unlike Giddens (1990 and 1991), who relies upon reflexivity to provide a sense of "ontological security" in the face of modernity's ever-changing, even chaotic, knowledge of the world (see also Beck 1992), Lash suggests that the experience of modernity is too contradictory and paradoxical for cognitive reflection to get any kind of handle on. Instead, we develop a kind of "aesthetic reflexivity" that allows us to "live with contingency." Thus, while the modernity of Enlightenment creates a world in which knowledge is dynamic and continuously updated—a process likened by Giddens to a "juggernaut"—Lash's "second modernity" goes beyond this understanding of change via cognitive reflection. In addition, it recognizes that there are few absolute answers to the questions generated by the rationalism of "first modernity." Enlightenment modernity, then, is recognized as a paradox. Heller (1999, 15) echoes this idea when she states that, "Reflected postmodern consciousness *thinks this paradox*; it does not lose it from sight, it lives with it."

There has been a great deal of writing about how the practices of exile, travel, and even tourism capture the ambivalence and contingency of modernity (e.g. Wilson 1956; Simmel 1971; Bradbury 1976; Fussell 1980; MacCannell 1989; Bauman 1991). The act of travel, of being displaced, has been said to express the modern subject's need to objectify the world while, paradoxically, subjectively experiencing it at the same time. Travel seems to provide both some critical distance from which to better understand the world combined with the stimulating intimacies of a new experience. One of the most emblematic figures, in this sense, has been that of the *flâneur*, the stroller gazing upon the street-spectacles of commodity fetishism and fashion with a revulsion ambivalently mixed with desire (Benjamin 1978; Tester

1994). Feminist critiques of this modern-subject-as-traveler have also been well established for some time (Wolff 1985; Wilson 1992; Wolff 1993; Kaplan 1996; Jokinen and Veijola 1997). Echoing these critiques, Lynda Johnston (2001) has argued that the traveler (or tourist) as modern subject has been universalized, abstracted, and disembodied. Her argument points out a crucial feature of the modern-subject-as-traveler trope which speaks to the broader issue of modernity's paradox. When the traveler is abstracted or disembodied, what was initiated as a project of escaping the dualisms of modernity, of expressing the contingency of modern life, has actually been reclaimed by those dualisms. The traveler simply becomes a category, a social role, a rational fix for the permanence of change. As suggested in the introduction to this volume, travel becomes more an homage to abstraction and categorization, an enactment of the subject-object binary. To resist the neat closure of such enactments, Johnston calls for a sustained focus on the embodied tourist, and specifically on the differences between men's and women's travel experiences.

The general problem being identified here is that of "finding yourself" through travel. In their imposition of an epistemological divide between subject and object, mind and body, the epistemological dualisms of modern rationalism inspire us to reflect upon the existential question of being and identity. Travel, broadly defined, has been conceived as a reflexive act in pursuit of these questions. And while the traveler has too often been abstracted and universalized as "the modern subject" without adequate accounting for its gendered, privileged, and classed positions, there remains a firmly entrenched desire for the refreshing stimulus of encounter, experience, and difference within the modern experience. Johnston's embodied tourist resists the hegemonic abstraction of the modern-subject-as-traveler and yet still longs for that subjective experience. Indeed, for Johnston, experience is marked by a radical embodiment of difference, otherness, and marginality, this being the kind of experience perhaps necessary to rupture, momentarily at least, modernity's dualisms. The message seems to be that it is through such ruptures that a more "authentic" sense of self can be attained. And in fact, tourism itself promises and even attempts to commodify these moments of radical departure from one's daily life.

That the tourism industry itself appropriates this desire for (a safe) encounter with otherness and difference should raise some interesting questions. Mark Neumann (1992, 177) has remarked that while tourist sites may be "inauthentic," they are nevertheless places where people work toward "self-realization" and meaning, "attempting to fill experiential vacancies that run through contemporary life." Neumann cites Patterson (1988) who, as we've seen, has argued that the (travel-induced) encounter with others prompts a self-consciousness that breaks away from the alienations of daily life and work. But Neumann also notices the problem inherent in finding oneself through tourism-mediated encounters. The reflexivity induced by tourism finds that "the self" cannot really escape the continuous process of objectification, thus reestablishing the dualism of modernity precisely at the moment we hope to escape it. In the end, all we discover is that we're tourists, just like everyone else. The sheer banality of our *role* as fugitives of modernity returns to us at every turn.

> In different ways, the ghosts of home tag along behind the station wagon and Winnebago, appearing along the road on occasion as disconcerting reminders of the difficulties that accompany the quest and the escape. While visitors may gaze with disappointment on the numbers who swell the roads and trails, and burgeon around the rim [of the Grand Canyon], some travelers find that their suspicions, anxieties and disappointment with tourism only reveal their own complicity in the gathering crowd. (Neumann 1992, 199)

And so, we may embody the tourist, and engender the tourist, but authenticity remains a paradox. Any attempt to bypass ontologically modernity's dualisms only reinforces their epistemological hold on us.

These concerns with ontology, with holistic experience rather than objective knowledge, suggest an intersection with phenomenology, which was initiated by Husserl as a critique of our taken-for-granted understandings of the object world. Husserl's project was to develop a method of disclosing the world by allowing "original experiences" to be seen. In many respects, it emerged as a critique of positivist science which took the subject-object binary at face value. For Husserl, positive science did not problematize ontologically the nature of things, but simply assumed their existence as objects without questioning the nature of consciousness in constructing them as such. Put this way, Husserl's critique of science expresses Lash's "second modernity" in its reflexivity and ontological orientation. By developing a theory of the intentionality of consciousness, Husserl sought to establish a link between phenomena and consciousness which moved beyond the dualism of subject-object. In "intentionality," Husserl sought to characterize the basic feature of consciousness as always directing itself to that which it is not. Consciousness, in other words, developed through direct experience of phenomena, and indeed, the object-world is inseparable from the meanings generated through intentional consciousness. As cited in Pickles (1985, 96), Husserl argued that the structure of intentionality is one where "the object appears as essentially determined by the structure of thinking itself; this thinking itself first gives meaning to the object and then continues to orient itself to the pole of identity which it itself has already created." It is, in other words, through intentional consciousness that any comprehension of the world is even possible in the first place.

While Husserl pursued these ideas in order to develop a more rigorous and more "ontologically secure" science, his project recalls the tourist's desire for a new sense of self through experience and reflection. Husserl was responding to the increasing power of scientific technology to eclipse any understanding of the central role of humans as subjects in charge of their world. Yet Husserlian phenomenology is significant in this respect because it seeks not to simply remind us of the inherent paradox of modernity, but rather to provide a more secure standpoint from which to negotiate modernity's dualisms. Having sought to erase the subject-object dualism as an epistemological given, in other words, Husserl proceeds to build an ontological basis for understanding "things themselves." Husserl recognized the ontological abyss opened up by the epistemological dualisms of the "first modernity" and sought to fill this with a philosophy of fundamental experience. Thus—and particularly for ontological thinkers like Heidegger—the "lifeworld" of our immediate, practical experience achieves a central position in phenomenology. Intentional consciousness, for Heidegger, is grounded in the world of everyday practical concerns, particularly work, instead of in abstract cognitive theorizing. Instead of simply embracing contingency, in other words, phenomenology anchors subjectivity in the "security" of one's environment and experience.

Compared to the escape and pursuit of difference expressed in travel, then, this is quite a different response to modernity's contingencies. While, as Pickles (1985) has argued, it may be a departure from Husserl himself to claim that phenomenology lends itself to a theory of place, spatially oriented practitioners of phenomenology have certainly focused more on place and dwelling, rather than displacement and travel, in response to that persistent need to overcome modernity's dualisms. The most prolific thinker in this regard has been Edward Casey (1993; 1997), who argues that place has been a casualty of Western epistemology because place-based experience is immediate and embodied, the very antithesis of the abstractions and dualistic thinking upon which Western scientific knowledge and rationalism has been based. Yet Casey is notable for not equating place with "security," as might easily be assumed. Instead, place is inherently deconstructive of the binary terms "that have enjoyed hegemonic power in Western epistemology and metaphysics" (1996, 36). The experience of place, he argues, always makes it clear that such binaries "deliver only a shadowy simulacrum of the experiences we have in that place" (1996, 36). One might say that place is authentic to the extent that it defies objectification and thus a dualistic approach to knowing.

While phenomenology fills modernity's ontological void with place and experience, the practice of travel and associated theories of exile, displacement, mobility, and tourism fill it with the ever-receding dream of authenticity. In this sense, travel only takes us *further from* authenticity because the practice of travel is an enactment of the subject-object binary, a binary which only renders authenticity impossible. Indeed we "find ourselves" through travel, but only because we do so by creating a self-other, subject-object dualism, that is, by "objectivating" our world. The apparent authenticity that Husserl sought, and which Casey (and Relph 1976) insists is to be found in place, cannot be narrated or represented at all, and to turn authenticity into an object of pursuit or knowledge is only to invite its death and burial by epistemology.

Such a scenario is proposed even by critics of phenomenology who find that it is a project ultimately reclaimed by rationalism's relentless epistemological categorizations and abstractions. Thus, Theodore Schatzki (2001) has noticed a parallel between phenomenology and Cartesianism. Initially, phenomenology breaks with the epistemological dualism of Enlightenment modernity: "Phenomenologists have forsaken the Cartesian ideas that mind is a substance and that a metaphysical gap looms between it and the physical world" (Schatzki 2001, 699) But, Schatzki continues, problems begin to develop once we consider the "reflexive attitude" of Husserl's project:

> Phenomenological accounts of lived experience are proffered, however, from a contemplative standpoint that is achieved through disengagement with, and a reflective stepping back from, that experience of the world. This disengaging retreat institutes a distanciation that approximates that of the holding at bay that Descartes achieved in his skeptical meditations (given which, the claim that the subject is a separate substance gains plausibility). In other words, this reflective stepping back creates a gap between I-here and experience/experienced world-there, the overcoming of which becomes an issue for any thinker who performs this maneouver. (Schatzki 2001, 699)

In many ways, according to this view, Husserl's project remains confined by the parameters of the subject-object dualism. For Husserl the point was less to erase this dualism than to enable scientists to reflect upon it and build scientific theory with the confidence of understanding the "essences" of things, rather than simply comprehending their "appearances."

Critics who have embraced the reflexive spirit of Husserl's project, if not its assumptions of the transcendental essence of the world, have sought to combine phenomenology's focus on experience and "lifeworld" with the importance of intersubjectivity and the experience of the body as ways of, once again, moving beyond the epistemological confines of Enlightenment modernity. And Casey (1997, 241) indeed seems to move in this direction when he insists that place is really a "body/place nexus," which paradoxically allows the conjoining of realism with transcendentalism and, thus, allows us to see how place and body are at once subject *and* object. This occurs, in part, according to Casey, because of intersubjectivity. If intersubjectivity confronts tourists with the problem of authenticity, unsettling our desire for exotic and meaningful experience with the reality of the other's indifference, then it also signals the problems inherent in any transcendental reduction. We cannot get *beyond* dualisms; we can only, as Heller puts it, "live with" their paradoxes. As Lash (1999, 149) writes, "Husserl had no satisfactory way of moving from the transcendental reduction of objects by the ego to the understanding of the 'alter ego' or 'other.' This shift in focus from the things to the other is a shift from subject-object relations to intersubjectivity." Lash observes that this was precisely the problem that Alfred Schutz confronted in phenomenology, his response being to develop an idea of "situated intersubjectivity." For Lash, Schutz's line of thought led him out of the domain of phenomenology proper and into that of hermeneutics. In turn, inquiry into the hermeneutics of everyday life leads one toward the body as a domain in which meaning and the experience of everyday life merge.

The body, then, has become a crucial focus among post-Heideggerian phenomenologists and their critics alike. Working with Bourdieu's idea of habitus, Casey, for instance, adopts the body as the key terrain upon which place and experience are inscribed and embedded in the subject: "Thanks to the inscriptive tenacity and expressive subjection of the body, places come to be embedded in us; they become part of our very self, our enduring character, what we enact and carry forward" (Casey 2001, 688). Yet while at the outset this focus on the body appears to return us to the embodiment that Johnston sees as necessary in accounting for intersubjective difference in the tourist experience, Casey's phenomenology was recently criticized by geographers for failing to overcome the abstract and universalizing distance of reduction. Casey's reliance on habitus, for instance, invites the criticism that Bourdieu's concept reduces human agency to one's actions determined by the material conditions of everyday existence (Entrikin 2001). Indeed, Jeffrey Alexander (1995, 136) has gone as far as to call habitus "a Trojan horse for [social structural] determinism." More problematic than habitus, however, is the abstract nature of Casey's body itself. As Barbara Hooper (2001) points out, power and difference are abstracted out of Casey's body; there are no "(other) bodies" in Casey's phenomenology, just "the body." Hooper's critique suggests that for all its focus on "being-in-the-world," there is something strikingly "unworldly" about the reductionism of phenomenology.

Casey does seem to reserve a place for the kind of intersubjectivity that the above critics have found wanting. It seems equally true, though, that to write (that is, to represent) the kind of places Casey seems to have in mind is clearly impossible, and that Casey himself is aware of this. The debate itself is indicative of how our reflexive impulses and desires for experience and embodiment in overcoming the epistemological dualisms of Enlightenment modernity ultimately find themselves reclaimed by those dualisms and by modernity's relentless process of abstraction. This is the larger problem that the tourist always encounters as well. The desire to "find yourself," to find a "real place," to experience the world anew—these desires only lead us to a paradox. Tourism expresses the impulse of Lash's "second modernity," but it also reveals how easily that ontological and existential impulse is colonized by our epistemological need for order and resolution. We cannot, in other words, turn to the body, or place, or everyday experience in the "lifeworld," for ontological security in a world of epistemological alienation. Reflexivity does not yield ontological answers, and does not unify the epistemological dualisms of modernity.

DE-REIFYING THE WORLD

For this reason, it seems that Edensor (2001) is right to argue that reflexivity is not necessarily the best way to conceive a touristic subjectivity. As he points out, many tourists seek not to actively or consciously "transcend the mundane," but merely act out habitually certain touristic practices because to do otherwise would interfere with the carefully prepared sense of relaxation and getting-away-from-it-all that forms a basic objective of the trip. But reflexivity does nevertheless help us understand those tourists who travel halfway around the world to see a village and retreat after less than two hours disappointed and dissatisfied. It's not that they simply didn't find authenticity, but that they understood, if only for a moment, the paradoxical nature of such a pursuit in the first place. Of course, they quickly backed away from this vista over the abyss of authenticity, retreating to the more comfortable belief that authenticity must be located *somewhere else*. For travel does not really permit a complete deconstruction of the subject-object / self-other dualism. To the contrary, travel ceaselessly rebuilds these binaries. As tourists they had no choice but to return to the search; for the journey itself is the whole point, after all. To get bogged down in place would disrupt rather than reward the project of "knowing" the world through travel.

But that placed moment of recognition is a crucial one. It is a moment that Peter Berger and Stanley Pullberg (1965) would identify as one of "dereification," in which we recognize our objectifications of the world for what they are, instead of assuming, as we typically do, that the world actually exists in the form in which we imagine or represent it. If the problem of phenomenology illustrates how, as Lash (1993) claims, the experience of modernity is too contradictory and contingent for reflexivity to resolve ontologically, then reflexivity becomes more an aesthetic form of existential hermeneutics, enabling us to experience moments of "de-reification" when they occur. Tourism is an aesthetics industry. Paradoxically it both provides for the possibility of "de-reification" at the same time that it seeks to commodify such moments, reintroducing alienation at the moment it disappears.

Berger and Pullberg argued that human subjectivity must continuously objectivate itself; it is a necessary human condition to know the self by establishing a subject-object dualism. Put this way, the impulse to escape such a dualism appears necessarily futile and philosophical reflection that provides resolution to this impulse only further mystifies a basic feature of subject formation with the promise of a world in which the "things themselves," their "essences," can be truly known. We can't help, Berger and Pullberg claim, but to "objectivate" our world, a process "whereby human subjectivity embodies itself in products that are available to oneself and one's fellow men as elements of a common world" (1965, 199). Further, "the moment in the process of objectivation in which man [sic] established distance from his producing and its product, such that he can take cognizance of it and make it an object of his consciousness" is called objectification (1965, 200). These are, they claim, necessary human processes, and because of them, humans are continuously "making their world" as they act to modify the given, structuring it into a meaningful totality (a process that is never complete). The world, in other words, must be made and remade over and over again. "The world remains real, in the sense of subjective plausibility and consistency, only as it is confirmed and reconfirmed" (1965, 201). This reminds us of the performative nature of tourism discussed briefly in this volume's introduction and by Edensor (2001), in which tourists re-enact the world, making it an object worth viewing or visiting. More significant for us here is the fact that such making and remaking is necessarily an intersubjective process; the world must be reconfirmed by others.

Yet, Berger and Pullberg continue, humans also find themselves forgetting that they themselves continuously make and remake the world. This "process by which the unity of the producing and the product is broken" is alienation (1965, 200). Such forgetting does not necessarily bring about a state of anxiety or even a sense of "lostness," but often may simply exist as one's everyday mode of existence. Indeed, living in alienation does tend to be the way many of us get on with our lives, since an alienated existence is usually easier to cope with than the ever-bracing sense of responsibility that accompanies the realization that we are always making and remaking our world. It is simply one of the more fundamental manifestations of the paradox of modernity that we make the world from which we are typically alienated. But in addition to alienation, Berger and Pullberg identify another tendency, which occurs as "a moment in the process of alienation in which the characteristic of thing-hood becomes the standard of objective reality" (1965, 200). This is the process of reification.

Reification is therefore a kind of double alienation. It means that not only have we forgotten that we make the world, but we also ascribe separate ontological status to the world that we've forgotten we ourselves made. In discussing the problems this causes, Berger and Pullberg focus on the reification of social structures and social institutions to point out how social roles have come to substitute for a nonalienated subjectivity. Here action itself becomes reified as the logical extension of social identities that are assumed to have an ontological status of their own. People themselves become little more than the embodiment of roles. "No one exists any longer, but roles interact in a sort of ectoplasmic exchange. The thief does not steal but is playing the role of thief, the judge does not judge but is playing the role of judge, and (last but not least) the criminologist does not understand either the thief's stealing or the judge's judging but is playing the role of social scientist" (1965, 206). They continue that,

> roles are reified by detaching them from human intentionality and expressivity, and transforming them into an inevitable destiny for their bearers. The latter may then act in the false consciousness that they "have no choice"—*because* they are bearers of this or that role. . . . The executioner who kills his victims mimes the prototypical action of the gods, of abstract justice or of the state in upholding right and punishing wrong—"ultimately" it is not he but these abstractions that engage in killing. . . . The reification of roles, on all possible levels of sophistication, thus produces a quasi-sacramental world, in which human actions do not express human meanings but rather represent, in priestly fashion, various super-human abstractions they are supposed to embody. Religious, ethical and "scientific" theories are then called upon to legitimate and further mystify the de-humanization that has occurred. (1965, 206–7)

Berger and Pullberg suggest three situations in which we suddenly see reification for what it is. These moments of "de-reification" include (1) catastrophes that disintegrate social structures and explode their taken-for-grantedness; (2) the crises of knowledge that ensue as a response to the "culture shock" of being confronted with alternative ways of perceiving the world and ordering one's life within it; and (3) marginal groups making their presence and views known within the dominant society (209–10).

While Berger and Pullberg identify cosmopolitan urban centers as places where culture shock and marginality are ever present, tourism also seemingly presents an activity offering similar opportunities for de-reification. Again, with Berger and Pullberg's alienated role-playing we are reminded of a key argument underlying many theories of performativity—that re-enactments leave vulnerable the taken-for-grantedness of the conventions they maintain (Butler 1990 and 1993). At least two kinds of disruption might occur as a result. One, mentioned by Edensor (2001) is when tourists consciously "play-up" their touristy roles with self-mocking irony. Something similar has been noted by Feifer (1985) in her categorization of "post-tourists." The other kind of disruption is what appeared to be happening to the American tourists when they visited the Miao village and momentarily saw (or perhaps refused to see) authenticity as the construction that it is. Put a slightly different way, we might be able to think of the tourist's search for authenticity as a *role* played by "the tourist," a reified act of producing a "quasi-sacramental world" of authentic cultures, real exoticism, and everything else we have come to expect of travel, adventure, and tourism. In these terms authenticity itself becomes a reification, an investment of ontological status upon that world that we *expect* or *hope* to see and experience in travel.

THE ABYSS OF AUTHENTICITY

According to Berman (1970, 75–159), it was precisely the predominance of social roles in masking people's "true identities" that led Rousseau to problematize the idea of authenticity. For Rousseau, men and women were always acting as if they were someone they were not, hiding behind masks of social propriety and the norms of fashion. "People cared only that a thing should be done well; no one worried about whether it should be done at all" (1970, 127). Thus, tyrants could be admired for their success at being tyrants, and this is no less true today when we hear, for instance, the perverse admiration expressed by some at the "cold professionalism" of the men who flew three commercial airliners into the World Trade Center and the Pentagon. Rousseau recognized alienation when he saw it, noticing that the men behind their masks didn't even know they were role-playing anymore. Recognizing the process whereby objectification becomes alienation, he wrote that the "social man knows only how to live outside himself, in the judgment of others; indeed, it is only from the judgment of others that he gains consciousness of his very existence" (cited in Berman 1970, 141).

Yet in alienation Rousseau also saw a solution, for if one could recognize objectification for what it was, the possibility of a new subjectivity emerged. As Berman puts it, referring to those moments when people realize they've merely been wearing masks, or playing roles, "At the core of their being, where their consciousness should have been, there was nothing at all. It was precisely this inner emptiness that liberated them from all moral inhibitions, and made things possible for them" (1970, 142). For Rousseau, only the world of children, of pure love, could provide the strength to face the paradox of modernity and become an authentic self again. This, for instance, seems to be the message in *Julie, or the New Eloise*.

Yet ultimately Rousseau came to believe that an authentic self was an impossible dream. More than this, it was a doomed quest that ultimately led one in the opposite direction, toward an increasingly inauthentic self. The more we pursued authenticity, the more we found it retreating beyond our grasp. The more we recognized the quest as doomed, that an authentic self was impossible, the more terrified we became. This terror drove us to reify the world with even greater conviction than before, and it was at this point that Rousseau saw tyranny and authoritarianism emerge, filling the abyss of authenticity with secure roles for a self readily consenting to be subjected to power. In such "inauthentic" societies, tyranny was always a threat for precisely the reasons discussed by Berger and Pullberg: reified action absolved one from personal responsibility and enabled ethics to be colonized by authoritarian power. To keep tyranny in check, Rousseau came to believe that the inauthentic society must be justly and humanely legislated by a liberal democratic state. "So long as modern men remain alienated from themselves, they will stand in need of a state to tell them who they are" (Berman 1970, 283).

And this is precisely the world, many would argue, that many modern tourists—those, presumably, traveling to Miao villages—find themselves escaping. The reflexive tourist recognizes the alienation and inauthenticity of the world, and takes to the road in response. In the process, however, we find ourselves "objectivating" and reifying authenticity itself, with plenty of help from an entire industry that has been built solely to commodify the aesthetics of reflective escape. It is in this sense, too, that Berman argues that any search for authenticity is doomed to "generate its antithesis." We are seduced by the *role* of the traveler, the adventurer, the exile, the tourist. We expect to have the experiences such roles are meant to entail. In our desire for escape we have merely recreated the double alienation of reification. One would suspect, following the course of events laid out by Rousseau, that the tourist's search for authenticity also implies the "threat of tyranny," and indeed many tourist places do suffer a tyranny of authenticity (Herzfeld 1991; Rogers 1996; DeLyser 1999). In broader terms, as Casey (1997, 338) has argued, the "escape" into a purer "space" of travel and mobility is *empowering* in that it evokes a sense of *control* over an otherwise uncontrollable world.

But tourism not only traffics in the reification of authenticity, but by the very transparency with which it commodifies and manipulates symbols and meanings, it also reveals with sometimes sharp clarity just how contrived the "real world" of objects can be. It is perhaps fitting, then, that in the Miao village visited by the Americans, the villagers expected the Americans to act like tourists but their assumptions about how the Americans would perform this role clearly backfired. This is partly because although the Americans recognized their role as tourists and perhaps implicitly knew the kind of behavior such a role entailed, they nevertheless rebelled against it in attempting to perform the more likeable role of knowledgeable aid workers and ambassadors of crosscultural exchange. The clash of expectations and assumptions about the roles played by tourist and villager alike produced a moment of de-reification for the Americans. Yet there is another intriguing dimension to this encounter that deserves exploration and perhaps offers the ultimate illustration of the abyss of authenticity that shadows the tourism experience.

The villagers were certainly not naïve about the fact that tourists arrived with specific expectations and that part of their responsibility in ensuring the success of the village as an ethnic tourist attraction involved meeting those expectations. This awareness came about through the numerous visits paid to the village by cultural workers and tourism officials who always took the opportunity to impress upon the villagers the crucial role they played in the preservation of Miao cultural heritage. It was made very clear to the villagers that *their* role was to "be authentic." At the same time, however, their awareness of their role as a tourist attraction came about through the fact that many villagers themselves (particularly village youth) had worked in the broader tourism industry in cosmopolitan metropolises of coastal China. Many, for instance, had been employed (and were still employed) at the China Folk Culture Villages theme park in Shenzhen, and in similar theme parks in other cities, such as Beijing and Guilin. There in the theme parks they understood what constitutes a successful tourist attraction and brought these ideas with them back to the village.

It seems profoundly ironic, therefore, that the villagers felt that in order to meet the expectations of tourists, they should model their reception routines and song and dance performances upon the theme parks, which they understood to be examples of successful tourism development (see Oakes 2006). It should be pointed out here that theme parks are themselves paradoxically marketed as "authentic reproductions" of some other real world. Thus, the Folk Culture Villages prides itself on its authenticity in reproducing the housing styles, culinary features, crafts, and songs and dances of China's different nationalities (Hitchcock et al. 1997). In other words, the theme park claims to be a model of the village at the same time that the village is claiming to be a model of the theme park. Such is the conundrum that authenticity gets one into. The villagers saw themselves as playing the role that they assumed tourists expected them to play. This was, they assumed, what one does when one becomes modern. The villagers believed tourism was their ticket to modernity, their path to a more comfortable life, an avenue that set them apart from their more traditional neighbors. That it was, but in more complex ways than they could comprehend.

The paradox of authenticity is that it vaporizes only when you look for it. I do not wish to claim here that there is no such thing as authenticity at all. Nor do I wish to claim, as Berman and (implicitly) Berger and Pullberg do, that authenticity merely involves a "truer" form of essential selfhood that reveals itself once the masks of alienation and reification are stripped away and we embrace the responsibilities of modern citizenship. While such an approach assumes that the performance of "roles" marks a kind of false consciousness that hides what is "really there," developments in performance theory question that there is indeed an essential foundation there to hide at all. If anything, what is "there" in terms of consciousness and identity is probably more of a *process* than a static being. But I leave such psychic and philosophical questions where they lie. At the same time, I have avoided writing off authenticity as a culturally specific social construction, something that has been ably demonstrated by others (see Cohen 1988; Bruner 1994; DeLyser 1999; Wang 1999; Hendry 2000). Instead, this chapter seeks to explore authenticity as a paradox, something that cannot simply be explained away by social science. To the extent that people again and again need to recognize that the subject is not the object, and that this doublet remains a shallow expression of being, authenticity exists to fulfill this need. Yet to the extent that this need leads one on a journey, a quest for some*thing* or some*where* "authentic," it will always recede and disappear from view, inexpressible in a modern language of binaries.

NOTE

1. "Miao" is the official classification of one of China's 55 minority nationalities. Outside of China, they are generally called Hmong, though there is considerable internal variation among and between these groups within and outside of China. For an ethnographic account of contemporary Miao cultural politics within China, see Schein 2000. For historical accounts of the Miao as the subjects of China's late-imperial efforts to colonize the southwestern frontier, see Diamond 1988, Diamond 1995, and Hostetler 2001.

Bibliography

3 Mustaphas 3. 1989. *Heart of Uncle*. Ryco.

Abu-Lughod, J. L. 1980. *Rabat*. Princeton, NJ: Princeton University Press.

Acland, C. 1998. IMAX Technology and the Tourist Gaze. *Cultural Studies* 12(3): 429–445.

Adams, K. M. 1984. "Come to Tana Toraja, Land of the Heavenly Kings": Travel Agents as Brokers in Ethnicity. *Annals of Tourism Research* 11(3): 469–485.

———. 2001. Danger-Zone Tourism: Prospects and Problems for Tourism in Tumultuous Times. In *Interconnected Worlds: Tourism in Southeast Asia*, ed. P. Teo, T. C. Chang, and K. C. Ho, 265–281. New York: Pergamon.

———. 2003a. Global Cities, Terror and Tourism: The Ambivalent Allure of the Urban Jungle. In *Postcolonial Urbanism: Southeast Asian Cities and Global Processes*, ed. R. Bishop, J. Philipps, and W. Yeo, 37–59. London and New York: Routledge.

———. 2003b. Museum/City/Nation: Negotiating Meaning and Identities in Urban Museums in Indonesia and Singapore. In *Theorizing the Asian City as Text,* ed. R. Goh and B. Yeoh, 135–158. Singapore: World Scientific Press/ Singapore University Press.

Adler, J. 1989. Origins of Sightseeing. *Annals of Tourism Research* 16(1): 7–29.

Agnew J. 1993. Representing Space: Space, Scale and Culture in Social Science. In *Place/Culture/Representation*, ed. J. Duncan and D. Ley, 251–271. London and New York: Routledge.

Agnew, J., and J. Duncan, eds. 1989. *The Power of Place: Bringing Together Geographical and Sociological Imaginations.* Boston: Unwin Hyman.

Albuquerque, Klaus de. 1998. Sex, Beach Boys and Female Tourists in the Caribbean. *Sexuality and Culture* 2: 87–112.

Alexander, J. 1995. The Reality of Reduction: The Failed Synthesis of Pierre Bourdieu. In *Fin de Siècle Social Theory*, ed. J. Alexander, 128–217. New York: Verso.

Alneng, V. 2003. "What the Fuck Is a Vietnam?": Touristic Phantasms and the Pop-colonization of (the) Vietnam (War). *Critique of Anthropology* 22(4): 461–490.

Anderson, B. 1983/1991. *Imagined Communities*. London: Verso.

Andrews, M. 1999. *Landscape and Western Art*. Oxford: Oxford University Press.

Andsager, J. L., and J. A. Drzewiecka. 2002. Desirability of Differences in Destinations. *Annals of Tourism Research* 29(2): 401–421.

Anon. 2000. Scoop: East Timor. Tourism Gets to Dili. *Lonely Planet Website*, www.lonelyplanet.com/scoop/asi/tim.htm., October 6.

Anton, D. J. 1995. *Diversity, Globalization and the Ways of Nature*. Ottawa: International Development Research Centre.

AP (Associated Press). 2001. White Monkeys, Earth-Color Men: Zapatistas Play on Color, Race. 12 March.

Appadurai, A. 1996. *Modernity at Large: Cultural Dimensions of Globalisation*. Minneapolis: University of Minnesota Press.

———, ed. 1986. *The Social Life of Things*. Cambridge: Cambridge University Press.

Armitage, J., and J. Roberts. 2003. From the Hypermodern City to the Gray Zone of Total Mobilization in the Philippines. In *Postcolonial Urbanism: Southeast Asian Cities and Global Processes*, ed. R. Bishop, J. Philipps, and W. Yeo, 87–101. London and New York: Routledge.

Arruda, M. 1996. The New World Order: Crises in Ethics and Rationality. Presentation to the XV National Conference of the Brazilian Bar Association (BBA). Foz do Iguazu. 4–8 September 1994. *Otherwise*. March/April.

Asia Pulse. 1999. http://wysiwyg://98/http://www.skali.com/business/eco/199903/05/eco19990305_07.html. August 19.

Atkinson, D., and D. Cosgrove. 1998. Urban Rhetoric and Embodied Identities: City, Nation, and Empire at the Vittorio Emanuele II Monument in Rome, 1870–1945. *Annals of the Association of American Geographers* 88: 28–49.

Bakhtin, M. 1984. *Rabelais and His World,* trans. H. Iswolsky. Bloomington: Indiana University Press.

Baranowski, S., and E. Furlough, eds. 2001a. *Being Elsewhere: Tourism, Consumer Culture, and Identity in Modern Europe and North America*. Ann Arbor: University of Michigan Press.

———. 2001b. Introduction. In *Being Elsewhere: Tourism, Consumer Culture, and Identity in Modern Europe and North America*, ed. S. Baranowski and E. Furlough, 1–31. Ann Arbor: University of Michigan Press.

Barber, B. 1996. *Jihad vs. McWorld: How Globalism and Tribalism Are Reshaping the World*. New York: Ballantine Books.

Barthes, R. 1985. *Valoisa huone* [Camera Lucida], trans. M. Lintunen, E. Sironen, and L. Lehto. Kansankulttuuri.

Batey, M. 1996. *Jane Austen and the English Landscape*. London: Barn Elms.

Baudrillard, J. 1983. *Simulations*. New York: Semiotext(e).

———. 1988a. *America*, trans. C. Turner. London: Verso.

———. 1988b. Consumer Society. In *Jean Baudrillard. Selected Writings*, ed. M. Poster. Palo Alto: Stanford University Press.

———. 1994. *Simulacra and Simulation.* Ann Arbor: University of Michigan Press.

Bauman, Z. 1991. *Modernity and Ambivalence.* Cambridge: Polity.

———. 1992. *Intimations of Postmodernity.* London and New York: Routledge.

———. 1994. Desert Spectacular. In *The Flaneur*, ed. K. Tester, 138–157. London and New York: Routledge.

———. 1996. From Pilgrim to Tourist—or a Short History of Identity. In *Questions of Cultural Identity*, ed. S. Hall and P. du Gay, 18–37. London: Sage.

BBC News. 2001a. Eyewitness: Street Violence in Genoa. 20 July.

———. 2001b. Genoa Gets Million-Dollar Aid Package. 23 July.

Beck, U. 1992. *The Risk Society: Towards Another Modernity.* London: Sage.

Beezer, A. 1993. Women and Adventure Travel. *New Formations* 21 (Summer): 119–130.

———. 2003. Negative Dialectics of the Desert Crash in *The English Patient.* In *Crash Cultures: Modernity, Mediation and the Material*, ed. J. Arthurs and I. Grant. London: Intellect.

Benjamin, W. 1974/1986. *Silmä väkijoukossa. Huomioita eräistä motiiveista Baudelairen tuotannossa*, trans. A. Alanen. Helsinki: Odessa.

———. 1978. Paris, Capital of the Nineteenth Century. In *Reflections: Essays, Aphorisms, and Autobiographical Writings*, ed. and trans. P. Demetz, 146–162. New York: Harcourt, Brace, Jovanovich.

Bennett, C. 2000. The Life of General Villa. *The Progressive Silent Film List.* Available online at: www.silentera.com/PSFL/data/L/LifeofGeneralVilla1914.html.

Berdai, M. H. 2000. Marche Municipal Place Jamaa el Fna. In *Place Jamaa al Fna. Journée d'études.* Marrakech: Municipalitè Marrakech Medina.

Berger, J. 1972. *Ways of Seeing.* Hammondsworth: Penguin.

Berger, P., and S. Pullberg. 1965. Reification and the Sociological Critique of Consciousness. *History and Theory* 4(2): 196–211.

Berman, M. 1970. *The Politics of Authenticity: Radical Individualism and the Emergence of Modern Society.* New York: Atheneum.

———. 1982. *All That Is Solid Melts into Air: The Experience of Modernity.* New York: Simon and Schuster.

Bey, H. 1991. *TAZ: T.A.Z. the Temporary Autonomous Zone, Ontological Anarchy, Poetic Terrorism.* Brooklyn: Autonomedia. Also available online at: www.t0.or.at/hakimbey/taz/taz.htm

Bhabha, H. 1994. *The Location of Culture.* London and New York: Routledge.

Bhabha, H. K. 1986. Signs Taken for Wonders: Questions of Ambivalence and Authority under a Tree Outside Delhi, May 1817. In *Race, Writing and Difference* ed. H. L. Gates, Jr. Chicago: University of Chicago Press.

Bhattacharyya, D. 1997. Mediating India: An Analysis of a Guidebook. *Annals of Tourism Research* 24(2): 371–389.

Bilkasis, S. 2000. Introduction. In *Place Jamaa al Fna. Journée d'études.* Marrakech: Municipalité Marrakech Medina.

Birkett, D. 1989. *Spinsters Abroad: Victorian Lady Explorers.* Oxford: Blackwell.

Bishop, R., and L. Robinson. 1998. *Night Market: Sexual Cultures and the Thai Economic Miracle.* London and New York: Routledge.

Bloch, E. 1929/1991. *Heritage of Our Times*, trans. N. Plaice and S. Plaice. Cambridge: Polity Press.

———. 1959/1973. *Das Prinzip Hoffnung*. Frankfurt: Suhrkamp.

Blunt, A. 1994. *Travel, Gender and Imperialism: Mary Kingsley and West Africa*. New York and London: Guildford.

Borghi, R. 2002. La costruzione dell'Oriente attraverso il paesaggio: il caso della Jamaa al Fna a Marrakech. In *Beni Culturali Territoriali Regionali. Siti e sedi rurali di residenza, culto, lavoro tra ricerca e didattica*, ed. P. Persi, 273–282. Urbino: Università di Urbino.

———. 2003. Dove finisce l'altra sponda. Tra Mediterrano e 'marocchinita' attraverso il turismo culturale di Marrakech. In *Orizzonte Mediterraneo*, ed. C. Minca, 145–169. Padoa: Cedam.

Bourdieu, P. 1977. Afterword. In *Reflections on Fieldwork in Morocco*, P. Rabinow. Berkeley: University of California Press.

———. 1984. *Distinction: A Critique of the Judgement of Taste*. London and New York: Routledge.

———. 1990. *The Logic of Practice*. Palo Alto: Stanford University Press.

Bradbury, M. 1976. The Cities of Modernism. In *Modernism, 1890–1930*, ed. M. Bradbury and J. McFarlane, 96–104. Harmondsworth: Penguin.

Braidotti, R. 1994. *Nomadic Subjects. Embodiment and Sexual Difference in Contemporary Feminist Theory*. New York: Columbia University Press.

Branch, M. P. 1999. Cosmology in the Casino. Simulacra of Nature in the Interiorized Wilderness. In *The Nature of Cities*, ed. M. Bennett and D. W. Teague, 277–298. Tucson: University of Arizona Press.

Brigham, J. 2002. Lighting Las Vegas. In *The Grit Beneath the Glitter*, ed. H. K. Rothman and M. Davis, 99–114. Berkeley: University of California Press.

Bruner, E. 1991. Transformation of Self in Tourism. *Annals of Tourism Research* 18(2): 238–250.

———. 1994. Abraham Lincoln as Authentic Reproduction: A Critique of Postmodernism. *American Anthropologist* 96(2): 397–415.

———. 1995. The Ethnographer/Tourist in Indonesia. In *International Tourism: Identity and Change*, ed. M. F. Lanfant, J. Allcock, and E. Bruner, 224–241. London: Sage.

Bryman, A. 1999. The Disneyzation of Society. *The Sociological Review* 47(1): 25–47.

Buie, S. 1996. Market as Mandala: The Erotic Space of Commerce. *Organisation* 3(2): 225–232.

Burland, J. 1988. Traveling Correspondence: Notes on Tourism. *Borderlines* 12 (Summer): 8–9.

Butler, J. 1990. *Gender Trouble*. London and New York: Routledge.

———. 1993. *Bodies That Matter. On the Discursive Limits of "Sex."* London and New York: Routledge.

———. 1997. *The Psychic Life of Power: Theories in Subjection*. Palo Alto: Stanford University Press.

Caballero, R. J., and M. L. Hammour. 2000. *Creative Destruction and Development: Institutions, Crises and Restructuring.* Cambridge, MA: National Bureau of Economic Research.

Campbell, F. F. 1999. The Spell of the Sensuous: Casino Atmosphere and the Gambler. In *The Business of Gaming*, ed. W. R. Eadington and J. A. Cornelius, 285–289. Reno: University of Nevada Institute for the Study of Gambling and Commercial Gaming.

Canetti, E. 1989. *Le voci di Marrakech.* Milano: Bompiani.

Cartier, C. 1998. Megadevelopment in Malaysia: From Heritage Landscapes to "Leisurescapes" in Melaka's Tourism Sector. *Singapore Journal of Tropical Geography* 19(2): 151–176.

Casey, E. 1993. *Getting Back into Place: Toward a Renewed Understanding of the Place-World.* Bloomington: Indiana University Press.

———. 1996. How to Get from Space to Place in a Fairly Short Stretch of Time: Phenomenological Prolegomena. In *Sense of Place*, ed. S. Feld and K. Basso, 13–52. Santa Fe: School of American Research Press.

———. 1997. *The Fate of Place: A Philosophical History.* Berkeley: University of California Press.

———. 2001. Between Geography and Philosophy: What Does It Mean to Be in the Place-World? *Annals of the Association of American Geographers* 91(4): 683–693.

Chaney, D. 2002. The Power of Metaphors in Tourism Theory. In *Tourism: Between Place and Performance,* ed. S. Coleman and M. Crang, 193–206. Oxford: Berghahn Books.

Chang, T. C. 1997. From "Instant Asia" to "Multi-faceted Jewel": Urban Imaging Strategies and Tourism Development in Singapore. *Urban Geography* 18(6): 542–562.

———. 2000a. Theming Cities, Taming Places: Insights from Singapore. *Geografiska Annaler B*(1): 35–54.

———. 2000b. Renaissance Revisited: Singapore as a "Global City for the Arts." *International Journal of Urban and Regional Research* 24(4): 818–831.

Christensen, J. 2002. Build It and the Water Will Come. In *The Grit beneath the Glitter*, ed. H. K. Rothman and M. Davis, 115–125. Berkeley: University of California Press.

Christiansen, E., and J. Brinkerhoff-Jacobs. 1997. The Relationship of Gaming to Entertainment. In *Gambling*, ed. W. R. Eadington and J. A. Cornelius, 11–48. Reno: University of Nevada Institute for the Study of Gambling and Commercial Gaming.

Claessen, C. 1993. *Worlds of Sense: Exploring the Senses in History and Across Cultures.* London and New York: Routledge.

Classen, C., D. Howes, and A. Synnott. 1994. *Aroma.* London and New York: Routledge.

Cleaver, H. 1998. The Zapatista Effect: The Internet and the Rise of an Alternative Political Fabric. *Journal of International Affairs* 51/2: 621–640.

Clifford, James. 1989. Notes on Theory and Travel. *Inscriptions* 5: 177–188.

——. 1992. Traveling Cultures. In *Cultural Studies*, ed. C. Nelson and P. Treichler, 96–116. London and New York: Routledge.

——. 1997. Traveling Cultures. In *Routes: Travel and Translation in the Late Twentieth Century*, 17–46. Cambridge, MA: Harvard University Press.

Cloke, P., and P. Perkins. 1998. "Cracking the Canyon with the Awesome Foursome": Representations of Adventure Tourism in New Zealand. *Environment and Planning D: Society and Space* 16(2): 185–218.

Cohen, E. 1972. Towards a Sociology of International Tourism. *Social Research* 39(1): 164–182.

——. 1988. Authenticity and Commoditization in Tourism. *Annals of Tourism Research* 15(3): 371–386.

Cohen, S., and L. Taylor. 1992. *Escape Attempts*. London and New York: Routledge.

Compagnon, A. 1997. Marcel Proust's Remembrance of Things Past. *Realms of Memory: The Construction of the French Past (2) Traditions*, ed. P. Nora, 211–246. New York: Columbia University Press.

Cooper, M. 1995. Searching for Sin City and Finding Disney in the Desert. In *Literary Las Vegas*, ed. M. Tronnes, 325–350. New York: Henry Holt.

Cosgrove, D., and S. Daniels, ed. 1988. *The Iconography of Landscape*. Cambridge: Cambridge University Press.

Craik, J. 1997. The Culture of Tourism. In *Touring Cultures: Transformations in Travel and Theory*, ed. C. Rojek and J. Urry, 113–136. London and New York: Routledge.

Crang, M., and S. Coleman 2002. Grounded Tourists, Travelling Theory. *Tourism: Between Place and Performance*, ed. M. Crang and S. Coleman. Oxford: Berghahn, 1–17.

Crawford, M. 1992. The World in a Shopping Mall. In *Variations on a Theme Park*, ed. M. Sorkin, 3–30. New York: Noonday.

Crick, M. 1989. Representations of Sun, Sex, Sights, Savings, and Servility: International Tourism in the Social Sciences. *Annual Review of Anthropology* 18: 307–344.

——. 1995. The Anthropologist as Tourist: An Identity in Question. In *International Tourism: Identity and Change*, ed. M. F. Lanfant, J. Allcock, and E. Bruner, 205–223. London: Sage.

Crouch, D. 1999. Introduction: Encounters in Leisure/Tourism. In *Leisure/Tourism Geographies: Practices and Geographical Knowledge*, ed. D. Crouch, 1–16. London and New York: Routledge.

Culler, J. 1981. Semiotics of Tourism. *American Journal of Semiotics* 1(1–2): 127–140.

Dann, G. 1996. The People of Tourist Brochures. *The Tourist Image: Myths and Myth Making in Modern Tourism*, ed. T. Selwyn, 61–82. Chichester: Wiley.

——. 1999. Writing Out the Tourist in Space and Time. *Annals of Tourism Research* 26(1): 159–187.

——. 2003. Noticing Notices: Tourism to Order. *Annals of Tourism Research* 30(2): 465–484.

Darby, H. C. 1948. The Regional Geography of Thomas Hardy's Wessex. *Geographical Review* 38: 426–443.

de Burlo, C. 1989. Islanders, Soldiers, and Tourists: The War and the Shaping of Tourism in Melanesia. In *The Pacific Theater: Island Representations of World War II*, ed. G. White and L. Lindstrom, 299–325. Honolulu: University of Hawaii Press.

de Wit, C. W. 1992. Food-Place Associations on American Product Labels. *Geographical Review* 83(3): 323–330.

Deleuze, G., and F. Guattari. 1980. *Mille Plateaux*. Paris: Editions de Minuit.

———. 1983. *Anti-Oedipus: Capitalism and Schizophrenia*, trans. B. Massumi. Minneapolis: University of Minnesota Press.

———. 1987. *A Thousand Plateaus: Capitalism and Schizophrenia*, trans. B. Massumi. Minneapolis: University of Minnesota Press.

DeLyser, D. 1999. Authenticity on the Ground: Engaging the Past in a California Ghost Town. *Annals of the Association of American Geographers* 89(4): 602–632.

Derrida, J. 1991. Ulysses Gramophone. *Between the Blinds*. New York: Columbia University Press.

Desforges, L. 1998. "Checking Out the Planet": Global Representations/ Local Identities and Youth Travel. In *Cool Places: Geographies of Youth Cultures*, ed. T. Skelton and G. Valentine, 175–192. London and New York: Routledge.

———. 2000. Traveling the World: Identity and Travel Biography. *Annals of Tourism Research* 27(4): 926–945.

Diamond, N. 1988. The Miao and Poison: Interactions on China's Southwest Border. *Ethnology* 27(1): 1–25.

———. 1995. Defining the Miao: Ming Qing, and Contemporary Views. In *Cultural Encounters on China's Ethnic Frontiers*, ed. S. Harrell, 92–116. Seattle: University of Washington Press.

Dienst, R. 1994. *Still Life in Real Time: Theory after Television*. Durham, NC: Duke University Press.

Diller and Scofidio. 1994. *Back to the Front: Tourisms of War*. Basse-Normandie, France: FRANC.

Dirlik, A. 1999. Place-Based Imagination: Globalism and the Politics of Place. *Review: A Journal of the Fernand Braudel Center for the Study of Economics, Historical Systems, and Civilizations* 22(2): 151–187.

Discover the Facts 2001. 2002. A Digest of Statistical Information on the Nevada Tourism Industry. Volume IX: Fourth Quarter. Nevada Commission on Tourism. 19 September 2002. www.travelnevada.com

Douglass, W. A., and P. Raento. 2004. The Tradition of Invention. Conceiving Las Vegas. *Annals of Tourism Research* 31(1): 7–23.

Drobnick, J. 2002. Toposmia: Art, Scent and Interrogations of Spatiality. *Angelaki* 7(1): 31–46.

Ducci, C. 2000. Una Perpetua Seduzione. *Traveller* 6: 108–123.

Duncan, J., and N. Duncan. 1988. (Re)reading the Landscape. *Environment and Planning D: Society and Space* 6(2): 117–126.

Dunning, J. H. 1993. *The Globalization of Business: The Challenge of the 1990s*. London and New York: Routledge.

Eco, U. 1986. *Travels in Hyperreality*. New York: Harcourt Brace Jovanovich.

Economist, The. 2001. After the Genoa Summit: Picking Up the Pieces. 26 July.

Edensor, T. 1998. *Tourists at the Taj*. London and New York: Routledge.
———. 2000. Walking in the British Countryside. *Body and Society* 6(3–4): 81–106.
———. 2001. Performing Tourism, Staging Tourism: (Re)Producing Tourist Space and Practice. *Tourist Studies* 1(1): 59–81.
———. 2002. *National Identity, Popular Culture and Everyday Life*. Oxford: Berg.
———. 2005. *Industrial Ruins: Space, Aesthetics and Materiality*. Oxford: Berg.
Edwards, J. E. 1992. The Americanization of Nevada Gambling. *Halcyon* 14: 201–216.
Elsrud, T. 2001. Risk Creation in Traveling: Backpacker Adventure Narration. *Annals of Tourism Research* 28(3): 597–617.
Entrikin, J. N. 1991. *The Betweenness of Place: Towards a Geography of Modernity*. Baltimore: Johns Hopkins University Press.
———. 2001. Hiding Places. *Annals of the Association of American Geographers* 91(4): 694–697.
Escobar, A. 2001. Culture Sits in Places: Reflections on Globalism and Subaltern Strategies of Localization. *Political Geography* 20(1): 139–174.
Expreso Chiapas. 1998. 19 February: 8
Fabian, J. 1983. *Time and the Other: How Anthropology Makes Its Object*. New York: Columbia University Press.
Farinelli, F. 1992. *I Segni del Mondo*. Florence: Nuova Italia.
Featherstone, M. 1987. Lifestyle and Consumer Culture. *Theory, Culture and Society* 4(1): 55–70.
———. 1991. *Consumer Culture and Postmodernism*. London: Sage.
Feifer, M. 1985. *Going Places: Tourism in History*. New York: Stein and Day.
Feinmann, J. P. 1998. Guevara y Marcos. *Página/12*. August 22.
Feld, S., and K. Basso, eds. 1996. *Senses of Place*. Santa Fe: School of American Research Press.
Findlay, J. M. 1986. *People of Chance*. New York: Oxford University Press.
———. 1990. Suckers and Escapists? Interpreting Las Vegas and Post-War America. *Nevada Historical Society Quarterly* 33(1): 1–15.
Flecker, K. 2003. Looking Down the Barrel. *NOW*. December 4–10: 20.
Flood, F. 2001. What Is It That Is Different about the Zapatistas? *Chiapas Revealed*. February: 1–12.
Flusty, S. 1994. *Building Paranoia: The Proliferation of Interdictory Space and the Erosion of Spatial Justice*. West Hollywood: The Los Angeles Forum for Architecture and Urban Design.
———. 1999. Field notes. Unpublished.
———. 2001. The Banality of Interdiction: Surveillance, Control, and the Displacement of Diversity. *International Journal of Urban and Regional Research* 25(3): 658–664.
Foley, M. 1995. Privatizing the Countryside: The Mexican Peasant Movement and Neoliberal Reform. *Latin American Perspectives* 84 (22/1) Winter: 59–76.
Forbes, H. O. 1885. *A Naturalist's Wanderings in the Eastern Archipelago: A Narrative of Travel and Exploration from 1978 to 1883*. New York: Harper and Brothers.

Foucault, M. 1978/1990. *The History of Sexuality. Volume I: An Introduction*, trans. R. Hurley. New York: Vintage.

——. 1979. *Discipline and Punish.* New York: Vintage.

——. 1982. The Subject and Power. *Critical Inquiry* 8/4 (Summer): 777–795.

Frankenberg, Ruth. 1993. *White Women, Race Matters: The Social Construction of Whiteness.* London: Routledge.

Franklin, A., and M. Crang. 2001. The Trouble with Tourism and Travel Theory? *Tourist Studies* 1(1): 5–22.

Friedman, B. 2000. *Designing Casinos to Dominate the Competition.* Reno: University of Nevada Institute for the Study of Gambling and Commercial Gaming.

Friedman, M. 1992. *Economic Freedom, Human Freedom, Political Freedom.* Hayward: California State University, Hayward; The Smith Center for Private Enterprise Studies.

Frisby, D. 1994. The Flaneur in Social Theory. In *The Flaneur*, ed. K. Tester, 81–110. London and New York: Routledge.

Frykman, J. 1994. On the Move: The Struggle for the Body in Sweden. In *The Senses Still: Perception and Memory as Material Culture in Modernity*, ed. C. Seremetakis, 63–85. Chicago: University of Chicago Press.

Fullagar, S. 2000. Desiring Nature: Identity and Becoming in Narratives of Travel. *Cultural Values* 4(1): 58–76.

——. 2001. Encountering Otherness: Embodied Affect in Alphonso Lingis's Travel Writing. *Tourist Studies* 1(2): 171–183.

Fussell, P. 1980. *Abroad: British Literary Traveling between the Wars.* New York: Oxford University Press.

FZLN (Frente Zapatista de Liberación Nacional). 1996. Zapatista Front of National Liberation. 22 October. Available online at: www.ezln.org/archivo/fzln/fzln.html

Gaonkar, D. P. 2001. On Alternative Modernities. In *Alternative Modernities*, ed. D. P. Gaonkar, 1–23. Durham, NC: Duke University Press.

Garcia, A. 2000. The March: The WTO-Battle in Seattle. *Changelinks* (January): 1, 7.

Garland, A. 1996. *The Beach.* London: Penguin.

Garlick, S. 2002. Revealing the Unseen: Tourism, Art and Photography. *Cultural Studies* 16(2): 289–305.

Gartner, W. C., and J. Shen. 1992. The Impact of Tiananmen Square on China's Tourism Image. *Journal of Travel Research* 30(4): 47–52.

Giddens, A. 1979. *Central Problems in Social Theory: Action, Structure and Contradition in Social Analysis.* London: Macmillan.

——. 1990. *The Consequences of Modernity.* Palo Alto: Stanford University Press.

——. 1991. *Modernity and Self-Identity.* Cambridge: Polity.

Gieryn, T. 2000. A Space for Place in Sociology. *Annual Review of Sociology* 26: 463–496.

Global Exchange, 1999. Reality Tours: Travel With US to See What's Really Happening. www.globalexchange.org/tours/auto/byCountry.html & www.globalexchange .org/tours/indonesiaItin1.html (Indonesia Itinerary, August 18).

Goffman, E. 1961. *Asylums.* Garden City: Anchor Books.

Golden, T. 2001. Revolution Rocks: Thoughts of Mexico's First Postmodern Guerrilla Commander. *The New York Times Review of Books*. 8 April.

Goss, J. 1999. Once-Upon-a-Time in the Commodity World: An Unofficial Guide to Mall of America. *Annals of the Association of American Geographers* 89(1): 45–75.

Gottdiener, M. 1997. *The Theming of America*. Boulder: Westview Press.

Gottdiener, M., C. C. Collins, and D. R. Dickens. 1999. *Las Vegas*. Oxford: Blackwell.

Goytisolo, J. 1982. *Makbara*. Paris: Editions du Seuil.

Graburn, N. 1983. The Anthropology of Tourism. *Annals of Tourism Research* 10(1): 9–33.

Graham, B., G. Ashworth, and J. Tunbridge. 2000. *A Geography of Heritage*. London: Arnold.

Gray, C. H. 1997. *Postmodern War: The New Politics of Conflict*. New York: Guildford Press.

Gregory, D. 1999. Scripting Egypt: Orientalism and the Cultures of Travel. In *Writes of Passage: Reading Travel Writing*, ed. J. Duncan and D. Gregory. London and New York: Routledge, 114–150.

Greider, W. 2001. The Right and US Trade Law: Invalidating the 20th Century. *The Nation*. 15 October. Available online at: www.thenation.com/doc.mhtml ?i20011015&sgreider

Gupta, A., and J. Ferguson, eds. 1997. *Culture, Power, Place: Explorations in Critical Anthropology*. Durham, NC: Duke University Press.

Hall, S. 1999. *Identiteetti* [Identity], trans. and ed. M. Lehtonen and J. Herkman. Tampere: Vastapaino.

Harvey, D. 1989. *The Condition of Postmodernity: An Inquiry into the Origins of Cultural Change*. Oxford: Blackwell.

Haug, F., et al. 1983. *Critique of Commodity Aesthetics: Appearance, Sexuality and Advertising in Capitalist Society*. Cambridge: Polity Press.

———. 1987. *Commodity Aesthetics: Ideology and Culture*. New York: International General.

———. 1992. *Female Sexualization. A Collective Work of Memory*, trans. E. Carter. London: Verso.

Hausladen, G. 2000. *Places for Dead Bodies*. Austin: University of Texas Press.

Heller, A. 1999. *A Theory of Modernity*. Oxford: Blackwell.

Hendry, J. 2000. *The Orient Strikes Back: A Global View of Cultural Display*. Oxford: Berg.

Hennock, M. 2003. Bali Tourism Struggles to Its Feet. *BBC News World Edition*. February 14.

Herzfeld, M. 1991. *A Place in History: Social and Monumental Time in a Cretan Town*. Princeton, NJ: Princeton University Press.

Hetherington, K. 1997. *The Badlands of Modernity*. London and New York: Routledge.

Hitchcock, M., N. Stanley, and S. K. Chung. 1997. The South-East Asian "Living Museum" and its Antecedents. In *Tourists and Tourism: Identifying with People and Places*, ed. S. Abram and M. Waldren, 197–221. Oxford: Berg.

Hochschild, A. 2000. Global Care Chains and Emotional Surplus Value. In *On the Edge: Globalization and the New Millenium*, ed. A. Giddens and W. Hutton. London: Sage, 130–146.

Hoisington, W. A. 1995. *Lyautey and the French Conquest of Morocco.* New York: St. Martin's Press.

Hooper, H. 2001. Desiring Presence, Romancing the Real. *Annals of the Association of American Geographers* 91(4): 703–715.

Hostetler, L. 2001. *Qing Colonial Enterprise: Ethnography and Cartography in Early Modern China.* Chicago: University of Chicago Press.

Hughes, G. 1998. Tourism and the Semiological Realization of Space. *Destinations: Cultural Landscapes of Tourism*, ed. G. Ringer, 17–32. London and New York: Routledge.

Hutnyk, J. 1996. *The Rumour of Calcutta: Tourism, Charity and the Poverty of Representation.* London: Zone Books.

IGWB. 1999. *International Gaming and Wagering Business* 20(6): 6.

Ingold, T., and T. Kurttila, 2000. Perceiving the Environment in Finnish Lapland. *Body and Society* 6(3–4): 186–196.

Insight Compact Guides: Venice. 1995. Singapore: Apa.

Irigaray, L. 1977/1985. *This Sex Which Is Not One* [Ce Sexe qui n'en est pas un], trans. C. Porter with C. Burke. Ithaca, NY: Cornell University Press.

Jacobs, J. 1996. *Edge of Empire: Postcolonialism and the City.* London and New York: Routledge.

Jallinoja, R. 2000. *Perheen aika* [The Time of the Family]. Helsinki: Otava.

Jansson, A. 2002. Spatial Phantasmagoria: The Mediatization of Tourism Experience. *European Journal of Communication* 17(4): 429–443.

Jansson, T. 1957. *Trollvinter* [Magic Winter]. Helsinki: WSOY.

Jay, M. 1992. Scopic Regimes of Modernity. In *Modernity and Identity*, ed. S. Lash and J. Friedman, 178–195. Oxford: Blackwell.

Johnson, N. 1995. Cast in Stone: Monuments, Geography and Nationalism. *Environment and Planning D: Society and Space* 13: 51–65.

Johnston, L. 2001. (Other) Bodies and Tourism Studies. *Annals of Tourism Research* 23(1): 180–201.

Jokinen, E., and S. Veijola. 1997. The Disoriented Tourist: The Figuration of the Tourist in Contemporary Cultural Critique. In *Touring Cultures: Transformations of Travel and Theory*, ed. C. Rojek and J. Urry, 23–51. London and New York: Routledge.

———. 2003. Mountains and Landscapes. Towards Embodied Visualities. In *Visual Culture and Tourism*, ed. N. Lübbren and D. Crouch, 259–278. Oxford: Berg.

Joyce, James. 1961. *Ulysses.* New York: Random House.

Kaes, A. 1989. *From Hitler to Heimat.* Cambridge, MA: Harvard University Press.

Kahn, J. 1997. Culturalizing Malaysia: Globalism, Tourism, Heritage and the City in Georgetown. In *Tourism, Ethnicity and the State in Asian and Pacific Societies,* ed. M. Picard and R. Wood, 99–127. Honolulu: University of Hawaii Press.

Kaplan, C. 1996. *Questions of Travel: Postmodern Discourses of Displacement.* Durham, NC: Duke University Press.

Karch, C., and G. Dann. 1981. Close Encounters of the Third World. *Human Relations* 34: 249–268.

Keskitalo, Anne, C. Keskitalo, M. Lüthje, S. Matala, J. Saarinen, and S. Veijola. 2000. Amenity Landscapes. Spaces of Mobility and Immobility. Unpublished research plan, University of Lapland (November).

Kirshenblatt-Gimblett, B. 1998. *Destination Culture: Tourism, Museums, and Heritage.* Berkeley: University of California Press.

Kivimäki, A., and P. Tuomisto. 2000. *Rooman keisarit.* Hämeenlinna: Karisto.

Klein, N. M. 1997. The Politics of Scripted Places: Las Vegas and Reno. *Nevada Historical Society Quarterly* 40(2): 151–159.

———. 2002. Scripting Las Vegas: Noir Naifs, Junking Up, and the New Strip. In *The Grit beneath the Glitter*, ed. H. K. Rothman and M. Davis, 17–29. Berkeley: University of California Press.

Klepacki, L. 1997. Signs of the Times. *International Gaming and Wagering Business* 18(1): 47–48, 50.

Koivunen, H. 1997. *Hiljainen tieto* [Quiet Knowledge]. Helsinki: Otava.

Kranes, D. 1995a. Play Grounds. *Journal of Gambling Studies* 11: 91–102.

———. 1995b. *Keno Runner.* Reno: University of Nevada Press.

———. 1999. Story Spaces: Any Casino's Romance & How It's Told. In *The Business of Gaming*, ed. W. R. Eadington and J. A. Cornelius, 291–302. Reno: University of Nevada Institute for the Study of Gambling and Commercial Gaming.

Kuiper, D. 2001a. Notes from the Front: The Wall Defines Two Americas in Quebec. *Los Angeles Weekly.* 4–10 May: 22–23.

———. 2001b. Out of Control: The Attack on Protesters and the Press in Genoa. *Los Angeles Weekly.* 27 July–2 August: 19.

Lach, D. 1965. *Asia in the Making of Europe.* Chicago: University of Chicago Press.

Laroui, A. 1995. *L'Histoire du Maghreb. Un essai de synthèse.* Casablanca: Centre Culturel Arabe.

Lash, S. 1993. Reflexive Modernization: The Aesthetic Dimension. *Theory, Culture, and Society* 10(1): 1–23.

———. 1999. *Another Modernity, a Different Rationality.* Oxford: Blackwell.

Latour, B. 1993. *We Have Never Been Modern,* trans. C. Porter. New York and London: Harvester Wheatsheaf.

Le Révérend, A. 1983. *Lyautey.* Paris: Fayard.

Lee, M. 1993. *Consumer Culture Reborn: The Cultural Politics of Consumption.* London and New York: Routledge.

Levi-Strauss, C. 1983. *The Raw and the Cooked,* trans. J. Weightman and D. Weightman. Chicago: University of Chicago Press.

Lewis, J. 2000. Terms of Resistance: Training at the Ruckus Society's Democracy Action Camp. *Los Angeles Weekly.* 11–17 August.

Lewis, M., and K. Wigen. 1997. *The Myth of Continents: A Critique of Metageography.* Berkeley: University of California Press.

Lewis, R. 1995. *Gendering Orientalism: Race, Femininity and Representation.* London and New York: Routledge.

Libra, C. 1995. Interview with Marcos. *La Journada.* 25 August. Available online at: http://flag.blackened.net/revolt/mexico/ezln/inter_marcos_consult_aug95.html

Light, D. 1995. Heritage as Informal Education. In *Heritage, Tourism and Society*, ed. D. Herbert, 117–145. London: Mansell.

Limerick, P. N. 1987. *The Legacy of Conquest*. New York: Norton.

Lindqvist, S. 2000. *Desert Divers*. Trans. J. Tate. London: Granta.

Lippard, L. 1999. *On the Beaten Track: Tourism, Art and Place*. New York: The New Press.

Littlejohn, D., ed. 1999. *The Real Las Vegas*. New York: Oxford University Press.

Littlewood, I. 2001. *Sultry Climates: Travel and Sex since the Grand Tour*. London: John Murray.

Löfgren, O. 1999. *On Holiday. A History of Vacationing*. Berkeley: University of California Press.

Lury, C. 1997. The Objects of Travel. In *Touring Cultures*, ed. C. Rojek and J. Urry, 75–95. London and New York: Routledge.

LVVPS. 1991. *Las Vegas Visitor Profile Study 1991*. Las Vegas: Las Vegas Convention and Visitors Authority.

———. 1996. *Las Vegas Visitor Profile Study 1996*. Las Vegas: Las Vegas Convention and Visitors Authority.

———. 2001. *Las Vegas Visitor Profile Study 2001*. Las Vegas: Las Vegas Convention and Visitors Authority.

Lyautey, G. H. 1927. *Paroles d'action*. Paris: Armand Colin.

———. 1995. *Paroles d'action*. Paris: Imprimerie Nationale Editions.

MacCannell, D. 1973. Staged Authenticity: Arrangements of Social Space in Tourism Settings. *American Journal of Sociology* 79: 589–603.

———. 1976. *The Tourist: A New Theory of the Leisure Class*. New York: Schocken.

———. 1989. *The Tourist: A New Theory of the Leisure Class*, 2nd ed. New York: Schocken.

———. 1992. *Empty Meeting Grounds*. London and New York: Routledge.

MacKinnon, M. 2001. WTO Finds a Haven: Qatar. *The Globe and Mail*. 9 February.

Macnaghten, P., and J. Urry. 2001. Bodies of Nature: Introduction. In *Bodies of Nature*, ed. P. Macnaghten and J. Urry, 1–11. London: Sage.

Maffesoli, M. 1988/1996. *The Time of the Tribes. The Decline of Individualism in Mass Society*. London: Sage.

Malamud, M. 1998. As the Romans Did? Theming Ancient Rome in Contemporary Las Vegas. *Arion* 6(2): 11–39.

———. 2001. The Greatest Show on Earth: Roman Entertainments in Turn-of-the-Century New York City. *Journal of Popular Culture* 35(3): 43–58.

Marcos, S. 1995. *Shadows of Tender Fury: The Letters and Communiqués of Subcomandante Marcos and the Zapatista Army of National Liberation*. New York: Monthly Review Press.

———. 1999. Teachers Are a Mirror and a Window. Presentation delivered to the Closing Session of the "Democratic Teachers and Zapatista Dream" Meeting. 1 August. Avaliable online at: http://flag.blackened.net/revolt/mexico/ezln/1999/marcos_teachers_close_aug.html

Marcos, S., and D. Domínguez. 1996. *The Story of Colors/La Historia de los Colores*, trans. A. Bar Din. Guadalajara: Ediciones Colectivo Callejero/Cinco Puntos Press.

Martinez, A. 1999. *24/7*. New York: Villard.

Massey, D. 1992. A Place Called Home? *New Formations* 17: 3–17.

———. 1993. Power Geometry and a Progressive Sense of Place. In *Mapping the Futures: Local Cultures, Global Change*, ed. J. Bird et al., 59–69. London and New York: Routledge.

Massey, D., and P. Jess, eds. 1995. *A Place in the World? Places, Cultures, and Globalization*. Oxford: Oxford University Press.

Maurois, A. 1931. *Lyautey*. Paris: Plon.

McAlister, M. 2001. *Epic Encounters*. Berkeley: University of California Press.

McClelland, L. F. 1998. *Building the National Parks*. Baltimore and London: The Johns Hopkins University Press.

McEwan, C. 2000. *Gender, Geography and Empire: Victorian Women Travellers in West Africa*. Aldershot: Ashgate.

McGregor, A. 2000. Dynamic Texts and the Tourist Gaze: Death, Bones and Buffalo. *Annals of Tourism Research* 27(1): 27–50.

McIntosh, A., and R. Prentice. 1999. Affirming Authenticity: Consuming Cultural Heritage. *Annals of Tourism Research* 26(3): 589–612.

Meethan, K. 2001. *Tourism in Global Society: Place, Culture, Consumption*. Basingstoke and New York: Palgave.

Meinig, D. W., ed. 1979. *The Interpretation of Ordinary Landscapes*. New York: Oxford University Press.

Meltzer, E. 2002. Performing Place: A Hyperbolic Drugstore in Wall, South Dakota. In *Tourism: Between Place and Performance*, ed. S. Coleman and M. Crang, 160–175. Oxford: Berghahn Books.

Merleau-Ponty, M. 1962. *Phenomenology of Perception*, trans. C. Smith. London and New York: Routledge and Kegan Paul.

Metcalfe, J. S. 1998. *Evolutionary Economics and Creative Destruction*. London and New York: Routledge.

Miles, S. 1998. *Consumerism: As a Way of Life*. London: Sage.

Mills, S. 1991. *Discourses of Difference: An Analysis of Women's Travel Writing and Colonialism*. London and New York: Routledge.

Minca C. 2001. Postmodern Temptations. In *Postmodern Geography: Theory and Praxis*, ed. C. Minca, 196–225. Oxford: Blackwell.

———. 2005. Bellagio and Beyond. In *Seductions of Place*, ed. C. Cartier and A. Lew, 103–120. London and New York: Routledge.

Minca, C., and R. Borghi. Forthcoming. Le lieu, la place, l'imaginaire: discours colonial et littérature dans la description de la Jamaa el Fna, Marrakech. *Expressions Maghrébin*.

Minister for Tourism. 2000. Allocution. In *Place Jamaa al Fna. Journée d'études*. Marrakech: Municipalitè Marrakech Medina.

Mintier, T. 1999. Indonesian Tourism Industry Battered by Images of Violence. www.cnn.com/ASIANOW/southeast/9909/26/indonesian.tourism/ September 26.

Mitchell, T. 1988. *Colonizing Egypt*. Berkeley: University of California Press.

———. 2000a. Introduction. In *Questions of Modernity*, ed. T. Mitchell, xi–xxvii. Minneapolis: University of Minnesota Press.

———. 2000b. The Stage of Modernity. In *Questions of Modernity*, ed. T. Mitchell, 1–34. Minneapolis: University of Minnesota Press.

Moehring, E. P. 1989. *Resort City in the Sunbelt.* Reno: University of Nevada Press.

Montes, R. 1995. Chiapas Is a War of Ink and Internet. *Reforma.* 26 April.

Morales, F. 2001. Welcome to the Free World: Gas Me-Stun Me-Shoot Me-Zap Me-Douse Me-Drug Me-Shut Me Up. *Covert Action Quarterly* 70. April–June: 6–13.

Morawski, S. 1994. The Hopeless Game of Flanerie. In *The Flaneur,* ed. K. Tester, 181–197. London and New York: Routledge.

Morley, D., and K. Robins. 1993. No Place Like Heimat: Images of Home(land). In *Space and Place: Theories of Identity and Location,* ed. E. Carter, J. Donald, and J. Squires, 3–31. London: Lawrence and Wishart.

Morris, M. 1988a. At Henry Parkes Motel. *Cultural Studies* 2(1): 1–16.

———. 1988b. Things to Do with Shopping Centres. *Grafts: Feminist Cultural Criticism,* ed. S. Sheridan, 193–224. London: Verso.

———. 1992. The Man in the Mirror: David Harvey's "Condition" of Postmodernity. *Theory, Culture and Society* 9: 253–279.

Morton, P. A. 2000. *Hybrid Modernities.* Cambridge, MA: MIT Press.

Muller, K. 1995. *East of Bali: From Lombok to Timor.* Lincolnwood: Passport Books.

Munt, I. 1994. The "Other" Postmodern Tourism: Culture, Travel and the New Middle Classes. *Theory, Culture and Society* 11(1): 101–123.

Murphy, L. 2001. Exploring Social Interactions of Backpackers. *Annals of Tourism Research* 28(1): 50–67.

MVRDV 2000. *Costa Iberica.* Barcelona: Actar.

Nabil, B. e Z. Abdelilah. 2000. La Place Jamaa El Fna un patrimoine oral. In *Place Jamaa al Fna. Journée d'études.* Marrakech: Municipalitè Marrakech Medina.

NACEC (North American Commission for Environmental Cooperation. 2001. *Summary of Environmental Law.* Chapter 15. Available online at: www.cec.org/pubs_info_resources/law_treat_agree/summary_enviro_law/publication/mx15.cfm?varlanenglish

Nash, R. 1983. *Wilderness and the American Mind.* 3rd ed. New Haven and London: Yale University Press.

Neumann, M. 1988. Wandering through the Museum: Experience and Identity in a Spectator Culture. *Border/lines* (Summer): 19–27.

———. 1992. The Trail through Experience: Finding Self in the Recollection of Travel. In *Investigating Subjectivity: Research on Lived Experience,* ed. C. Ellis and M. Flaherty, 176–201. London: Sage.

Nielsen, N. K. 1999. Knowledge by Doing: Home and Identity in a Bodily Perspective. In *Leisure. Tourism Geographies. Practices and Geographical Knowledge,* ed. D. Crouch, 277–289. London and New York: Routledge.

Nordland, R., and C. Dickey. 2001. First Blood. *Newsweek.* 30 July: 20–23.

Nugent, D. 1995. Northern Intellectuals and the EZLN. *Monthly Review* 47 (July-August): 24–138.

Oakes, T. 1997. Place and the Paradox of Modernity. *Annals of Association of American Geographers* 87(3): 509–531.

———. 1998. *Tourism and Modernity in China.* London and New York: Routledge.

———. 1999. Eating the Food of the Ancestors: Place, Tradition and Tourism in a Chinese Frontier River Town. *Ecumene* 6(2): 123–145.

———. 2005. Tourism and the Modern Subject: Placing the Encounter between Tourist and Other, 36–55. In *Seductions of Place*, ed. C. Cartier and A. Lew. London and New York: Routledge.

———. 2006. The Village as Theme Park: Mimesis and Authenticity in Chinese Tourism. In *Translocal China: Linkages, Identities and the Reimagining of Space*, ed. T. Oakes and L. Schein. London and New York: Routledge.

O'Connell Davidson, J., and J. Sanchez Taylor. 1999. Fantasy Islands: Exploring the Demand for Sex Tourism. In *Sun, Sex and Gold: Tourism and Sex Work in the Caribbean*, ed. K. Kempadoo, 37–54. Lanham, MD: Rowman & Littlefield.

Oppenheimer, A. 1996. Guerrillas in the Mist: What Do Mexico's Rebels Want? *The New Republic* 214/25, 17 June: 22.

Orwell, G. 1954. Marrakech. In *A Collection of Essays*, 180–187. New York: Doubleday Anchor Books.

Paasi, A. 1991. Yhteiskuntatutkimuksen kielestä ja metodologisista implikaatioista: teoriaa ja empiirisiä esimerkkejä [About the Language and Methodological Implications of Social Studies: Theory and Empirical Examples]. *Terra* 103(3): 293–241.

Parets, R. T. 1998. Making a Grand Entrance. *International Gaming and Wagering Business* 19(11): 15, 20, 22, 24.

Parker, R. E. 1999. Las Vegas: Casino Gambling and Local Culture. In *The Tourist City*, ed. D. R. Judd and S. S. Fainstein, 107–123. New Haven and London: Yale University Press.

Parnwell, M. 1998. Tourism, Globalisation and Critical Security in Myanmar and Thailand. *Singapore Journal of Tropical Geography* 19(2): 212–231.

Pasztory, E. 2001. Nostalgia for Mud. *The Pari Journal: A Quarterly Publication of the Pre-Colombian Art Research Institute* 2(1) mesoweb.com/pari/publications/journal/03/mud.html

Patterson, D. 1988. *Literature and Spirit: Essays on Bakhtin and His Contemporaries*. Lexington: University Press of Kentucky.

Paz, O. 1982. *The Labyrinth of Solitude,* trans. L. Kemp, Y. Milos, and R. Phillips Belash. New York: Grove/Atlantic.

———. 1994. The Media Spectacle Comes to Mexico. *New Perspectives Quarterly* 11/2, Spring: 59–61.

Pelton, R. Y., C. Aral, and W. Dulles. 1998. *Fielding's The World's Most Dangerous Places.* Redondo Beach, CA: Fielding Worldwide, Inc.

Pennell, C. R. 2000. *Morocco since 1831.* New York: New York University Press.

Phillips, J. 1999. Tourist-Oriented Prostitution in Barbados: The Case of the Beach Boy and the White Female Tourist. In *Sun, Sex and Gold: Tourism and Sex Work in the Caribbean*, ed. K. Kempadoo, 183–200. Lanham, MD: Rowman & Littlefield.

Phipps, P. 1999. Tourists, Terrorists, Death and Value. In *Travel Worlds: Journeys in Contemporary Cultural Politics*, ed. R. Kaur and J. Hutnyk, 74–93. London and New York: Zed Books.

Picard, M. 1996. *Bali: Cultural Tourism and Touristic Culture*. Singapore: Archipelago Press.

Pickles, J. 1985. *Phenomenology, Science, and Geography: Spatiality and the Human Sciences.* Cambridge: Cambridge University Press.

Pileggi, N. 1995. *Casino.* New York: Simon and Schuster.

Pine, B. J., and J. H. Gilmore. 1999. *The Experience Economy.* Boston: Harvard Business School Press.

Pitts, W. J. 1996. Uprising in Chiapas, Mexico: Zapata Lives—Tourism Falters. In *Tourism, Crime and International Security Issues*, ed. A. Pizam and Y. Mansfield, 215–227. Chichester: Wiley.

Pizam, A., and Y. Mansfield, ed. 1996. *Tourism, Crime and International Security Issues.* Chichester: Wiley.

Pocock, D. 1992. Catherine Cookson Country: Tourist Expectation and Experience. *Geography* 77: 236–243.

Polanyi, M. 1983. *The Tacit Dimension.* Gloucester: Peter Smith.

Political Fabric. *Journal of International Affairs* 51/2, Spring: 621–640.

Poyner, A. M. 1998. Watering Las Vegas. *Geography* 83(1): 37–45.

Poynter, J. 1993. *Tour Design, Marketing and Management.* Englewood Cliffs, NJ: Regents/Prentice Hall.

Pratt, M. L. 1992. *Imperial Eyes: Travel Writing and Transculturation.* London and New York: Routledge.

Pred, A. 1986. *Place, Practice, and Structure: Social and Spatial Transformation in Southern Sweden: 1750–1850.* Totowa, NJ: Barnes and Noble.

Press, C., Jr. 1978. Reputation and Respectability Reconsidered: Hustling in a Tourist Setting. *Caribbean Issues* 4: 109–119.

Probyn, E. 1996. *Outside Belongings.* London and New York: Routledge.

Pruitt, D., and S. La Font. 1995. For Love and Money: Romance Tourism in Jamaica. *Annals of Tourism Research* 22(2): 422–440.

Rabelais, F. 1955. *Gargantua and Pantagruel,* trans. J. M. Cohen. Baltimore: Penguin Books.

Rabinow, P. 1977. *Reflections on Fieldwork on Morocco.* Berkeley: University of California Press.

———. 1989. *French Modern.* Chicago: Chicago University Press.

Raento, P. 2003. The Return of the One-Armed Bandit: Gaming in the West. In *Western Places, American Myths*, ed. G. J. Hausladen, 225–252. Reno: University of Nevada Press.

Raento, P., and W. A. Douglass. 2001. The Naming of Gaming. *Names* 49(1): 1–35.

Rajagopal, A. 2001. The Violence of Commodity Aesthetics: Hawkers, Demolition Raids and a New Regime of Consumption. *Social Text* 19(3): 91–113.

Rajanti, T. 1995. Talvinen tarina kulttuurista [A Winter Story on Culture]. *Tiede and Edistys* 2: 148–155.

Ramírez Cuevas, J. 2000. The Body as a Weapon for Civil Disobedience (and Other New Forms of Political Activism), trans. Irlandesa. *La Journada.* 15 October. Available online at: www.infoshop.org/news5/white_monkeys.html.

Reisner, M. 1986. *Cadillac Desert: The American West and Its Disappearing Water.* New York: Viking.

Relph, E. 1976. *Place and Placelessness.* London: Pion.

Report from Nurío, Michoacán. 2001. Available online at: http://mexico.indymedia .org/local/webcast/uploads/zapatistassgmqyd.txt.

Reynolds, S. 1998. *Energy Flash: A Journey through Rave Culture and Dance Music.* London: MacMillan.

Richter, L. 1992. Political Instability and Tourism in the Third World. In *Tourism and the Less Developed Countries*, ed. D. Harrison, 35–46. London: Belhaven.

Ricoeur, P. 1965. *History and Truth*, trans. by C. Kelbley. Evanston: Northwestern University Press.

Riikonen, H. 1997. Aluetietoisuuden sisältö paikallisyhteisössä. Sukupolvet ja muistinvaraiset alueet [The Contents of Regional Consciousness in a Local Community. Generations and Memorised Regions]. In *Tila, paikka ja maisema. Tutkimusretkiä uuteen maantieteeseen* [Space, Place and Landscape. Explorations in the New Geography], ed. T. Haarni, M. Karvinen, H. Koskela, and S. Tani, 170–189. Tampere: Vastapaino.

Riley, P. 1988. Road Culture of International Long-Term Budget Travelers. *Annals of Tourism Research* 15(3): 313–328.

Ritzer, G., and A. Liska. 1997. "McDisneyization" and "Post-Tourism": Complementary Perspectives on Contemporary Tourism. In *Touring Cultures: Transformations of Travel and Theory*, ed. C. Rojek and J. Urry, 96–109. London and New York: Routledge.

Rivet, D. 1988. *Lyautey et l'institution du Protectorat français au Maroc, 1912–1925.* Paris: L'Harmattan.

Roberts, D. 1988. Beyond Progress: The Museum and the Montage. *Theory, Culture and Society* (5): 543–557.

Robertson, G., M. Mash, L. Tickner, J. Bird, B. Curtis, and T. Putnam, eds. 1994. *Travellers' Tales: Narratives of Home and Displacement.* London and New York: Routledge.

Robles, F. 2001. Zapatistas Desbordan el Zócalo. *La Opinión.* 12 March: 1, 12.

Rogers, M. 1996. Beyond Authenticity: Conservation, Tourism, and the Politics of Representation in the Ecuadorian Amazon. *Identities* 3(1–2): 73–125.

Rojek, C. 1995. *Decentring Leisure: Rethinking Leisure Theory.* London: Sage.

———. 1997. Indexing, Dragging and the Social Construction of Tourist Sights. In *Touring Culture: Transformations of Travel and Theory*, ed. C. Rojek and J. Urry, 52–74. London and New York: Routledge.

Rojek, C., and J. Urry, eds. 1997a. *Touring Cultures: Transformations of Travel and Theory.* London and New York: Routledge.

———. 1997b. Transformations of Travel and Theory. In *Touring Culture: Transformations of Travel and Theory*, ed. C. Rojek and J. Urry, 1–19. London and New York: Routledge.

Romney, L., and J. F. Smith. 2001. At End of Trek, Marcos Declares Indians' "Hour." *Los Angeles Times.* 12 March: 1, 4.

Ronfeldt, D. F., J. Arquilla, G. E. Fuller, and M. Fuller. 1998. *The Zapatista "Social Netwar" in Mexico.* Santa Monica: RAND Corporation.

Room, A. 1982. *Dictionary of Trade Name Origins.* London and New York: Routledge and Kegan Paul.

Rose, G. 1993. *Feminism and Geography: The Limits of Geographical Knowledge.* Minneapolis: University of Minnesota Press.

Rothman, H. K., and M. Davis, eds. 2002. *The Grit beneath the Glitter.* Berkeley: University of California Press.

Routledge, P. 1996. Critical Geopolitics and Terrains of Resistance. *Political Geography* 15: 509–531.

Runte, A. 1987. *National Parks: The American Experience.* 2nd rev. ed. Lincoln: University of Nebraska Press.

Russell, M. 1988. *The Blessings of a Good Thick Skirt: Women Travellers and Their World.* London: William Collins.

Ryan, C., ed. 1997. *The Tourist Experience: A New Introduction.* London: Cassell.

Said, E. 1978. *Orientalism.* London and New York: Routledge and Kegan Paul.

Saldanha, A. 2002. Music Tourism and Factions of Bodies in Goa. *Tourist Studies* 2(1): 43–62.

Sanchez Taylor, Jacqueline. 2001. Dollars Are a Girl's Best Friend? Female Tourists' Sexual Behaviour in the Caribbean. *Sociology* 35(3): 749–764.

Savage, M. 1995. Walter Benjamin's Urban Thought: A Critical Analysis. *Environment and Planning D: Society and Space* 13(2): 201–216.

Scham, A. 1970. *Lyautey in Morocco.* Berkeley: University of California Press.

Schatzki, T. 2001. Subject, Body, Place. *Annals of the Association of American Geographers* 91(4): 698–702.

Schein, L. 1999. Performing Modernity. *Cultural Anthropology* 14(3): 361–395.

———. 2000. *Minority Rules: The Miao and the Feminine in China's Cultural Politics.* Durham: Duke University Press.

Schleiffer, R. 2000. *Modernism and Time: The Logic of Abundance in Literature, Science and Culture 1880–1920.* Cambridge: Cambridge University Press.

Schreider, H., and F. Schreider. 1960. From the Hair of Siva: *Tortuga II* Explores the Ganges. *National Geographic* 118(4): 445–503.

———. 1961. Indonesia: The Young and Troubled Island Nation. *National Geographic* 119(5): 579–625.

———. 1962. East from Bali by Seagoing Jeep to Timor. *National Geographic* 122(2): 236–279.

Schwartz, D. 2003. *Suburban Xanadu.* London and New York: Routledge.

Selwyn, T. 1996. Introduction. In *The Tourist Image*, ed. T. Selwyn, 1–31. Chichester: Wiley and Sons.

Sennett, R. 1994. *Flesh and Stone.* London: Faber.

———. 1999. *The Corrosion of Character. The Personal Consequences of Work in the New Capitalism.* New York and London: W. W. Norton.

Seremetakis, C., ed. 1994a. *The Senses Still: Perception and Memory as Material Culture in Modernity.* Chicago: University of Chicago Press.

Seremetakis, C. 1994b. The Memory of the Senses, Part One: Marks of the Transitory. In *The Senses Still: Perception and Memory as Material Culture in Modernity*, ed. C. Seremetakis, 1–18. Chicago: University of Chicago Press.

──── . 1994c. The Memory of the Senses, Part Two: Still Acts. In *The Senses Still: Perception and Memory as Material Culture in Modernity*, ed. C. Seremetakis, 23–43. Chicago: University of Chicago Press.

──── . 1994d. Implications. In *The Senses Still: Perception and Memory as Material Culture in Modernity*, ed. C. Seremetakis, 123–145. Chicago: University of Chicago Press.

Shemeligian, B. 2000. The Venetian Gets Its Legs. *Casino Journal* 13(6): 30–32, 34.

Shields, R. 1991. *Places on the Margin: Alternative Geographies of Modernity*. London and New York: Routledge.

──── . 1992. A Truant Proximity: Presence and Absence in the Space of Modernity. *Environment and Planning D: Society and Space* 10: 181–198.

──── . 1994. Fancy Footwork: Walter Benjamin's Notes on Flanerie. In *The Flaneur*, ed. K. Tester, 61–80. London and New York: Routledge.

Shiva, V. 1993. *Monocultures of the Mind; Perspectives on Biodiversity and Biotechnology*. Penang: Zed Books and Third World Network.

Silverman, D. 1986. *Selling Culture*. New York: Pantheon.

Simmel, G. 1950. *The Sociology of Georg Simmel*, ed. K. H. Wolff. New York: Free Press.

──── . 1971. The Stranger. In *On Individuality and Social Forms: Selected Writings*, ed. and trans. D. Levine, 143–149. Chicago: University of Chicago Press.

──── . 1990. *The Philosophy of Money*, 2nd enlarged ed., trans. T. Bottomore and D. Frisby. London and New York: Routledge.

──── . 1995. The Metropolis and Mental Life. In *Metropolis: Centre and Symbol of Our Times*, ed. P. Kasinitz, 30–45. London: Macmillan.

Sironen, E. 1993/1995. Laajavuoren maisemaa lukiessa [Reading the Landscape of Laajavuori Mountain]. In Esa Sironen, *Urheilun aika ja paikka* [Research Reports on Sport and Health 100], 199–224. Jyväskylä: Research Center for Sport and Health Sciences.

Skoglund, K., and M. Hermiö. 2002. Kesämökit 2001 [Summer Cottages 2001]. *Tilastokeskus* 5. Asuminen: *SVT*.

Slater, D. 1997. *Consumer Culture and Modernity*. Cambridge: Polity Press.

Smart, B. 1994. Digesting the Modern Diet: Gastro-Porn, Fast Food and Panic Eating. In *The Flâneur*, ed. K. Tester, 158–180. London and New York: Routledge.

Smith, J. F. 1991. Bugsy's Flamingo and the Modern Casino-Hotel. In *Gambling and Public Policy*, ed. W. R. Eadington and J. A. Cornelius, 499–518. Reno: University of Nevada Institute for the Study of Gambling and Commercial Gaming.

Smith, V. 1996. War and Its Tourist Attractions. In *Tourism, Crime and International Security Issues*, ed. A. Pizam and Y. Mansfield, 247–264. Chichester: Wiley.

Sørensen, A. 2003. Backpacker Ethnography. *Annals of Tourism Research* 30(4): 847–867.

Sorkin, M., ed. 1992. *Variations on a Theme Park*. New York: Noonday.

Spanier, D. 1992. *Welcome to the Pleasuredome*. Reno: University of Nevada Press.

St. Clair, S. 1943. Timor: A Key to the Indies. *National Geographic* 84(3): 355–384.

Stallybrass, P., and A. White. 1986. *The Politics and Poetics of Transgression*. London: Methuen.

Stewart, S. 1984. *On Longing: Narratives of the Miniature, the Gigantic, the Souvenir and the Collection*. Baltimore: Johns Hopkins University Press.

———. 1999. Prologue: From the Museum of Touch. In *Material Memories: Designs and Evocation*, ed. M. Kwint, C. Breward, and J. Aynsley, 17–36. Oxford: Berg.

Stoller, P. 1994. "Conscious" Ain't Consciousness: Entering the "Museum of Sensory Absence." In *The Senses Still: Perception and Memory as Material Culture in Modernity*, ed. C. Seremetakis, 109–121. Chicago: University of Chicago Press.

Sugden, I. 1998. http://homepages.ihug.co.nz/~stu/fret/ian_sugden.html (downloaded August 15, 1999).

Taussig, M. 1993. *Mimesis and Alterity: A Particular History of the Senses*. London and New York: Routledge.

Tester, K., ed. 1994. *The Flâneur*. London and New York: Routledge.

Thompson, Craig J., and Tambyah Siok Kuan. 1999. Trying to Be Cosmopolitan. *Journal of Consumer Research* 26 (December): 214–241.

Tomlinson, J. 1991. *Cultural Imperialism*. London: Pinter Publishers.

Torres, R. 2002. Cancun's Tourism Development from a Fordist Spectrum of Analysis. *Tourist Studies* 2(1): 87–116.

Touraine, A. 1995. *Critique of Modernity*, trans. D. Macey. Oxford: Blackwell.

Touri, A. 2000. Place Jamaa El Fna: sauvegarde et mise en valeur d'un patrimoine unique. In *Place Jamaa al Fna. Journée d'études*. Marrakech: Municipalitè Marrakech Medina.

Tuan, Y.-F. 1974. *Topophilia. A Study of Environmental Perception, Attitudes, and Values*. Englewood Cliffs, NJ: Prentice-Hall.

Turco, A. 1995. Delacroix in Marocco: indagine sull'altrove. *Terra d'Africa* 4: 315–354.

Turner, V. 1986. *The Anthropology of Performance*. New York: Performing Arts Journal Publications.

UCB (United Colors of Benetton). 1998. *Enemies*. Published by *Newsweek*.

Urry, J. 1990. *The Tourist Gaze*. London: Sage.

———. 1992. The Tourist Gaze Revisited. *American Behavioural Scientist* 36: 172–186.

———. 1995. *Consuming Places*. London and New York: Routledge.

———. 2000. *Sociology Beyond Societies: Mobilities for the Twenty-First Century*. London and New York: Routledge.

———. 2002a. Mobility and Proximity. *Sociology* 36(2): 255–274.

———. 2002b. *The Tourist Gaze*, 2nd ed. London: Sage.

———. 2004. Social Networks, Travel, and Talk. *British Journal of Sociology*.

Usborne, C. V. 1936. *The Conquest of Morocco*. London: S. Paul and Co. Ltd.

Veijola, S., and E. Jokinen. 1994. The Body in Tourism. *Theory, Culture and Society* 11(3): 125–151.

Venier, P. 1997. *Lyautey avant Lyautey*. Paris: L'Harmattan.

Venturi, R., D. S. Brown, and S. Izenour. 1972. *Learning from Las Vegas*. Cambridge: MIT Press.

Villafuerte, A. A. 2001. The Zapatistas in the Fox Era. *Voices of Mexico* 55, April-June: 15–18.

Visitor Statistics: 1970 to Present. 2002. Las Vegas Convention and Visitors Authority, Las Vegas. 19 September 2002. www.vegasfreedom.com.

Wainwright, M. 2003. Last Post for Britain's Card Habit? *The Guardian*. July 24.

Wagner, Ulla. 1977. Out of Time and Place—mass tourism and charter trips. *Ethnos* 42: 38–52.

Wallace, A. R. 1869. *The Malay Archipelago*. Singapore: Oxford University Press.

Walton, J., and D. Seddon. 1994. *Free Markets and Food Riots: The Politics of Global Adjustment*. London and New York: Blackwell.

Wang, N. 1996. Logos-Modernity, Eros Modernity, and Leisure. *Leisure Studies* 15(2): 121–135.

——. 1999. Rethinking Authenticity in Tourism Experience. *Annals of Tourism Research* 26(2): 349–370.

——. 2000. *Tourism and Modernity: A Sociological Analysis*. Oxford: Pergamon.

——. 2002. The Tourist as Peak Consumer. In *The Tourist as the Metaphor of the Social World*, ed. G. Dann, 281–295. Wallingford: Cab International.

Wasko, J. 2001. *Understanding Disney*. Cambridge: Polity.

Watson, G. L., and J. Kopachevsky. 1994. Interpretation of Tourism as Commodity. *Annals of Tourism Research* 21(3): 643–660.

Watson, J. 2001. Subcomandante Marcos Not Only Inspires and Leads, He Sells. Associated Press. March 1.

Weber, M. 1978. *Economy and Society*, vols. 1 and 2, ed. G. Roth and C. Wittich. Berkeley: University of California Press.

White, G. 1997. Museum/Memorial/Shrine: National Narrative in National Spaces. *Museum Anthropology* 21(1): 8–26.

White, R. 1991. *It's Your Misfortune and None of My Own*. Norman: University of Oklahoma Press.

Wilbaux, Q. 2000. La Place Jamaa el Fna de Marrakech. Etude architecturale. In *Place Jamaa al Fna. Journée d'études*. Marrakech: Municipalitè Marrakech Medina.

Williams, S., and G. Bendelow. 1998. *The Lived Body: Sociological Themes, Embodied Issues*. London and New York: Routledge.

Wilson, C. 1956. *The Outsider*. Boston: Houghton Mifflin.

Wilson, D. 1993. Tourism, Public Policy and the Image of Northern Ireland Since the Troubles. In *Tourism in Ireland: A Critical Analysis*, ed. B. O'Connor and M. Cronin, 138–161. Cork: Cork University Press.

Wilson, E. 1991. *Sphinx in the City: Urban Life, the Control of Disorder, and Women*. London: Virago Press.

——. 1992. The Invisible Flâneur. *New Left Review* 191: 90–110.

Wolff, J. 1985. The Invisible Flâneuse: Women and the Literature of Modernity. *Theory Culture and Society* 2(3): 37–46.

——. 1993. On the Road Again: Metaphors of Travel in Cultural Criticism. *Cultural Studies* 7(2): 224–239.

Wolfwood, T. 1997. Who is Ramona? *Third World Resurgence* 84. August. Unnumbered.

Wordsworth, William. 1888. Imagination and Taste, How Impaired and Restored. In *The Complete Poetical Works*, with an introduction by John Morley. London: Macmillan and Co.

Wylie, J. 2002. Becoming-icy: Scott and Amundsen's South Polar Voyages, 1910–1913. *Cultural Geograhies* 9(3): 249–265.

Ya Basta! 2001. New York City Ya Basta! Collective Calls for All Bodies to Resist the FTAA. 13 February. Available online at: www.infoshop.org/news6/padded_yabasta.html

Yoneyama, L. 1995. Memory Matters: Hiroshima's Korean Atom Bomb Memorial and the Politics of Ethnicity. *Public Culture* 7(3): 499–527.

Young, J. E. 1995. *The Texture of Memory: Holocaust Memorials and Meaning.* New Haven, CT: Yale University Press.

Zapatistas. 1998. *Zapatista Encuentro: Documents from the 1996 Encounter for Humanity and Against Neoliberalism.* New York: Seven Stories Press.

Zelinsky, W. 1967. Classical Town Names in the United States. The Historical Geography of an American Idea. *Geographical Review* 57(4): 463–495.

———. 2001. The Geographer as Voyeur. *Geographical Review* 91(1–2): 1–8.

Index

About the Contributors

Kathleen M. Adams is associate professor of anthropology at Loyola University Chicago. She is coauthor of *Home and Hegemony: Domestic Service and Identity Politics in South and Southeast Asia* and is currently completing a book on tourist art and identity politics in Tana Toraja, Indonesia. Her publications have appeared in *American Ethnologist, Museum Anthropology, Ethnology, Ethnohistory,* and other journals.

Mike Crang is a reader in geography at the University of Durham. He has written on social memory, museums, and heritage, and works as well on theories of space-time and electronic media. He is the co-editor of the journals *Time & Society* and *Tourist Studies,* and the edited collections *Tourism: Between Place and Performance* (with Simon Coleman), *Thinking Space* (with Nigel Thrift), *Virtual Geographies* (with Phil Crang and Jon May), and he wrote the text *Cultural Geography.*

Tim Edensor teaches cultural geography at Manchester Metropolitan University. He is the author of *Tourists at the Taj* (1998), *National Identity, Popular Culture and Everyday Life* (2002), and *Industrial Ruins: Space, Aesthetics and Materiality* (2005). Edensor has also written about cultures of walking and driving, the film *Braveheart,* and performing rurality, as well as several pieces on aspects of tourism.

Steven Flusty is assistant professor of geography at York University in Toronto, Canada. His focal interest is the everyday practices of global formation, a topic he has addressed most fully in *De-Coca-Colonization: Making the Globe from the Inside Out* (2003). His work has appeared in assorted electronic media and a selection of academic, professional, and popular journals of varying degrees of repute. Dr. Flusty also practices as an architectural and urban design consultant, in which capacity he has visited his own sensibilities upon the unsuspecting cities of three continents.

Jessica Jacobs is currently an honorary research fellow at the Open University and at the Council for British Research in the Levant where she is carrying out research on the geographical imaginations of the "Levant" in contemporary European tourist practice. Her past research, carried out in the resorts of Sinai, Egypt, centered on the idea of the "Orient" in "romance" tourism and the role of tourist places in negotiating modernity.

Claudio Minca is professor of human geography at the University of Newcastle. He has written widely on geographical representations, tourism, and postmodernism in geography and is the author of *Spazi Effimeri* (1996) and *Spazio e Politica* (with Luiza Bialasiewicz, 2004) and the editor of *Introduzione alla Geografia Postmoderna* (2001), *Postmodern Geography* (2001), and *Orizzonte Mediterraneo* (2003).

Tim Oakes is associate professor of geography at the University of Colorado at Boulder. He is the author of *Tourism and Modernity in China* (1998) and co-editor of *Translocal China: Linkages, Identities, and the Reimagining of Space* (2006). His work focuses on Chinese cultural geography, tourism, and regional development.

Pauliina Raento is an Academy of Finland senior research fellow and reader in human geography at the University of Helsinki, Finland. Her work on American casino gambling, Basque nationalism, and Finnish political and cultural geographies has appeared in numerous edited volumes and journals, including *Annals of Tourism Research*, *The Geographical Review*, *Names*, and *Political Geography*. Her research on Las Vegas has been funded by the Academy of Finland (1998–2001, 2003–2008) and hosted by the University of Nevada (Reno); University of Minnesota (Minneapolis); and University of Helsinki.

Soile Veijola is a Finnish sociologist whose research interests range from feminist critique of theories of tourism (mostly coauthored with Eeva Jokinen), analyses of sexed orders in team sport, and the gendered and numbered construction of the social. She is currently working as an acting professor of cultural studies of tourism at the University of Lapland.

Ning Wang is professor of sociology at Zhongshan University (Sun Yat-Sen University), Guangzhou, People's Republic of China. He is the author of *Tourism and Modernity: A Sociological Analysis* (2000) and of *The Sociology of Consumption* (2001).